Handbook of Research on Cultural and Cross-Cultural Psychology

Edited by
Chandan Maheshkar
Department of Management, CDGI, Indore, India
East Nimar Society for Education (ENSE), Indore, Indore
Jayant Sonwalkar
Institute of Management Studies, University of Indore, India

Cognitive Science and Psychology
VERNON PRESS

www.vernonpress.com

In the Americas:
Vernon Press
1000 N West Street, Suite 1200
Wilmington, Delaware, 19801
United States

In the rest of the world:
Vernon Press
C/Sancti Espiritu 17,
Malaga, 29006
Spain

Cognitive Science and Psychology

Library of Congress Control Number: 2023937930

ISBN: 978-1-64889-914-0

Also available: 978-1-64889-701-6 [Hardback]; 978-1-64889-779-5 [PDF, E-Book]

Cover design by Vernon Press. Cover background designed by coolvector / Freepik.

Table of Contents

List of Figures   **vii**

List of Tables   **ix**

Preface   **xi**

Chandan Maheshkar
Department of Management, CDGI, Indore, India
East Nimar Society for Education (ENSE),
Indore, Indore

Jayant Sonwalkar
Institute of Management Studies (IMS),
University of Indore, India

Acknowledgements   **xv**

Chapter 1   **Culture-Driven Behaviors: A Perspective on Cultural and Cross-Cultural Psychology**   **1**

Chandan Maheshkar
Department of Management, CDGI, Indore, India
East Nimar Society for Education (ENSE),
Indore, Indore

Jayant Sonwalkar
Institute of Management Studies,
University of Indore, India

Chapter 2   **Emotions: The Missing Link in Cultural Diversity Research**   **23**

Arti Sharma
Indian Institute of Management (IIM) Indore, India

Sushant Bhargava
Indian Institute of Management (IIM) Jammu, India

Chapter 3   **Moral Development in Cultural Psychology**   **39**

Namrata Chatterjee
Sulhaa Healthcare, Delhi, India

Alankrita Kumar
Sulhaa Healthcare, Delhi, India

Chapter 4   **Wisdom: Cultural and Cross-Cultural Understanding with a Systematic Review of Empirical Studies**   53

Roshan Lal Dewangan
Kazi Nazrul University, Asansol, West Bengal, India

Hari Narayanan V.
Indian Institute of Technology Jodhpur, Rajasthan, India

Rajib Ghosh
Kazi Nazrul University, Asansol, West Bengal, India

Chapter 5   **Human Values: Related Concepts and Types**   71

Eisha Rahman
Research Associate, Military Mind Academy, Pune, India

Mubashir Gull
Department of Applied Psychology, GITAM School of Humanities and Social Sciences, Visakhapatnam, India

Akbar Husain
Aligarh Muslim University, UP, India

Chapter 6   **Shaping Reality through Interaction: Thoughts on Cultural Specifications**   97

Cserkits Michael
University of Vienna, Austria

Chapter 7   **Dealing the Responses Contaminated with Social Desirability Bias while Studying Socially Stigmatized Behaviors**   111

Salman A. Cheema
School of Applied Science, National Textile University Faisalabad, Pakistan

Irene L. Hudson
Mathematical Sciences, School of Science, Royal Melbourne Institute of Technology (RMIT), Melbourne, Australia

Muhammad Naveed
Faisalabad Medical University, Pakistan

Arslan Khan
Department of Statistics, Quaid-i-Azam University Islamabad, Pakistan

Farooq Shah
Department of Statistics, University of Peshawar, Pakistan

Zawar Husain
Department of Statistics, the Islamia University, Bahawalpur, Pakistan

Chapter 8   **The Use and Method of Psychodrama as a Research Method in Cultural and Intercultural Psychology**   137

Ezgi Gül Ceyhan
Muğla Sıtkı Koçman University, Turkey

Chandan Maheshkar
Department of Management, CDGI, Indore, India
East Nimar Society for Education (ENSE), Indore, Indore

Chapter 9   **Cross-cultural Collectivistic and Individualistic Comparison between Vietnamese and Western Cultures**   153

Tuan, V. V.
Hanoi Law University, Vietnam

Anh, H. B.
Hanoi Law University, Vietnam

Chapter 10   **The Psychology of Acculturation: Losing My Religion**   181

Janelle Christine Simmons
AmeriCorps VISTA – AARP Foundation, New York, USA

Chapter 11   **Culture and Its Influence on Peoples' Behavior towards Education of Persons with Disabilities in Nigeria**   195

Odirin Omiegbe
University of Delta, Agbor, Nigeria

Chapter 12   **Native Country and Its Influence on Social
Support and Cultural Shock among Foreign
Students**   221

Feba Thomas
*Xavier Institute of Management & Entrepreneurship,
Kalamassery, Kochi, India*

Chapter 13   **African Culture and Traditions Matter:
Managing Psychological Wellbeing During
and After a Crisis**   237

Wandile Fundo Tsabedze
*Department of Psychology, University of South
Africa, South Africa*

Siboniso Collin Gumedze
*Department of Psychology, University of South
Africa, South Africa*

Mpho Maotoana
*University of Limpopo, Department of Psychology,
Sovenga, Limpopo, South Africa*

Mokoena, Patronella Maepa
*Sefako Makgatho Health Sciences University,
South Africa*

Chapter 14   **Cultural Influences on Motivation Theories
and their Application**   253

Bhawna Tushir
Christ (Deemed to be) University, Delhi NCR, India

Garima Joshi
*All India Institute of Medical Sciences (AIIMS),
New Delhi, India*

Vatsal Priyadarshi Pandey
*Department of Psychology, Lakshmibai College
Delhi University, New Delhi, India*

About the Contributors   275

Index   283

List of Figures

Figure 2.1: The conceptual framework of cross-cultural diversity and emotions   28

Figure 4.1: Preferred Reporting Items for Systematic Reviews and Meta-Analyses (PRISMA)   60

Figure 6.1: First sketch of the cultural scape approach   106

Figure 7.1: Odds of contraceptive use estimated through the multilevel logistic regression model with masking parameter $p = 0.90$ 126

Figure 7.2: Estimated effects of determinants of contraceptives use, through the multi-level logistic regression model with $p = 0.90$, across all divisions   130

Figure 7.3: Display of predicted probabilities with respect to region Age and WDM controlling for age and boys, estimated through the multi-level logistic regression model with $p = 0.90$ 132

Figure 9.1: Contrastive differences of cultural constructs between two cultures according to average means   172

Figure 10.1: Berry's Acculturation Model   187

List of Tables

Table 1.1:	Differences in Collectivism and Individualism	6
Table 1.2:	Difference between High and Low Power Distance	7
Table 1.3:	Difference between Masculinity and Femininity	9
Table 1.4:	Difference between Short-term and Long-term Orientation	10
Table 1.5:	Difference between Indulgence and Restraint	10
Table 4.1:	Details of search strategies	59
Table 4.2:	Studies included in the review	61
Table 7.1:	Descriptive of micro and macro variables at national and divisional level	115
Table 7.2:	Estimates of logistic regression – national and divisional level	117
Table 7.3:	Estimates of fixed effects with respect to the varying extent of masking	123
Table 7.4:	Measures of model assessment	124
Table 7.5:	Estimated variability of the random effects averaged over all divisions	126
Table 7.6:	Estimates of multi-level logistic regression for all divisions – $p = 0.90$	128
Table 9.1:	Attributes of cultural orientation of horizontal and vertical individualism and collectivism	163
Table 9.2:	Vertical/Horizontal individualism and collectivism	164
Table 9.3:	Characteristics of Vertical and Horizontal Individualism and Collectivism	165
Table 9.4:	Comparison of collectivistic and individualistic degrees between Western cultures and Vietnamese culture	171
Table 12.1:	Participants Demographic Profile (N=100)	227
Table 12.2:	Descriptive Statistics, Reliability (Cronbach's Alpha) and Correlation Matrix	228
Table 12.3:	Mean, Standard Deviation, & Anova between Native Country on Culture shock (N=100)	229
Table 12.4:	Regression Coefficient of Social Support and Culture Shock	229

Preface

Chandan Maheshkar

Department of Management, CDGI, Indore, India
East Nimar Society for Education (ENSE), Indore, Indore

Jayant Sonwalkar

Institute of Management Studies (IMS), University of Indore, India

A significant proportion of behavioral attributes and values in a human system are determined by respective cultures and interactions with other cultures. Cultural and cross-cultural psychology has emerged as an interdisciplinary area that explores how a culture regulates society and its business, how cross-cultural interactions affect the psychology of individuals and societies, behavioral variability under various cultural conditions, and how to harmonize the cultural diversities. Organizationally and philosophically, cultural and cross-cultural psychology differs from other areas of social sciences. It is a common phenomenon that as people engage with cultural practices, their thoughts, feelings, and behaviors come to reflect their cultural values and beliefs. As a process, people formulate, replicate, transform and/or transmit their cultural practices in their daily social and/or business interactions.

This '*Handbook of Research on Cultural and Cross-cultural Psychology*' starts with the essentials of culture, its relationship with human psychology, and the origin of cultural and cross-cultural psychology. The book is focused on dynamics that amplify knowledge, skills, and behaviors relevant to deal with different cultural and cross-cultural issues. It considers the relationships between the cultural theory and practices, explaining what the character of these relationships might be?

This book seeks to discuss why and how cultural/cross-cultural psychology should be focused on and help to deal with the behavioral/psychological challenges caused by a culture in diverse settings to diverse groups of people.

Chapter 1, by the editors of this book, introduces cultural and cross-cultural psychology and enlightens how culture is a significant dimension of human beings. This chapter explores culture-driven behavior involving individual, national and international perspectives. Authors have attempted to discover the paradigm shift due to globalization that considerably encouraged cross-cultural interaction and promoted a multicultural society and organizations.

Chapter 2, by Arti Sharma and Sushant Bhargava, examines emotions based on their socio-cultural roots. This chapter proposed a conceptual model emphasizing the missing link of emotions in mainstream cultural diversity research. This model intends that "the historical and ecological understanding of emotions embedded within a culture constructs the perception of inclusion and exclusion within individuals." Also, the chapter enlightened the theoretical and practical implications of holding emotions as an indispensable element of cultural diversity.

Chapter 3, by Namrata Chatterjee and Alankrita Kumar, focuses on *moral development in cultural/cross-cultural psychology*. The chapter explores the psychological impact of culture on approaches toward morality and ethics, the prominent theories of moral development, and diverse aspects of morality.

Chapter 4, by Roshan Lal Dewangan, Hari Narayanan V. and Rajib Ghosh, describes the wisdom in a cross-cultural context. They explored two databases (APA PsycArticles® and PubMed) with a mixed methodology to comprehend the notion of *wisdom*. They inform that there is overlap in wisdom conception from one culture to another, and cultural uniqueness lies in prioritizing some features of wisdom over others.

Chapter 5, by Eisha Rahman, Mubashir Gull and Akbar Husain, concentrates on human values. The chapter is based on the sociological perspective that values are critically linked with society and its people and reflect in almost functions. It discusses the nature of values and elements related to human values, including valence, attitude, life patterns, understanding behavior, enduring belief, and societal norm.

Chapter 6, by Cserkits Michael, highlights the anthropological view of space, place, and scape. In this chapter, the author underlines social constructivism concerning functionalism and historicism. This chapter will help understand the relationship between culture and constructed scapes. It clarified that the 'cultural scape' model could be applied in cross- or intercultural social interactions to mitigate perceptions of what is often called 'reality'.

Chapter 7, by Salman A. Cheema, Irene L. Hudson, and colleagues, deals with social desirability bias while studying socially stigmatized behaviors. The study deals with the situation where data have already been collected, and an initial analysis reveals the patterns pointing towards the existence of *social desirability bias*. Authors have demonstrated the applicability of the proposed model by studying the contraceptive behaviors and their deriving factors in a multi-linguistic, culturally diverse and relatively more rigid society.

Chapter 8, by Ezgi Gül CEYHAN and Chandan Maheshkar, advocates the use of psychodrama as a research method in cultural and intercultural psychology. This chapter claims psychodrama is a convenient methodology for psychological analysis of self-reflection, creativity, social emotions and role-based psychological revitalization.

Chapter 9, by Tuan, V. V. and Anh, H. B., presents a cross-cultural collectivistic and individualistic comparison between Vietnamese and Western cultures. The chapter voiced that long-lost or imperiled cultural entities have to be preserved and developed before they disappeared. In this way, the chapter is advocating that knowing well the nature of cultural differences between Vietnamese and Western cultures can avoid such issues.

Chapter 10, Janelle Christine Simmons discusses acculturation, a process of cultural assimilation, where the dominant culture of the society typically adapts. The chapter addresses mainly how a person acculturates without losing themselves, and becoming a citizen of another country does require rejecting one's religious/cultural beliefs.

Chapter 11, by Odirin Omiegbe, presents the culture and its influence on people's behavior, in particular reference to the education of persons with disabilities in Nigeria. The chapter introduces various cultural terminologies of Nigerian Culture and reveals different cultural practices with shocking examples and cases. The chapter reveals barbaric cultural and religious practices that impede the education of persons with disabilities and emphasizes making citizens aware to stop such practices. This chapter is a unique contribution to help Nigerian society and others, in general, remove deeply rooted superstitions in cultural practices.

Chapter 12, by Feba Thomas, reveals the native country and its influence on social support and culture shock among students studying abroad. The chapter emphasizes social support as a coping strategy for reducing the cultural shock that international students face in the assimilation process from their home country to the host country. This chapter indicates that cultural shock can be reduced significantly if social support is received from the families.

Chapter 13, by Wandile Fundo Tsabedze, Siboniso Collin Gumedze, Mpho Maotoana and Mokoena Maepa, presents African Culture and traditions towards its role in maintaining psychological well-being during and after turbulent times. It is a case about how Emaswati, an African nation, has been culturally affected due to the Covid-19 pandemic. The chapter presents different cultural aspects (such as, *"kufukama"* and *"Ubuntu"*) used in Emaswati/Africa, which communicate its cultural philosophy, social beliefs, and richness of values.

Chapter 14, by Bhawna Tushir, Garima Joshi and Vatsal Priyadarshi Pandey, reviews the cultural influence on Motivation Theories. In this chapter, the authors discuss major motivation theories and the role of motivation in different developmental aspects, such as ethics, motivational imbalance, and innovative motivation. The measures of examination that have been made from achievement motivation speculations are examined in this chapter, emphasizing recent advancements.

Acknowledgements

In the Name of God, Most Gracious, Most Merciful

This book is a collection of numerous research works by authors and researchers from different countries related to cultural and cross-cultural behavior/psychology and its contribution to cultural psychology. We want to thank all the researchers, reviewers, and individuals whose sincere efforts have helped us complete this multi-author volume in the best possible manner.

Special thanks to all the reviewers who gave their precious time and made sincere efforts to review all the manuscripts. Their honest suggestions and advice helped us enrich the quality of the chapters of the book.

We are grateful to all the researchers and authors who have contributed their work to this handbook. Also, we thank the people who permitted our researchers and authors to carry out research and develop it through their state-of-the-art descriptions of situations of all times to make this book a significant contribution to the field.

We are immensely thankful to our family members, friends and colleagues for encouraging us to publish this research work. Their love, sacrifice and support helped us focus and continue in this direction. Their confidence in us helped us rise above the times of self-doubt and uncertainty throughout the journey.

In the end, we wish to pray to the Almighty for his kindness and eternal grace on us at all times to help us accomplish our goals.

Chapter 1

Culture-Driven Behaviors: A Perspective on Cultural and Cross-Cultural Psychology

Chandan Maheshkar

Department of Management, CDGI, Indore, India
East Nimar Society for Education (ENSE), Indore, Indore

Jayant Sonwalkar

Institute of Management Studies, University of Indore, India

Abstract: Culture is the dynamic frame of reference that offers almost every context of human endeavors. It strongly influences cognitive, affective and psycho-motor domains of human behavior. This chapter has presented how cultural and cross-cultural contexts regulate human behavior at different levels (i.e., individual, intra-societal, and inter-societal). From the anthropological, psychological, and sociological basis, cultures can be compared and contrasted based on some specific dimensions of cultural variability, such as individualism-collectivism, high-low context, masculinity-femininity, power distance, and uncertainty avoidance. Value orientation is the most influential attribute of any culture, which guides and reflects in people's behaviors; however, it varies across cultures. Significantly, the chapter offers a sense of cultural elements and their role in the fabrication of different behaviors in different cultural and cross-cultural contexts. Thus, critical thinking, perception, intelligence, and emotions were discussed particularly. The chapter establishes that people cannot be separated from their cultures.

Keywords: Behavior, Cross-Cultural Psychology, Multiculturalism, Diversity, Cultural Beliefs, Societal Competence, Human Development, Collectivism, Individualism

***

Introduction

A major proportion of behavioral attributes and values in a human system are determined by respective cultures and interactions with other cultures. Cultural and cross-cultural psychology has emerged as an interdisciplinary area that explores how a culture regulates society and its businesses, how cross-cultural interactions affect psychologies of individuals as well as societies, behavioral variability under various cultural conditions, and how to harmonize cultural diversities. Organizationally and philosophically, cultural and cross-cultural psychology differs from other areas of social sciences. It is a common phenomenon that as people engage with cultural practices, their thoughts, feelings, and behaviors come to reflect their cultural values and beliefs. As a process, people formulate, replicate, transform and/or transmit their cultural practices in their daily social and/or business interactions.

Cultural psychology and cross-cultural psychology differ in a few aspects. Cross-cultural psychology studies cultural effects on human behavior by comparing the components of at least two cultures. Cultural psychology revolves around the relationships between culture and human psychology within that culture and the resultant behaviors. Broadly, it deals with behavioral tendencies such as identity, emotions, social behaviors, and relationship dynamics (like friendship, love, and affection). As an academic discipline, it is an interdisciplinary area of study that covers psychology, anthropology, philosophy and languages to comprehend how a culture, its practices and institutions regulate the thoughts, beliefs, and actions of both an individual and a group of individuals. Very specific in nature, cross-cultural psychology explores patterns between two or more cultures based on their underlying differences and similarities. Objectively, cultural psychology functions intra-culturally and cross-cultural psychology functions inter-culturally; however, both study the influence of cultural norms on individuals' psychology and behavioral patterns (e.g., thinking, attitudes).

Exploring the many roles of culture and its interaction with other cultures is particularly significant because globalization and the rise of extreme manifestation affect the perceptions of culture and seriously damage societies. An in-depth exploration of a culture and its practices on an individual's behavior and collectively on society will lead to an increased awareness of culture-driven behaviors of people and society.

Theoretical Underpinnings

Theoretically, a socio-psychological perspective suggests behavior as a function of the people and their environment. However, the environment, or context wherein behavior originates, is very complicated to conceptualize and assess. It is difficult to segregate people from their environment (i.e., a fabrication of content and contexts) and/or isolate the cultural aspects that they always experience in their entirety. In the case of cross-culture, segregating oneself from his/her socio-cultural environment is not so difficult when he/she works in other cultures (Maynard & Barney, 2018, Maheshkar & Sharma, 2018). It can be observed that the socio-cultural content and contexts of other cultural environments may influence people's behavior, possibly because they contrast sharply with content and contexts familiar to their own socio-cultural environment.

Epistemology of Cultural Psychology

Cultural psychology studies how cultural traditions and social practices regulate, express, and transform the human psyche, resulting in deviations in human personality and emotions. It is settled on human existential uncertainty (the search for meaning and purpose) and the intended creation of the 'own worlds' (Shweder, 1999). According to the principle of existential uncertainty, humans are greatly inclined to acquire and use meanings, patterns, and resources from their socio-cultural environment. This socio-cultural environment is also organized and attributed in a way to make meanings, patterns, and resources available to acquire and use. The core of cultural psychology is that a socio-cultural environment has no existence without people acquiring meanings, patterns, and resources out of it. In contrast, people hold their subjectivity and mental state changing through the process of acquiring and using meanings, patterns, and resources from their socio-cultural environment (Shweder, 2008, 1999).

Mainly, cultural psychology believes that the socio-cultural contexts make human behavior meaningful wherein it happens (Segal et al., 1999). As Shiraev and Leavy (2010) mentioned, "cultural psychology advocates the idea that mental processes are essentially the products of an interaction between culture and the individual."

Cultural psychology attempts to understand the influence of cultural content and context on people's inherent central processing mechanism and the resultant behaviors. It offers interpretations of the central processing mechanism of the mind. According to cultural psychology, the mind is content-driven, context-specific, and stimulus-bound. As a result, it interprets observed patterns dependent on context, content, stimuli strength, and comprehension modes. It combines some of the attributes of general psychology, cross-cultural psychology, ethno-psychology, and psychological anthropology. Based on the content and contexts, culture can be identified and studied into two major types – traditional, nontraditional, or contemporary. Traditional culture is deep-rooted in customs, principles, and rules established in the past and transferred from generation to generation. Contemporary culture is nontraditionally based on new ideas, principles, and practices typically influenced by scientific knowledge, technological developments, and business and political organizations.

Epistemologically, reasoning is the process that uses knowledge and experiences to reason. A cultural frame of society significantly influences people's expectations and endeavors that may have consequences for them to reason regarding events and objects they have not experienced; thus, they have no direct knowledge about them (Maynard & Barney, 2018).

Epistemology of Cross-Cultural Psychology

The socio-cultural environment varies regionally throughout the world. People's actions and behaviors may vary considerably, constituted and developed in different socio-cultural settings. These culture-specific differences have very acute psychosomatic effects on the behaviors of people of one culture in other cultures. According to Shiraev and Leavy (2010), "cross-cultural psychology is the critical and comparative study of cultural effects on human psychology." Any cross-cultural investigation draws conclusions only based on at least two samples representing two different cultures. It is because cross-cultural psychology is a comparative field that analyzes psychological and behavioral differences and the core reasons for these differences. Mainly, cross-cultural psychology studies the relations between cultural norms and behaviors and how socio-cultural factors, sometimes dissimilar, influence particular human actions (Segall et al., 1990, Shiraev & Leavy, 2010). For example, India witnessed the Mughals and British during different time intervals. How did Mughals and their Islamic culture and Christians and their Western culture influence Indian culture, values, and behaviors in their respective era? In this case, cross-cultural psychology studies cross-cultural interactions and the consequent influences on one's culture, values, and behaviors. It considers not only diversity between different cultures but also ascertains psychological/behavioral commons (Berry et al., 1992; Lonner, 1980, Shiraev & Leavy, 2010).

Cross-cultural psychology provides culturally sensitive measures for comparing cultures. Its central advantage is that it gives culture-specific generalizations. It identifies cultural patterns—such as masculinity and femininity, indulgence and restraint, and power distance—that comprise *Etic* and *Emic* attributes (Triandis, 2000). It not only identifies culture-specific elements but also compares and contrasts the same phenomena in different cultures.

Cultural Dichotomies

Collectivism and Individualism

The cultural philosophy of '*self*' and '*common good*' determines the social orientation of different cultures. Some cultures are very much inclined toward collectivism and promote intra-cultural and inter-cultural cooperation. Other cultures, typically contemporary, stress individualism and personal autonomy. These cultural attributes significantly influence human behavior, particularly value systems.

Collectivism is a set of behaviors based on humanistic values that care for the community, organization, or society to which one belongs. It refers to people's interdependence in a group/society/organization—in multifarious ways—they belong. Group/societal norms in collectivist culture are fundamental to regulating individual and/or group behavior. Collectivist people/societies usually prefer strategies, which are cooperative and improve harmony for conflict resolution (Shiraev & Leavy, 2010). It respects long-standing relationships and promotes group goals. Collectivists can easily give up their personal benefits for the *common good*. Collectivism is context-centric than the content, e.g., one's facial expressions, eye contact, tone of voice, and appearance are the most precise indicators of how an individual feels about what he/she is presenting and why.

Individualism is a complex behavior rooted in the concern for individual independence, including *self* and family to which one belongs, contradictory to collectivistic culture. The individualist philosophy of '*self*' considers individuals autonomous and exclusively responsible for deciding whether or not to share resources (Reykowski, 1994; Triandis, 1999). Individualists deny that traditions, religious institutions (i.e., the temple, the church, etc.), and other social organizations can impose limitations on individuals. They resist the collectivist cultures' values and principles that prioritize social roles, responsibilities, and collective goals. Improvement in socio-economic status is a growing trend in individualist cultures. It exhibits that individualists believe that improving one's socio-economic status is closely tied to being autonomous and motivated to attain individual goals.

Collectivism focuses on the significance of society, while individualism is centered on the rights and concerns of every individual. Where harmony and selflessness are admirable qualities in collectivist societies, autonomy and personal identity are advanced in individualistic societies (Cherry, 2022). The mentioned cultural differences are determined and can affect different functional aspects of society. Studies reported that people/societies with higher levels of collectivism are more dependent and less likely to be disloyal to groups to which they belong or are associated (Le Febvre & Franke, 2013). Converse to this, individualists are more rational than collectivists.

Table 1.1: Differences in Collectivism and Individualism

Collectivism	*Individualism*	*Studies*
Collectivists use *groups* as the units for analyzing social behavior.	Individualists use *individuals* as the units for analyzing social behavior.	Triandis (1999)
Collectivists have long-term thinking because their in-groups often include both ancestors and descendants.	Individualists often have short-term thinking because they only consider themselves and think of immediate gratification.	Lincoln et al. (1986) Triandis (1999)
Collectivist people are more inclined to the success of their groups.	Individualists are mainly concerned with their gratification and success.	Nickerson (2021)
In interpersonal situations, collectivist attributes: Relationships, Roles, Norms, Cooperation, Common Good, etc.	In interpersonal situations, individualist attributes: Personality, Ability, Attitude, perceived rights, etc.	Gudykunst et al. (1994), Singelis (1994) Miller (1994) Nickerson (2021)
Subordination of individual goals into group goals.	Individual goals are usually associated with '*Self*' and personal orientation.	Triandis (1990, 1999) Schwartz (1994) Wagner & Moch (1986)
The wellbeing of collectivists depends on good relationships, which closely connect to the norms of the group to which they belong.	The wellbeing of individualists depends on the gratification of '*self*' and emotional attachment to self-satisfaction.	Suh et al. (1998)
Collectivists emphasize absolute relatedness	Individualists emphasize rationality	Triandis (1999)
Collectivist societies are both simple and hold tight bonds.	Individualist societies are both complex and hold loose bonds.	Triandis (1999) Cherry (2022)
Collectivism is commonly observed in traditional societies. Example: China, India, Indonesia, and Brazil	Collectivism is commonly observed in nontraditional societies. Example: USA, UK, Canada, Australia, and Germany	Cherry (2020)
Personality traits are disciplined, selfless, responsive, reliant, generous, yielding, uniformed, politically correct, sensitive, and fellowship-seeking.	Personality traits are more independent, determined, self-assured, emotional stability, solitary, free-willed, leadership, innate, assertive, strong-willed, dominant, and objective.	Nickerson (2021) Shweder (1999)

Power Distance

It is the potency of social hierarchy in different societies. The concept *of power distance communicates that people at the lower levels of this social hierarchy have no equal power and have to accept that power is not equally distributed in* society. People at the lower levels of the social hierarchy in their cultures/societies have observed that they expect equal distribution of power. Opposite this, those at the top of the social hierarchy don't want to share or lose the power they hold.

The power distance is used to measure to what extent people at all the levels of the social hierarchy are satisfied with their position and the present state of this hierarchy. Thus, it can be claimed that evaluation of social hierarchies and how cultures change while a time interval. The most appreciated use of power distance is assessing the acceptance rate of cultural norms and determining the consequential effects when a culture or social hierarchy changes. People are very respectful to those at higher levels of social hierarchy (*figures of authority*) in cultures exhibiting high power distance and, as a general rule, accept an unequal division of power. On the other hand, people explicitly question social hierarchy, institutions and concerned authority and look forward to being a part of decisions that affect them.

Table 1.2: Difference between High and Low Power Distance

Low Power Distance	High Power Distance
▪ The use of power is legitimate and is subject to criteria of good and bad	▪ Power is a basic fact of society antedating good or bad. Its legitimacy is irrelevant
▪ Parents treat children as equals	▪ Parents teach children obedience
▪ Older people are neither respected nor feared	▪ Older people are both respected and feared
▪ Student-centric education	▪ Teacher-centric education
▪ Hierarchy means inequality of roles, established for convenience	▪ Hierarchy means existential inequality
▪ Subordinates expect to be consulted	▪ Subordinates expect to be told what to do
▪ Pluralist governments are based on a majority vote and change peacefully	▪ Autocratic governments based on cooperation and changes by revolution
▪ Corruption is rare; scandals end political careers	▪ Corruption is frequent; scandals are covered up
▪ Income distribution in society is relatively even	▪ Income distribution in society is very uneven
▪ Religions stressing the equality of believers	▪ Religions with a hierarchy of priests

Source: Hofstede, 2011, p. 9

In cross-cultural settings, power distance is a significant aspect that inadvertently influences human behavior, which directly contributes to the *cultural norms* of cross-cultural societies and organizations (Ji et al., 2015). Cultural norms emerged from people's perceptions and their acceptance of power inequality. These social norms generate diverse responses while confronting the same state of affairs or environment. There are four essential factors influencing a cross-cultural society and/or organization's levels of power distance (House et al., 2004), which are:

1. The Predominant Religion or Cultural Philosophy;

2. The Democratic Principles of the Government;

3. The Presence of Strong and Responsible Middle Class; and

4. The Proportion of Immigrants in Total Population.

Cultural Dimensions Theory

The cultural dimension theory given by Geert Hofstede is a scheme used to describe the cultural differences across nations, how culture influences the values of people to which they belong, and how these values regulate their behaviors (Adeoye & Tomei, 2014; Nickerson, 2022). This theory enables to appreciate insights into other cultures that can make people more effective in cross-cultural communication. If Hofstede's theory is adequately understood and applied, this can be helpful in reducing the level of frustration and anxiety while interacting with other cultures.

Hofstede's Cultural Dimensions

1. Power Distance Index (PDI): The PDI is described as "the extent to which the less powerful members of organizations and institutions (like the family) accept and expect that power is distributed unequally". As already described, the power distance, inequality and power in the society/organization are perceived by its members or lower levels of social hierarchy. A higher level of the PDI shows that social hierarchy is visibly in existence, whereas a lower level of the PDI demonstrates people's endeavors to distribute power (Hofstede, 2011).

2. Individualism v/s Collectivism (IDV): It expresses the "degree to which people in a society are integrated into groups".

3. Uncertainty Avoidance (UAI): It is coping with anxiety by controlling uncertainty. As Hofstede (2011) mentioned, it is "a society's tolerance for ambiguity". Cultures with a high level of uncertainty avoidance have acceptance of social norms and prefer structured conditions. People are more open to uncertainty in cultures with a low level of uncertainty avoidance;

thus, comparatively, they take risks to a greater extent, make quick decisions without any idea of potential results, and are more open to others. According to Snitker (2010), uncertainty avoidance influences decisions and processes in multifarious ways.

4. Masculinity v/s Femininity (MAS): It is about how people value masculine and feminine cultural roles. It is also referred to as task versus person orientation, whereas gender traits are assessed through emotional roles in different cultures. Masculine cultures value competence, power, ambitions, autonomy, success and assertiveness. Feminine cultures are more inclined to have relationships, cooperation, quality of life, and care for others uniformly with men and women. Masculine cultures are more sensitive to the elements that constitute men's social and work roles than women's social and work roles, while low masculine cultures allow more significant overlap in men's and women's roles.

Table 1.3: Difference between Masculinity and Femininity

	Masculinity	**Femininity**
Value Orientation	Highest emotional and social role discrimination between genders	Least emotional and social role discrimination between genders
Autonomy	Men at large and limited Women have their choice of career	Essentially, Men and Women both have their choice of career
Social-emotional Role	Respect for the strong	Empathy for the weak
Behavioral Trait	Men are, and women may be assertive and ambitious	Men and Women are modest and supportive
Work & Life	Work first, then family	A balance between work and family
Decision-Making	Fathers deal with facts, and mothers with feelings	Both fathers and mothers deal with facts and feelings
Social Norms	Girls cry; boys don't; they should be strong and can't express emotions	Both Boys and Girls may cry; they should not fight back
Religious View	Focuses on God	Focuses on fellow human beings
Attitude toward Sexuality	Moralistic: sex is a way of performing	Matter-of-Fact: sex is a way of relating

5. Long-term v/s Short-term Orientation (LTO): It expresses a society's association with time horizon, i.e., the extent to which a society encourages delayed satisfaction or physiological and social needs of its people. Long-term orientation stresses pragmatic values, future, adaptation and success. Short-term orientation focuses more on the present, instant needs, adaptation, and quick results.

Table 1.4: Difference between Short-term and Long-term Orientation

	Short-term Orientation	**Long-term Orientation**
Life Philosophy	A reasonable person is always the same	A reasonable person adapts to the circumstances
Personal Control & Stability	Low	High
Moral Code	There are universal guidelines about what is good and evil	What is good and evil depends upon the circumstances
Traditions	Sacrosanct	Adaptable to changed circumstances
Social Responsibility	Service to others is an important goal	Thrift and perseverance are essential goals
Economic Orientation	Social spending and consumption	Large savings and investments
Hopefulness	Success and failure to luck	Success to effort and failure to lack of effort

Table 1.5: Difference between Indulgence and Restraint

	Indulgence	**Restraint**
Life Perception	Personal control of life	Life depends on others doing
Freedom of Speech	High: seen as a primary concern	Low: not a primary concern
Emotions	Retain and remember most positive emotions	Less inclined to remember positive emotions
Level of Optimism & Joy	High: free gratification	Low: strict social norms
Education vs Birthrate	Educated population with a higher birthrate	Educated population with a lower birthrate
Sport Participation	Most people actively involved	Fewer people actively involved
Sexual Norms	Lenient	Stricter
Leisure	Higher importance	Lower importance

6. Indulgence v/s Restraint (IND): It is about how society allows its members to fulfill their needs and to what extent. Abstractly, a society's cultural norms give its people the degree of freedom to attain their desires. This dimension offers a measure of societal propensity and control.

Culture Drives Behavior

Culture is an inseparable and differentiating aspect of humans. It is a part of their identity and significantly impacts their beliefs about life. Their dependence on culture is exceptional and surprising too. Culture is a dynamic force in a society comprised of its people's shared values, beliefs and behaviors. It directs people's decisions and actions at a cognitive level, strongly impacting their socio-economic and psychological wellbeing and success. Behaviors are the most visible reflection of a culture. The type of culture to which a person belongs, either collectivistic or individualistic, profoundly influences his/her beliefs and behaviors. For example, a person born in a collectivistic culture, where the social norms are strongly followed, does not uphold individualistic behavior. In contrast, a person who grew up in an individualistic culture has greater autonomy in what to believe and behave (Gantt, 2020).

The shared social norms constitute behaviors generally regarded as *"common sense"* and cultural practices of the society as well as its people's philosophies and values. Social norms restrict people from questioning their culture's ideology and formation—such as rituals, roles, responsibility, honor system, and group dynamics. People perceive culture as eminence in life that regulates their level of impetus. Their culture-originated impetus drives their behaviors, critical thinking, decision-making, individual growth and level of satisfaction. Recent studies outlined possible ways people learn cultural concepts during childhood and the cultural practices they observe and experience in adulthood influence their cognitive processes and behaviors (Kitayama & Park, 2010; Pogosyan, 2017).

Every culture holds certain collectivist and individualist beliefs; however, more importance is given to being extroverted in individualistic cultures. Collectivistic cultures promote behaviors appropriate to most people. Giving importance to others' perspectives to promote collective harmony is an optimistic aspect of collectivistic cultures, whereas it is not as much in individualistic cultures. According to Smith (2014), people from individualistic cultures are considerably inclined to develop independent self-construal that they "strive for self-expression, uniqueness and self-actualization, acting autonomously based on their own thoughts and feelings, and pursuing their own goals" (p. 160). The trait extroversion propels individualistic thoughts and behaviors; thus, more diversity can be observed in the population. There is a greater need for social interaction if a culture promotes extrovert personality traits (Gantt, 2020). Individualistic societies encourage extreme assertive behaviors, but when these societies' people support these behaviors, the exchange of ideas increases. It may significantly enhance people's level of motivation.

There is not always necessary that the converse of extroversion is introversion (Gantt, 2020). It means that less introverted people are possibly less socially inclined, but this does not signify that they don't like socializing. It has been observed that these people prefer to socialize in small groups, usually with close friends or most trusted people from their professional circle. People from individualistic cultures look more contented than collectivists. It may be due to their success in getting attention. According to Gantt (2020), "being noticed is a psychological reward."

An individual's consolidated behavior is the sum total of his/her core human nature, culture, and personality (Matsumoto, 2007). Personality determines one's preferences, which guide individual lives (Samli, 2012). Because of their preferences, people prioritize their choices and endeavors. In this way, they underline their endeavors and establish and follow specific life patterns. Different cultures promote different values and different associated behavioral patterns. These differing behavioral patterns reflect and emphasize culture-specific behaviors. The possibility of having common or specific behavioral traits within cultures results from "being *born and bred* within the same society." Here, it is also necessary to clarify that caste is not synonymous with culture. However, racial identity is a mix of social, historical and political contexts, and thus people's racial and cultural identities often share many similarities.

It is a usual phenomenon that culture has a dominant influence on people's perspectives and behaviors that often they are not aware. In the context of more culturally diverse settings, such unobserved beliefs and behaviors can lead to preventable conflicts. Once people become aware of such possibilities, they can take thoughtful steps toward a better and more thorough understanding of them. People who belong to a particular society should be mindful that their beliefs and practices can influence others' behavior and be influenced by the expectations and practices of people from other cultures.

Human Behavior in Cultural and Cross-Cultural Situations

Culture is robustly associated with all psychological processes and influences probable facets of one's behavior, such as perception, attitude, motivation, and judgment (Triandis, 2000; Maheshkar & Sharma, 2018). According to Shiraev and Leavy (2010), "human behavior is not only a 'result' or 'product' of cultural influences; people are also free, active, and rational individuals who are capable of exercising their own will." Thus, it can be believed that cultural psychology considers culture as a person's inside processor of psychological states. Cross-cultural psychology considers culture as an independent variable. It refers to culture outside the person, i.e., a culture's interaction with other cultures and its influences on a person's culture to which he/she belongs and his/her behaviors. These influences may be positive and/or negative to a person's behavior.

Human Behavior in Intra-Cultural Situations

Human behavior, in socio-cultural context, is basically engaged with relationships with people (i.e., family, friends, and work), reactions to behaviors of each others, and linkages with abundant societal and individual forces that lead them. An intra-cultural situation refers to the culture context in which all the members of the society have similar backgrounds. For example, communication between two or more people essentially belong to the same culture, thus a dialogue between two Chinese people who grew up in mainland China would be intra-cultural because they have the same cultural belonging and backgrounds.

Culture provides a reasonably established context for human development (Segall et al., 1999, Maheshkar, 2016). For investigating human behaviors and their effects, culture, in a real sense, considered as a pre-specified environment. Human behavior emerges in, and shaped and controlled by environmental elements. According to Ember and Ember (1985), "culture encompasses the learned behaviors, beliefs, and attitudes that are characteristic of people in a particular society or population" (p.166). A culture contains knowledge, skills, and attitudes that are taught to and learned by people and thus shared by them over the generations, thus more or less, it is adaptive (Segall, 1999, Moore & Lewis, 1952). As an action field, culture not only stimulate different behaviors, but also control these behaviors through stipulated conditions '*social/cultural norms*' (Boesch, 1991).

Different behaviors are the products of genetic inheritance and experiences with various intra-cultural contexts. The conditions in which people develop within the intra-cultural contexts are regulated by the interaction of their social learning and inherited genetic competence. Primarily, every person born in a particular culture and its intra-cultural settings (e.g., community, social class, language, and religious practices) play vital role in their development. The attributes of an intra-cultural setting affect how people learn to think and behave in the initial years of their age. It is the reason behind the substantial similarity in the ways of responding to the influence of similar pattern. And later, they come into contact of other inter-cultural influencers. Intra-culturally inspired behavioral patters—such as lingual dexterity, body language, humor, and social role—are deeply rooted in the human mind that people usually use without being fully aware of them.

Every culture holds somewhat varying patterns of living and sustaining—social norms and roles, tradition of food and clothing, religions, beliefs and values, behavioral expectations from others, and attitudes toward other cultures. Within a culture, there may be various sub-cultural groups differentiated with geography, ethnic origin, or social class. If a culture is central in a large province, its values and practices can be accepted as true and promoted not only by its people, but also by governments (e.g., Hinduism in India).

Human Behavior in Cultural and Cross-Cultural Situations

Human behavior in a cross-cultural or multi-cultural context is the resultant response due to critical cultural effects on human psychology. A cross-cultural situation is formed when at least two different cultural groups interact; in which people need a particular set of critical skills, mainly critical thinking, emotional intelligence, and respect for diversity. Diversity is the central part the cross-cultural situations. Human psychology struggles with *inclusion-exclusion phenomenon* caused by this cultural diversity, in which particular human activities are influenced by numerous and sometimes divergent social and cultural forces.

Critical Thinking

Thinking is an indispensable trait of humans. It is an intrinsic mechanism behind almost every act people do and closely linked with other behavioral traits, such as learning and problem-solving. Thinking is usually prone to be simplistic, biased, rigid, lethargic, or just casual. The meta-thoughts (*thoughts about thought*) can provide people with specific strategies for inquiry and problem-solving.

For describing phenomena, the way people use reflects their thinking as an aggregation of values, biases, preferences, and cultural orientation. It can reveal many aspects of their thinking and its reflection can be seen in their behavioral responses. No phenomena are homogeneous to and heterogeneous from each other because of the dimensions or variables involved. So, one's thinking and its varied effects on other behavioral components and overall personality depending on the dimensions and/or variables selected for evaluation purposes. The assimilation bias is a significant barrier to clear thinking, which caused distortions, misinterpretation, and invalidation (Shiraev & Leavy, 2010).

It can be observed as the most significant attribute of thinking that people personally engage in and then closely stick to their beliefs, cultural values, societal norms, and interpretations. This *belief importunity* can usually lead them to freely modify (exaggerate or reduce) or ignore facts that appear contrary to their reality. In the case of cross-culture setting, it can create culture-led conflicts.

Perception

People's experience with their environment stimulates them to think and make interpretations, fabricates their expectations—known as perceptual set—about the environment they belong, or its objects or events that may be deviated from the reality. People of one culture have common perceptual sets and do not necessarily develop in people from other cultures (Shiraev & Leavy, 2010). There are numerous factors—that may cause differences in consciousness and perception of people—varying across the cultures, depending upon: 1) people's psychosomatic order, socio-economic status, and hereditary and 2) culture's environmental conditions, socialization norms, and acculturation practices. Self-concept, which refers to how people perceive and consider themselves, is an important dimension for interpreting cross-cultural differences in behavior, cognition, and emotions. For example, western cultures encourage individualist self-concept, where the *self* is an autonomous entity, which emphasizes on one's individuality and independence. On the other hand, most of Asian cultures emphasize on collectivist self-concept, where the *self* is rational, interconnected, and harmonious to one's self and the others (Pogosyan, 2017). Here, consciousness directs human behavior in adaptive manner in particular cultural environment. One's consciousness is dependent on his/her socialization experiences, which typically influenced by cultural and cross-cultural factors and shared collective experiences (Shiraev & Leavy, 2010). People's cultural environment determines which abilities will improve in them, and which remain deprived. As the knowledge of the world increases, their consciousness broadens that increases their perceptual clarity.

Intelligence or Cultural Intelligence

Intelligence refers as an individual's competence to be successful in terms of conceptualizing the ways through which personal standards can be achieved within the particular socio-cultural context. When cultural elements considered, people can effectively use their abilities. As Sternberg and Grigorenko (2004) mentioned, "intelligence is always displayed in a cultural context." The core mental processes of intelligence and the mental representations upon which they perform principally transcend cultures. For example, problem-solving in all cultures following almost same process, however, the problems may vary to different extent. People's ability to solve problems linked with their well-being; but attitude of and the efforts made for problem-solving varies from culture to culture. Here, if overall performance toward problem-solving assessed, it means mental processes and representations have been assessed in a cultural context (Sternberg & Grigorenko, 2004).

In the case of cross-cultural settings, term intelligence evolved as *cultural intelligence*, which refers to one's adaptability to new cultural settings (Ersoy, 2014; Maheshkar & Sharma, 2018). The constructs of cultural intelligence and why people differ in effectiveness toward adapting new cultural settings are a major interest of cross-cultural psychology. System approach viewed *cultural intelligence* as a mechanism of interaction between knowledge, skills, and attitudes based on cultural meta-cognition. It allows people to adjust to accept or reject cultural elements of a cross-cultural setting for responding to other cultures effectively (Thomas et al., 2008). Cultural intelligence is a major determinant of leadership (Kim & Van Dyne, 2011; Ersoy, 2014; Maheshkar & Sharma, 2018) that linked with cultural adaptation, decision-making, communication processes, trust-building, and performance in an intercultural or cross-cultural environment (Ng et al., 2009; Maheshkar & Sharma, 2018).

Emotions

Emotions are people's conditional expressions and behavior, which can be *positive or negative* and *internal or external*. As a psychological phenomenon, emotions are "*internal*", which outburst through expressions and behavior depending upon the nature of emotions i.e. *positive or negative* (Niedenthal et al., 2006). Emotions in interpersonal relationships enable people to relate and decide their priorities for each other. There are various studies claiming that emotions are universal phenomena and always culturally influenced because of the patterns of reaction are social constructions (e.g., Darwin, 1998; Richeson & Boyd, 2005; Miyamoto & Ryff, 2011). Culture provides a framework to recognize and interpret emotions and related behavioral responses; however, there are significant cultural deviations in social norms and consequences. It can be observed that collectivists are less likely to express emotions toward maintaining social harmony. For example, Japanese are low in self-expression, either verbal or non-verbal (Miyahara, 2000). Emotional self-control in collectivistic cultures is typically more than individualistic cultures (Niedenthal et al., 2006). Individualists freely express their emotions and willing to have selected closer relationships (Rakahashi et al., 2002).

Cross-culturally, emotions can influence people to accept, avoid and reject others, respect or disregard others, care or disgust others, and control or be dedicated to some (Shiraev & Leavy, 2010). Emotional practices vary across cultures due to cultural differences in the established and idiosyncratic emotional responses (Lim, 2016; Mesquita & Walker, 2002; Russell, 1998; Markus & Kitayama, 1991). According to Laukka & Elfenbein (2020), "people can recognize emotional expressions via nonverbal behavior across cultural divides, and yet they do so better when staying within their own cultural boundaries." It is an important notion in regards to evaluating emotional disturbances—"excess and/or deficiency in emotions" or "variations in constituents of emotions" (Mesquita & Walker, 2002, Kring, 2001). Emotional arousal is an important aspect of affective experience. According to Lim (2016), there are considerable "cultural differences in the levels of emotional arousal between the West and the East." People from Western cultures have more inclination for high arousal emotions than low arousal emotions, whereas, in Eastern cultures, people have low arousal emotions more than high arousal emotions.

Moreover, motive or motivation expresses an individual's goal-directed behavior caused through his/her internal drive(s), such as self-efficacy, achievement, and intrinsic competence (Bandura 2002). The specific factors vary across the cultures that drive behavior. For example, achievement motivation is higher in individualistic cultures than in collectivistic cultures (Sagie et al. 1996). Psychological well-being is the most needed aspect of human psychosomatic order, where intrinsic motives—autonomy, relatedness, and competence—play a significant role and vary cross-culturally (Ryan & Deci, 2000). For example, Nguyen et al. (2021) mentioned that "westerners are more promotion-focused (and less prevention-focused) than Easterners," which gives an apparent basis to explore meta-motivational comparisons across the cultures.

Conclusion

Culture considerably influences human behavior; thus, it is fundamental to differences and similarities in behaviors. A culture expresses a cluster of symbolic meanings, values, norms, rituals and inherited history, which gives a frame of reference to the cognitive, affective and psycho-motor domains of humans to behave in specific ways in different situations. It influences probable dimensions of cognitive processes, behaviors, and describes the relationships among these processes and behavioral factors. This review-based chapter makes it comprehensible that human behavior continuously varies in response to environmental influences. Human beings learn how to behave essentially from cultural learning, mediated mainly through socialization and enculturation processes. There is no homogeneity across the cultures, which can be examined on specific cultural factors, such as those described by Hofstede. In cultural and cross-cultural contexts, human behavior includes developing and altering cognitive and affective behaviors—values and attitude, perception, critical thinking, emotional intelligence, intercultural relations, acculturation and tolerance. An improved understanding of cultural and cross-cultural influences on behavior can allow being more effective in cultural interactions and maintain psychological equilibrium.

References

Adeoye, B. & Tomei, L. (2014). Effects of information capitalism and globalization on teaching and learning. Information Science Reference.

Cherry, K. (2020). Individualist Culture and Behavior. Retrieved on March 27, 2022 from https://www.verywellmind.com/what-are-individualistic-cultures-2795273

Cherry, K. (2022). What is a Collectivist Culture? Retrieved on March 27, 2022 from https://www.verywellmind.com/

Darwin, C. (1998). The expression of emotions in man and animals. London.

Ersoy, A. (2014). The Role of Cultural Intelligence in Cross-Cultural Leadership Effectiveness: A Qualitative Study in the Hospitality Industry. Journal of Yasar University, 9(35), 6099-6260.

Gantt, L. M. (2020). Lynda Gantt: How does culture affect behavior? Retrieved on April 2, 2022 from https://santamariatimes.com/

Gudykunst, W. B., Matsumoto, Y., Ting-Toomey, S., Nishida, T., & Karimi, H. (1994). Measuring self construals across cultures: a derived etic analysis. Paper presented at the International Communication Association Convention in Sydney, Australia, July.

Hofstede, G. (2011). Dimensionalizing Cultures: The Hofstede Model in Context. Online Readings in Psychology and Culture, 2(1). https://doi.org/10.9707/2307-0919.1014

House, R. J., Hanges, P. J., Javidan, M., Dorfman, P. W., Gupta, V. (2004). Culture, Leadership, and Organizations The GLOBE Study of 62 Societies. Sage.

Ji, Y., Zhou, E., Li, C., & Yan, Y. (2015). Power Distance Orientation and Employee Help Seeking: Trust in Supervisor as a Mediator. Social Behavior & Personality, 43(6): 1043–1054. https://doi.org/10.2224/sbp.2015.43.6.1043

Kim, Y. J. & Van Dyne, L. (2011). Cultural Intelligence and International Leadership Potential: The Importance of Contact for Members of the Majority. Applied Psychology: An International Review, 61(2), 272-294. https://doi.org/10.1111/j.1464-0597.2011.00468.x

Kring, A. M. (2001). Emotion and psychopathology. In T. J. Mayne, & G. A. Bonanno (Eds.), Emotions (pp. 337–360). Guilford Press

Laukka, P. & Elfenbein, H. A. (2020). Cross-Cultural Emotion Recognition and In-Group Advantage in Vocal Expression: A Meta-Analysis. Emotion Review, 13(1), 3-11. https://doi.org/10.1177/1754073919897295

Lim, N. (2016). Cultural differences in emotion: differences in emotional arousal level between the East and the West. *Integrative Medicine Research*, 5(2), 105-109. https://doi.org/10.1016/j.imr.2016.03.004

Lincoln, J. T., Hanada, M., & McBride, K. (1986). Organizational structures in Japanese and U.S. manufacturing. Administrative Science Quarterly, 31, 338–364.

Maheshkar, C. (2016). HRD Scholar-Practitioner: An Approach to Filling Research, Theory and Practice Gaps. In Hughes, C. & Gosney, M. W. (Eds.), Bridging the Scholar-Practitioner Gap in Human Resource Development (pp 20-46). USA: IGI Global. https://doi.org/10.4018/978-1-4666-9998-4.ch002

Maheshkar, C. (2019). A study of evaluation of competency mapping scales in management education. Doctoral Thesis. University of Indore, India.

Maheshkar, C., & Sharma, V. (2018) (Eds.). Cross-cultural Business Education: Leading Businesses around the Cultures. In Handbook of Research on Cross-Cultural Business Education (pp. 1-35). IGI Global. https://doi.org/10 .4018/978-1-5225-3776-2.ch001

Markus, H.R. & Kitayama, S. (1991). Culture and the self: implications for cognition, emotion, and motivation. Psychological Review, 98(2), 224-253. https://doi.org/10.1037/0033-295X.98.2.224

Matsumoto, D. (2007). Culture, Context, and Behavior. Journal of Personality, 75(6), 1285-1320. https://doi.org/10.1111/j.1467-6494.2007.00476.x

Maynard, A. E. & Barney, D. E. (2018). Epistemologies: Cultural and Methodological Considerations. Human Development, 61, 368–375. https://doi.org/10.1159/000495119

Mesquita B. & Walker, R. (2002). Cultural differences in emotions: a context for interpreting emotional experiences. Behaviour Research and Therapy, 41(7), 777–793. https://doi.org/10.1016/S0005-7967(02)00189-4

Miller, J.G. (1994). Cultural diversity in the morality of caring: Individually-oriented versus duty-based interpersonal moral codes. Cross-Cultural Research, 28(1), 3–39. https://doi.org/10.1177/106939719402800101

Miyahara, A. (2000). Toward Theorizing Japanese Communication Competence from a Non-Western Perspective. American Communication Journal, 3(3), 279-292.

Miyamoto, Y. & Ryff, C. (2011). Cultural differences in the dialectical and non-dialectical emotional styles and their implications for health. Cognition and Emotion, 25(1), 22-30. https://doi.org/10.1080/02699931003612114

Ng, K. Y., Van Dyne, L. & Ang, S. (2009). Developing Global Leaders: The Role of International Experience and Cultural Intelligence. In Mobley, W.H., Wang, Y. & Li, M. (Eds.), Advances in Global Leadership (pp. 225-250). https://doi.org /10.1108/S1535-1203(2009)0000005013

Nguyen, T., Togawa, T., Scholer, A. A., Miele, D. B., & Fujita, K. (2022). A Cross-Cultural Investigation of Metamotivational Beliefs About Regulatory Focus Task-Motivation Fit. Personality and Social Psychology Bulletin, 48(5), 807-820. https://doi.org/10.1177/01461672211025423

Nickerson, C. (2021). Understanding Collectivist Cultures. Retrieved on April 25, 2022 from https://www.simplypsychology.org/what-are-collectivistic-cultures.html

Niedenthal, P. M., Silvia, K-G., & Francois, R. (2006). Psychology of Emotion Interpersonal, Experiential, and Cognitive Approaches (pp. 5, 305-342). Psychology Press.

Pogosyan, M. (2017). How Culture Wires Our Brains. Retrieved on April 5, 2022 from https://www.psychologytoday.com/us/blog/between-cultures/201701/how-culture-wires-our-brains

Richeson, P. J. & Boyd, R. (2005). Not by genes alone: How culture transformed human evolution. University of Chicago Press.

Russell, J.A. (1994). Is there universal recognition of emotion from facial expression? A review of the cross-cultural studies. Psychological Bulletin, 115(1), 102-141. https://doi.org/10.1037/0033-2909.115.1.102

Ryan, R. M., & Deci, E. L. (2000). Self-determination theory and the facilitation of intrinsic motivation, social development, and well-being. American Psychologist, 55(1), 68–78. https://doi.org/10.1037/0003-066X.55.1.68

Sagie, A., Elizur, D., & Yamauchi, H. (1996). The structure and strength of achievement motivation: a cross-cultural comparison. Journal of Organizational Behavior, 17(5), 431-444. https://doi.org/10.1002/(SICI)1099-1379(199609)17:5<431::AID-JOB771>3.0.CO;2-X

Samli, A.C. (2013). Culture Driven Values. In: International Consumer Behavior in the 21st Century. New York, NY: Springer. https://doi.org/10.1007/978-1-4614-5125-9_4

Schwartz, S. H. (1994). Beyond individualism and collectivism: new cultural dimensions of values. In U. Kim, H.C. Triandis, C. Kagitcibasi, S-C. Choi, & G. Yoon (Eds.), Individualism and collectivism: Theory, method, and applications (pp. 85–122). Sage.

Shiraev, E. B. & Leavy, D. A. (2010). Cross-Cultural Psychology: Critical Thinking and Contemporary Applications, 4e. Boston, MA: Allyn & Bacon.

Shweder, R. A. (1999). Why Cultural Psychology?. Ethos, 27(1), 62-73. https://doi.org/10.1525/eth.1999.27.1.62

Shweder, R. A. (2008). The Cultural Psychology of Suffering: The Many Meanings of Health in Orissa, India (And Elsewhere). Ethos, 36(1), 60–77.

Singelis, T. M. (1994). The measurement of independent and interdependent self-construals. Personality and Social Psychology Bulletin, 20(5), 580–591. https://doi.org/10.1177/0146167294205014

Smith (2014). Cited in Importance Of Culture On Human Behavior. Retrieved on April 24, 2022 from https://www.123helpme.com/essay/Importance-Of-Culture-On-Human-Behavior-709645

Snitker, T. V. (2010). The impact of culture on user research. In Schumacher, R. M. (Ed.), Handbook of Global User Research, p.257-277. Morgan Kaufmann. https://doi.org/10.1016/B978-0-12-374852-2.00009-4

Sternberg, R. J., & Grigorenko, E. L. (2004). Intelligence and culture: how culture shapes what intelligence means, and the implications for a science of well-being. Philosophical transactions of the Royal Society of London. Series B, Biological sciences, 359(1449), 1427–1434. https://doi.org/10.1098/rstb.2004.1514

Suh, E., Diener, E., Oishi, S., & Triandis, H. C. (1998). The shifting basis of life satisfaction judgments across cultures: emotions versus norms. Journal of Personality and Social Psychology, 74(2), 482-493. https://doi.org/10.1037/0022-3514.74.2.482

Takahashi, K. N., O., Antonucci, T. C., & Akiyama, H. (2002). Commonalities and differences in close relationships among the Americans and Japanese: A comparison by the individualism/collectivism concept. International Journal of Behavioral Development, 26(5), 453–465. https://doi.org/10.1080 /01650250143000418

Thomas, D. C., Elron, E., Stahl, G., Ekelund, B. Z., Ravlin, E. C., Cerdin, J-L., Poelmans, S., Brislin, R., Pekerti, A., Aycan, Z., Maznevski, M., Au, K., & Lazarova, M. B. (2008). Cultural intelligence: Domain and Assessment. International Journal of Cross-Cultural Management, 8(2), 123–143. https://doi.org/10.1177/1470595808091787

Triandis, H. C. (1990). Cross-cultural studies of individualism and collectivism. In J. Berman (Ed.), Nebraska symposium on motivation, 1989 (pp. 41–133). University of Nebraska Press.

Triandis, H. C. (1994). Culture and social behavior. McGraw-Hill.

Wagner, J. A., III, & Moch, M. K. (1986). Individualism–collectivism: Concept and measurement. Group and Organizational Studies, 11(3), 280–304. https://doi.org/10.1177/105960118601100309

Chapter 2

Emotions: The Missing Link in Cultural Diversity Research

Arti Sharma

Indian Institute of Management (IIM) Indore, India

Sushant Bhargava

Indian Institute of Management (IIM) Jammu, India

Abstract: Cultural diversity recognizes the presence of different cultures and acknowledges their underlying values and distinctiveness. A large section of cultural diversity research is rooted within the basic emotion theory (e.g., Ekman & Friesen, 1969, 1971), arguing for the universalistic nature of emotions while marginalizing the discussion on the socio-cultural rooting of emotions (Valsiner, 2007). While addressing this gap, the present work attempts to bring forth a conceptual model emphasizing the missing link of 'emotions' in mainstream cultural diversity research. This model proposes that the historical and ecological understanding of emotions embedded within a culture constructs the perception of inclusion and exclusion within individuals. It has been suggested that the interplay of emotions at the individual, group, and societal level shapes the experience of inclusion and exclusion, which may help in multicultural understanding and reconstruction or deconstruction of the worldview. Further, the chapter discusses the theoretical and practical implications of having emotions as an essential tenet in cultural diversity research.

Keywords: Cultural Diversity, Emotions, Inclusion & Exclusion, Surface-level Diversity, Deep-level Diversity, Organizational Culture

***

Introduction

The pace of globalization and technological advancements has facilitated interactions among individuals with diverse backgrounds, beliefs, and cultures

(Mazur, 2010). Organizations are becoming increasingly diverse with visible acceptance of different cultures in work units (Ely & Thomas, 2001). This composition of workers from various cultural groups attributes to the cultural diversity within the organizations (Seymen, 2006). Historically, cultural diversity is understood as a combined function of culture viewed as an ongoing conscious mobilization of cultural differences (Bosler & Bauman, 1992) and diversity of the human mind (Appadurai, 1996).

Interestingly, scholars in cultural diversity have indicated that cultural differences can form the basis of stereotypes or social categorization and, at the same time, can go unrecognized due to their presence beneath the level of consciousness (Stahl et al., 2010). Scholars have demonstrated this with the manifestation of cultural diversity in situations concerning higher education (Guo & Jamal, 2007; Mostafa & Lim, 2020); management leadership (Duchatelet, 1998); human rights; universal ethics; cultural disagreements (Fleischacker, 1999); and cultural polarization (Flache, 2018), establishing cultural diversity as an outcome of various visible or invisible factors rooted within the culture (Groeschl & Doherty, 2000). It has led to the skewed advancement of the research on cultural diversity towards the surface level characteristics, for instance, age, gender, race, language, norms, lifestyle, etc. (Fleury, 1999; Zakaria, 2000; Wright & Noe, 1996). It is asserted that over-reliance on this perspective has led to the myopic conceptualization of cultural diversity with respect to only surface-level attributes while overlooking the underlying deep-level characteristics such as attitudes, beliefs, and emotions that shape the overall social and cultural differences.

In essence, cultural diversity is based on surface-level attributes beyond conceptualization. Cultural diversity is a complex system of beliefs and behavior that recognizes and respects the group's diversity and acknowledges and values the socio-cultural differences encouraging an inclusive culture to empower all in the organization or society (Rosado, 2006). It is known from studies that culture is a generic representation of mutually shared values, symbols, and meanings derived dynamically through social interactions, thereby shaping the affective and behavioral responses of individuals (Jenkins, 1992). Psychological anthropologists have emphasized that emotions are mediated by culture (Kleinman & Good, 1985; Rosaldo, 1984; Shweder et al., 1984). In fact, facial expressions of emotions play a crucial role in ascertaining culture-specific features to dwell deeper into understanding the shared meaning and affective responses of a culture (Jack et al., 2012; Jenkins, 1991). Scholars have indicated that these distinctive characteristics embedded within the culture shape the understanding of emotions, which plays a crucial role in the idea of inclusion and exclusion (Stevens et al., 2008).

According to Social Identity Theory (Tajfel & Turner, 1979) and Self-Categorization Theory (Turner et al., 1987), individuals identify with a group having similar characteristics. Thus, in a culturally homogenous group, the similarity of culture facilitates instant identification with the group, while in a culturally diverse group, the identification is much lower among the members (Chattopadhyay et al., 2004; O'Reilly et al., 1989; Tsui et al., 1992), serving as the dominant trigger of inclusion and exclusion (Otten & Jansen, 2014; Mazur, 2010). Parallelly, borrowing from the anthropological view of emotions as culturally wrapped universals (Beatty, 2005), we intend to move forward from the scholarly discussions on the emotional underpinnings of diversity through distinctive and observable impacts on different aspects of organizational work. Though emotions are a crucial human attribute in determining the effects of cultural diversity in organizational work, they remain neglected in targeted exploration and beyond cursory treatments as far as theory development/application is concerned. It is especially important for realizing and developing insights about culturally-induced inclusion and exclusion, which are central to workforce management.

For this, a conceptual model is proposed to advance the discourse on emotions as a missing link in cultural diversity research. Through this model, we attempt to discover a) the criticality of emotion in predicting how cultural diversity shows up in various situations and b) how these emotion-related attributes of diversity combine to dictate human responses of significance to organizational work in the global workplace. With this, it is intended to contribute to the under-explored line of inquiry in cultural diversity research and attempts to bring emotions to the forefront of cross-cultural diversity studies. As the model deals explicitly with workforce diversity in organizations, thus model explanation is limited to the domain of organizational and management studies.

Literature Review

Diversity is asserted as a unidimensional construct pressing on the patterns of inclusion or exclusion due to visible or less visible differences within a workgroup (Jehn et al., 1999). The visible heterogeneity within the workgroup reflecting the overt demographic attributes is referred to as surface level (Ely & Thomas, 2001; Mannix & Neale, 2005), while the less visible psychological characteristics such as attitudes, personality, values, and emotions are termed as deep-level diversity attributes (Barsade et al., 2000; Harrison et al., 1998; Roberson, 2019). Based on the similarity or differences of these characteristics, the sense of mutual identification and the way of perceiving is developed among the individuals, which is evident in the culture-specific communication styles, attitudes, and behavioral responses (Seymen, 2006). Based on this understanding, cultural diversity is defined as an outcome of the interaction of visible demographic characteristics and underlying values (Hurn & Tomalin, 2013).

Interestingly, scholars have indicated that cultural diversity can source both surface-level and deep-level diversity characteristics (Harrison et al., 1998; Stahl et al., 2010). For instance, studies report the surface-level attributes of cultural diversity in racial, ethnicity and nationality (Ely & Thomas, 2001; Mannix & Neale, 2005). These conceptualizations emphasize the primary dimensions of diversity, or the surface-level diversity characteristics such as race, ethnicity, gender, and age (Maier, 2002) solely, indicating the salience of visible differences to trigger the similarity attraction and social categorization processes within the workgroup laying the foundation of inclusion and exclusion (Haas, 2010).

Inclusion and exclusion are the founding stone of diversity research (Nkomo et al., 2019). Individuals tend to identify the commonalities and explore culturally constructed differences for inclusion or exclusion (Halse, 2018). Here, inclusion refers to "the degree to which individuals experience treatment from the group that satisfies their need for belongingness and uniqueness" (Shore et al., 2011, p. 1265). On the other hand, exclusion refers to "the process through which individuals or groups are wholly or partially excluded from full participation in the society within which they live" (De Haan, 2000, p.26). These patterns of inclusion and exclusion lay the differentiating characteristics for diversity (Shore et al., 2011), prominently in the context of cultural diversity (Hulse & Stone, 2007; Jönhill, 2012).

A few studies attempted to study the deep-level characteristics of cultural diversity regarding culture-specific values and attitudes of members within a workgroup (Hofstede, 1980; House et al., 2004; Kirkman & Shapiro, 2001). However, these studies focused on the biological and universalist aspect of emotions (e.g., Ekman, 1973; Kitayama & Markus, 1994; Mesquita & Frijda, 1992; Scherer & Wallbott, 1994), suggesting them as a natural phenomenon driven by autonomic biological mechanisms uniform across cultures (Ratner, 2000). It has marginalized the discussion on the socio-cultural rooting of emotions (Valsiner, 2007), calling for attention to the deep-level diversity characteristics in cultural diversity. Simultaneously, authors have questioned the overreliance on surface-level attributes (Litvin, 1997) and have demonstrated the dynamic nature of diversity while suggesting that less visible attributes may become more prominent in contrast to visible attributes over time (Harrison et al., 1998; Nkomo, 2021). They argue that diversity is inherently contextual, socially constructed, and culturally bound (Triandis, 1996), with a greater reliance on subjective feeling and objectively categorizing members (Garcia-Prieto et al., 2003). It inspires to draw the attention of the research fraternity to argue for emotions as the missing link in cultural diversity research. Emotions are indigenous to each individual, and scholars have touched upon the role of emotions in different situations of work (Ashkanasy et al., 2002; Garcia-Prieto et al., 2003). However, the discussion on emotions in mainstream cultural diversity research is deficient. The rationalist perspective of cultural diversity has highlighted the role of cognition for inclusion and exclusion, which is a myopic way of looking at both in a broad sense. Though Hofstede and Bond's (1984) cultural dimensions demonstrate the differences in emotions across cultures, these have surprisingly not been adopted much in the cultural diversity research. Hence, this gap is addressed by cementing the place of emotions in cultural diversity research through the proposed model in the subsequent section. Adopting an individual perspective (as the proposed model does) allows us to look at diversity from the perspective of their membership and other aspects of personal identity. However, more recent and detailed research analyses have covered other aspects of diversity-oriented identity. These systematic treatments do not fall into our purview of exploring the place of emotions in diversity models (see Devine & Ash, 2022, for one such treatment).

Conceptual Framework

Culture plays a definitive role in constructing and preserving social identity (Hopkins & Reicher, 2011) and, thereby, interpreting diversity for each individual. Social Identity works at all levels (the individual, group, or societal/organizational) to dictate behavioral actions and patterns. There are numerous social components to every aspect of human interaction. Diversity is uniquely positioned in this milieu of influences on human life and social interactions (Flache, 2018). It is crucial to approach the subject from multiple angles simultaneously to make sense of the complex influences of cultural diversity on human interactions and observe their impact on organizational/administrative work. The proposed model serves this purpose by modeling the change in behavior through cultural diversity and related interventions as a series of value changes (Shore et al., 2011). The model distills varied and deep conclusions from the literature on the topics of interest. As we have seen, diversity creates differences in emotional responses among individuals. However, culture is so deeply embedded in human understanding and expression that it is impossible to isolate its effects entirely. Therefore, the focus is on the components of diversity that are affected by training and intervention (Mazur, 2010). It demonstrates how and where emotions meld with behavior in the context of cultural diversity.

Till now, scholarly literature has explored and interpreted the emotional underpinnings of diversity through distinctive and observable impacts on different aspects of organizational work. The model development based on theory integration and observations from practice is valuable in furthering the discipline and understanding of the subject concerned (Fleischacker, 1999). The proposed model uses the visible characteristics of the diversity-emotion relationship as representative labels. Here, the interplay of various characteristics among each other was considered. In this way, it was intended to discover a) the criticality of emotion in predicting how cultural diversity shows up in various situations and b) how those emotion-related attributes of diversity combine to dictate human responses of significance to organizational work in the global workplace. Therefore, the model explanations are limited to the domain of organizational work and may not be generalizable to other situations where the highlighted relationships may manifest. Figure 2.1 presents the model as emergent from existing perspectives on cultural diversity in the scholarly literature.

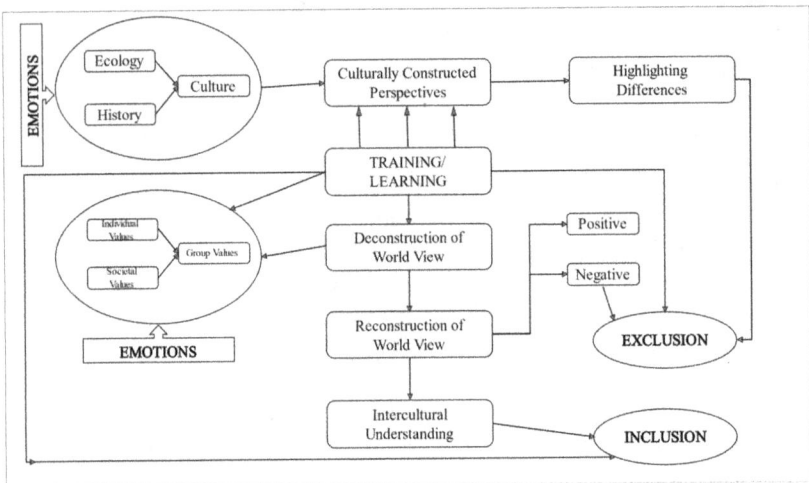

Figure 2.1: The conceptual framework of cross-cultural diversity and emotions

Links between culture, cultural diversity, and emotions are difficult to establish without going slightly deeper into the inherent (and sometimes non-obvious) characteristics. Cultural diversity guides behavior through its surface- and deep-level components. Therefore, both components are essential to finding the place of emotions in traditional and modern work environments and related dynamics of diversity. Further, we use inclusion and exclusion as outcomes to demonstrate how the presence or absence of triggered emotional responses borrow from and shape manifestations of diversity [*see (Shore et al., 2011, p. 1265) and (Haan, 2000, p. 26) for definitions*]. The interpretation of inclusion and exclusion are extensions to models of diversity vis-à-vis its evolving character as technology continues to routinize and facilitate interactions among individuals with differing origins in beliefs and culturally rooted responses or understandings of situations. However, behavior and behavioral change are central to the model, enhancing its value for practitioners who find cultural diversity at their workplace inalienable to their work practices and processes. Prior research has acknowledged the variability in interactions and behavior across contexts where multicultural or intercultural participation is involved (Ferraro & Cummings, 2007). However, the place of underlying emotions and their reflection in determining expressed behavior and/or formation of attitudes and values remains unclear, especially where the complex phenomena of inclusion and exclusion are concerned.

While emotions have a direct part to play in building an individual's worldview, they indirectly affect the consequences of that worldview. This worldview may be apparent in multiple instances of behavior, but not all behavior may be of organizational relevance in all situations. Also, the organization may primarily be interested in changing certain displayed cases of behavior for any individual. Behavioral change has previously been rooted in culture or culture change through multiple pathways (Cleveland et al., 2016; Glenn, 2004; Landrine & Klonoff, 2004). Hence, cultural diversity has a profound and subtle impact on workplace behavior, the mechanisms that merit scholarly consideration and integration. The construction and deconstruction of existing worldviews are essential to any training program or intervention and contribute to relatively permanent changes in values. These values are interconnected in the levels of influence each individual is exposed to within the organization. For instance, research supports such changes at the level of the team (Garcia-Prieto et al., 2003), as also, if only distally, at the leadership level (Duchatelet, 1998). Inclusion and exclusion are essential behavioral consequences of cultural diversity (Otten & Jansen, 2014). Even starting from the student level, diversity continues to play out (Guo & Jamal, 2007; Mostafa & Lim, 2020). Given the macro nature of the eventual effects of cultural diversity and its ever-present influences even outside of organizational work, it is prudent to include inclusion and exclusion with emotions to lend a corporate character to the whole scheme of influences emanating from cultural diversity.

This model also considered that the historical and ecological understanding of emotions embedded within a culture constructs the perception of culture within individuals. This perception is further learned and refined due to the experiences of an individual while interacting with other individuals, groups, and society at large. At the surface level, these cultural differences can be highlighted and frame boundaries for exclusion, which can cause the deconstruction of pre-existing worldviews. For instance, the individual may drop favorable notions about one culture upon being excluded or mistreated. Based on this experience, one can reconstruct the worldview in a positive or negative light. It is propounded that this new meaning of the world will resonate at a deeper level of cultural diversity, which may influence the intercultural understanding of individuals from different cultures. It may further align with their inclination towards diversity inclusion. Through this model, it has been attempted to bring emotions as the central idea of discussion in cultural diversity models. Yet, with diversity being all-encompassing in its effects and manifestations, emotions remain but a part of the actual impact – albeit a critical one. This attempt does not intend to assert any apportioning of the effects of diversity on emotions (or vice versa) but merely build pathways to possible associations and provide glimpses of some implications through the following sections.

Discussion and Theoretical Implications

Emotions are universal in their occurrence and impact. Therefore, their management is rapidly gaining importance as workplaces become global. The focus is on the modern workplace and organizations since other aspects of emotions are primarily personal and only expressed through social interactions (Nummenmaa et al., 2012; Lopes et al., 2005). The expression of emotions becomes unique to the individual as societies become more diverse. Still, that expression may remain non-regular or non-consistent outside work or organizational settings. Organizations are of many types, sometimes prompting observation of diversity within their boundaries (see literature on the ecology of organizations starting from Hannan & Freeman, 1977). It is challenging to bring out the facets in a single model. However, management situations have been shown to – a) carry adequate weight in the sustenance of both emotions and diversity (e.g., Vigoda-Gadot & Meisler, 2010; Knight et al., 1999), and b) to be situated in organizational boundaries (Brinkerhoff, 2008; Suresh et al., 2017; Wen, 2011). Hence, they are used here to show the missing place of emotions in cultural diversity.

Modern society is a confluence of multi-objective individuals and groups. When the individual faces culture, cultural diversity, and emotions as commonplace social phenomena, identity distinction becomes important (Cole & Salimath, 2013; Mitchell & Boyle, 2017; Phinney, 1996). However, those same individuals and groups are also the founding units of organizations that hold relatively more continuity in their existence (Smeekes & Verkuyten, 2015). Hence, the objective of this attempt is to find the place of emotions vis-à-vis some aspects of organizations. Therefore, on the left-hand side of the model, the place of emotions in the pattern of influences has been shown in contrast with the right-hand side, where elements of organizations have been shown (see Figure 2.1). The implications of the relationships are described in the guise of indicative labels. There may be other levels at play in different situations, and those overlooked situational factors better highlight the place of emotions in cultural diversity. As such, emotions are not reduced in their impact in this representation but are slightly segregated for clarification of the flow of influences in the overall pattern. As regards inclusion and exclusion, they are depicted as stages through which CCD and emotions together cast their power over the individual. For instance, perception, realization, or the creation of prevailing differences leads to feelings of exclusion or disconnection. For the same reason, reconstructions of world view or world view generally come into the picture (Knoblauch & Wilke, 2016; Barber, 2020). World views are critical to the existence of distinctive effects of diversity and therefore necessitate inclusion in a holistic model. Also, world views are considered indisputable only in the interim, as far as they affect the emotions and attitudes to eventually engage with cultural diversity (Wolf et al., 1994; Hobsbawm & Ranger, 2012).

Culture and emotions here are not seen directly through conventional modes of observation but at two ends of a pattern of influences (interchangeably, it may be argued by some). Both are deeply studied phenomena and hold such a degree of subjectivity in any representation that a single model cannot capture the entire spectrum of details when the two are taken up together. Additionally, cultural diversity assumes its place at the intersection of embedded cultural and emotional norms in a globalized world and organizations. Hence, cultural diversity ceases to be merely an issue to be handled by those in management roles within those organizations. Though its benefits and detriments have been known for a long, integration is still required to inculcate modern realities. There are also lingering issues relating to ethics in the manifestation and handling of cultural diversity (Fleischacker, 1999). The extension of diversity to emotions can resolve these issues. Measuring emotions is fraught with ethical and methodological complexities, especially in the internet age and online work. Increasingly, the process orientations of diversity-sensitive interventions (as highlighted in the model) are becoming more apparent through research (Ely & Thomas, 2001). Aside from the direct theoretical advantages, a more holistic inclusion of diversity in models depicting the forms in which cultural diversity (in general and cross-cultural diversity in particular) is visible in human interactions can be seen as having some powerful intervention-oriented practical implications.

Practical Implications

The presented model details the successive effects of training on emotions through the changes in an individual's worldview. These effects are often implicit where cultural diversity or other kinds of diversity are concerned in organizations. Here, they have been considered explicitly to enhance immediate practical significance. Training and learning are critical for the adjustment of individuals in any organization and the perception and experiences of diversity and emotions where interventions are being considered (Otaye-Ebede, 2018). To enable the model's adaptability to different organizational contexts, emotions are shown at definitive places within the model – first as essential contributors to the eventual experience of cultural diversity and second as contributors to the building of relevant values. However, despite the narrowness of the theoretical relations outlined here, emotions are much more deeply ingrained with the other labels. It can lead to the discovery of further implications for the experiences of cultural diversity as the individual navigates the organization through time. Therefore, there exists ample scope for emotional anchoring of cultural diversity models–thereby contributing to the theoretical advancements in psychological contexts of cultural diversity. Emotions are an integral part of an individual and are firmly embedded in the culture. Thus, there is a need for empirical studies to understand the interplay of surface and deep-level diversity attributes in cultural diversity.

Subsequently, with the aid of this model, a practitioner might be able to generate new insights while asserting the missing link of emotions, which can help them understand or explain the psychological attributes of cultural diversity. It is also likely to enable them to design an inclusive workplace with effective interventions addressing the emotional differences among individuals. The insights from our model may also serve as a handy tool for building an effective workforce attuned to the emotional attributes inherent in specific cultures such that a conducive and congenial work environment can be created and sustained. Through this model, the academician and the industrialist may understand the role of emotions in handling diversity in digital space and online communities. Thus, culturally sensitive training for all the stockholders is also highlighted for reaping the maximum advantage of a diverse workforce. In this manner, emotions are considered related to diversity only in terms of their place in organizations and managerial work. However, this chapter only highlights the much-overlooked missing link of emotions in the models of cultural diversity. It is expected that the labels provided would aid adaptation and translation to other aspects of human interactions (dyadic or social). Future work may additionally bring into consideration and context the similarly divergent views on diversity using the proposed model as a basis through the exploration of systematic review-based insights.

Conclusion

This study exhibits that emotions are indeed a "missing piece" in the holistic conceptualizations of cultural diversity. The context of organizational work has been considered in describing the presented model and extending it to include other observed influences as labels. It is critical since organizations and other work settings are where cultural diversity comes into play most extensively with emotions and related behavior. The literature review draws from established lines of research to find evidence for the eventual place of emotions in cultural diversity. Notably, it was found that the variation and prevalence of worldview and feelings of exclusion and inclusion are prominent in the patterns of influence in the workplace. Culture cannot be reduced to emotions, and the reverse is also untrue. However, when seen together, diversity assumes additional significance as viewed in its form of cultural diversity. Implications in organizational work are thus enormous, and further explorations of the model relationships are fruitful given the current volatility in the world scenario.

References

Appadurai, A. (1996). *Modernity at large: Cultural dimensions of globalization* (Vol. 1). University of Minnesota Press.

Ashkanasy, N. M., Härtel, C. E., & Daus, C. S. (2002). Diversity and emotion: The new frontiers in organizational behavior research. *Journal of management, 28*(3), 307-338.

Barber, M. D. (2020). Alfred Schutz. In *The Routledge Handbook of Phenomenology and Phenomenological Philosophy* (pp. 616-624). Routledge.

Barsade, S. G., Ward, A. J., Turner, J. D., & Sonnenfeld, J. A. (2000). To your heart's content: A model of affective diversity in top management teams. *Administrative science quarterly, 45*(4), 802-836.

Beatty, A. (2005). Emotions in the field: What are we talking about?. *Journal of the Royal Anthropological Institute, 11*(1), 17-37.

Bosler, R., & Bauman, D. J. (1992). Meeting Cultural Diversity with Personal Conviction: The Teacher as Change Agent and Transformational Leader.

Brinkerhoff, D. W. (2008). The state and international development management: Shifting tides, changing boundaries, and future directions. *Public Administration Review, 68*(6), 985-1001.

Chattopadhyay, P., Tluchowska, M., & George, E. (2004). Identifying the ingroup: A closer look at the influence of demographic dissimilarity on employee social identity. Academy of Management Review, 29(2), 180–202.

Cole, B. M., & Salimath, M. S. (2013). Diversity identity management: An organizational perspective. *Journal of business ethics, 116*(1), 151-161.

De Haan, A. (2000). Social exclusion: Enriching the understanding of deprivation. *Studies in social and political thought, 2*(2), 22-40.

Devine, P. G., & Ash, T. L. (2022). Diversity training goals, limitations, and promise: a review of the multidisciplinary literature. *Annual review of psychology, 73*, 403.

Duchatelet, M. (1998). Cultural diversity and management/leadership models. *American Business Review, 16*(2), 96.

Ekman, P. (1973). Cross-cultural studies of facial expression. *Darwin and facial expression: A century of research in review, 169222*(1).

Ekman, P., & Friesen, W. V. (1969). The repertoire of nonverbal behavior: Categories, origins, usage, and coding. *semiotica, 1*(1), 49-98.

Ekman, P., & Friesen, W. V. (1971). Constants across cultures in the face and emotion. *Journal of personality and social psychology, 17*(2), 124.

Ely, R. J., & Thomas, D. A. (2001). Cultural diversity at work: The effects of diversity perspectives on work group processes and outcomes. *Administrative science quarterly, 46*(2), 229-273.

Ferraro, P. J., & Cummings, R. G. (2007). Cultural diversity, discrimination, and economic outcomes: an experimental analysis. *Economic Inquiry, 45*(2), 217-232.

Flache, A. (2018). Between monoculture and cultural polarization: Agent-based models of the interplay of social influence and cultural diversity. *Journal of Archaeological Method and Theory, 25*(4), 996-1023.

Fleischacker, S. (1999). From cultural diversity to universal ethics: three models. *Cultural Dynamics, 11*(1), 105-128.

Fleury, M.T.L. (1999). The management of culture diversity: lessons from Brazilian companies. *Industrial Management & Data Systems, 99*(3), 109-14.

Garcia-Prieto, P., Bellard, E., & Schneider, S. C. (2003). Experiencing diversity, conflict, and emotions in teams. *Applied psychology, 52*(3), 413-440.

Groeschl, S., & Doherty, L. (2000). Conceptualising culture. *Cross Cultural Management, 7*(4), 12-17.

Guo, S., & Jamal, Z. (2007). Nurturing cultural diversity in higher education: a critical review of selected models. *Canadian Journal of Higher Education, 37*(3), 27-49.

Haas, H. (2010). How can we explain mixed effects of diversity on team performance? A review with emphasis on context. *Equality, Diversity and Inclusion: An International Journal.*

Halse, C. (2018). Theories and theorising of belonging. In *Interrogating belonging for young people in schools* (pp. 1-28). Palgrave Macmillan, Cham.

Hannan, M. T., & Freeman, J. (1977). The population ecology of organizations. *American journal of sociology, 82*(5), 929-964.

Harrison, D. A., Price, K. H., & Bell, M. P. (1998). Beyond relational demography: Time and the effects of surface-and deep-level diversity on work group cohesion. *Academy of management journal, 41*(1), 96-107.

Hobsbawm, E., & Ranger, T. (Eds.). (2012). *The invention of tradition.* Cambridge University Press.

Hofstede, G. 1980. Culture's consequences: International differences in work-related values. Sage.

Hofstede, G., & Bond, M. H. (1984). Hofstede's culture dimensions: An independent validation using Rokeach's value survey. *Journal of cross-cultural psychology, 15*(4), 417-433.

House, R. J., Hanges, P. J., Javidan, M., Dorfman, P. W., & Gupta, V. (Eds.). (2004). *Culture, leadership, and organizations: The GLOBE study of 62 societies.* Sage publications.

Hulse, K., & Stone, W. (2007). Social cohesion, social capital and social exclusion: A cross cultural comparison. *Policy Studies, 28*(2), 109-128.

Hurn, B. J., & Tomalin, B. (2013). Multiculturalism and diversity. In *Cross-cultural communication* (pp. 191-207). Palgrave Macmillan.

Jack, R. E., Caldara, R., & Schyns, P. G. (2012). Internal representations reveal cultural diversity in expectations of facial expressions of emotion. *Journal of Experimental Psychology: General, 141*(1), 19.

Jenkins, J. (1992). The meaning of expressed emotion: Theoretical issues raised by cross-cultural research. *American journal of psychiatry, 149*(1), 9-21.

Jenkins, J. H. (1991). Anthropology, expressed emotion, and schizophrenia. *Ethos, 19*(4), 387-431.

Jönhill, J. I. (2012). Inclusion and exclusion—A guiding distinction to the understanding of issues of cultural background. *Systems Research and Behavioral Science, 29*(4), 387-401.

Kirkman, B. L., & Shapiro, D. L. (2001). The impact of cultural values on job satisfaction and organizational commitment in self-managing work teams: The mediating role of employee resistance. *Academy of Management journal, 44*(3), 557-569.

Kitayama, S. E., & Markus, H. R. E. (1994). *Emotion and culture: Empirical studies of mutual influence* (pp. xiii-385). American Psychological Association.

Kleinman, A., Good, B. J., & Good, B. (Eds.). (1985). *Culture and depression: Studies in the anthropology and cross-cultural psychiatry of affect and disorder* (Vol. 16). University of California Press.

Knight, D., Pearce, C. L., Smith, K. G., Olian, J. D., Sims, H. P., Smith, K. A., & Flood, P. (1999). Top management team diversity, group process, and strategic consensus. *Strategic management journal, 20*(5), 445-465.

Knoblauch, H., & Wilke, R. (2016). The common denominator: The reception and impact of Berger and Luckmann's The Social Construction of Reality. *Human Studies, 39*(1), 51-69.

Litvin, D. R. (1997). The discourse of diversity: From biology to management. *Organization, 4*(2), 187-209.

Lopes, P. N., Salovey, P., Côté, S., Beers, M., & Petty, R. E. (2005). Emotion regulation abilities and the quality of social interaction. *Emotion, 5*(1), 113.

Maier, C., (2002). Leading Diversity – A Conceptual Framework. St Gallen: Institute for Leadership and HR Management.

Mannix, E., & Neale, M. A. (2005). What differences make a difference? The promise and reality of diverse teams in organizations. *Psychological science in the public interest, 6*(2), 31-55.

Mazur, B. (2010). Cultural diversity in organisational theory and practice. *Journal of intercultural management, 2*(2), 5-15.

Mesquita, B., & Frijda, N. H. (1992). Cultural variations in emotions: a review. *Psychological bulletin, 112*(2), 179.

Mitchell, R., & Boyle, B. (2015). Professional diversity, identity salience and team innovation: The moderating role of openmindedness norms. *Journal of Organizational Behavior, 36*(6), 873-894.

Mostafa, H., & Lim, Y. (2020). Examining the relationship between motivations and resilience in different international student groups attending uS universities. *Journal of International Students, 10*(2), 306-319.

Nkomo, S. M. (2021). Reflections on the continuing denial of the centrality of "race" in management and organization studies. *Equality, Diversity and Inclusion: An International Journal.*

Nkomo, S. M., Bell, M. P., Roberts, L. M., Joshi, A., & Thatcher, S. M. (2019). Diversity at a critical juncture: New theories for a complex phenomenon. *Academy of Management Review, 44*(3), 498-517.

Nummenmaa, L., Glerean, E., Viinikainen, M., Jääskeläinen, I. P., Hari, R., & Sams, M. (2012). Emotions promote social interaction by synchronizing brain activity across individuals. *Proceedings of the National Academy of Sciences, 109*(24), 9599-9604.

O'Reilly, C. A., Caldwell, D. F., & Barnett, W. P. (1989). Work group demography, social integration, and turnover. *Administrative Science Quarterly, 34*, 21–37.

Otaye-Ebede, L. (2018). Employees' perception of diversity management practices: scale development and validation. *European Journal of Work and Organizational Psychology, 27*(4), 462-476.

Otten, S., & Jansen, W. S. (2014). Predictors and consequences of exclusion and inclusion at the culturally diverse workplace. In *Towards Inclusive Organizations* (pp. 75-94). Psychology Press.

Phinney, J. S. (1996). Understanding ethnic diversity: The role of ethnic identity. *American Behavioral Scientist, 40*(2), 143-152.

Ratner, C. (2000). A cultural-psychological analysis of emotions. *Culture & Psychology, 6*(1), 5-39.

Roberson, Q. M. (2019). Diversity in the workplace: A review, synthesis, and future research agenda. *Annual Review of Organizational Psychology and Organizational Behavior, 6*, 69-88.

Rosado, C. (2006). What do we mean by "managing diversity". *Workforce diversity, 3*(1), 1-15.

Rosaldo, M. Z. (1984). *Toward an anthropology of self and feeling.*

Scherer, K. R., & Wallbott, H. G. (1994). Evidence for universality and cultural variation of differential emotion response patterning. *Journal of personality and social psychology, 66*(2), 310.

Seymen, O. A. (2006). The cultural diversity phenomenon in organisations and different approaches for effective cultural diversity management: a literary review. *Cross Cultural Management: An International Journal.*

Shore, L. M., Randel, A. E., Chung, B. G., Dean, M. A., Holcombe Ehrhart, K., & Singh, G. (2011). Inclusion and diversity in work groups: A review and model for future research. *Journal of management, 37*(4), 1262-1289.

Shweder, R. A., Le Vine, R. A., LeVine, R. A., & Economiste, R. A. L. (Eds.). (1984). *Culture theory: Essays on mind, self and emotion.* Cambridge University Press.

Smeekes, A., & Verkuyten, M. (2015). The presence of the past: Identity continuity and group dynamics. *European Review of Social Psychology, 26*(1), 162-202.

Stahl, G. K., Maznevski, M. L., Voigt, A., & Jonsen, K. (2010). Unraveling the effects of cultural diversity in teams: A meta-analysis of research on multicultural work groups. *Journal of international business studies, 41*(4), 690-709.

Stevens, F. G., Plaut, V. C., & Sanchez-Burks, J. (2008). Unlocking the benefits of diversity: All-inclusive multiculturalism and positive organizational change. *The journal of applied behavioral science, 44*(1), 116-133.

Suresh, L., Bodik, P., Menache, I., Canini, M., & Ciucu, F. (2017, September). Distributed resource management across process boundaries. In *Proceedings of the 2017 Symposium on Cloud Computing* (pp. 611-623).

Tajfel, H., & Turner, J. C. (1979). An integrative theory of intergroup conflict. In W. C. Austin & S. Worchel (Eds.), *The Social Psychology of Intergroup Relations* (pp. 33–47). Brooks/Cole

Triandis, H. C. (1996). The psychological measurement of cultural syndromes. *American psychologist, 51*(4), 407.

Tsui, A. S., Egan, T. D., & O'Reilly, C. A. (1992). Being different: Relational demography and organizational attachment. *Administrative Science Quarterly, 37,* 549–579

Turner, J. C., Hogg, M. A., Oakes, P. J., Reicher, S. D., & Wetherell, M. S. (1987). *Rediscovering the social group: A Self-Categorization Theory.* Basis Blackwell.

Valsiner, J. (2007). *Culture in minds and societies: Foundations of cultural psychology.* SAGE.

Verkuyten, M., & Yildiz, A. A. (2007). National (Dis)identification and Ethnic and Religious Identity: A Study Among Turkish-Dutch Muslims. *Personality and Social Psychology Bulletin, 33*(10), 1448–1462. https://doi.org/10.1177/0 146167207304276

Vigoda-Gadot, E., & Meisler, G. (2010). Emotions in management and the management of emotions: The impact of emotional intelligence and organizational politics on public sector employees. *Public Administration Review, 70*(1), 72-86.

Wen, J. J. (2011). Gender and management across boundaries. *The Business Review, Cambridge,* 212-218.

Wolf, E. R., Kahn, J. S., Roseberry, W., & Wallerstein, I. (1994). Perilous ideas: Race, culture, people [and comments and reply]. *Current anthropology, 35*(1), 1-12.

Wright, P.M. & Noe, R.A. (1996). Management of Organizations. Irwin McGraw-Hill.

Zakaria, N. (2000). The effects of cross-cultural training on the acculturation process of the global workforce. *International Journal of Manpower, 21*(6), 492-510. https://doi.org/10.1108/01437720010377837

Chapter 3

Moral Development in Cultural Psychology

Namrata Chatterjee
Sulhaa Healthcare, Delhi, India

Alankrita Kumar
Sulhaa Healthcare, Delhi, India

Abstract: Moral development constitutes a complex system of cognitive and affective components and socio-cultural influences such as media, legal frameworks, and religious, ideological, and social norms. Philosophers have theorized the cultural impact of individuals and societies on morality under the ambit of cultural relativism. In this chapter, systematically discussing the prominent theories of moral development, the psychological impact of culture on approaches toward morality and ethics was explored. Further, distinct aspects of morality were examined, as theorized by philosophers and psychologists, such as moral realism versus moral relativism and heteronomous morality versus autonomous morality. With the help of examples, the various factors that influence the development of moral reasoning and subsequent moral action, including the evolutionary correlation between culture and moral development, collectivistic versus individualistic societal factors, and moral dynamism in terms of temporality, were also investigated. Finally, the possibility of a universal code and its distinction from pragmatic relativism, employing the Moral Foundations Theory as a theoretical framework explored.

Keywords: Moral Development, Cultural Psychology, Cultural Relativism, Moral Judgment, Heteronomy, Autonomy, Moral Realism

***

Introduction

Moral development refers to the process of forming beliefs and attitudes that govern moral decision-making and related behaviors in an individual's life. To engage in the discourse pertaining to moral development, it is imperative to clarify specific terms. Morality has been defined as a system of beliefs relating to right conduct, against which behavior is judged to be acceptable or unacceptable (APA Dictionary of Psychology, 2020).

The concept of morality, including moral judgment and reasoning, has been a part of both philosophical and psychological studies in academic research. In psychological academia, the development of morality in individuals has been reported as an active part of developing personality and cognitive patterns, starting from childhood, focusing on the dynamism of moral action throughout an individual's lifespan. For example, one of the earliest understandings of moral action was posited by the founder of psychodynamic theory, Sigmund Freud, who attributed moral judgment and subsequent behavior to the superego—the morality principle of personality. Further, from the perspective of evolutionary psychology, humans have been studied as social animals because we tended to live in communities, a practice formerly necessary for survival; thus, with time, giving rise to the relevant moral principles and questions of help, reciprocity, team formation, group norms, and rules of right conduct.

Jean Piaget and Lawrence Kohlberg provide us with extensive insight into how moral development takes place and the role of subjective, cognitive, emotional, and social developmental processes as contributing factors. Piaget took the cognitive route to understand moral development in children and talked about mutual autonomy. He proposed two stages, namely heteronomous moral realism and autonomous moral relativism (Cam et al., 2012). Kohlberg adopted Piaget's criteria for cognitive development and argued that moral reasoning develops according to the universally prevalent sequence of three stages—pre-conventional, conventional, and post-conventional. He founded the modern field of moral psychology with his declaration that the answer was one (he was a monist) and developed a grand theory that unified moral psychology as the study of the progressive development of a child's understanding of justice (Naito, 2013). He further proposed that all cultures use universal concepts of morality: "All individuals in all cultures use the same thirty basic categories, concepts, or principles" (Kohlberg, 1971, p. 175). Thus, given this context, it may be established that human cognition and behavior function in a complex network of conditioning, individual beliefs, and ideas, as well as the culture and environment surrounding individuals.

Cultural Psychology in Moral Development

To understand moral development in its entirety, it is essential to see its correlation with culture. From the viewpoint of cultural psychology, cultures are all-embracing constructs that form relatively coherent patterns of thought and action, with the patterns of one culture different from another. Individuals are predisposed to participate in culture and accept and reproduce their culture's dominant orientation and norms. Cultural messages are communicated to members via several mechanisms, such as explicit instruction, media and literature, and participation in socially prescribed forms of behavior (Wainryb & Recchia, 2014).

Moral identity in an individual develops due to the need to curb impulsive, innate desires and yearnings. Incorporating socially acceptable behavior through rules, norms, and roles and responsibilities are required to benefit others and secure the same rights and benefits. This idea has been discussed in the political-philosophy theory known as the Social Contract Theory, which argues that people have an unwritten and implicit agreement with the group or culture in which they function, in order to gain the security and safety, inclusivity, and cultural privileges like reciprocity, from the socio-cultural construct, in turn giving up on their innate state of being, thereby developing patterns of moral reasoning and subsequent moral action.

Despite moral development being regarded as a purely cognitive, subjective, and individual process by early contributors to the field, many researchers have argued the need to involve a cultural lens in the discourse; this points toward the understanding that while some moral concepts may be similar in most cultures, its functioning and manifestation may differ significantly. The primary conflict in this sphere is the apparent subjectivity of moral ideas and values. Descriptive moral relativism posits that moral positions on significant matters differ culturally. On the contrary, cultural relativism suggests that culturally held values that appear to be conflicting may not necessarily be so (e.g., killing superannuated parents) (Duncker, 1939). Given this, an action may be morally sound depending on its "meaning" rather than its cultural context. This distinction enables the investigation of overarching moral ideas that guide moral development in different cultures and societies. It emphasizes that cultural differences in moral judgment do not necessarily imply disparities in the central moral ideas of different societies. It gives rise to whether the world may be ready for a universal moral code as theorized in the Moral Foundations Theory (Haidt & Joseph, 2008). The theory seeks to understand how and why morality varies vastly across cultures and yet illustrates many similarities and recurrent themes. It provides the perspective that several innate and universally available psychological systems form the foundations of "intuitive ethics." Each culture, then, constructs virtues, narratives, and institutions based on these foundations, thereby creating the unique systems of morality that may be recorded around the world, nuanced geographically as well as temporally.

Review And Themes

Autonomous Moral Development and Culture

Despite moral development having its roots embedded in the necessity of surviving in a culture or social structure, primary contributors sought to emphasize individual cognitive development of moral judgment and reasoning. It aimed to establish some universal concepts, patterns, and hierarchy of stages that each person goes through, spread across their lifetime, more or less regardless of their environment. For this reason, early philosophers and psychologists such as Jean Piaget, Lawrence Kohlberg, Carol Gilligan, and others focused their study and understanding of morality and ethical behavior as a niche, unidirectional method.

The criticism for this arose due to the advent of research on the subject matter in non-Western countries. It was largely felt that the principles of the existing theories of moral development catered to a limited audience and lacked the required inclusivity and cultural lens. Thus, the debate on moral development and patterns of moral reasoning can be comprehended by whether morality is learned (or conditioned) by the social construct a person lives in or if it is subjectively reasoned with as an individual goes through life experiences and forms a cumulative understanding of what is generally right and wrong; this includes the understanding of the extent to which morally acceptable behavior is necessary for survival in a particular culture.

Taking Kohlberg's (1958) theory into account, he established that children learn and develop moral reasoning solely based on the principle of justice. That is to say, if a child, and later adult, deems an act or decision to be fair and just in a given scenario, they will proceed in that direction irrespective of their personal experiences, influences from primary caregivers, or social influences like media, literature, legal frameworks, and political and religious affiliations. The sequential 6-stage model proposed by Kohlberg begins with children's focus on the avoidance of punishment by authority figures through obedience (Stage 1) and potentially ends with an endorsement of universal principles of justice and rights (Stage 6). Such a monistic view of morality later came into scrutiny with the formation and entry of various cultures into the discourse.

Further research on this theory, in the context of cultural psychology, resulted in findings that indicated the possibility that the first four stages of Kohlberg's theory are universal; however, it is essential to emphasize the fact that their manifestation and functioning in varying cultures may be poles apart, along with personal motivations for the same being multifarious.

Many researchers focus on understanding moral development since Kohlberg disagrees with the question of inclusivity of diverse cultures, including cross-cultural interactions.

These researchers contend that focusing on concepts of justice, fairness, and harm to individuals and excluding concepts of interdependence, social harmony, and the role of cultural socialization in non-Western settings. This concern is grounded in Western philosophical thought and in the cultural milieu in which Kohlberg developed his theory in the Midwestern United States in the 1950s. Although Western notions of individualism may have been appropriate to describe his theory at the time and place, those same notions may not represent universal moral principles applicable to all people of all cultures (Jia & Krettenauer, 2017, p. 2).

For example, India, being a collectivist culture, gives immense importance to religious affiliations, familial traditions, principles of obedience and compliance, and the authority of older family members. Therefore, the question of a just act or decision seldom becomes the basis of moral judgment. Instead, cultural ideals get attached to an individual in ways that become their natural course of reasoning. Whether these ideals are later modified to fit individual experiences and perceptions and to what extent may also depend on cultural influences. Further, the manifestation of evolved moral understanding as moral action is also subject to how accepting individual environments may be of such changes.

Carol Gilligan (1982) was another contributor to moral development; she laid extensive emphasis on gender differences in moral reasoning and action. Her work proclaimed two kinds of ethics: the ethics of care for women and ethics of justice for men. She criticized Kohlberg for generalizing his research on all genders despite the prime sample consisting of males. However, later criticized by cultural psychologists, Gilligan's claim on moral development based on two absolute principles—justice and care. Understanding moral reasoning in terms of just two principles, specific to particular genders, cannot prove to be dependable.

To illustrate further, we take into account the work of one of the oldest researchers in moral and cognitive development—Jean Piaget. Piaget (1932) talked about moral heteronomy and moral autonomy. Through his moral judgment studies based on cognitive functioning in moral scenarios, Piaget found that younger children (aged four to seven) thought in terms of moral realism or moral heteronomy. These terms connote absolutism, in which morality is seen in terms of fixed and unchangeable rules; guilt is regarded to be determined by the extent of violation of rules rather than by intention. For later stages (aged 10 +), he found that rules have arbitrariness and are formed by mutual consent for reasons of fairness and equity. This applied equally to society's laws, game rules, and familial standards of behavior. Here, both moral realism and moral relativism provide a sound basis for moral reasoning but again lack the role of cultural influences that govern or at least significantly influence moral behavior.

For example, the role of media in today's world is heavily influenced by national laws and political affiliations. Most of the information received on and analysis done of one's own culture and that of others is through what one learns from the avenues of media and literature. These moral messages are bound to impact conditioning in terms of morality and hold power to strengthen or weaken autonomous moral principles, i.e., principles based on the innate need of people to remain compliant with their group or culture. Similarly, the laws set by the government of one's country, religious affiliations and traditions, as well as ideological beliefs taught at an early age are bound to create mental dissonances that may be considered under the ambit of moral dilemmas.

Thus, the assumption that sufficient research has been done in a wide range of socio-cultural settings cannot go unquestioned, which puts the matter of autonomous morality under stringent observation. It also indicates the need to contemplate how many cultures (and varieties of the same) need to be studied to claim these universal moral principles adequately; the usual criteria of chance error may be misleading. Additionally, these factors—age, gender, diverse religions, etc.—need to be inclusive of the varying aspects of a culture (Snarey, 1985).

Having said that, it has also been reiterated through combined research in multiple fields, including affective neuroscience, cognitive development, cross-cultural studies, and studies done on non-human primates, that all humans rely on a set of complex, evolved, and learned norms that are put in place to encourage community members to adopt certain perspectives that can guide and promote prosocial interactions. These moral norms are so important for social functioning that there appears to be a universal moral grammar through which certain moral norms—fairness, altruism, trust, and cooperation—are sacredly held. For example, take how a single social instrument—reciprocity—underpins compliance to these norms across socio-cultural settings and time (Feldman Hall et al., 2018).

Morality in Collectivist versus Individualistic Cultures

As discussed above, moral reasoning and moral action have come to be understood in terms of cultural ideals and their influence on the same. In addition to this, with the advent of globalization, cross-cultural interactions now pave the way for the incorporation of an eclectic process of moral development and judgment. Understanding moral development in terms of cultural and cross-cultural psychology requires the careful cognizance of the proposition that societies are divided into two kinds - collectivist versus individualistic.

Most of the research done in moral psychology was on Western ideals and perspectives, owing to sample taking are limited to the Western population. With the advent of research in different fields of psychology in Eastern cultures and the like, the importance of cultural influences and dynamism of human cognition and behavior was reported. In terms of moral development, a clear distinction between moral realism and moral relativism has been established, paving the way forward for understanding the processes of moral development with varying degrees of cultural influences, the role of media and the law, and religious and ideological differences in inter- and intra-socio-cultural settings. Here, ethnocentrism may be seen to be of importance, as it is through the consolidated ideals of the morality of one's own culture that a person judges the moral principles of another culture, which is bound to influence their own perceptions well. It is argued that people around the world may share the same moral foundations, ethical codes, and moral reasoning, but there is much disagreement about their relative importance across cultures (Jia & Krettenauer, 2017; Norenzayan & Heine, 2005).

Moral development in cultures is grounded in the perspective that individuals formulate social and moral ideals through participation in and reflection on social interactions of different kinds. Cultures with an individualistic orientation emphasize social experience around autonomous persons, relatively detached from their community and motivated to attain freedom and personal goals. As for collectivist cultures, the focus is on family, community, and interpersonal relationships. Thus, members of such cultures are identified by their interdependent roles and the social responsibilities they work along (Wainryb & Recchia, 2014).

Collectivist and individualistic cultures are also seen to have divergent views on morality owing to an evident difference in the dynamics of their members and respective social worlds. Moral development in individualistic cultures revolves around furthering their conceptions of freedom, personal choice, independence, and justice. It can be considered working on autonomous morality, as described by Piaget. On the other hand, collectivistic cultures seem to have a morality structure that is heavily interconnected to the societal norms, duties and roles prescribed to their members and focused on maintaining the smooth cultural functioning of the society they inhabit.

Hardy and Carlo (2005) explain a concept that talks about the role of an individual in moral functioning and moral action. Moral identity refers to "the degree to which being a moral person is important to an individual's identity"

(Hardy & Carlo, 2005, pp. 212). In individualistic cultures, moral identity plays a vital role as the emphasis is laid on what the individual's moral judgment deems fit in a given scenario that their personal experiences have presumably shaped. To say that moral identity is not an active and significant part of collectivistic moral structures would be wrong, as more research is required to understand the correlation. However, it can be safely recognized that moral identity in collectivistic societies plays a role in determining the causes of certain moral decisions and achieving a delicate balance between moral realism and cultural relativism.

Being a moral person results from a desire to be consistent with one's moral concepts, through which individuals are motivated to gain independence from social conventions. In contrast, people from Eastern cultures consider a highly moral person to be socially oriented. In this moral orientation, people tend to define themselves in the context of collectivism and an interdependent self (Markus & Kitayama, 1991). Social relationships and group membership are linked to the motivation to adjust to the demands of others and to maintain harmony within one's group (Markus & Kitayama, 1991). Being a moral person in Eastern societies may reflect group norms more than an individual's morality.

From the perspective of Confucianism, understandings of morality help to socialize individuals by encouraging them to suppress personal desires in social interactions and to eliminate "Xiao Wo," personal-centered actions, by emphasizing "Da Wo," societal-centered actions instead (Hwang, 1999). As a consequence of Eastern ideology, a highly moral person, "I," is transformed into "we" and, consequently, feelings of society within the group are strengthened (Jia & Krettenauer, 2017, p. 3).

How socio-cultural influences shape and change moral development and subsequent moral actions, in both collectivistic and individualistic cultures can be understood by taking the example of abortion laws in India and the USA. When discussing decisions to be made concerning a person's body and physical health, objectively speaking, neither the law nor the society should ideally have a say. However, as discussed in this chapter previously, social norms, cultural ideals and traditions, and the resulting legal system have a massive role in making a person's moral identity and consequent moral judgment. Abortion, or induced miscarriage, has been legal in the USA since the 1973 case of Roe v. Wade (the first abortion case to be taken to the Supreme Court). Since then, it has been ensured that every state consists of at least one abortion clinic. On the contrary, the Indian Penal Code, 1860 (IPC) makes abortion a criminal offence under Section 312, even after 50 years of the Medical Termination of Pregnancy Act. This distinction results from a difference in moral viewpoints in both countries - the USA is recognized as an individualistic culture, and India is of a collectivistic orientation. The moral understanding of abortion in India is shadowed by ancient cultural ideals that view abortion at par with murder, which has essentially contributed to the existence of a congruent legal framework. The emphasis on independence, justice, freedom, and an overall significance of personal liberty in moral decision-making allows the culture of the USA to accept the same.

However, the distinction of cultures in terms of collectivism versus individualism has met with criticism owing to an overemphasis on cultural homogeneity as well. Anthropologists and developmental psychologists have argued that the principles of autonomy and interdependence are not mutually exclusive but interwoven in development, coexisting in the thoughts and actions of people in all societies. For example, Asian societies are characterized as high on collectivism and low on individualism and Latin American societies are characterized as high on both values (Wainryb & Recchia, 2014).

Moral Dynamism and Temporal Influences

The advancement of civilization, as a process, remains persistent and unceasing to date. Technological innovations have contributed to remarkable lifestyle and social developments over time. Social changes affect the overall culture of communities and groups; this phenomenon is valid for all societies and cultures. Thus, culture is a function of time. Accordingly, apart from extant inter-cultural differences, all cultures undergo intra-cultural changes as well. Such changes, driven by time, have prompted a shift in the perception of morality. To illustrate: circuses were widely celebrated recreation mediums in the late nineteenth and early twentieth centuries. The use of wild and exotic animals in circuses was an accepted truth that did not arise as a moral question until recently; several countries have now banned the use of wild animals in circuses. Further, zoological gardens have now come to face scrutiny claiming that it is immoral to cage wild animals for recreation. This shift in the perception of animal use demonstrates a temporal, cultural change made possible by a shift in the scope of morality. In the case described above, the scope of moral judgment expanded with time to include animal welfare in recreational use. Such shifts in moral perceptions can be observed across cultures. However, it is worth exploring whether this change in the scope of morality evidences a temporal disparity between the core moral beliefs of cultures across the globe. It may be argued that the foundational moral themes—care/harm, fairness/cheating, loyalty/betrayal, authority/subversion, sanctity/degradation, and liberty/oppression— presently postulated in the MFT have remained unaffected by the passage of time. Outside of the MFT framework as well, it may be affirmed that certain moral beliefs and values, shared by people across cultures and over time, remain unchanged despite the apparent change in the scope of morality.

To take the example of mass media, there is a stark change in the nature of socially permissible content to be broadcasted. Here, it is essential to note a distinction: the temporal difference in media contents does not reflect the creators' morality but the moral consciousness of society at large. Another notable point is that social acceptance is not an indicator of morally sound action. Media produces the most acceptable content at any given point in time. It also exerts considerable influence on people's understanding of morality. Take Tamborini's (2012) Model of Intuitive Morality and Exemplars (MIME), which demonstrates short-and-long-term processes of media's influence on morality and vice-versa. According to this study, whether or not media content is received positively by an audience depends on the audience's moral inclinations. Additionally, repeated exposure to a particular moral construct may shape the audience's attitude towards it in the long term. The latter suggests a distinct temporal effect on morality caused by mass media.

Changes in law prompted by morality make an excellent case demonstrating temporal differences in the moral sphere, as practically enforced by society. In 1789, voting rights were granted only to men who owned property following the French Revolution. It was only later, in the early nineteenth century, that Western movements toward universal suffrage demanded the removal of property ownership as a prerequisite for voting rights. Further, the social practice of exchanging dowry has been a widely accepted and practiced tradition in India for centuries. It was only in 1961 that the exchange of dowry was criminalized in the country. These cases highlight the influence of socially sanctioned morality on legal frameworks. Per Honore (2002):

> The connection between law and critical morality is necessary for that it is not contingent. It applies to every law and every legal system. The proposed interpretation of every law in every legal system can legally be challenged on the ground that it is not morally defensible, whether the challenge succeeds or fails in a particular instance (p. 494).

Given this, it may be established that the moral defensibility of laws changes with time, demonstrating that the changing scope of morality is closely related to legal outcomes.

Another interesting element in the investigation of temporally shifting moral spheres is that of religion. The religious understanding of moral behavior posits that morally correct attitudes adhere to the word of God. The primary reason behind this may be the position of absolute and inarguable moral authority granted to God. However, the interpretation of morally acceptable behaviors as dictated by religion, and people's adherence to the same, has transformed with time. As generations progress, more and more people are moving away from religion-based morality and adopting a more contextually nuanced understanding of morality. This phenomenon can be understood by employing Kohlberg's (1981) moral development theory: individuals' earliest stage of moral development arises due to the fear of punishment and the social rewards associated with obedience. Parallelly, most religions control behavior by instilling the fear of punishment after death upon rejecting religious norms. Likewise, the possibility of a blissful afterlife depends on how obedient one has been to the word of God. On the contrary, the final stage of moral development is based on universal moral principles and abstract reasoning, which deems an act as moral or immoral based on contextual evidence rather than a pre-set of rules or norms. With a decreasing trend in religious fanaticism, individuals globally are attracted to the idea of independent moral decision-making as described by Kohlberg's (1981) final stage of moral development. Interestingly, this universal understanding of morality is also an integral part of the MFT by Haidt and Joseph (2008), which refer to it as "moral intuitions."

Further, temporal changes in social norms prompted by environmental and technological developments contribute to changes in the scope of morality. After civilization's advent and subsequent development, a wide range of activities was incorporated within the moral ambit: business ethics, sports ethics, and professional ethics, all contributed to the broadening scope of morality over time. While these sub-aspects may be regarded merely as rules or norms, all are founded on an innate moral basis.

A Case of Moral Diversity

To further illustrate culturally determined moral differences, let us take the case of moral vegetarianism. As its first premise, this construct deems the production of meat unethical. Because meat consumption is closely related to production, it concludes that meat consumption is immoral. According to DeGrazia (2009), sentient animals have a moral status, i.e., how they are treated is a moral question and not a matter of how their treatment may indirectly affect human beings. Thus, the interests of sentient non-human animals are of independent moral importance. It is an essential theme in vegetarian culture; however, it appears to be rejected by non-vegetarians. Bandura (2015) proposed the concept of moral disengagement as a psycho-social mechanism that enables individuals to sanctify a possibly harmful behavior as not being harmful or even benevolent. It may serve as a basis to understand how meat consumers morally disengage from meat consumption behavior; they do not consider consuming meat a matter of moral importance. Given the available information on the cruel practices of animal husbandry and rearing worldwide, it may be asked how this is possible, mainly for consumption. The findings of Tillman et al. (2018) indicated that the experience of shame is positively related to moral disengagement, suggesting that shame may prompt an individual to disengage from the behavior that causes shame morally. This may be a potential reason for the moral disengagement of meat consumers with their dietary choices. Further, many cultures do not subscribe to the notion that meat consumption may be immoral. Many religious and ethnic communities even pray to or worship the animals they intend to use for consumption. This illustrates the complex processes involved in determining which questions may be included under the ambit of morality. Establishing the morality of an action per se, only by the action itself, may not be effective. Instead, it is essential to examine what potentially moral matters mean to individuals in their cultural contexts.

Further, consider the Eskimo practice of killing superannuated parents. One may argue that killing another human being, especially one's parents, is immoral. However, Eskimo cultures deem it an act of care and benevolence. They justify this by presenting that old age is especially cruel in the harsh climatic conditions of the northern circumpolar region. Thus, while the act itself is nonconforming, the universal "moral intuition" that inspires it is care. This example demonstrates the claim that moral behaviors constitute diverse and dynamic elements influenced by culture. It also reiterates the universality of certain elements that drive moral behavior globally, such as care.

This approach may also enable the reconciliation of morally diverse attitudes globally. By avoiding generalizations in moral judgment and considering the contextual situations where morally significant actions are taking place, it is possible to reach a stage of moral understanding. This does not necessitate or warrant agreement on all matters but prevents irreconcilable differences. Thus, this approach does not necessarily result in a positive outcome but works toward avoiding potentially adverse outcomes.

Conclusion

This study explores the mutual influences that psychology and morality exert on each other. We have extensively discussed moral development by employing global and contextual examples and referencing extant literature in the field. The study of moral development in the cultural context is an important research subject, now more than ever, due to the continued increase in global interactions in the past few decades. Cross-cultural interactions may present the problem of moral disagreements, leading to discord and disharmony. This is especially so because morality as a construct is often very profoundly valued by cultures and individuals; thus, moral disagreements may potentially prove harmful to the global reception of cultural behaviors deemed morally harmful.

This study contributes to the relevant literature on morality, social psychology, cultural psychology, and cultural studies. It has the potential to inform future research to a considerable extent. However, it has a few limitations. As is often the case with narrative reviews, this study may not meet the criteria for adequately mitigating researchers' bias. Further, the criteria for including articles that have informed this study have not been explicitly stated. It is recommended that future studies employ a systematic review method to clarify the inclusion criteria for literature better and effectively prevent researchers' bias.

References

APA Dictionary of Psychology. (2020). American Psychological Association. Retrieved October 24, 2021, from https://dictionary.apa.org/morality

Bandura, A. (2015). Moral Disengagement: How People Do Harm and Live with Themselves (1st ed. 2016). Worth Publishers.

Cam, Z., Cavdar, D., Seydoogullari, S., & Cok, F. (2012). Classical and Contemporary Approaches for Moral Development. *Educational Sciences: Theory & Practice*, 12(2), 1123–1125. https://eric.ed.gov/?id=EJ987841

DeGrazia, D. (2009). Moral Vegetarianism from a Very Broad Basis. *Journal of Moral Philosophy*, 6(2), 143–165. https://doi.org/10.1163/174552409x402313

Duncker, K. (1939). The Influence of Past Experience upon Perceptual Properties. *The American Journal of Psychology*, 52(2), 255. https://doi.org/10.2307/1416111

Feldman Hall, O., Son, J. Y., & Heffner, J. (2018). Norms and the Flexibility of Moral Action. *Personality Neuroscience*, 1. https://doi.org/10.1017/pen.2018.13

Gilligan, C. (1982). In A Different Voice: Psychological Theory and Women's Development (1st ed.). Harvard University Press.

Haidt, J., & Joseph, C. (2008). The moral mind: How five sets of innate intuitions guide the development of many culture-specific virtues, and perhaps even modules. In P. Carruthers, S. Laurence, & S. Stich (Eds.), The innate mind: Vol. 3: Foundations and the future (1st ed., pp. 367–391). Oxford University Press. https://doi.org/10.1093/acprof:oso/9780195332834.003.0019

Hardy, S. A., & Carlo, G. (2005). Identity as a Source of Moral Motivation. Human Development, 48(4), 232–256. https://doi.org/10.1159/000086859

Honore, T. (2002). The Necessary Connection between Law and Morality. *Oxford Journal of Legal Studies*, 22(3), 489–495. https://doi.org/10.1093/ojls/22.3.489

Hwang, K. K. (1999). Filial Piety and Loyalty: Two Types of Social Identification in Confucianism. *Asian Journal of Social Psychology*, 2(1), 163–183. https://doi.org/10.1111/1467-839x.00031

Jia, F., & Krettenauer, T. (2017). Recognizing Moral Identity as a Cultural Construct. *Frontiers in Psychology*, 8. https://doi.org/10.3389/fpsyg.2017.00412

Kohlberg, L. (1958). The development of modes of moral thinking and choice in the years 10 to 16 (Thesis). University of Chicago.

Kohlberg, L. (1971). From Is to Ought: How to Commit the Naturalistic Fallacy and Get Away with It in the Study of Moral Development. New York: Academic Press.

Kohlberg, L. (1981). The Philosophy of Moral Development Moral Stages and the Idea of Justice (1st ed.). Harper & Row. https://doi.org/10.1111/j.2044-8295.1982.tb01814.x

Markus, H. R., & Kitayama, S. (1991). Culture and the self: Implications for cognition, emotion, and motivation. *Psychological Review*, 98(2), 224–253. https://doi.org/10.1037/0033-295x.98.2.224

Moralfoundations (2021). Moral Foundations Theory | MoralFoundations.Org. Retrieved on September 23, 2021 from https://moralfoundations.org/

Naito, T. (2013). Moral Development. In K. D. Keith (Ed.), *The Encyclopedia of Cross-Cultural Psychology* (pp. 891–897). Wiley. https://doi.org/10.1002/978 1118339893.wbeccp367

Norenzayan, A., & Heine, S. J. (2005). Psychological Universals: What Are They and How Can We Know? *Psychological Bulletin*, 131(5), 763–784. https://doi.org/10.1037/0033-2909.131.5.763

Piaget, J. (1932). The moral judgment of the child. Harcourt.

Snarey, J. R. (1985). Cross-cultural universality of social-moral development: A critical review of Kohlbergian research. *Psychological Bulletin*, 97(2), 202–232. https://doi.org/10.1037/0033-2909.97.2.202

Tamborini, R. (2012). Model of intuitive morality and exemplars. In R. Tamborini (Ed.), Media and the moral mind (1st ed., pp. 453–474). Routledge. https://doi.org/10.4324/9780203127070

Tillman, C. J., Gonzalez, K., Whitman, M. V., Crawford, W. S., & Hood, A. C. (2018). A Multi-Functional View of Moral Disengagement: Exploring the Effects of Learning the Consequences. Frontiers in Psychology, 8. https://doi.org/10.3389/fpsyg.2017.02286

Wainryb, C., & Recchia, H. (2014). Moral lives across cultures: Heterogeneity and conflict. In M. Killen & J. G. Smetana (Eds.), *Handbook of moral development* (2nd ed., pp. 259–278). Psychology Press. https://doi.org/10.43 24/9780203581957.ch12

Chapter 4

Wisdom: Cultural and Cross-Cultural Understanding with a Systematic Review of Empirical Studies

Roshan Lal Dewangan
Kazi Nazrul University, Asansol, West Bengal, India

Hari Narayanan V.
Indian Institute of Technology Jodhpur, Rajasthan, India

Rajib Ghosh
Kazi Nazrul University, Asansol, West Bengal, India

Abstract: The history of wisdom starts with human civilization. However, scientific exploration to understand its nature is hardly 50 years old. Theoretical understanding grasped through ancient literature and historical account suggests cultural diversity in the conception of wisdom. This study tried to overview the wisdom concept from different cultural perspectives. Two databases (APA PsycArticles® and PubMed) were explored for English journal articles with an implicit (or mix of implicit and explicit) method to understand the concept of wisdom. A total of 4019 articles were screened, and ten were selected for the final review. Empirical studies exploring wisdom conception mainly represented North American, European and Asian perspectives. Overall, it was found that very few studies have explored cultural conception and cross-cultural understanding of wisdom empirically. Empirical explorations are in their initial stage. Findings suggest there is overlap in wisdom conception from one culture to another, and cultural uniqueness lies in prioritizing some features of wisdom over others.

Keywords: Wisdom, Culture, Cultural Differences, Cultural Uniqueness, PRISMA, Cross-cultural studies

***

Introduction

Where is the wisdom we have lost in knowledge? Where is the knowledge we have lost in information?

- T S Elliot in Choruses from the Rock

This question reverberates in current times with much more acuity. When immense information bombards each moment, like "the juicy piece of meat carried by the burglar to distract the watchdog of the mind" (McLuhan, 1994), constructing knowledge from information becomes a humungous task the odds against wisdom become much more profound. In such a scenario, post-truth becomes the norm, and even *alternate facts* emerge. Further, when humanity is faced with innumerable challenges, including the impending destruction of life-supporting systems, it is even said that "humanity is in a race between sagacity and catastrophe" (Walsh, 2015).

The search for wisdom has been present in different cultures since ancient times. If it were *Sophia* for ancient Greeks, ancient Indians talked of *Prajna*. Often it remained an ideal to be pursued for most humans. Given the difficulty in meeting the standards of that ideal, there have been much more knowledgeable people than wise humans. If the method for acquiring knowledge is definite, it is not the case with wisdom. In fact, the way wisdom is understood varies widely. It is even called "the most complex characteristic that can be attributed to individuals or cultures" (Birren & Cheryl, 2005).

To begin with, let us consider some major approaches to the understanding of wisdom. Plato's *Apology* contains the humility theory of wisdom, presenting Socrates as a wise person because of his humble claims regarding knowledge (Hamilton & Cairns, 1978). Of course, as Sharon Ryan highlights, all humble people are not necessarily wise (Ryan, 2020). What matters is the ability to distinguish between what one knows and what one does not know.

Among various practices, Ancient Greek belief systems that promoted logical thought and understanding had the most effect on the concept of wisdom in Western culture (Robinson, 1990). According to many Greek philosophers, wisdom is primarily about understanding the truth while also being familiar with nature around the world. For Socrates (470–399 B.C.), "Virtue is wisdom", and for Plato (428–348 B.C.), "Wisdom is the core of knowledge about good" (cited in Wang et al., 2021). Aristotle distinguished between theoretical and practical wisdom (Aristotle, 1941). The former is primarily a matter of knowledge in different domains, whereas the latter is the ability to lead a good life. Maintaining a distinction between knowledge and wisdom suggests that, though some knowledge is necessary for wisdom, a mere increase in knowledge is insufficient to make one wiser. Similarly, merely possessing the theoretical knowledge of leading a good life is not sufficient to be wise if the person fails to apply it in everyday contexts.

If the humility theory of wisdom stresses the quality of being realistic and moderate in one's claims to knowledge, the quality of temperance is present in many accounts of wisdom. As Philo of Alexandria ascertained, "every person who is in training for wisdom, leading a blameless, irreproachable life, chooses neither to commit injustice nor return it unto others...As their goal is a life of peace and serenity, they contemplate nature nor everything found within her..." (cited in Hadot, 1995, p. 264). Such serenity is possible because, as Bernard Groethyusen puts it in his words, "the sage never ceases to have the whole constantly present to his mind" (as cited in Hadot, 1995, p. 251). This is the ability "to see a World in a Grain of Sand" (Blake, 1987).

Two features stand out in the above accounts: One is looking at oneself as part of the all-encompassing whole. The other is to keep moderation when it comes to claims regarding knowledge or other kinds of behavior. A similar commitment is central to ancient Indian accounts of wisdom as well. Consider the well-known statement in Chandogya Upanishad, 'Tat tvam asi (you are that)', which means that the individual is one with the absolute reality (Krishnananda, 1977). Even if one discounts the metaphysical implications of the notion of the soul, there is indeed a clear message against the tendency to overlook the whole in everyday life because of the separative way in which one understands one.

Similarly, Yoga means union, whereby the self is united with the ultimate reality. Though Yoga is widely understood to refer to various physical postures, there are eight important aspects to Yogic practice (Iynegar, 1996). They restrain sense organs, non-possession, and meditation. This suggests that moderation in different aspects of life is the key to Yogic practice, which can maintain peace and equanimity.

Consider the account of an enlightened person given in the Bhagavad Gita. The term Stithaprajna is used to refer to a person of steady wisdom who is defined as "One whose mind remains undisturbed amidst misery, who does not crave for pleasure, and who is free from attachment, fear, and anger, is called a sage of steady wisdom" (Mukundananda, 2021), means, a wise person does not get easily perturbed by the uncertainty in the conditions of life and can maintain equanimity regardless of the outcome of his actions. The notion of acting without getting attached to its results follows from this account.

All these accounts of wisdom have in common that they all point to the need to go beyond the mundane, conflict-prone approach to life. Consider a dictionary definition of wisdom. "Insight and knowledge about oneself and the world and sound judgment in the case of difficult life problems" (Grimm & Grimm, 1984). Knowledge of oneself is an important feature here, and the same is emphasized in ancient accounts. Whether it be the cosmic consciousness of Stoics or the union in Yoga, they are matters of knowing the fundamental nature of oneself. One becomes aware of oneself as an integrally related entity or forms a part of all that exists.

That wisdom is much more than a mere accumulation of knowledge is clear from the distinction between reasonableness and rationality. As Rawls (2005) highlights, rationality is primarily a matter of pursuing one's interests, but reasonableness includes a sense of fairness and cooperation (Rawls, 2005). That means the kind of moderation or balance constituting wisdom is closer to reasonableness. Similarly, moral concern is intrinsic to reasonableness, and a wise person is expected to be morally upright as well. On similar grounds, Clayton (1982) distinguishes between intelligence and wisdom. Knowledge is common in both intelligence and wisdom. However, the knowledge of intelligence can be impersonal and can remain narrow in its scope and application. On the other hand, wisdom demands using knowledge with a broader perspective. Intelligence may lead to using the knowledge of splitting an atom for building nuclear weapons, but wisdom would never support such a move to build weapons of mass destruction (Clayton, 1982).

Thus, one can see a clear picture of the various accounts of wisdom in different traditions. It is not difficult to notice a connection between humility theory and the task of leading a life of overall balance. To be able to distinguish between what one knows and does not know is to overcome the attitude of what Kahneman (2011) calls– "What you see is all there is (WYSIATI)." The automatic mode of judging often proceeds under the assumption that there is nothing more than what we know (Kahneman, 2011). Whenever people come across something, it can be automatically imbued with the feeling that one knows, even if one does not know much about it. Reducing such automatic judging has been central to practices such as mindfulness by observing everything without judging. It can have implications not just for the feeling of knowing but also in other areas. When a person reacts to a statement angrily, that too is an automatic reaction, and the practice of non-judgmental observation can also mitigate such reactions.

There have been attempts to contrast Eastern and Western accounts of wisdom. Takahashi (2000) argues that western traditions take an analytical approach, whereas Eastern traditions are analytic and synthetic (Takahashi, 2000). In a cross-cultural study, it was found that Americans and Australians tend to associate wisdom with knowledge, whereas Japanese and Indians give more importance to the ability to be discreet, which amounts to judicious use of knowledge by considering various social and emotional factors (Takahashi

& Bordia, 2000). Similar views regarding the analytical and knowledge-based approach of the Western notion of wisdom have been mentioned in some other studies (Clayton & Birren, 1980; Csikszentmihalyi & Rathunde, 1990). Thus, it is often concluded that the Western notion of wisdom is more analytic by stressing the aspect of knowledge. The Eastern notion of wisdom is more synthetic by stressing direct experience.

This difference can have deeper roots in the way things are perceived and how the nature of the individual is understood. Based on empirical studies, it is claimed that, even in perceptual processes such as categorization, there is a difference between Westerners and Asians (Nisbett & Miyamoto, 2005). The former focuses on an object oblivious to its context, whereas Easterners appreciate the context much more. Further, the way the individual is understood is different in Western and Eastern cultures. If Western culture is more individualistic Eastern culture is traditionally more collective (Nisbett, 2004).

Though such differences certainly exist, Takahashi is cautious enough to point out that there is no dichotomy between the Western and the Eastern understanding of wisdom and different characteristics can be seen in both traditions (Takahashi, 2000). For instance, Stoics appreciated the need to have cosmic consciousness and Eastern traditions certainly gave importance to the pursuit of knowledge. It can well be the case that different traditions emphasized different aspects of thinking at different times, resulting in divergent world views. For instance, Hadot (1995) argues that Christianity usurped the philosophical concern with the way of life and, as a result, philosophy became a theoretical pursuit in the Middle Ages. This might have played a significant role in shaping the Western notion of wisdom, oriented more towards analysis and knowledge.

Some recent developments in the psychology of wisdom try to do justice to multiple aspects of wisdom. Consider Sternberg's balance theory of wisdom (Sternberg, 1998). Sternberg explained wisdom as a balance among multiple interests, such as intrapersonal and interpersonal, to achieve the common good. Additionally, there must be a balance among three courses of action: adaptation to the existing environment, shaping the environment to suit one's or other's needs and selecting new environments. He considers tacit knowledge as the key to wisdom. That means a wise person possesses tacit knowledge on handling life situations and acts in a manner aligned with the goal of the common good.

Psychologists have proposed several other models of wisdom. A recent one is the polyhedron model (Karami et al., 2020), according to which wisdom is constituted by features such as knowledge, self-regulation, reflectivity, sound judgment, moral maturity, openness, creativity, dynamic balance and synthesis etc. Here one can see a clear commitment to multiple aspects of wisdom, such as knowledge, moral sense and overall balance. This certainly requires a change in the dominance of one mode of functioning of thought. As Labouvie-Vief (1990) mentions, the Western tradition emphasizes logical, objective and analytical modes of thinking. This results in understating the role of an experiential, holistic way of thinking. Wisdom, according to Labouvie-vief, amounts to the balance between these two modes of thinking. That means wisdom is much more than cold cognition because factors like emotion and direct experience are significant elements of wisdom. That means experiential understanding and logical or abstract analysis are of equal importance, and one should not be adulated at the expense of another.

The upshot of the above discussion is that though wisdom as an ideal has been pursued in different traditions, some cultures emphasize knowledge-related aspects of wisdom, whereas others give more importance to emotional regulation and direct experience than abstract knowledge. While knowledge has been growing exponentially in our times, this hardly ensures that it is utilized in a way that benefits everybody. For the latter to happen, it is essential that the current fragmented, instrumentalist way of looking at the world has to give room for holistic and experiential approaches.

Core of Wisdom: Culture

According to wisdom scholars Paul Baltes and Ursula Staudinger, "cultural memory is the mother of wisdom" (Baltes & Staudinger, 2000). Indeed, wisdom is frequently defined as the idealized conduct of life in some of the oldest written works. Researchers claimed that ethical and religious codes depicted in the historical text were similar to those found in other ancient cultures of different regions such as Africa, China, and Mesopotamia (Assmann, 1994). The relationship between culture and wisdom could be understood through the lens of the original concept of renowned anthropologist Kluckhohn, which later Georgas and Mylonas (2006) modified this adage to read: "Cultures are like all other cultures, like some other cultures, like no other culture" (Georgas & Mylonas, 2006).

When comparing Western and non-Western wisdom traditions, there is much overlap in the notions of wisdom. For example, Jeste and Vahia (2008) contrasted modern Western notions of wisdom with those contained in the ancient Hindu text Bhagavad Gita, stressing Gita-wisdom components such as knowledge of life and awareness of the life, self-detachment/contentment, self-regulation/equanimity, compassion, and sacrifice, and the integration of these practices for the benefit of one's social environment. Similar concepts may be found in different faiths in the West, Middle East, and East Asia.

It also appears that people from many cultures have a lot in common when it comes to wisdom. Existing research suggests that wisdom incorporates cognitive abilities, particularly those related to self-reflection, life judgments, decisions, and socio-emotional abilities such as emotion control and kindness. Simultaneously, we noticed various culture-specific patterns relating to the development of wisdom.

The existing evidence that should reflect a cultural and cross-cultural understanding of wisdom is reviewed, given the above account. Though theoretical understanding reflected in religious texts and philosophical accounts, suggests that cultural differences exist in the conceptualization of wisdom. It was desired to know whether this historical account of wisdom also resonated in the voice of native people; what do the empirical studies on the conception of wisdom in various cultures suggest?

Methodology

Article Search Strategy

This systematic review followed the method as prescribed by PRISMA. Two databases, viz. PubMed and APA PsycArticles® were searched for publications dated until December 24, 2022. Strings (keywords) used for searching the articles are given in Table 4.1.

Table 4.1: Details of search strategies

Database	Search String (Keywords)	Filter
APA PsycArticles®	(ab(wisdom) OR ab(wise)) AND (ft(implicit) OR ft(explicit) OR ft(psychology))	Scholarly Journal, Journal articles, English Language
PubMed	((Wisdom[Title/Abstract]) OR (Wise[Title/Abstract])) AND ((Implicit[Text Word]) OR (Explicit[Text Word]) OR (Psychology[Text Word]))	Journal articles, English Language

Review Method

Firstly, the title and abstract of the resulting articles from databases were screened with a special focus on keywords. Selected articles in the first stage were then read to evaluate the selection criteria. Articles that used any implicit method or a mix of implicit and explicit methods to explore wisdom concepts were selected for the review. Articles that met the selection criteria were then reviewed in full.

Data Synthesis

Findings were arranged around cultural similarity of study samples and cross-cultural comparison.

Results

Database searches resulted in total 4195 articles (1504 from PubMed and 2691 from APA PsycArticles®). Total number of unique articles was 4019 as 176 duplicate articles were removed. Ninety-nine articles were found eligible for screening on methodology section to meet the eligibility criteria, where only ten articles were found eligible for final selection (see Figure 4.1).

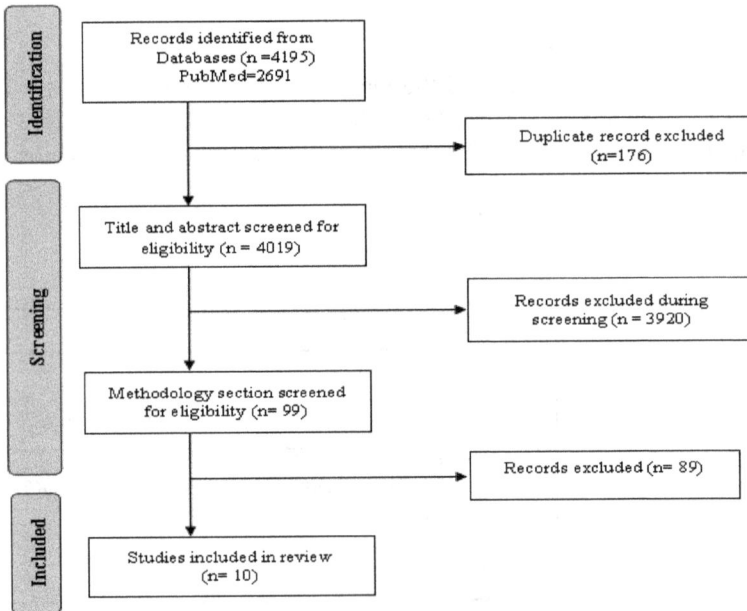

Figure 4.1: Preferred Reporting Items for Systematic Reviews and Meta-Analyses (PRISMA)

Study Characteristics

Out of ten articles (see Table 4.2), only one article (Grossmann et al., 2012) directly compares two cultures. Other articles either investigated the conception of wisdom among native people (Hu et al., 2018; Kaluzna-Wielobób, 2014; Sternberg, 1985), contextual and experiential factors that can lead to wisdom (Mahdavi et al., 2020; Yang, 2017), characteristics based on which wise persons were nominated (Weststrate et al., 2016; Weststrate & Glück, 2017) or emotional quality of nominated wise persons (Grossmann et al., 2019). Studies have used a diverse range of samples, with participants ranging from 18–99 years, with different educational and professional backgrounds. All the studies have used semi-structured interviews to elicit wisdom conception, nomination, and responses from wise persons.

Table 4.2: Studies included in the review

SN	Authors	Sample's Country	Continent
1.	Hu et al. (2018)	Mainland China	Asia
2.	Grossmann et al. (2012)	Japan and United States of America (USA)	Asia vs. North America
3.	Grossmann et al. (2019)	Austria, Germany	Europe
4.	Kaluzna-Wielobób (2014)	Poland	Europe
5.	Mahdavi et al. (2020)	Iran	Asia
6.	Sternberg (1985)	USA	North America
7.	Weststrate and Glück (2017)	Germany	Europe
8.	Weststrate et al. (2016)	USA and Canada	North America
9.	Yang (2017)	Taiwan	Asia
10.	Yamada et al. (2022)	USA	North America

Review of Studies from Different Cultures

North American

Sternberg's (1985) study is considered pioneering in understanding the implicit meaning of wisdom. In a series of studies in the USA, he found that American professors and laypersons considered wisdom very close to intelligence. However, wisdom was conceptualized in three dimensions: 1) reasoning ability and sagacity (e.g., considers advice is fair); 2) learning from ideas and environment and (good) judgment; 3) expeditious use of information and perspicacity.

Weststrate et al. (2016) asked 209 North American (i.e., Canadian and American) participants (aged 21–99 years) to provide exemplars of a wise person. Many nominated wise persons were male and were from various domains of public life. Politicians, social activists and spiritual figures were top nominees. In another study, they asked American participants (N= 202, 18-75 years old) to rate the top 13 wisdom nominees, taken from the first study, based on nominees' similarity to each other (1 very dissimilar- 6 very similar). Multi-dimensional scaling produced the three best-fitting dimensions. These dimensions are identified as practical prototype (including Abraham Lincoln, Benjamin Franklin, Winston Churchill, Thomas Jefferson and Barack Obama), philosophical prototype (including Socrates, King Solomon and Albert Einstein) and benevolent prototype (including Jesus Christ, Martin Luther King Jr., Mahatma Gandhi, Mother Teresa and Nelson Mandela).

Wisdom is considered one of the factors closely linked with successful aging in different cultures (Ardelt, 1994; Baltes, Smith, & Staudinger, 1992; Howell & Peterson, 2020; Nam & Cho, 2018). However, empirical finding presented recently from 1,549 community-dwelling adults in San Diego shows mixed results. In their study, Yamada et al. (2022) asked these community-dwelling adults aged between 21 to 99 years to define successful aging. Several themes emerged from the content analysis; wisdom contents (intelligence, spirit, generosity, faith and knowledge) were one of them. Though, explicit wisdom measure assessed by 3-D wisdom scale was statistically associated with the self-rated successful aging in the lower-successful-aging subgroup (but not in high successful-aging subgroup), the theme of wisdom was mentioned by only 10.6% of the participants in that subgroup. It seems physical health and social support availability is still top more priority in successful ageing.

European

To explore Polish conception of wisdom, Kaluzna-Wielobób (2014) questioned (through a questionnaire) to 304 Polish citizens (18–85 years old) about their conception of wisdom. She found that most of the participants conceptualized wisdom in terms of "…balancing own profits with concern for others and relation to existential problems, such as meaning and direction of life", which was in accordance with the popular conceptualization of wisdom (Baltes & Staudinger, 2000; Sternberg, 1998). However, participants "…lack the consciousness that wisdom is associated with: acting for common (global) good, deep and conscious reflection of value system, the consciousness of limited nature of knowledge and logical thinking and developing relativistic and dialectic thinking."

As a part of a study, Germans nominated 82 persons as wise; these wise persons have the following qualities: "cognitive competencies (e.g., knowledge, life experience, problem-solving, intelligence), concern for others (e.g., sensitivity, generosity, helping, guidance), positive attitudes (e.g., humor, trust, positive thinking), and transcendence (e.g., spirituality, feeling connected to nature)" (Weststrate & Glück, 2017). It was also reported that wisdom nominees used more exploratory and redemptive processing than the normal group processing their difficult life experiences. Exploratory processing was identified when the reflection to gain insight within or life circumstance made (i.e., meaning-making) and when changes in self were attributed to the life experience (i.e., personal growth). Emotional processing of and settlement with the life events was identified as redemption.

Grossmann et al. (2019) reported five studies, out of which two are relevant to this study's purpose. In study-1, they analyzed transcripts from a study conducted by Glück and Bluck (2013) in Austria. Emotional responses of the people nominated as wise by peer groups were compared with a control group. Participants replied about their emotional experience during a conflicting challenge in the original interview. Results indicated that compelling themes were more in the narratives of the wisdom nominees than in the control group. Further, the themes contained various emotions among the wisdom nominees than in the control group. In study-2 with the German sample, they found that emodiversity (intensity and variety in the use of emotions) was associated with each aspect of wise reasoning (i.e., intellectual humility, consideration of diverse perspectives, self-transcendence, and compromise). Researchers concluded that wise reasoning could be catered through balanced emotional life.

Asian

Taiwanese (375; 19–92 years old) reported that learning from life experience was associated with the development of wisdom, whereas wisdom also fosters openness to new learning (Yang, 2017). In a study conducted in Mainland China to understand the implicit theory of Chinese wisdom, Hu et al. (2018) interviewed 50 older adults (age 60–80 years) and 50 younger adults (age 20–30 years). Participants were asked to provide examples of a wise person and their meaning of wisdom. Historical figures (scholars and leaders) were the popular prototype of a person with wisdom. Common themes that emerged in the conceptualization of wisdom were cognitive abilities (knowledge-seeking, reflective thinking, reasoning, comprehension and generalization ability, etc.) and practical and social skills. Different from popular Western conceptualization, some new themes, transcendental interest and a positive mindset also emerged.

In an Iranian study by Mahdavi et al. (2020), 21 health professionals were interviewed in the context of conceptualization of managerial wisdom in the hospital settings. Individual variables (experience, personality and values), organizational factors (spiritual atmosphere and organizational values) and social solidarity were identified as three causal factors to realize practical wisdom in the hospital settings. Cognitive (knowledge and decision-making abilities) and managerial skills to implement cognitive abilities into work were identified as the core capacity of practical wisdom. The goal of practical wisdom was identified as the well-being of stakeholders and organizations along with social capital development.

This study investigated how culture (Japanese and American) and age influence wisdom (e.g., recognition of multiple perspectives, the limits of personal knowledge, and the importance of compromise) in the context of approaching social conflict (Grossmann et al., 2012). In this study, Japanese younger and middle-aged participants displayed wiser reasoning than the Americans in interpersonal and inter-group conflict while answering "What do you think will happen after that?" and "Why do you think it will happen this way?". This finding was interpreted in the cultural context; Americans experience more and more diverse conflicts than the Japanese, so the Japanese showed more wisdom and reasoning till middle age. Americans with richer experience showed more wisdom reasoning than Japanese at an older age.

Discussion

A consensual matter can be considered wise. Hence, the conceptualization of wisdom should follow the prominent cultural practice. The findings reflect American emphasis on analytical ability and European emphasis on empathy. Sternberg's study shows that North Americans consider sagacity a key feature of wisdom in addition to intelligence. Wisdom is not just a matter of having good intelligence but the ability to use that intelligence reasonably. Thus, the notion of fairness or reasonableness becomes central to wisdom. A similar emphasis is evident in European accounts of wisdom. Though Polish people acknowledge concern for others as central to wisdom, this does not amount to the concern for grand notions like global good. That is to say, a wise person can undoubtedly consider the interest of others, but this is far away from the cosmic consciousness that Stoics talked about. Studies on Germans and Austrians clearly show that emotional factors are considered to play a significant role in wisdom. Here again, wisdom is understood to be more than mere knowledge. This implicit differentiation between wisdom and intelligence is also reflected in explicit conceptualization. For example, Ardelt (2004) has added reflective and affective dimensions and cognitive while conceptualizing wisdom. Wisdom scholars, both American and European, agree that wisdom is a unique concept and can be differentiated from similar concepts (e.g., intelligence and spirituality) (Jeste et al., 2010). However, it is unclear whether there is a consensus on points of difference between wisdom and other similar concepts.

Studies on Asian conceptions of wisdom (Hu et al., 2018; Yang et al., 2017) suggest many wisdom characteristics match American and European conceptions of wisdom. However, the conceptualization of wisdom can be affected or based on emphasizing particular characteristics. For example, Taiwanese Chinese people's characterization of a wise person as, apart from being knowledgeable and empathic towards others, "a wise person be able to bring harmony and joy to home and society, rather than be beyond suffering" (Yang, 2001) might explain differences between Taiwanese conceptualization of wisdom and conceptualization of wisdom in other cultures. This necessary ability of wise people to bring *positive effects* within and surrounding, along with other identified characteristics (e.g., cognitive, affective), has resulted in the *process model of wisdom* (Yang, 2008).

Thus, the lay views discussed here broadly do justice to the account that tries to capture the difference between Western and Eastern understanding of wisdom in analytic and synthetic outlooks. Simultaneously, this difference need not be understood in mutually exclusive terms. Westerners do not restrict wisdom to mere knowledge. The importance of emotional factors and broad-mindedness is well appreciated in Western understanding of wisdom. Similarly, the Eastern account does not overlook the role of knowledge in wisdom. The difference is mainly a matter of emphasis, which, in turn, can be due to various cultural and historical factors.

Furthermore, implicit and explicit conceptualizations have suggested that even wisdom can have *types*, as reflected in Weststrate et al.'s (2016) finding, where wisdom nominees were dimensioned in three prototypes (i.e., practical, philosophical, and benevolent). Earlier, based on its emergence, Staudinger et al. (2005) suggested categories of wisdom. Personal wisdom emerges from one's own life experience, whereas general wisdom comes from the observation of others' life. They have further suggested that these two types of wisdom may not coincide. In Buddhist philosophy, wisdom, referred to as *paññā*, can be divided into three types: learned paññā, reflective paññā and meditative paññā (Bhikkhu, 2017). As mentioned in the introduction section of this chapter, Aristotle distinguished between theoretical and practical wisdom. It suggests that this ancient distinction of wisdom is still embodied within people, and it will be interesting to explore it in different cultures.

Though a systematic review did not find any study from India, this study is pertinent here to represent the Indian perspective. In an attempt to examine whether Indians have similar descriptions of wisdom as people from other parts of the world have, Sharma and Dewangan (2017) asked participants (n=170) to nominate a wise person and give the characteristics of the nominated wise person(s). In the second stage of the same study, they prepared a list having 25 characteristics of a wise person. This list was based on Trowbridge's (2005) review, the MORE experience model (Glück & Buck, 2013) and ten leadership virtues prepared by Green and Gini (2013). Sharma et al. (2017) asked their participants to opt for as many as most appropriate characteristics, from the list, of a wise person. More than 50% of the participants identified 14 characteristics (Good Judgment, intelligence, vision, self-control etc.) out of 25 as the most appropriate of a wise person. Most of the characteristics provided by the participants for their nominated wise persons were convergent with the characteristics prepared in the list. However, they found some uniqueness, and different trends from Western, in their study. Very young (age 40 or below) people were identified as wise in this study, whereas mostly nominated wise people were 50 years older than those in other parts of the world. They cited Yang's (2008) observation behind this finding, "Eastern believes in both action and its effect, the participants were influenced by the success of these nominees in their respective areas". Thus, in this modern era, where it might be challenging to find 'pure' Western or Eastern practice, cultural and contextual factors still play an important role in practical (wisdom) terms.

The review performed has certain limitations. Publication bias is one of the significant limitations; when looking for implicit studies, some possibilities published work in non-English journals, published and unpublished dissertations and reports have not been included in this review. Though two large databases were explored, many journals are not indexed in the databases used. So, caution must be taken when inference is made based on this review.

Conclusion

Nisbett (2004) challenged psychological tradition which generalized cognitive process as universal, and emphasized upon socio-cultural differences. Early populated naïve theories, which were generalized across the world were flattened by the later evidence. Cross-cultural validation of health-related measures, health-care systems, engineering and infrastructure, pedagogy, and many other aspects of human survival has proven how cultural understanding can optimize human living. The applied value of wisdom studies especially demands cultural acceptance, which is not possible without earthing wisdom on local geopolitical and cultural grounds. However, the impact of globalization must be considered parallelly. Migration-immigration and *global village* are significant world phenomena that have mitigated cultural differences to a large extent. Thus, research on wisdom at a cross-cultural level is pertinent for a comprehensive understanding of wisdom and to ensure effective implications of results.

A systematic review of two databases suggests that very few studies have empirically addressed cultural conception and cross-cultural understanding of wisdom. The theoretical discussion provides ground to reason culture as a significant factor in discerning the concept of wisdom. However, empirical exploration is in its initial stage of delving into the nuances of the cultural conception of wisdom. Initial findings suggest overlap from one culture to another, and cultural uniqueness lies in prioritizing some features of wisdom over others.

References

Ardelt, M. (1994). Wisdom in the later years: A life course approach to successful aging. Chapel Hill: The University of North Carolina.

Aristotle. (1941). Nichomachean Ethics. In R. McKeon (Ed.), *The Basic Works of Aristotle* (pp. 935–1112). Random House.

Baltes, P. B. (2004). *Wisdom as Orchestration of Mind and Virtue Paul B. Baltes Max Planck Institute for Human Development, Berlin Book in preparation, 2004.*

Baltes, P. B., Smith, J., & Staudinger, U. M. (1992). Wisdom and successful aging. In T. B. Sonderegger (Ed.), Nebraska symposium on motivation 1991: Psychology and aging (pp. 123–167). University of Nebraska Press.

Baltes, P. B., & Staudinger, U. M. (2000). *A Metaheuristic (Pragmatic) to Orchestrate Mind and Virtue Toward Excellence.* 55(1), 122–136. https://doi.org/10.1037//000 3-066X.55.1.122

Bhikkhu,B. (2017). *Under the Bodhi Tree: Buddha's Original Vision of Dependent Co-arising.* Simon and Schuster.

Birren, J. E., & Cheryl, M. S. (2005). Wisdom in history. In R. J. Sternberg & J. Jordan (Eds.), *A handbook of wisdom* (pp. 3–31). Cambridge University Press.

Blake, W. (1987). Auguries of Innocence. In A. Ostriker (Ed.), *William Blake: The complete poems* (pp. 506–510). Penguin Books.

Clayton, V. (1982). Wisdom and Intelligence: The Nature and Function of Knowledge in the Later Years. *The International Journal of Aging & Human Development, 15*(4), 315–321. https://doi.org/10.2190/17TQ-BW3Y-P8J4-TG40

Clayton, V. P., & Birren, J. (1980). The development of wisdom across the life span: A reexamination of an ancient topic. *Life-Span Development and Behavior, 3,* 103–105.

Csikszentmihalyi, M., & Rathunde, K. (1990). The psychology of wisdom: An evolutionary interpretation. In R. J. Sternberg (Ed.), *Wisdom: Its nature, origins, and development* (pp. 25–51). Cambridge University Press.

Georgas, J., & Mylonas, K. (2006). Cultures are Like All Other Cultures, Like Some Other Cultures, Like No Other Culture. In *Indigenous and cultural psychology: Understanding people in context.* (pp. 197–221). Springer. https://doi.org/10.1 007/0-387-28662-4_9

Glück, J., & Bluck, S. (2013). The MORE Life Experience Model: A Theory of the Development of Personal Wisdom. In *The Scientific Study of Personal Wisdom* (pp. 75–97). Springer Netherlands. https://doi.org/10.1007/978-94-007-7987-7_4

Green, R., & Gini, A. (2013). *Ten Virtues of Outstanding Leaders*. John Wiley & Sons.

Grimm, J., & Grimm, W. (1984). *Deutsches Wörterbuch*. Deutscher Taschenbuch-Verlag.

Grossmann, I., Karasawa, M., Izumi, S., Na, J., Varnum, M. E. W., Kitayama, S., & Nisbett, R. E. (2012). Aging and wisdom: culture matters. *Psychological Science, 23*(10), 1059–1066. https://doi.org/10.1177/0956797612446025

Grossmann, I., Oakes, H., & Santos, H. C. (2019). Wise reasoning benefits from emodiversity, irrespective of emotional intensity. *Journal of Experimental Psychology. General, 148*(5), 805–823. https://doi.org/10.1037/xge0000543

Hadot, P. (1995). *Philosophy as a Way of Life: Spiritual Exercises from Socrates to Foucault* (A. I. Davidson (Ed.)). Oxford: Blackwell.

Hamilton, E., & Cairns, H. (Eds.). (1978). Socrates' defense (apology). In *The Collected Dialogues of Plato* (pp. 3–26). Princeton University Press.

Howell, B. M., & Peterson, J. R. (2020). "With Age Comes Wisdom:" a Qualitative Review of Elder Perspectives on Healthy Aging in the Circumpolar North. *Journal of Cross-cultural Gerontology, 35*(2), 113-131.

Hu, C. S., Ferrari, M., Liu, R.-D., Gao, Q., & Weare, E. (2018). Mainland Chinese Implicit Theory of Wisdom: Generational and Cultural Differences. *The Journals of Gerontology. Series B, Psychological Sciences and Social Sciences, 73*(8), 1416–1424. https://doi.org/10.1093/geronb/gbw157

Iynegar, B. (1996). *Light on the Yoga Sutras of Patanjali*. Haper Collins Publishers.

Jeste, D. V., Ardelt, M., Blazer, D., Kraemer, H. C., Vaillant, G., & Meeks, T. W. (2010). Expert consensus on characteristics of wisdom: A Delphi method study. *The gerontologist, 50*(5), 668-680.

Jeste, D. V, & Vahia, I. V. (2008). Comparison of the conceptualization of wisdom in ancient Indian literature with modern views: focus on the Bhagavad Gita. *Psychiatry, 71*(3), 197–209. https://doi.org/10.1521/psyc.2008.71.3.197

Kahneman, D. (2011). *Thinking, fast and slow*. Farrar, Straus and Giroux.

Kaluzna-Wielobób, A. (2014). Do individual wisdom concepts depend on value? *Polish Psychological Bulletin, 45*(2), 112–127. https://doi.org/http://dx.doi.org/10.2478/ppb-2014-0016

Karami, S., Ghahremani, M., Parra-Martinez, F. A., & Gentry, M. (2020). A Polyhedron Model of Wisdom: A Systematic Review of the Wisdom Studies in Psychology, Management and Leadership, and Education. *Roeper Review, 42*(4), 241–257. https://doi.org/10.1080/02783193.2020.1815263

Krishnananda, S. (1977). *The Chhandogya upanishad*. Rishikesh: The Divine Life Society.

Labouvie-Vief, G. (1990). Wisdom as integrated thought: historical and developmental perspectives. In R. J. Sternberg (Ed.), *Wisdom: Its nature, origins, and development* (pp. 52-84). Cambridge University Press.

Mahdavi, A., Ardabili, F. S., Kheirandish, M., Ebrahimpour, H., & Daryani, S. M. (2020). Presenting a Model of Managerial Practical Wisdom in Hospitals. *Management, 24*(2), 20–48. https://doi.org/http://dx.doi.org/10.2478/manment -2019-0045

McLuhan, M. (1994). *Understanding media: The extensions of man.* MIT press.

Mukundananda, S. (2021). *Chapter 2, Verse 56 – Bhagavad Gita, The Song of God – Swami Mukundananda.* https://www.holy-bhagavad-gita.org/chapter/2/ verse/56

Nam, M. J., & Cho, Y. M. (2018). The Effect of basic psychological needs and wisdom on successful aging in the elderly. Korean Journal of Adult Nursing, 30(1), 70-78.

Nisbett, R. E. (2004). *The geography of thought: How Asians and Westerners think differently... and why.* Free Press.

Nisbett, R. E., & Miyamoto, Y. (2005). The influence of culture: Holistic versus analytic perception. *Trends in Cognitive Sciences, 9*(10), 467–473. https://doi .org/10.1016/j.tics.2005.08.004

Rawls, J. (2005). *Political liberalism.* Columbia University Press.

Ryan, S. (2020). *Wisdom (Stanford Encyclopedia of Philosophy).* http://seop.illc. uva.nl/entries/wisdom/

Sharma, A., & Dewangan, R. L. (2018). Indian Socio-Cultural Conception of Wisdom: Does it Follow Universal Understanding?. Journal of Psychology, 6(1), 5-19.

Staudinger, U.M., Dörner, J., & Mickler, C. (2005). Wisdom and personality. In R. Sternberg & J. Jordan (Eds.) *A Handbook of Wisdom: Psychological Perspectives* (pp. 191–219). Cambridge Univ. Press

Sternberg, R. J. (1985). Implicit Theories of Intelligence, Creativity, and Wisdom. *Journal of Personality and Social Psychology, 49*(3), 607–627. https://doi.org/10 .1037/0022-3514.49.3.607

Sternberg, R. J. (1998). A Balance Theory of Wisdom: *Review of General Psychology, 2*(4), 347–365. https://doi.org/10.1037/1089-2680.2.4.347

Takahashi, M. (2000). Toward a culturally inclusive understanding of wisdom: Historical roots in the East and West. *International Journal of Aging and Human Development, 51*(3), 217–230. https://doi.org/10.2190/H45U-M17W-3AG5-TA49

Takahashi, M. & Bordia, P. (2000). The concept of wisdom: A cross-cultural comparison. *International Journal of Psychology, 35*(1), 1–9. https://doi.org/ 10.1080/002075900399475

Trowbridge, R. (2005). The scientific approach to wisdom (Unpublished Ph.D. Thesis). Union Institute & University, Cincinnati, OH.

Walsh, R. (2015). What is wisdom? Cross-cultural and cross-disciplinary syntheses. Review of General Psychology, 19(3), 278-293. https://doi.org/10.1037/GPR0000 045

Wang, Z.-D., Wang, Y.-M., Li, K., Shi, J., & Wang, F.-Y. (2021). The comparison of the wisdom view in Chinese and Western cultures. *Current Psychology 2021,* 1–12. https://doi.org/10.1007/S12144-020-01226-W

Weststrate, N. M., Ferrari, M., & Ardelt, M. (2016). *The Many Faces of Wisdom: An Investigation of Cultural-Historical Wisdom Exemplars Reveals Practical, Philosophical, and Benevolent Prototypes.* https://doi.org/10.1177/01461672 16638075

Weststrate, N. M., & Glück, J. (2017). Hard-earned wisdom: Exploratory processing of difficult life experience is positively associated with wisdom. *Developmental Psychology, 53*(4), 800–814. https://doi.org/10.1037/dev0000 286

Yamada, Y., Shinkawa, K., Shimmei, K., Kim, H. C., Daly, R., Depp, C., Jeste, D. V., & Lee, E. E. (2022). Latent subgroups with distinct patterns of factors associated with self-rated successful aging among 1,510 community-dwelling Americans: potential role of wisdom as an implicit promoter. Aging & mental health, 1–8. Advance online publication. https://doi.org/10.1080/ 13607863.2022.2087207

Yang, S. Y. (2001). Conceptions of wisdom among Taiwanese Chinese. *Journal of Cross-cultural psychology, 32*(6), 662-680.

Yang, S. Y. (2008). Real-life contextual manifestations of wisdom. The International Journal of Aging and Human Development, 67(4), 273-303. https://doi.org/10.21 90/AG.67.4.a.

Yang, S. Y. (2017). The Complex Relations between Wisdom and Significant Life Learning. *Journal of Adult Development,* 24(4), 227–238. https://doi.org /10.1007/S10804-017-9261-1

Chapter 5

Human Values: Related Concepts and Types

Eisha Rahman

Research Associate, Military Mind Academy, Pune, India

Mubashir Gull

Department of Applied Psychology,
GITAM School of Humanities and Social Sciences,
Visakhapatnam, India

Akbar Husain

Aligarh Muslim University, UP, India

Abstract: Values institute a critical element of self-concept and function as a person's supervisory compass. Moreover, one's decisions often reflect the values and beliefs; therefore, understanding values could evince a detailed account of people's behavior. The values are so indelibly knitted into the patterns of human language, thought, and behavior that they have intrigued philosophers, psychologists, and sociologists for aeons. Nevertheless, their quick-silverness and intricacy have left us ignorant of the laws governing them. Because values are deeply ingrained in every aspect of an individual's life, scholars worldwide have remained enthralled by their magnificence. Also, since its inception, the values have been central to psychology and have been described numerously over the decades. However, the advent of empirical and theoretical methods in social psychology provided a scientific way of probing this phenomenon during the 1960s. This chapter is an effort in this direction and presents an overview of fundamental human values. It discusses the nature of values and spells out the elements related to human values, viz., valence, attitude, life patterns, understanding behavior, enduring belief, and societal norm. Moreover, based on the acronym, the chapter expounds on the types of values, namely, vocational, achievement, leadership, universal, extrinsic, and spiritual. At the heart of the chapter is the idea that values form a circular structure and reflect the assertive role of values in human motivation.

Keywords: Values, Vocational Values, Achievement Values, Leadership Values, Extrinsic Values, Spiritual Values, Culture

***

"Values are the very core of our behavior, the motive force of our lives."

- Swami Yuktananda

Introduction

Individuals' decisions often mirror the values ingrained in their belief system and cast a marked influence on diverse aspects of human lives. Moreover, they govern one's behavior patterns, thoughts, and actions, so scholars have addressed them extensively. Some have described it as an ideal code of conduct (Kluckhohn, 1951), while others, like Rokeach (1969), traced it as an ingrained conviction. Moreover, Feather (1975) has explored it as a precursor of feeling rather than a solitary manifestation of a belief system.

A comprehensive theory of human values must therefore delineate its course of development. More specifically, it must incorporate at least three different scales of time: (i) slow, for the centuries of growth of our civilization through history; (ii) fast, for the fleeting years of our technological breakthrough; and (iii) in between the years (past independence) our values have developed. Thus, to give a clear account of how values came into an institution, we must address questions associated with diverse aspects related to values, such as:

Origin:	Where do the values come from?
Heredity:	Are we all born with the values?
Function:	How do values operate?
Embodiment:	What are they made of?
Interaction:	How do they communicate or interact?
Learning:	How do we develop new values or modify old ones?
Forgetting:	How do we discard old values?
Character:	What are the most critical kinds of values?
Authority:	What happens when we disagree?
Competence:	How do values affect our ability to work efficiently and uprightly?

Personality: How do the values develop our personality?

Integration: What do values imbue in us for unity?

Awareness: How do values influence our consciousness or self-awareness?

Environment: Do the values develop in ecology?

Education: How should we address values in society?

Perception: Wh does the individual perceive him/herself as good and others as bad?

Influence: What are the factors that influence values?

As evident from the questions mentioned above, values are composed of innumerable strands; thus, it may seem a challenging and daunting task to address and evaluate them comprehensively. However, if we see them as a unified whole, each question will start connecting with the other, providing an answer to the enigma of values. A theory thus established is radical and offers an eclectic outlook for the entire notion.

Values and its Dimension

The concept of values has been extensively explored by scholars like Spranger (1928), Vernon and Allport (1931), Dukes (1955), Maslow (1967, 1968), Rokeach (1967; 1968, 1973, 1979, 2008), Husain (1983), Spranger (1928), Schwartz (1992, 2012, 2017), Nazam and Husain (2016), and Vecchione et al. (2019). They all have addressed its comprehensive framework and integral role in developing and tailoring personality. Vernon and Allport (1931) contend that values have broad functions common to all personalities. They state that values have six significant types: theoretical, economic, aesthetic, social, political, and religious. On the other hand, Duke (1955) states that values emphasize each person's expression of himself as an individual. Further, Morris (1956) has classified values into operational values (conception of desirable), conceived values (symbolically indicated object), and object values (properties of the object) based on the actual direction of the respective behavioral preferences. However, the values share a common element of preference, giving origin to the unified value of the preference. The importance of preference as a constituent of value has also been apprehended by Allport (1961). According to him, values are beliefs upon which a man acts by preference.

The role of values in the development and organization of personality has also been explored by Maslow (1967). He studied values about need gratification by classifying them as higher and lower-order needs while predominantly focusing on higher-order needs. Maslow (1968) has further shed light on the expression of values, as the individuals get governed by the rigorous impulse to maximize their potential in the direction of self-actualization.

Rokeach (1967) classified values into terminal and instrumental based on interpersonal or intrapersonal orientation. He further subdivided these values into personal, social, and moral competencies. He defined the terminal values in terms of eternal objectives, which are worthy of governing people's state of affairs throughout life. On the other hand, an instrumental value was considered a means to fulfill the terminal goals. They are the codes of conduct preferable to the self and others across diverse situations. Sheth (1995) classified values as moral, ethical, and socio-political values. According to him, moral and ethical values are usually ingrained in life's religious and spiritual realms. In contrast, socio-political values are rooted in the complex regulation of social hierarchy.

Values: Origin and Conflict

Value as a catalyst steers our course of action towards uprightness. Therefore, it has been probed since time immemorial. Some scholars believe that the values get imbued in people's lives in response to the approval and disapproval of significant others, especially parents. This process of weighing the worth of their actions ensues from the virtues inculcated in them since birth. However, others argue that it has a neurobiological grounding (Damasio, 2005). Irrespective of this fact, these standards of right and wrong giving rise to a personal sense of worth, regret, or guilt stems from one's superego (McLeod, 2016) and are the controlling force of inappropriate and irresistible impulses. They develop as people internalize the standards of desirable codes of conduct from their significant others, such as parents, siblings, kin, friends, teachers, and close acquaintances.

The process of value internalization is fairly governed by the theory of social learning, which states that children learn by observing and imitating their models (Bandura, 1961). Eventually, these values get modified (Rokeach, 2008) as we and our boundaries grow. This modification leads to the admiration of new models and prepares one for further responsibilities and roles. However, the process is not plain sailing, as individuals are peculiar and follow different standards to act upon (Schwartz, 2012). Thus, the discrepancy between the standards of self and the models gives rise to the sense of intrapersonal and interpersonal conflicts.

Different people have different value systems, yet almost everyone thinks that their values are reasonable and that what they do is right. Values sometimes lead us to rationalize or explain our acts that are not keeping up with the norms of society and thereby form an integral part of our identities. During periods of life when our values are in flux, such as during adolescence, we may experience what Erikson (1970) has labeled as an identity crisis. Hence, the behavior of individuals gets purposeless, i.e., without meaning, ensuing from the impediment in the growth of personal values. Regardless, these values are crucial in today's society. They ignite the human element while interacting with other beings. Moreover, they instill a sense of positive character, create a bond of humanity, and persuade consideration for others.

Though value is being explored and bifurcated in recent times in terms of their generation, i.e., whether they are fostered by science or not (Bronowski, 2011), still the central part of its exploration is related to the influence of diverse life aspects in its determination. More specifically, if we trace the roots of its origin, we come to know that values get instituted in early childhood and continue to develop and modify as we interact with our family and friends or participate in social organizations such as educational institutions, religious shrines, or cultural groups (Rokeach, 1968). It ensures that our interaction implants the seed of learning via observation, imitation, and modeling (Bandura, 1961). Rokeach posited that values are subjective to individual differences and individuals prioritize specific values based on their experiences and level of maturation. Moreover, these value priorities moderate our attitudinal and behavioral decision-making patterns (Rohan, 2000). Thus, Rokeach (1979) advocated that developing a healthy personality and prosperous society depends on the relative stability of the values, i.e., our values must be both flexible and stable. The notion of flexibility, in this case, serves as a prerequisite for meeting the requirements of changing scenarios. At the same time, the aspect of stability facilitates its continuity across diverse facets of life.

The postulation of value is swayed by sundry life aspects such as the understanding of self, others, society, and culture (Rokeach, 1979; Zavalloni, 1980), social and cultural change, and socio-economic development (Feather, 1975). At the idiosyncratic level, they expound on one's self-image and orientations (subjective, cultural, and behavioral) (Rokeach, 1973; Triandis et al., 1972). Moreover, they facilitate the substantial prediction of one's attitudes, predispositions, preferences, and explicit behaviors (Sagiv et al., 2017). Since values form a vital part of the normative order of a society, thus the exploration of sociocultural development entails a thorough investigation of value structure (Williams, 1979).

Attempts have been made from time to time to define and classify values comprehensively. However, the concept of value has eluded a pervasive explication. It may ensue from the dynamic nature of value and the fact that values are subjective to the changes (Husain, 1988, p.49). Therefore, psychologists have posited the need to address diverse factors in understanding the value system.

Values: Need and Importance

The cognitive constructs or values chart life's behavioral inclination (Renner, 2003) and beget personal goals. Moreover, they demarcate the irrational means assumed to fulfill these goals. Values constitute an essential part of our identities; they drive us to look inwards and act judiciously. They are critical to diverse aspects of our lives, such as feelings articulation, family affairs, role portrayal, and career. Therefore, values entail genuineness and rationality; they must be apposite to the sense of self, allowing ourselves and others to flourish.

Values inculcate an impulse to do something great in his life. It enhances our inner spirit and imbues a sense of spirituality. Values activate one's mind and attitude to adopt a righteous path and do hard work. This universal construct facilitates the transformation of personality and imbues meaning in life. Moreover, it trains one's mind to adopt spiritual thinking and conform to social ethics.

Vedas spell out that values are the ultimate test when there is a controversy between alternative paths of action. Values influence an individual's perception and significantly influence our proclivity to desire. According to Frankl (1963), values relate to three broad approaches. For instance, the first is experiential values, which the loved one feels towards others. Through this love, one can enable the beloved to develop meaning, and by doing so, one may develop meaning itself. The second approach is creative values, i.e., "doing a deed." It includes the creativity involved in art, music, writing, invention, etc. The third is attitudinal values, including virtues such as compassion, bravery, and a good sense of humor.

However, the concept of value is extensive and may be interpreted concerning sundry concepts. Therefore, this account takes a new approach to understand values, i.e., the acronym approach.

Six Critical Human Values Based On Acronyms

Vocational Values

Vocational values have their functional role in the work-related process. They affect an individual's vocational behavior, such as organizational commitment, work motivation, job satisfaction, and organizational functioning. Vocational values include affiliation, altruism, balance, competence, creative expression, flexibility, harmony, teamwork, and tranquillity. In their review, Schwartz and Surkiss (1999) mentioned four important vocational values: intrinsic, extrinsic, social, and prestige (p. 49). Vocational values are essential for the success of organizational setups. However, the effect of vocational values on an individual's job performance depends on how much an individual's values are congruent with the vocational values. According to them, work values are specific expressions of general values in the work setting (p. 54). In contrast, Alderfer (1972), Borg (1990), Crites (1961), Pryor (1987), Mottaz (1985), and Rosenberg (1957) have identified three common work values. These values are intrinsic or self-actualization, extrinsic or security or material, and social or relational. However, Schwartz and Surkiss (1999) stated that these three values do not represent higher-order values. Therefore, the researchers posited the fourth work value, i.e., self-enhancement.

Aspiration Values

According to Gull et al. (2022), this value represents the trait of ambition. A high level of aspiration value suggests rigorous efforts on the part of an individual towards achieving a goal. Sometimes being too achievement-oriented may come in the way of being morally right; thus, conscience-oriented aspiration levels are the best. This value represents three sub-values: accomplishment, achievement, and ambition. The value of accomplishment denotes acts of nobility towards self and others. The achievement value signifies achieving under others' pursuit and welfare, and the ambition value symbolizes the intense desire to achieve something. This type of value includes personal success through demonstrating competence according to social standards (success, capability, ambition, and influence) (Schwartz, 1992). These values determine how to shape our lives.

Leadership Values

There is a widespread need for confidence in leadership, business, education, government, and many other places in today's world. Every leader needs to regain and maintain trust. Value-based leaders engage their employees and help them flourish in life, boosting productivity, creativity, and financial return. Leadership values are based on the idea that the effectiveness of laws and other regulations begins and ends with the ethicality of individual managers and company owners. Besides, it reflects on the fundamental change in understanding of what is meant by "effective leadership" and who is a "successful leader" Žydžiūnaitė (2018). People who have clear principles are honest and congruent in their deeds, inspire others, and feel a greater sense of gratitude than they expect in return. These are the qualities of effective and successful leadership. According to Kraemer (2011), four basic principles of leadership values are self-reflection, balance, true self-confidence, and genuine humility. Value-based leadership may not be a cure for everything, but it is good to start with. Hence, leading and evaluating success based on values is the best way to build a high-performance culture.

Universal Values

Values were acknowledged as true universals and seen as worthy of explaining socially significant activities that contributed to the aspects of truth, beauty, and suitable life forms. The value of "utility" sub-served the continuance of individual and social life. According to Sorokin (1998), these concepts can explain the socially significant human activity and may represent the true universals. Universal values surpass the material realm and involve the spiritual life (Cowell, 1970).

People universally agree upon specific values such as honesty, equality, freedom, and justice. These are highly ethical and moral and become the guiding principle of one's life. Universalism includes understanding, appreciation, tolerance, and protection for the welfare of people and nature (Broadminded, Wisdom, Social Justice, Equality, A World at Peace, A World of Beauty, Unity with Nature, Protecting the Environment) (Schwartz, 1992). The value of universal brotherhood is not a new concept, and many have contemplated it. Universal values develop the ability to share good qualities among ordinary people.

Extrinsic and Intrinsic Values

Values reflect feelings and emotions. Extrinsic values form an individual's attitude and behavior and make strong impressions in one's mind. According to Linley (2009), "intrinsic values refer to aspirations for affiliation with friends and family, autonomy and self-direction, personal growth, and community involvement. In contrast, extrinsic values are concerned with aspirations for financial success, fame, and attractive appearance" (p.3). Thus, intrinsic values motivate a person towards non-tangible self-satisfactory variables, whereas extrinsic values motivate one towards having a materialistic gain.

Both could provide satisfaction and enhance well-being depending upon what a person values. Maslow (1959) claimed the necessity of intrinsic values as they are necessary "to avoid sickness and to achieve the fullest humanness" (p. 312). So, what are those intrinsic and extrinsic values? Intrinsic values are more communal and incorporate the social well-being of an individual, such as the feeling of affiliation, belongingness, and self-acceptance. On the other hand, extrinsic values are more self-serving, such as social popularity, financial success, and physical attractiveness. Intrinsic values directly satisfy people's basic psychological needs and foster their growth and thriving. Contrarily, the extrinsic values are less directly satisfying to needs and growth striving. In short, they foster ego excessively and lead to social compassion.

Spiritual Values

Spiritual values are generally considered the measure of ethical behavior. The most important spiritual value is honesty. Honesty refers to a facet of moral behavior and denotes positive virtuous attributes such as truthfulness and straightforwardness. Another typical spiritual value related to ethical behavior is integrity. Integrity is the consistency of actions, values, methods, measures, principles, expectations, and outcomes. Spiritual values develop and lead to the Self. Spiritual values are more significant than any other type of value. Spiritual life is stable; it cannot be changed.

According to Husain et al. (2012), "spiritual values are very much embedded in the teaching of religions such as the religion of Islam." Values raised in the Holy Qur'an are a whole way of life. The primary objective of the Holy Qur'an is to transform human values into a life of an individual and into a 'system of obedience to God' (Islam). Examples of spiritual values are piety, love, truthfulness, kindness, and wisdom (p. 496). Spiritual values are directly related to the adoption of certain lifestyle habits, such as diet, alcohol use, and sexual practices.

Spiritual values nurture temperament (Cleveland, 2014) and personality (Koessel, 2011; Simpson et al., 2007). They give a new meaning to people in terms of spiritual living. Moreover, they develop the power to fulfill the desired purpose. If righteous people practice sincerity and determination, their faith gets fostered, and they can achieve their purpose. A righteous person leads a remarkable life. The power of prayer and spiritual values helps maintain our spiritual living.

Spiritual values enhance spiritual life, which minimizes stress (Powers et al., 2007) through effective control of the mind and thought. Spiritual values strengthen the attitude and mind. The best way to lead a spiritual life is to follow the values which God has described in the Holy Scriptures (Maathai, 2010).

Spiritual values harmonize and enrich one's spiritual life. They help him/her acquire a positive and spiritual foundation in life. Moreover, spiritual living radiates the vision of hope (Espedal, 2021) and activates the states beyond the physical aspect (Idler, 2008). They also help people spiritually transform their energy and life and make life worth living. Spiritual life engenders the realization of *dharma* and helps discover the supreme Self and attain spiritual enlightenment (Holloway, 2003).

Spiritual values encourage and support spiritual living and make people peaceful and self-confident. The power of spiritual living lies in the peaceful state of mind and doing spiritual practices in the form of meditation, prayer, and service to humanity (Wuthnow, 2001). Spiritual values are dynamic, not static; their full, fiery power transforms our minds (Karakas & Sarigollu, 2019).

Spiritual values such as harmony, unity, peace, spiritual discipline, forbearance, and truthfulness strengthen in adversity and help prevent inevitable hardship and difficulties. They help transform thoughts and bring stability to mind, which is necessary for confronting and resolving adversity in life and righteous actions (Manning, 2019). Spiritual values give purpose and meaning to life (Krok, 2015).

Values and Related Concepts

Valence

Valence is the affective component of an event, object, or situation that engenders a sense of appeal or unwillingness to do something. They often categorize emotions as negative or positive based on their valence of boon or bane. Valence reflects the "hedonic tone" about the effect, feelings, accomplishment or no accomplishment of goals, approach or avoidance behaviors, and norm accordance or infraction.

Research proffer that the perceived valence of an environmental stimulus impacts an individual's choice (Lerner & Keltner, 2000), which in turn is assumed to be influenced by values (Feather, 2021; French & Kahn, 1962), i.e., an associate structure kindling the sense of good or bad. Therefore, values form an essential component in governing the valence of stimulus and the ensuing direction of behavior (Feather, 1975, pp. l3-17). In other words, values influence the attractiveness of recourse and govern the hedonic tone of behavior, thereby increasing the likelihood of behavior engagement (Feather, 1988). Thus, people act in ways that facilitate value attainment and vice-versa (Sagiv & Schwartz, 1995).

Attitude

An attitude is a relatively stable arrangement of beliefs, which engenders a preferential response to environmental stimuli. In other words, it is a predisposed state of mind that influences thought and action. This complex acquired construct characterizes a person. It is feeling about oneself and the world that can be explicit (conscious) or implicit (unconscious). This learned disposition leads to the evaluation of stimuli in a certain way (positive or negative) and thereby influences one's behavior. Therefore, researchers have extensively explored the link between the two. More explicitly, studies suggest that behavior is a function of attitude (Ajzen, 1989; Bechler, 2021; Marcinkowski & Reid, 2019; Rokeach & Kliejunas, 1972) relating to sundry conceptual categories or attributes of objects and situations based on their relative importance (Conner et al., 2021).

Regardless, the link between behavior and attitude is not aligned (Chaiklin, 2011). This misalignment may ensue from the influence of the intervening variable value. Since an individual's values are factors of his attitude, researchers have probed its influence on the attitude and behavior linkage (Bardi & Schwartz, 2003; Maio & Olson, 1995; Rokeach, 1973). Studies unveil those values are the critical link between personality traits and attitudes (Olson & Maio, 2003; Yik & Tang, 1996) and are significant predictors of behavior and attitudes. More explicitly, the value system people acquire and develop affects their attitudes, regulating perception and thinking.

Rokeach (1971) also argued that predicting behavior from attitudes entails considering attitudes toward both objects and situations. Moreover, the researcher posited that a person's beliefs, attitudes, and values should be aggregated (Rokeach, 1979). Boer and Fischer (2013) further expounded on the relationship between value and attitude by probing how social attitudes are related to personal values based on the moral foundation theory (Haidt & Joseph, 2007) and Schwart'z theory (1992). Their study found that self-transcendence values positively related to fairness and prosocial attitude, and conservation values related to purity/religious and political attitudes. In contrast, in-group/identity attitudes did not consistently relate to value dimensions. It can be concluded that value is an essential determinant of attitude and must be probed to ensure a thorough understanding of attitude.

Life Pattern and Circumstances

Values reflect an individual's perspective on life and behavior patterns. They regulate our lifestyle patterns, which in turn affect our health. Moreover, Milbrath (1981) suggested that quality of life emanates from fulfilling life values and lifestyle goals. Furthermore, sociocultural factors and one's beliefs on the functioning of the world cast an influence on lifestyle. Therefore, lifestyle patterns regulated by values are not autonomous; life circumstances impact and get impacted by values. More specifically, the relationship between values and life circumstances is two-way because value-based choice affects life circumstances and influences value functioning.

According to Schwartz and Bardi (1997), people adapt their values to life circumstances. For example, a wealthy individual can continue with his or her power values more efficiently than an individual with conformity values (obedience and honor). They further suggested that individuals can readily attain and downgrade the importance of values if their pursuit is blocked.

Furthermore, Gouveia et al. (2015) suggested that developmental patterns of life, i.e., increase in age, also impact levels of fundamental value. They observed the linear and curvilinear patterns of transitions across the lifespan and propounded that value change is consistent with biopsychosocial development. They also stated that values have specific functions for each development stage.

In contrast, the value change ensuing from major life events is often substantial. For instance, migration to a culturally different society posits pressure to conform to a new set of values. Immigration studies of longitudinal nature also bear evidence of this by revealing a mean-level change in values (Bardi et al., 2014; Lönnqvist et al., 2011). The change in value resulting from major life events is further supported by Kohn & Schooler (1983). Their longitudinal research on working conditions determined persistent features of work that changed values.

Researchers further advocated that values are relatively stable and may not change unless significant or long-term changes in life circumstances happen (Sorthiex et al., 2019). Thus, temporary and usual changes, viz., commencing and culminating a course, class, or job, evince minor changes in values (Arieli et al., 2020).

The mean-level change ensuing from drastic social change supports the notion of the relative stability of value. For instance, in contrast to fatherhood, motherhood engenders a shift in value priorities of protection over openness to change (Lönnqvist et al., 2018). Therefore, it becomes evident that values are subject to change with drastic changes in the situation, roles, and responsibilities. The impact of critical external circumstances on value change is further supported by Bojanowska et al. (2021). Their study revealed that values of self-direction, security, conformity, humility, caring, and universalism increased, and the hedonistic value decreased due to a major life crisis.

Understanding Behavior

Values set the standards and guidelines which govern behavior. They are crucial to understanding behavior. If not all, values affect most behaviors and are essential for predicting and explaining the value-behavior relationship. Thus, researchers have probed the relationship in sundry contexts to address questions like "Does the full range of different values relate to common, recurrent behaviors?", "Which values relate more strongly to behavior than others?" and "Do relations among different values and behaviors exhibit a meaningful overall structure?" (Bardi & Schwartz, 2003). The study revealed that stimulation and traditional values strongly correlate to the behaviors that express them. Moreover, they found that the relationship between behavior and value is not exclusive but subject to normative pressures.

The feature ignites research interest in this direction is the association between values, behaviors, and behavioral intentions. It is associated with consumer behavior (Janssens, 2020), social dilemmas and conflict resolution (Bond et al., 2004; Feather, 1995), child-rearing and care (Gaunt, 2005), negotiation (Brett & Okumura, 1998), eco-friendly behavior (de Groot & Steg, 2008; Nordlund & Garvill, 2002; Poortinga et al., 2004; Stern, 2000), and political orientation (Caprara et al., 2006; Thorisdottir et al., 2007).

The effect of values is both direct, i.e., people are likely to act in ways that align with values (Sagiv & Schwartz, 1995) and indirect, i.e., values affect one's focus of attention (de Dreu & Boles, 1998) and interpretation of information (Sattler & Kerr, 1991), which in turn, affects the way one behaves. Initially, we choose our values, and then values start guiding our behavior via the notion of value priority. According to Schwarts, Sagiv, and Boehnke (2000), "high priority values are chronic goals that guide people to seek out and attend to value-relevant aspects of a situation." Aride and Pàmies-Pallisé (2019) aimed to understand the factors involved in the relationship between human values and behavior. Their study identified the concept of "consequences" as a critical factor in understanding the influence of human values on behavior.

Enduring Belief

An individual's standard of behavior or appraisal of something as important is affected by beliefs, i.e., the idea that something is true (Schwitzgebel, 2011). This conviction is often a function of probabilities or matters of faith emanating from experiences, socio-cultural norms, and knowledge imbued by others (Goldman, 1979). In other words, a potential conviction is not a belief, for it becomes one only after acceptance of it as truth. This process is subjective, and every individual evaluates the potential belief in their way. Once accepted, this belief becomes a part of the belief system and evokes a sense of fortification. In due course of time, these beliefs become steadfast and stable, thereby engendering the construct of values. These stable, long-lasting beliefs govern what is essential and become standards of judgment. This development of belief into values is a function of steadfast commitment.

Ramsey (1931) stated that belief is a map, and it is something by which we steer. Individuals in a society have specific beliefs as well as shared values. Rokeach (1973) has suggested the following definition:

A value is an enduring belief that a specific mode of conduct or end-state of existence is personally or socially preferable to an opposite or converse mode of conduct or an end–state of existence. A value system is an enduring organization of beliefs concerning preferable modes of conduct or end-state of existence along the continuum of relative importance.

Values are enduring, but personal and social change would be impossible if they were entirely stable. If values were volatile, continuity of human personality and society would be impossible. Thus, all conceptions of human values have to account for both their enduring and dynamic character. Values persist in the individual because they become a part of his sense of identity (Erikson, 1959). Rokeach (1973) and Allport (1935) also stressed this enduring characteristic of values in their definition of values. Moreover, unlike an attitude, a value is impressive to action and belief about the preferable and a preference for the preferable (Lovejoy, 1950).

Milfont et al. (2016) have investigated the rank-order stability and mean level difference in core values. They also aimed to examine whether age and sex moderate stability and change. They revealed that all values are prioritized among women except for conservation value, and the stability of values decreases after 50 years of age. Older adults and women placed greater emphasis on values relating to the welfare of others and the preservation of traditional practices and stability (Self-Transcendence and Conservation values). In contrast, younger individuals and men tend to highly value the pursuit of status, power, and independent thought and behavior (Self-Enhancement and Openness to Change).

Societal Norm

Norms are standards of behavior that ensure social order and stability and reflect the ought of behavior in a given situation (Elster, 1989). In contrast, values govern the judgment of right or wrong (Sagiv et al., 2017). Values are abstract constructs, whereas norms are specific guidelines. More explicitly, norms are accepted standards of being or doing things shared by group members. For instance, some social norms are apologizing for mistakes, greeting people, and asking for an excuse. These norms are subject to socio-cultural changes. For example, religious etiquettes and practices of individuals are varied.

The norm is implemented and acknowledged because it creates order and stability. People seek acceptance and fear alienation; therefore, they succumb to the norms of society. Moreover, ethnographic evidence (Sober & Wilson, 1998), evolutionary theory (Boyd et al., 2003), and laboratory studies (Fehr & Gächter, 2002) indicate that norms can only be adhered to and maintained if there is retribution for violation. It is entailed because individuals with a high value of self-interest are likely to violate norms.

Since norms are not ingrained, they are subject to influence. Values are one such catalyst that influences norm conformity. Therefore, researchers have probed norms in relation to values (Kaiser, 2005; Kelsen, 1966; Mukařovský, 2015; Oreg & Katz-Gerro, 2006; Stern et al., 1999). Moreover, Sorokin (1998) advocates that every value presupposes a norm of conduct. It ensures that values describe personal standards of what is valuable. Also, their ability to shape one's behavior provides an essential basis for understanding individuals' perceptions, attitudes, behavior, and personality. Kesberg and Keller (2018) examined the association between the endorsement of human values and situation characteristics. They found that the variance in the experience of the negatively connoted situation was due to individual differences. They also found that power was related to experiencing tricky situations, whereas reversed patterns emerged for universalism and benevolence. The tradition was related to experiencing more aversive situations, while self-direction was related to experiencing fewer situations high in adversity. Thus, it be can deduced that values are subject to individual pursuits. In other words, values engender individual discretion. Thus, it entails a standard of order, i.e., norms, which are an essential part of society representing the standard of society's acceptable behaviors. Therefore, it is essential to consider the principles individuals believe, i.e., values, and principles accepted by society, i.e., norms.

Moreover, every individual has their own set of values, i.e., social, vocational, achievement, moral, and spiritual values, and focus on their world. Therefore, people conflict because everybody lives in their world and follows different values for different purposes. Thus, it is imperative to acknowledge norms and values as essential aspects of society.

Discussion

The values are a core aspect of Self. They form early in life as hierarchies of priorities (Homer & Kahle, 1988) and remain relatively stable as guiding principles throughout the life course (Feather, 1975). Rokeach (1979) asserts that these core values can be ordered into hierarchies of importance or value systems and reflect underlying needs and societal demands. Changes in fundamental values are assumed to have widespread effects upon thought and action, having significant implications for attitudes and beliefs and personal and social behavior. Thus, the role of values is paramount, and the research on personal values is expanding rapidly worldwide. In the space available, the researchers have numbed some critical concepts. The researchers have delved into the realm more explicitly and provided an overview of values, origin, need, types, and related concepts.

Integrating research from multiple arenas reveals that values are constant guides across domains. Vocational values, for instance, affect one's vocational behavior (Dawis, 1991), such as organizational commitment, work motivation, job satisfaction, and organizational functioning. Moreover, they govern the choice of vocation and envoke the spirit of commitment (Sheikh et al., 2012). Though they are changing over time (Gribbons & Lohnes, 1965), their influence on vocational choices and behavior remains paramount.

Vocation values are essential for vocational wellness and include affiliation, altruism, balance, competence, creative expression, flexibility, harmony, teamwork, and tranquility. These are varied across cultures, yet they form an essential constituent in all cultures (Bruni & Smerilli, 2009). It ensures that people are either preparing for vocational life or living one. Thus, a significant part of one's life is devoted to vocational endeavors; therefore, vocational values hold immense importance. Therefore, the value of vocation becomes one of the principal values to be addressed.

Another value of importance is the value of aspiration. This value is posited for its substantial role in deriving an individual's behavior. Every being has a thirst for success, demonstrated through competence. However, this drive may become a cause for concern if it defies social standards. Therefore, the value of aspiration has been advocated by researchers (Gull et al., 2022; Schwartz, 1992). The chapter further proposes the value of leadership, which is another critical drive. Every organization entails leadership to prosper (D'Innocenzo et al., 2021). However, leadership follows diverse styles (Alheet et al., 2021; Pratt & Putra, 2022). Thus, their impact is varied and can be both positive and negative. Thus, it is essential to ensure that a sound value system governs the core of leadership. It is entailed to ensure that the function of leadership to steer towards productivity is not compromised (Matthews, 2021). Since value-based leaders engage their employees and help organizations and employees flourish altogether, they are vital (Godbless, 2021). Leadership values are based on the idea that the effectiveness of laws and other regulations begins and ends with the ethicality of individual managers and company owners. Besides, it reflects on the fundamental change in understanding of what is meant by "effective leadership" and who is a "successful leader" (Žydžiūnaitė, 2018).

Values are subject to cultural variations, yet they share a universal core. Thus, it is imperative to address universal values (Sorokin, 1998). Hence, the researchers have highlighted this concept and suggested that they surpass the material realm and involve the spiritual life (Cowell, 1970). These values reflect the notion of understanding, appreciation, tolerance, and protection for the welfare of people and nature. The concept is vital because the universal sacredness of human life bonds every being into an organic unity and credits a privileged ontological status to humankind. In other words, individuals' universal solidarity is unquestioned; it is hemmed into our being as a moral species (Christians & Traber, 1997). Therefore, universal values hold importance and entail exploration.

The values are further influenced by the force of motivation, i.e., extrinsic and intrinsic. The resultant extrinsic and intrinsic value forms another critical type of value. The extrinsic values form an individual's attitude and behavior and make strong impressions in one's mind. They are concerned with aspirations for financial success, fame, and attractive appearance. In contrast, Linley (2009) suggests that intrinsic values refer to aspirations for affiliation, autonomy, personal growth, and community involvement. Thus, intrinsic values motivate a person towards non-tangible self-satisfactory variables, whereas extrinsic values motivate one towards having a materialistic gain. All in all, they both are critical to human functioning.

Spirituality is a significant and universal aspect of the human experience. Human beings are spiritual beings with human experience (De Chardin, 2018). Thus, spiritual value is another core value. They help us acquire a positive and spiritual foundation in life. Moreover, spiritual living radiates the vision of hope (Espedal, 2021) and activates the states beyond the physical aspect (Idler, 2008). They help spiritually transform our energy and life and make life worth living. Spiritual values engender the realization of *dharma* and help discover the supreme Self and attain spiritual enlightenment (Holloway, 2003).

When similar values underlie and motivate behavior in different domains (e.g., self-direction and universalism values underlying tolerance and political activism), we can recognize the meaning these behaviors share and learn from one domain about the other. Therefore, the chapter sheds light on the values of different types and cognizes the readers of the critical factors that govern human behavior despite cultural diversity.

Values portray an ideal culture – the standard embraced by society. However, the actual functioning of society is distinct; in the authentic culture, authorities and people constantly strive to prevent or repair the issues of life. People act in ways that facilitate value attainment and vice-versa (Sagiv & Schwartz, 1995). This descriptive account offers that the perceived valence of an environmental stimulus impacts an individual's choice (Lerner & Keltner, 2000), which is assumed to be influenced by values (Feather, 2021). Thus, valence is essential in the context of value exploration. More explicitly, the value system people acquire and develop affects their attitudes, regulating their perception and thinking. Rokeach (1971) posited that a person's beliefs, attitudes, and values should be aggregated (Rokeach, 1979).

An individual's standard of behavior or appraisal of something as important is affected by beliefs, i.e., the idea that something is true (Schwitzgebel, 2011). This conviction is often a function of probabilities or matters of faith emanating from experiences, socio-cultural norms, and knowledge imbued by others (Goldman, 1979). Once accepted, this belief becomes a part of the belief system and evokes a sense of fortification. These beliefs become steadfast and stable in time, thereby engendering the construct of values (Rokeach (1973). Thus, the researchers have next delineated values to enduring beliefs.

Sorokin (1998) advocates that every value presupposes a norm of conduct. Values are catalysts that influence norm conformity. Therefore, researchers have probed norms with values (Kaiser, 2005; Kelsen, 1966; Mukařovský, 2015; Oreg & Katz-Gerro, 2006; Stern et al., 1999). Values are subject to individual pursuits and engender individual discretion. Thus, it entails a standard of order, i.e., norms, which are an essential part of society representing the standard of society's acceptable behaviors. Therefore, it is essential to consider both the principles individuals believe, i.e., values, and principles accepted by society, i.e., norms.

Conclusion

There has been much dispute amongst scholars of varying disciplines regarding the exact definition of the value, but it is generally agreed that it grinds human behavior and society. The present authors proposed an approach to the unanimity on the basic definition of values. Values, i.e., moral and social, may be defined as 'good' or 'bad' because it has the reason that its most fundamental levels in the value system must incorporate a general statement as to what exactly constitutes good or bad. Goodness or badness differs from individual to individual or from society, i.e., society and the particular type of relationship between the persons. The conceptual model of values suggests the nuances of psychosocial and spiritual factors related to values, such as valence, attitude, life pattern and circumstances, understanding behavior, enduring belief, and societal norm. It probes the role of values in fostering and transforming an individual's life into positive development across the life span. Furthermore, the values such as vocational, aspiration, leadership, universal, extrinsic and intrinsic, and spiritual have been delineated. Their role in cultivating human capacities to imbue resources to grow successfully across the life course has also been elucidated.

Society must naturally be based on truth and non-violence. It is not possible without belief in God. Values uplift individuals; it helps them grow. Though values seem to be an individual behavior, it covers all aspects of society in terms of result. Therefore, to meet the challenge of life in the face of change, i.e., overpopulation, technological development, pollution, rural development, intergroup conflict, unemployment, drug addiction, etc., the most significant thing is to determine intricate values in human beings. It is critical for developing countries with limited resources and unlimited needs. People, in general, need to be educated, keeping in view their needs, attitudes, and perceptions to meet the various challenges of socioeconomic change and development and improve people's general quality of life. Thus, the researchers hope that this chapter will render benefits and direction to the researchers in identifying core concepts related to values and their types.

References

Ajzen, I. (1989). Attitude structure and behavior. In Breckler, S.J. and Greenwald, A.G., Eds., *Attitude structure and function*, Lawrence Erlbaum, Hillsdale, 241-274.

Alderfer, C. P. (1972). *Existence, relatedness and growth: Human needs in organizational settings.* Free Press.

Alheet, A., Adwan, A., Areiqat, A., Zamil, A., & Saleh, M. (2021). The effect of leadership styles on employees' innovative work behavior. *Management Science Letters, 11*(1), 239-246.

Allport, G. W. (1935). *A handbook of social psychology.* Clark University Press.

Allport, G. W. (1961). *Pattern and growth in personality.* Holt, Rinehart & Winston.

Aride, O., & Pàmies-Pallisé, M.-M. (2019). From values to behavior: Proposition of an integrating model. *Sustainability, 11*(21), 6170. https://doi.org/10.3390/su11216170

Arieli, S., Sagiv, L., & Roccas, S. (2020). Values at work: The impact of personal values in organisations. *Applied Psychology, 69*(2), 230-275.

Bandura, A. (1961). Psychotherapy as a learning process. *Psychological Bulletin, 58*(2), 143.

Bardi, A., & Schwartz, S. H. (2003). Values and behavior: Strength and structure of relations. *Personality and Social Psychology Bulletin, 29*(10), 1207-1220.

Bardi, A., Buchanan, K. E., Goodwin, R., Slabu, L., & Robinson, M. (2014). Value stability and change during self-chosen life transitions: Self-selection versus socialization effects. *Journal of Personality and Social Psychology, 106*(1), 131.

Bechler, C. J., Tormala, Z. L., & Rucker, D. D. (2021). The attitude–behavior relationship revisited. *Psychological Science, 32*(8), 1285-1297.

Berry, J. W. (2005). Acculturation: Living successfully in two cultures. *International Journal of Intercultural Relations, 29*(6), 697-712.

Boer, D., & Fischer, R. (2013). How and when do personal values guide our attitudes and sociality? Explaining cross-cultural variability in attitude–value linkages. *Psychological Bulletin, 139*(5), 1113–1147. https://doi.org/10.1037/a0031347

Bojanowska, A., Kaczmarek, Ł. D., Koscielniak, M., & Urbańska, B. (2021). Changes in values and well-being amidst the COVID-19 pandemic in Poland. *Plos One, 16*(9), e0255491.

Bond, M. H., Leung, K., Au, A., Tong, K. K., & Chemonges-Nielson, Z. (2004). Combining social axioms with values in predicting social behaviours. *European Journal of Personality, 18*(3), 177-191.

Borg, I. (1990). Multiple facetisations of work values. *Applied Psychology: An international Review, 39*, 401-412.

Boyd, R., Gintis, H., Bowles, S., & Richerson, P. J. (2003). The evolution of altruistic punishment. *Proceedings of the National Academy of Sciences, 100*(6), 3531-3535.

Brett, J. M., & Okumura, T. (1998). Inter and intra cultural negotiation: US and Japanese negotiators. *Academy of Management Journal, 41*(5), 495-510.

Bronowski, J. (2011). *Science and human values.* Faber & Faber.

Bruni, L., & Smerilli, A. (2009). The value of vocation. The crucial role of intrinsically motivated people in values-based organizations. *Review of Social Economy, 67*(3), 271-288.

Caprara, G. V., Schwartz, S., Capanna, C., Vecchione, M., & Barbaranelli, C. (2006). Personality and politics: Values, traits, and political choice. *Political Psychology, 27*(1), 1-28.

Chaiklin, H. (2011). Attitudes, behavior, and social practice. *Journal of Sociology & Social Welfare, 38*, 31.

Cheney, G. (2018). *Values at work.* Cornell University Press.

Christians, C. G., & Traber, M. (Eds.). (1997). *Communication ethics and universal values.* Sage Publications.

Cleveland, R. E. (2014). *Psychometric reanalysis of happiness, temperament, and spirituality scales with children in faith-based elementary schools.* Seattle Pacific University.

Conner, M., Wilding, S., Van Harreveld, F., & Dalege, J. (2021). Cognitive-affective inconsistency and ambivalence: Impact on the overall attitude–behavior relationship. *Personality and Social Psychology Bulletin, 47*(4), 673-687.

Cowell, F. R. (1970). *Values in human society: The contributions of P.A. Sorokin in sociology.* Porter Sargent.

Crites, J. O. (1961). Factor analytical definitions of vocational motivation. *Journal of Applied Psychology, 43*, 426-433.

Damasio, A. (2005). The neurobiological grounding of human values. In *Neurobiology of human values* (pp. 47-56). Springer.

Dawis, R. V. (1991). Vocational interests, values, and preferences. In M. D. Dunnette & L. M. Hough (Eds.), *Handbook of industrial and organizational psychology* (pp. 833–871). Consulting Psychologists Press.

De Chardin, P. T. (2018). *The phenomenon of man.* Lulu Press, Inc.

De Dreu, C. K., & Boles, T. L. (1998). Share and share alike or winner take all?: The influence of social value orientation upon choice and recall of negotiation heuristics. *Organizational Behavior and Human Decision Processes, 76*(3), 253-276.

De Groot, J. I., & Steg, L. (2008). Value orientations to explain beliefs related to environmental significant behavior: How to measure egoistic, altruistic, and biospheric value orientations. *Environment and Behavior, 40*(3), 330-354.

D'Innocenzo, L., Kukenberger, M., Farro, A. C., & Griffith, J. A. (2021). Shared leadership performance relationship trajectories as a function of team interventions and members' collective personalities. *The Leadership Quarterly, 32*(5), 101499.

Dukes, W. F. (1955). Psychological studies of values. *Psychological Bulletin, 52*(1), 24-50.

Elster, J. (1989). Social norms and economic theory. *Journal of Economic Perspectives, 3*(4), 99-117.

Erikson, E. H. (1959). *Identity and life cycle: Selected papers.* W. W. Norton.

Erikson, E. H. (1970). Autobiographic notes on the identity crisis. *Daedalus,* 730-759.

Espedal, G. (2021). "Hope to see the soul": The relationship between spirituality and hope. *Journal of Religion and Health, 60*(4), 2770-2783.

Feather, N. T. (1975). *Values in education and society.* Free Press.

Feather, N. T. (1988). Values, valences, and course enrollment: Testing the role of personal values within an expectancy-valence framework. *Journal of Educational Psychology, 80*(3), 381.

Feather, N. T. (1995). Values, valences, and choice: The influences of values on the perceived attractiveness and choice of alternatives. *Journal of Personality and Social Psychology, 68*(6), 1135.

Feather, N. T. (Ed.). (2021). *Expectations and actions: Expectancy-value models in psychology.* Routledge.

Fehr, E., & Gächter, S. (2002). Altruistic punishment in humans. *Nature, 415*(6868), 137-140.

Frankl, V. E. (1963). *Man's search for meaning: An introduction to logotherapy.* NY: Pocket.

Gaunt, R. (2005). The role of value priorities in paternal and maternal involvement in child care. *Journal of Marriage and Family, 67*(3), 643-655.

Godbless, E. E. (2021). Moral leadership, shared values, employee engagement, and staff job performance in the university value chain. *International Journal of Organizational Leadership, 10*(1).

Goldman A.I. (1979) What is Justified Belief?. In: Pappas G.S. (eds) Justification and Knowledge. Philosophical Studies Series in Philosophy. Springer, Dordrecht. https://doi.org/10.1007/978-94-009-9493-5_1

Gouveia, V. V., Vione, K. C., Milfont, T. L., & Fischer, R. (2015). Patterns of value Change during the life span: Some evidence from a functional approach to values. *Personality and Social Psychology Bulletin, 41*(9), 1276–1290. https://doi.org/10.1177/0146167215594189

Gribbons, W. D., & Lohnes, P. R. (1965). Shifts in adolescents' vocational values. *The Personnel and Guidance Journal, 44*(3), 248-252.

Gull, M., Rahman, E., & Husain, A. (2020). Reliability, validity and factor structure of values scale. Sage Preprint Sage Submissions. Preprint. https://doi.org/10.31124/advance.12138732.v1

Haidt, J., & Graham, J. (2007). When morality opposes justice: Conservatives have moral intuitions that liberals may not recognize. *Social Justice Research, 20*, 98-116. doi: 10.1007/sll211-007-0034-z

Holloway, J. (2003). Make-believe: Spiritual practice, embodiment, and sacred space. *Environment and Planning A, 35*(11), 1961-1974.

Homer, P. M., & Kahle, L. R. (1988). A structural equation test of the value-attitude-behavior hierarchy. *Journal of Personality and Social Psychology, 54*(4), 638.

Husain, A. (1988). Value preferences among Indian and Somalian students. Personality Study and Group Behaviour, 8, 49-53.

Husain, A., Rahman, S., & Khan, A. (2012). Human values – A running commentary based on literary texts. *Man in India, 92*(3-4), 491-504.

Idler, E. (2008). The psychological and physical benefits of spiritual/religious practices. *Spirituality in Higher Education Newsletter, 4*(2), 1-5.

Janssens, K., Lambrechts, W., Keur, H., & Semeijn, J. (2020). Customer value types predicting consumer behavior at Dutch grocery retailers. *Behavioral Sciences, 10*(8), 127.

Kaiser, F. G., Hübner, G., & Bogner, F. X. (2005). Contrasting the theory of planned behavior with the value-belief-norm model in explaining conservation behavior. *Journal of Applied Social Psychology, 35*(10), 2150-2170.

Karakas, F., & Sarigollu, E. (2019). Spirals of spirituality: A qualitative study exploring dynamic patterns of spirituality in Turkish organizations. *Journal of Business Ethics, 156*(3), 799-821.

Kelsen, H. (1966). Norm and value. *California L. Review, 54*, 1624.

Kesberg, R., & Keller, J. (2018). The relation between human values and perceived situation characteristics in everyday life. *Frontiers in Psychology, 9*, 1676. https://doi.org/10.3389/fpsyg.2018.01676

Kluckhohn, C. (1951). Values and value-orientations in the theory of action: An exploration in definition and classification. In T. Parsons & E. Shils (Eds.), *Toward a general theory of action* (pp. 388-433). Harvard University Press.

Koessel, K. C. (2011). *The relationship between spirituality and personality*. Western Michigan University.

Kohn, M. L., & Schooler, C. (1983). *Work and personality: An inquiry into the impact of social stratification*. Greenwood.

Kraemer Jr., H. M. J. (2011). The only true leadership is values-based leadership. *Forbes Magazine, 26*. https://www.forbes.com/2011/04/26/values-based-leadership.html#288ceff2652b

Krok, D. (2015). Striving for significance: The relationships between religiousness, spirituality, and meaning in life. *Implicit Religion, 18*(2), 233-257.

Lerner, J. S., & Keltner, D. (2000). Beyond valence: Toward a model of emotion-specific influences on judgement and choice. *Cognition & Emotion, 14*(4), 473-493.

Linely, P. A. (2009). Children's intrinsic and extrinsic values: Sources of internalization and implications for well-being. Unpublished manuscript, University of Leiceroter, U.K.

Lönnqvist, J. E., Jasinskaja-Lahti, I., & Verkasalo, M. (2011). Personal values before and after migration: A longitudinal case study on value change in Ingrian–Finnish migrants. *Social Psychological and Personality Science, 2*(6), 584-591.

Lönnqvist, J. E., Leikas, S., & Verkasalo, M. (2018). Value change in men and women entering parenthood: New mothers' value priorities shift towards conservation values. *Personality and Individual Differences, 120,* 47-51.

Lovejoy, A. O. (1950). Terminal and adjectival values. *Journal of Philosophy, 47,* 593-608.

Maathai, W. (2010). *Replenishing the earth: Spiritual values for healing ourselves and the world.* Image.

Maio, G. R., & Olson, J. M. (1995). Relations between values, attitudes, and behavioral intentions: The moderating role of attitude function. *Journal of Experimental Social Psychology, 31,* 266–285.

Manning, L., Ferris, M., Narvaez Rosario, C., Prues, M., & Bouchard, L. (2019). Spiritual resilience: understanding the protection and promotion of well-being in the later life. *Journal of Religion, Spirituality & Aging, 31*(2), 168-186.

Marcinkowski, T., & Reid, A. (2019). Reviews of research on the attitude–behavior relationship and their implications for future environmental education research. *Environmental Education Research, 25*(4), 459-471.

Maslow, A. H. (1967). A theory of metamotivation: The biological rooting of the value-life. *Journal of Humanistic Psychology, 7*(2), 93-127.

Maslow, A. H. (1968). Some educational implications of the humanistic psychologies. *Harvard Educational Review, 38*(4), 685-696.

Maslow, A. H. (Ed.) (1959). *New knowledge in human values.* Harper.

Matthews, S. H., Kelemen, T. K., & Bolino, M. C. (2021). How follower traits and cultural values influence the effects of leadership. *The Leadership Quarterly, 32*(1), 101497.

McLeod, S. A. (2016). Id, ego and superego. *Simply Psychology, 3,* 1-4.

Milbrath, L. W. (1981). Values, lifestyles and basic beliefs as influences on perceived quality of life. In *The Quality of Life: Systems approaches* (pp. 235-241). Pergamon.

Milfont, T. L., Milojev, P., & Sibley, C. G. (2016). Values stability and change in adulthood: A 3-Year longitudinal study of Rank-Order stability and mean-level differences. *Personality and Social Psychology Bulletin, 42*(5), 572–588. https://doi.org/10.1177/0146167216639245

Morris, C. (1956). *Varieties of human value.* University of Chicago Press. https://doi.org/10.1037/10819-000

Mottaz, C. J. (1985). The relative importance of intrinsic and extrinsic rewards as determinants of work satisfaction. *Sociological Quarterly, 26,* 365-385.

Mukařovský, J. (2015). Aesthetic function, norm and value as social facts (excerpts). *Art in Translation, 7*(2), 282-303.

Nazam, F., & Husain, A. (2016). Exploring spiritual values among school children. *International Journal of School and Cognitive Psychology, 3*(2), 1-5.

Nordlund, A. M., & Garvill, J. (2002). Value structures behind proenvironmental behavior. *Environment and Behavior, 34*(6), 740-756.

Olson, J. M., & Maio, G. R. (2003). Attitudes in social behavior. In M. J. Lerner & T. Millon (Eds.), *Handbook of psychology: Personality and social psychology*. NY: John Wiley and Sons, Inc.

Oreg, S., & Katz-Gerro, T. (2006). Predicting proenvironmental behavior cross-nationally: Values, the theory of planned behavior, and value-belief-norm theory. *Environment and Behavior, 38*(4), 462-483.

Poortinga, W., Steg, L., & Vlek, C. (2004). Values, environmental concern, and environmental behavior: A study into household energy use. *Environment and Behavior, 36*(1), 70-93.

Powers, D. V., Cramer, R. J., & Grubka, J. M. (2007). Spirituality, life stress, and affective well-being. *Journal of Psychology and Theology, 35*(3), 235-243.

Pratt, T. J., & Putra, E. D. (2022). Leadership types. In *Encyclopedia of tourism management and marketing*. Edward Elgar Publishing.

Pryor, K.G.L. (1987). Differences among differences: In search of general work preference dimensions. *Journal of Applied Psychology, 72*, 426-433.

Ramsey, F. P. (1931). *General Propositions and Causality.* http://www.dspace.cam.ac.uk/handle/1810/194722

Renner, W. (2003). Human values: A lexical perspective. *Personality and Individual Differences, 34*(1), 127-141.

Rohan, M. J. (2000). A rose by any name? The values construct. *Personality and Social Psychology Review, 4*(3), 255-277.

Rokeach, M, (1967). *Value Survey,* Sunnyvale, CA: Halgren Tests.

Rokeach, M. (1968). The role of values in public opinion research. *Public Opinion Quarterly, 32*(4), 547-559.

Rokeach, M. (1969). Part I. Value systems in religion. *Review of Religious Research,* 3-23.

Rokeach, M. (1971). Long-range experimental modification of values, attitudes, and behavior. *American Psychologist, 26*(5), 453.

Rokeach, M. (1973). *The nature of human values.* Free press.

Rokeach, M. (1979). *Understanding human values.* Free Press.

Rokeach, M. (2008). *Understanding human values.* Simon and Schuster.

Rokeach, M., & Kliejunas, P. (1972). Behavior as a function of attitude-toward-object and attitude-toward-situation.

Rosenberg, M. (1957). *Occupational and values.* IL: Free Press.

Sagiv, L., Roccas, S., Cieciuch, J., & Schwartz, S. H. (2017). Personal values in human life. *Nature Human Behaviour, 1*(9), 630-639.

Sattler, D. N., & Kerr, N. L. (1991). Might versus morality explored: Motivational and cognitive bases for social motives. *Journal of Personality and Social Psychology, 60*(5), 756.

Schwartz, S. H. (1992). Universals in the content and structure of values: Theoretical advances and empirical tests in 20 countries. In M.P. Zanna (Ed.), *Advances in experimental social psychology.* (Vol.25, pp. 1-65). Academic Press.

Schwartz, S. H. (2012). An overview of the Schwartz theory of basic values. *Online Readings in Psychology and Culture, 2*(1), 11.

Schwartz S.H. (2017) The refined theory of basic values. In: Roccas S., Sagiv L. (eds) Values and behavior. Springer, Cham. https://doi.org/10.1007/978-3-319-56352-7_3

Schwartz, S. H., & Bardi, A. (1997). Influence of adaptation to communist rule on values priorities in Eastern Europe. *Political Psychology, 18*, 385-410.

Schwartz, S. H., Sagiv, L., & Boehnke, K. (2000). Worries and values. *Journal of Personality, 68* (2), 309-346.

Schwartz, S. H., & Surkiss, S. (1999). Basic individual values, work values and the meaning of work. *Applied Psychology: An International Review, 48*(1), 49-71.

Schwitzgebel, E. (2011). Belief. In *The Routledge companion to epistemology* (pp. 40-50). Routledge.

Sheikh, K., Rajkumari, B., Jain, K., Rao, K., Patanwar, P., Gupta, G., & Sundararaman, T. (2012). Location and vocation: Why some government doctors stay on in rural Chhattisgarh, India. *International Health, 4*(3), 192-199.

Sheth, N. R. (1995). Values in search of an identity. *Journal of Human Values, 1*(1), 75-91.

Simpson, D. B., Newman, J. L., & Fuqua, D. R. (2007). Spirituality and personality: Accumulating evidence. *Journal of Psychology and Christianity, 26*(1), 33.

Sober, E., & Wilson, D. S. (1998). Unto others. *Cambridge/Mass.*

Sorokin, P. A. (1998). *On the practice of sociology.* University of Chicago Press.

Spranger, E. (1928). *Types of men. The psychology and ethics of personality.* Niemeyer.

Stern, P. (2000). Toward a coherent theory of environmentally significant behavior. *Journal of Social Issues, 56*(3), 407-424.

Stern, P. C., Dietz, T., Abel, T., Guagnano, G. A., & Kalof, L. (1999). A value-belief-norm theory of support for social movements: The case of environmentalism. *Human Ecology Review*, 81-97.

Thorisdottir, H., Jost, J. T., Liviatan, I., & Shrout, P. E. (2007). Psychological needs and values underlying left-right political orientation: Cross-national evidence from Eastern and Western Europe. *Public Opinion Quarterly, 71*(2), 175-203.

Triandis, H. C., & Vassiliou, V. (1972). Interpersonal influence and employee selection in two cultures. *Journal of Applied Psychology, 56*(2), 140.

Vecchione, M., Alessandri, G., Roccas, S., & Caprara, G. V. (2019). A look into the relationship between personality traits and basic values: A longitudinal investigation. *Journal of Personality, 87*(2), 413-427.

Vernon, P. E., & Allport, G. W. (1931). A test for personal values. *The Journal of Abnormal and Social Psychology, 26*(3), 231-248.

Williams Jr, R. M. (1979). Change and stability in values and value systems: A sociological perspective. *Understanding Human Values, 15*, 46.

Wuthnow, R. (2001). Spirituality and spiritual practice. *The Blackwell Companion to Sociology of Religion*, 306-320.

Yik, M. S. M., & Tang, C. S. (1996). Linking personality and values. *Personality and Individual Differences, 21*, 767–774.

Zavalloni, M (1980). Values. In H. Triandis & R. W. Brislin (Eds.), *Handbook of cross-cultural psychology*, Vol. 5. Boston: Allyn & Bacon.

Zimmerman, M. J. (2002). Intrinsic vs. extrinsic value. Retrieved from https://plato.stanford.edu/entries/value-intrinsic-extrinsic/

Žydžiūnaitė, V. (2018). Leadership values and values-based leadership: What is the main focus? *Applied Research in Health and Social Sciences: Interface and Interaction, 15*(1), 43-58 https://doi.org/10.2478/ARHSSS-2018-0005

Chapter 6

Shaping Reality through Interaction: Thoughts on Cultural Specifications

Cserkits Michael
University of Vienna, Austria

Abstract: In this paper, it has been argued that the possible impact of implementing two schools of thought together is based on the current limitations of two social sciences – Sociology and Anthropology. Based on the Anthropological view of space, place, and scape, these concepts are intertwined with Social Constructivism and their implementations by Berger and Luckmann (2010). The outcome will be a new approach to understanding the role of culture and its connotation shaped by various variables throughout human forms of existence. Hence, the 'cultural scape' model could be applied in cross- or intercultural social interactions to mitigate different perceptions of what is often called 'reality'.

Keywords: Cultural Scape, Social Constructivism, Social Anthropology, Functionalism, Historicism, Shaping Reality

***

Introduction

Constructivism is a very useful tool to argue against deterministic and ego-centered views of the world. In its very essence, constructivism states that reality is not exclusively constructed and that there is a thing that can be called a "material world"[1] - a part of the world that exists outside the constructed reality (Knorr-Cetina, 1993, p. 558).

It is noteworthy to state already at the beginning that some aspects of social constructivism are not part of this chapter. Especially radical social constructivism, with prominent members such as Luhmann (2007), von Glasersfeld (1996), or

---

[1] Again the author would like to state that the given viewpoints are more common to social and interactive constructivism and are not applicable in a radical view.

Cottone (2013), has out of the point of view of the author several limitations in helping us (in a very reasonable way) how to understand our surrounding scapes, their outcomes, and in fact, ourselves. Additionally, its three main theses (there is no free will, there is no mind, there is no absolute truth) are to a high extent more philosophical than sociological questions and cannot add any value to the following discussion. For example, Luhmanns "*Systemtheorie*" tries to convince his followers that arbitrariness is no inherent part of systems (Luhmann, 2007, p. 221). North (2016) has already shown that the idea of Radical Social Constructivism is logically incoherent (p.114). In the following pages, the author would like to argue against this view and include several aspects of arbitrariness and fuzziness when combining two theories together. For this approach, the chapter will follow the roots of social constructivism and interactive constructivism, with their very different philosophical implications and possible outcomes for the cultural and social scape. But what for? Well, the benefit of this attempt can be twofold: On the one hand, it is possible to describe the "culturally embeddedness" of the actors in interactive constructivism. On the other hand, readers could create a better understanding of the way how people (or to speak in constructivist terms, actors) shape their reality, and therefore understand them. This is even very succinct for social constructivism, with "language and knowledge" as the starting point for the construction of reality. Even if one would never get to the deep bottom of the mind of the other - a problem which was already stated and very cleverly argued by Schütz (2004, p. 222) - we can handle their experience and their actions in a more precise way: A field where every intercultural activity can benefit from.

Social Constructivism and Functionalism

Social constructivism - first initiated by Berger and Luckmann (2010) - starts with social interaction. It is the basis for further processes like *Institutionalization* - habitualized actions that are reciprocally performed by actors - or *Socialization*. It is, therefore, necessary to deal with this concept more in detail and point at the shortfalls and possible traps within it.

In the course of Peter L. Berger's and Thomas Luckmann's treatise "The Social Construction of Reality", the two authors already come to the thesis that a sociology of knowledge has to deal primarily with "everyday knowledge", i.e., the knowledge of the environment surrounding us, which is always present in a concise way (p. 16). In their view, it is this immanent reality of the everyday world that modern sociology of knowledge has to fathom. Referring to several authors of the phenomenological theory of action, such as Alfred Schütz (their intellectual father) but also structural-functionalists like Talcott Parson, a picture emerges which strongly reminds of the tradition of the former Heidegger -

student Gehlen. Sociology of knowledge per se is, based on the historical development, already since its origins strongly philosophically saturated and with the corresponding vocabulary pregnant with meaning. This historical fact, to which the two authors also pay some attention as part of their chain of argumentation, is only slightly taken into account. But how is it then possible for them to reconstruct the deeper structures of meaning?

As already mentioned, the fact that Berger and Luckmann limit themselves strongly to a functionalist way of looking at reality is already striking when dealing with them. To an extent that goes far beyond the normal sense of proportion, they argue about the unspoken superfluity of considering ideologies, which in their view do not shape the essence of society. The author does not agree with the two sociologists on this point. In fact, the history of the last 200 years shows us the opposite. From the author's point of view, it is precisely the great ideologies of the early eighteenth and nineteenth centuries that saturated society and changed its view of the world. This is also supported by the thoughts of Bonnemann (2017), who states that the way we experience the world and sort it along social categories is always inseparable from social needs; hence they are always subject to social interests (p. 36) and an ideological implication. Sensibly, this very statement would be a point of criticism for the two authors, since here they are already referring back to the world as "objectified." Berger and Luckmann do not go beyond the level of the first order when considering the objectivation of the actions according to meaning (p.20). They do consider the actions, the meaning subjectively meant by them, as Weber saw it, but their view is shaped from that of a researcher. The step to the meta-level, i.e., the environment of the action, is not made from their perspective. There is a decidedly scientific consideration of the construction of the co-world of the action, as well as in the broadest sense of the conditions of the co-world, its barriers, limits, and filtering possibilities, but a view of the third, uninvolved observer of the action is missing. Therefore, this is one of the most important points in holistically phenomenological action, as Schütz argued already before them and to whom they repeatedly refer. Berger and Luckmann's view resembles Gehlen in many ways, if not his teacher Heidegger. Based on a naturalistic-functionalistic view of the meaningfulness of actions, the orderly-purposeful sequence of sequences, a mechanistic picture of the world is inevitably formed. Indirectly, then, they thus bypass the question of the empiricism of their theory and refer to a kind of formative process that cannot be captured by purely empirical means (see Hay, 2016) for his critique on their view on institutionalism). This early rejection of the constraints of empiricism and its sister, statistics, diffuses the theory into an abstract one, which even evades the touchstone of time and thus immunizes itself against any criticism.

Social Constructivism and Historicism

The second paving stone on the road of Berger and Luckmann's chain of argumentation is their historicism. In an almost unconcerned manner, the two authors have succumbed, consciously or unconsciously, to the temptation to reintroduce their historical relationizm, a legacy of Hegel, in a veiled way, quasi via the back door of the discussion of principles. Hegel, whose stage of world events was history and the inseparable "determination" of nation-states (Popper, 2006, p. 13), again resembles the way Berger and Luckmann set out the path of the sociology of knowledge through the centuries. Once again, on a functionalist basis, each individual stage of cognition is illustrated, which, unspoken, of course, subsumes itself in ever more highly developed forms of understanding reality. Only once does the obvious tendency to favor Hegel's view of the world, of history, indeed of the deeper meaning of our *Dasein*, betray itself: *"Historicism, especially as expressed in the work of Wilhelm Dilthey, was an immediate precursor of the sociology of knowledge"* (Berger/Luckmann, 1977, p. 7). Hegel's legacy, which - according to Popper, created a veritable armory of arguments against freedom (Popper, 2006, p. 78), thus also propagates itself in Berger and Luckmann's chain of argumentation when considering the construction of reality. Indirectly, this could be interpreted as an admission by the authors that the individual is already per se inevitably chained to his fate, and it is only granted to him to experience at least a certain degree of understanding from the surrounding fellow world due to external circumstances. The researcher, who would go to the meta-level of the environment, would be warned to evaluate their typifications of such kind as generally valid. For what is the "essence" of man? What is associated with this term at all? The sensory world of the sociologist should be sharpened just in this point, so that the recognizing and reflecting social scientist, takes into account in a kind of multidimensional matrix the individual relevant aspects of the object to be observed phenomenologically.

Recent Approaches in Social Constructivism

"Social constructivism in this sense assumes that social reality is built on, by and through social actions." (Knoblauch, 2013, p. 299) Social constructivism therefore always starts with the interaction between at least two actors and their outcome - language and knowledge - is further constructing the surrounding reality (Knežić 2017, p. 297).

Here lies the big difference when comparing it with interactive constructivism, as the starting point for this theoretical framework is still the single actor or participant[2]. The single actor constructs a meaning of experience which is solely for further implications and realizations of the constructed world (Reich, 2010). Exactly the single actor (hence it is preferred to use the active term in the following pages) is culturally embedded - a fact that is underrepresented in social constructivism - which led to specific, culturally connotated observations. *"As members of a particular culture, we observe within the given context of this culture. In always being cultural participants as well as observers, the freedom of our observations is limited"* (Reich, 2007, p. 13). A similar approach can be found in Neubert (2008) who, with the common base of Dewey's pluralistic philosophy and pragmatic viewpoint, pleads for an embedded, context-related view in constructivist approaches. *"Intelligence, for Dewey, is something that has been developed out of human experiences in a long process of cultural history."* (Neubert, 2008, p. 91)

In recent research, Knoblauch (2019) suggested modifying Social Constructivism along two main axes: First, a shift from the subject to the relation gives more emphasis to the social position (or relation) of the single social actor to others (p. 285). Second, the role of language - which is, in a sole constructivist viewpoint, a matter of objectivation – should be taken more into account. Even if such newer approaches acknowledge the role of language and social position in social constructivism, they are still lacking the intertwined interaction with the already preexisting material world (the scape). Keller (2019), on the other hand, reactivates the theses by Berger and Luckmann as a whole and argues that they in itself must be seen as a part of discursive practice which has started more than 50 years ago. In reflecting on their main treatise: *"As it happens, it seems that yesterday's crossover easily becomes today's purified tradition and will be challenged by other crossovers to come. For better or for worse, this is the way transformations happen."* (p. 323)

In the next pages, a common understanding of the field of research will be created with the anthropological concept of "scape" and the different forms of social constructivism. After this short adjustment of the theoretical frame, the paper will further discuss the implications, overlaps, and fruitful outcomes of a possible merger of the two different fields.

The Anthropological Approach

Space is everywhere, and the events and behaviors that interest social scientists occur in and through space. [...] The effects of space stem from its role in causality, which assume that spatial contact must be

---

[2] It would be discussable if the ontological implications of starting with "actor" as still active conotated entity would be others than with "participant" as passive one.

made between and among interacting objects. [...] The effect of space depends on how the spatial arrangement of these objects influences their interactions. [...] The territorial rules about in/out of place not only enable the elements of a system and the flows within it to take place, but also constrain or prevent other interactions through space. (Sack, 1999, p. 830)

When arguing that space is everywhere, this raises the question of whether space is the same everywhere? The concept of one space that is the same for all is neither true nor realistic. Space as the three-dimensional vague object is valid for all humans in terms of gravity and the possibility to survive (when reaching a specific height, the oxygen level gets too low to breathe). Only these two main parameters are the same for all human beings - the rest is culture-, space- and period-specific.

Sack used the term "interaction" to show that the arrangement of objects in space is the result of human presence in the world. The world itself is consisting of three main parameters: Space, resources, and humans. Interaction can therefore only take place between these three entities. The mode of interaction, the results, and the spatial order that emerges out of the interaction differ as human existence differs around the world. Space is in this view more than just a physical entity, it is the possibility to create and to solve the own subsistence and to project internal feelings into the external world. This may be through arts, social organization, or other forms of interaction. Space is a term used to refer to our externalized thoughts. Appadurai (1990) created the term "Scape" to better match the concept for the problems of the twenty-first century. The concept of Scape is useful when analyzing global dynamics, as there is a more or less intertwined situation everywhere on the globe.

Additionally, the concept of the scape is contradictory to the notion or assumption that a fixed space is the prerequisite for a closed, homogenous, or authentic culture (Kreff, 2011, p. 351). The causality argument (fixed space leads to fixed culture) is no longer valid. Maybe some conclusions can be drawn about space regarding culture, but the one doesn't predict the other (there is nothing like a fixed causality). Ingold (2000) supports this argument when talking about *taskscapes*. Scape is, in Ingold's conception, the experience that has been made alive. Landscapes are therefore visible-made taskscapes (pp. 154) as the product of the interaction between humans and resources. So if the composition of the resources changes the mindset, the taskscape also changes its appearance. The connection between space and humans should again not be mistaken as causality, even if a strong affective relationship exists between them.

When talking about space, we often have to face the dichotomy between nature and culture, between continuity and discontinuity (de Castro, 2002, p. 778), which directly leads us to the polysemic notion of space. We could identify space as one prerequisite to human existence, we could set limits within which human existence is possible and we could contain that landscape is an inherent part of space. But how space affects humans, or how humans affect space is a highly complex and mutual process that is neither easy to understand nor necessarily logical. To approach space as a given entity, one that influences the mindset of humans that inhabit a specific area, is too hasty and leads to an ethnocentric viewpoint, confounding correlation for causality. Instead, space is a complex field that emerges between the interactions of humans with their surroundings, reproducing social interaction into the physical world. Aside from the purely spatial dimension - beginning with the medieval city as a combination of fortress and market – space in an anthropological view has to keep in mind the historical component of the scape. As it stems from the interaction of humans with the physical world that each interaction is unique and creates a solely non-comparable path in understanding, interpreting, and explaining natural circumstances, a comparison from a single viewpoint is hardly possible. Lerch (2014) has emphasized that cultural comparison 'beyond reason' opens new problems for the integration of humankind into natural and social sciences. From his point of view, the analysis has to start already before the emergence of reflexive studies (p. 195). What is so startling about this approach is that it neither uses a naturalistic (reducing the human body to pure chemical processes) or culturalistic (reducing the human nature to skills and reason) avenue, but rather tries to adept an analytical scheme presented by Ernest Cassier and Helmut Plessner. *"Both offer a concept for the different forms of science in the 'comprehension of expression' (Ausdrucksverstehen), and both develop a new concept of what it is to be a human being"* (p. 196). This approach can best be understood as integrative and focuses on an adept and enabling individual which is both – autonomous and part of an already present scape. As it refers much to Dilthey (1989), who has understood social interaction as a priori existing in the physical world, it offers a possible path for a further translation to the sociological aspects of time, space and meaning. Dilthey, being one of the intellectual fathers of Alfred Schütz (who later inspired Berger and Luckmann) can be seen as a starting point for a transition from a pure Anthropological to a more Sociological approach.

Culture and Constructed Scapes

As it was discussed in the previous sections, the landscape is visible made taskscape, the direct interaction between humans and resources. If an actor relies on the prerequisite to constructivism (except the radical one), that there is something like a material world that exists independent of our knowledge or observation, then it is possible to identify this material world as the *resource* of scape (e.g., Wacquant, 2012, as a very similar way how cultural-economic anthropology deal's with this issue). The starting point therefore in a merged scenario would neither be the social interaction that creates knowledge or language, nor the individual actor which makes meaning of his or her experience. Instead, we would have a dialectical interaction between the resource and the actor.

Through his actions, the actor performs and creates experience, which will lead to meaning. In order to structure the plenty amount of all experiences and subjective meanings, the actor invented language.

Wittgenstein precisely stated: *The limits of my language mean the limits of my world.* The author would add to this quotation that the resources, the material world which is a prerequisite for human existence, limits the possibility of meaningful experiences and therefore shapes the local structural system - language[3]. Language and knowledge - the classified and meaningful experience of the resources - lead to a selective process in further development. Innovation in this system is therefore seen as the adaption and implementation of resources other than in the surrounding scape in the existing structural system of the performing language. As now the borders of the possible experience are limited through the resources, also the performance, the acts of the actor are limited through it. This leads to locally specific accumulation of knowledge, which further marks the environmental scape (that is, what interactive constructivism calls "culturally embedded"). The local scape adepts to the actors and their performance and gets through the historic process - as also time is seen in the physical sense as a prerequisite existing entity outside human existence - further shaped. For sure, the notion and experience of time can be differentiated due to the given resources and the outcoming scapes, but the linear, one-directed flow of the physical time for all living and dead material is the same.

The now adapted scape, which has been shaped through the performance of actors, saves - or in a more metaphoric way memorizes - the permanent presence of the actors as well as their ongoing or long-closed actions. In this manner, the scape (the overall present space) divides into different areas of

---

[3] As an example, in each language we can observe a specific differentiation regarding the specific surrounding, e.g. the different Arab pronunciations for "camel" or the specific shapes of "white snow" in the Eskimo-Aleut language family. These specific meanings and experiences can only occur in a given environment that already provides the possibility of experience (see Mualem 2002 for the philosophical basis).

specialization according to the local structural system. In Social Anthropology, we would now speak of place.

> A place is an area in which people live together, and thus a key concept in geographic analysis. [...] The contents of a place - who is there, when - vary, therefore: when one is in a place, and who with, are major influences on individual and group socialization and behavior (Johnston, 1999, p. 612).

Place is, in contrast to space, not available for everyone. Places are predefined, at least two-dimensional entities that can harbor actors or resources. When talking about a place, the author follows the logic of Johnston and states the central issue: who is there when? The 'who' refers to the actor that inhabits the place, their mindset as well as the objects they use to create their individual taskscape. The 'when' refers to the point in history – imagined or not – when actors claim specific interests in specific places. Here we can see another distinction between space and place. *"Space refers to the abstract conception of physical location and its contents. Spaces become places when individuals and groups assign meanings and social significance to them."* (Zieleniec, 2013, p. 953).

The now specialized scapes - or places - are limited in two possibilities: On the one side, the number or degree of specialization is limited due to the possible resources that are already preexisting in the surroundings. If there are limited numbers of possible choices that can be converted into meaningful experiences, the lower the possible distinction in the division of scapes would be. All scapes are in such a sense socially constructed.

On the other side, the already shaped structural system, language, and knowledge, limit the possible meaningful experiences that can be experienced. If there is no possible scheme or way to modify a resource or a scape in a way that is accessible to the human mind, then it cannot be included. This statement concludes that actors, and especially humans, have a common psychic basis. Adolf Bastian was the first Anthropologist that talked about the so-called 'psychic unity of mankind', a theoretical framework that would support the present assumptions. Caldararo (2011) has reviewed the approach in a very critical way and attacked especially the linear-evolutionistic outcomes of this assumption (from which the author also definitely distances), but nevertheless, he also concludes that a common sole for all human activity - and therefore including 'actor activity' - is existing.

Culture in this approach can therefore be seen as the sum of the specialized scapes which evolved through the impact of the actors over time, and the additional limitations imposed by resources and knowledge/language.

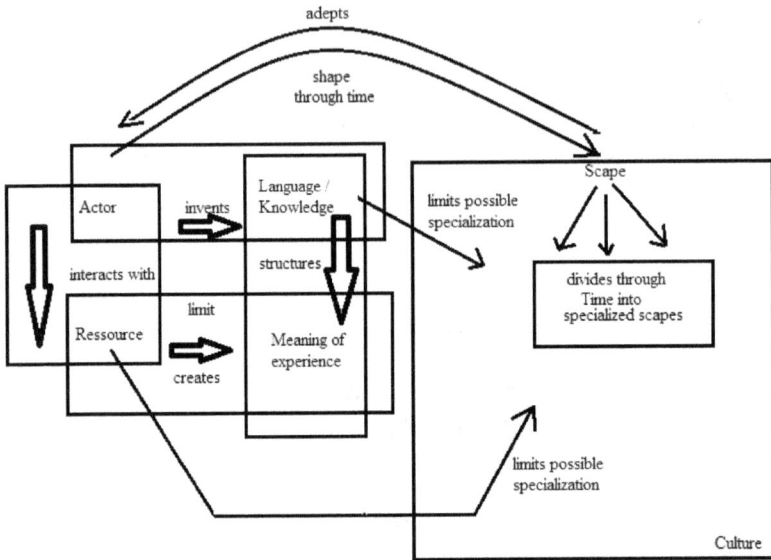

Figure 6.1: First sketch of the cultural scape approach

Culture is, therefore, a very interconnected, intertwined, and fluid construct, but never the less a construct of the involved actors as well as the material world. The reciprocal appearance of culture is seen in the way it adepts - via the overall scape as the sum of the specialized places - to the actions of the actors. As soon as the actor changes the way it interacts with the given resources he will therefore change all the other variables in this interconnected relationship. Some might now step forward and shout, that this will now rely on the single actor as a starting point, but we have to consider that the actor is not a loose entity. Instead, the actor is bound to other variables. Consider the possibility that the resources would change; they can also start a completely new development in the creation of meaningful experiences, which further interact with language as their structural system. In this approach, each option will influence - in the long run - culture. The author hereby wants to clearly state that he deliberately didn't use the word "cyclic", even if, at first glance, someone would get the impression of such a cyclic movement. Instead, it is tried to convince the interested reader that there is absolutely no cyclic movement in this approach. With such a cyclic movement, this approach would bind itself to a single starting and a single endpoint. Additionally, cyclic movements tend to be interpreted post hoc as evolutionary, as we intend to view such movements as linear upwards processes.

But the opposite - a fluid and vivid flux of possibilities - is the intention of the author. Even culture as the outcome of the interaction of several entities can therefore via several specialized places influence the appearance and perception of the actor and therefore initiate a change in the whole process. The author also wants to state that none of the above-mentioned variables is superior to another. We can highlight the role of the actor as well as those of language or the resource. All would have the same chance and influence to the others regardless of their position in the cycle. One question cannot be answered with this approach: What, or who, was first? The actor, the resource, or the scape? Similar to the chicken-and-egg problem, this question remains unanswered as the frame cannot explain *when* the involving factions evolved, but only *how*.

Conclusion

In the previous sections, it was the goal to – even very roughly - sketch the main effects of scape/place/space as well as social constructivism in order to give the interested reader a basic understanding of the cultural scape approach. It was then the aim to merge the separate approaches and invent a new approach in understanding culture. This theoretical frame relies heavily on actors who construct via language and knowledge meaningful experience, but it also involves the material world with the concept of resource and scape (as well as time), which are in their essence (in German: *Wesen*) independent of our existence. Making them understandable and integrating them into our structural system for further shapings of reality is another part of the approach. With the limitations and the division of scapes into places, the author hopes to pay enough attention to the very specific and historically unique division of the tremendous amount of existing scapes, each of them a product of the interaction of local structural systems, resources, and actors with their performance. As already mentioned at the beginning, time as a variable was integrated to not fell into the same historicity that Berger and Luckmann promoted, but rather to contribute to the possibility of change, as with time our structural system may change and to involve the possibility of innovation as the integration of resources other than yet currently available.

In times where skepticism and pessimism regarding scientific research are on the everyday agenda, we have to have a closer look at their philosophical grounds and try to figure out how they can help us better understand ourselves and others.

Hence the proposed framework is conceptual in the present state. Empirical examination of the stated framework would be a separate study, which would go beyond the scope of this handbook. The author can only encourage scholars to test the framework on real-life examples and is looking forward for empirical results.

References

Appadurai, A. (1990). Disjuncture and Difference in the Global Cultural Economy. *Public Culture, 2*(2), 1-24.

Barnard, A. & Spencer, J. (2002). *Encyclopedia of Social and Cultural Anthropology*. Routledge.

Berger, P. L. & Luckmann, T. (2010). *Die gesellschaftliche Konstruktion der Wirklichkeit – Eine Theorie der Wissenssoziologie*. (23th Ed.). Fischer Taschenbuch Verlag.

Bonnemann, J. (2017). Licht und Schatten der Begriffe. Zwischen Sozialkonstruktivismus und Mythos des Gegebenen: Adorno mit Merleau-Ponty. *Deutsche Zeitschrift für Philosophie, 65*(1), 34-50.

Byron, K. (2013). *Encyclopedia of Philosophy and the Social Sciences*. SAGE Publications.

Caldararo, N. L. (2011, June 6). *The Psychic Unity of Mankind: The Origins of Anthropology, the Anti-Slavery Movement, Cultural Relativism and Man's 'Unique' Nature*. SSRN. https://ssrn.com/abstract=1858882

Cassirer, E. (1963). *The Philosophy of Symbolic Forms. Volume Three: The Phenomenology of Knowledge*. (Trans. Ralph Manheim). Yale University Press.

Cottone, R. R. (2013, September 1). A paradigm shift in counseling philosophy. *Counseling Today*. Retrieved from https://ct.counseling.org/2013/09/a-paradigm-shift-in-counseling-philosophy/

de Castro, E. V. (2002) Society. In Barnard, A. & Spencer, J. (Eds.), *Encyclopedia of Social and Cultural Anthropology* (pp. 774-785). Routledge.

Dilthey, W. (1989). Introduction to the Human Sciences. In Makkreel, R. A. & Rodi, F. (Eds.), *Selected Works Volume I*, Princeton University Press.

Garrison, J. (2008). *Reconstructing Democracy, Recontextualizing Dewey Pragmatism and Interactive Constructivism in the Twenty-First Century*. Ithaca State University of New York Press.

Hay, C. (2016). Good in a crisis: the ontological institutionalism of social constructivism. *New Political Economy, 21*(6), 520-535, DOI: 10.1080/135634 67.2016.1158800.

Ingold, T. (2000). *The Perception of the Environment. Essays on livelihood, dwelling and skill*. Routledge.

Johnston, R. J. (1999). Place. In Kuper, A. & Kuper, J. (Eds.), *The Social Science Encyclopedia 2nd Ed.* (p. 612). Routledge.

Keller, R. (2019). The discursive construction of realities. In Pfadenhauer, M. & Knoblauch, H. (Eds.), *The Legacy of The Social Construction of Reality* (pp.310-324). Routledge.

Knežić, I. (2017). The Problem of Language Grounding as a Specific Human Feature in the Philosophy of Thomas Hobbes and Thomas Reid. *Synthesis Philosophica*, 64(2), 295–309.

Knoblauch, H. (2013). Communicative Constructivism and Mediatization. *Communication Theory, 23*, 297-315.

Knoblauch, H. (2019). From the social to the communicative construction of reality. In Pfadenhauer, M. & Knoblauch, H. (Eds.), *The Legacy of The Social Construction of Reality* (pp.275-291). Routledge.

Knorr-Cetina, K. (1993). Strong Constructivism -- from a Sociologist's Point of View: A Personal Addendum to Sismondo's Paper. *Social Studies of Science, 23*, 555-563.

Kreff, F. (2011). Scapes. In Kreff, F., Knoll, E.M.& Gingrich, A. (Ed.), *Lexikon der Globalisierung* (pp. 351-352). transcript Verlag.

Lerch, H. (2014) Anthropology as a Foundation of Cultural Philosophy. The connection between Human Nature and Culture by Helmuth Plessner and Ernst Cassirer. In de Mul, J. (Ed.), *Plessner's Philosophical Anthropology. Perspectives and Prospects* (pp. 195-210). Amsterdam University Press.

Luhmann, N. (2007). Erkenntnis als Konstruktion. In Luhmann, N. (Ed.) *Aufsätze und Reden,* (pp. 218-242). Reclam.

Mualem, S. (2002). Borges and Wittgenstein on the Borders of Language: The Role of Silence in "The God's Script" and the Tractatus Logico-Philosopicus. *Variaciones Borges, 14*, 61-78.

Neubert, S. (2008). Dewey's Pluralism Reconsidered - Pragmatist and Constructivist Perspectives on Diversity and Difference In Garrison, J., *Reconstructing Democracy, Recontextualizing Dewey Pragmatism and Interactive Constructivism in the Twenty-First Century,* (pp. 89-117). Ithaca State University of New York Press.

North, A. (2016). A Millennial Mistake: Three Arguments Against Radical Social Constructivism. *Journal of Counseling & Development, 94*, 114-122.

Plessner, Helmuth. (1980). *Gesammelte Schriften.* Suhrkamp.

Popper, K. R. (2006). *Die offene Gesellschaft und ihre Feinde. Band II Falsche Propheten: Hegel, Marx und die Folgen.* J. C. B. Mohr.

Reich, K. (2007). Interactive Constructivism in Education. *Education and Culture, 23*(1), 7-26.

Reich, K. (2010). *Systemisch-konstruktivistische Pädagogik.* Beltz.

Sack, R. (1999). Space. In Kuper, A. & Kuper, J. (Eds.), *The Social Science Encyclopedia 2nd Ed.* (p. 830). Routledge.

Schütz, A. (2004). *Der Sinnhafte Aufbau der sozialen Welt. Eine Einleitung in die verstehende Soziologie.* UVK Verlagsgesellschaft mbH.

von Glasersfeld, E. (1996). *Radical Constructivism. A way of knowing and learning.* Routledge.

Wacquant, L. (2012). Three steps to a historical anthropology of actually existing neoliberalism. *Social Anthropology/Anthropologie Sociale, 20*(1), 66-79.

Zieleniec, J. L. A. (2013). Social Theories of Space. In Byron, K., *Encyclopedia of Philosophy and the Social Sciences* (pp. 952-955). Sage.

Chapter 7

Dealing the Responses Contaminated with Social Desirability Bias while Studying Socially Stigmatized Behaviors

Salman A. Cheema
School of Applied Science, National Textile University
Faisalabad, Pakistan

Irene L. Hudson
Mathematical Sciences, School of Science, Royal Melbourne Institute of Technology (RMIT), Melbourne, Australia

Muhammad Naveed
Faisalabad Medical University, Pakistan

Arslan Khan
Department of Statistics, Quaid-i-Azam University Islamabad, Pakistan

Farooq Shah
Department of Statistics, University of Peshawar, Pakistan

Zawar Husain
Department of Statistics, the Islamia University, Bahawalpur, Pakistan

Abstract: This research primarily focuses on the proposition of a hybrid strategy capable of entertaining the socially masked responses when stigmatized behaviors are under study. The suggested approach respects that individuals' behaviors are embedded within their distinctive socio-cultural fabrics, and the "need for social approval" phenomenon is likely to affect the respondent's responses. It is anticipated that ignoring the effects of varying cultural streams prevalent in society may result in un-cohesive estimates projecting the social psychology. The study deals with the situation where data have already been collected, and an initial analysis reveals the patterns pointing towards the existence of *social desirability bias*. The proposed scheme allows investigators to work with the same data while considering the presence of desirability bias by incorporating a masking parameter in the model. The applicability of the proposed model is demonstrated by studying the contraceptive behaviors and their deriving factors in a multi-linguistic, culturally diverse and relatively more rigid society. Notably, the likely prevalence of social desirability bias in the stated social profile remains highly expected.

Keywords*:* Data masking, Desirability Bias, Multi-level Modeling, Social Desirability, Stigmatized Behaviors, Survey Research

***

Introduction

Face-to-face interviewing constitutes probably the most popular data collection intervention in social research to explore the group structures embedded in varying socio-cultural orientations. One of the most lamented complications coined with the aforementioned gathering practice remains the likely prevalence of social desirability bias (SDB). The SDB most commonly emerges due to respondents' discomfort and belief that a specific response may expose their social standing (Mneimneh et al., 2015; Meisters et al., 2020). As a result, the respondents commence providing answers that they judge socially acceptable instead of reflecting on their actual status about the issue (Groves et al., 2009 & Schröder & Schmiedeberg, 2020). A deeper investigation into the literature reveals that many researchers have raised a red flag to warn of the ability of social desirability bias to creep into survey research while piercing unanticipated gaps. For example, Gill (1993) looked into a different aspect of this bias by tagging it as the *conspiracy of courtesy*. He argued that the warmth of rural societies towards strangers is one of the possible factors in the tendency toward responding deemed to please their *guest* (interviewer). In addition, Schaeffer (2000) suggested two layers of the respondent's information storage process; public information, which creates a public image, and private information, which reflects the truth. The first layer is considered to be the mother of desirability bias. The fundamental effect of SDB is the masking of the actual response and thus poses a serious threat to the validity of the findings (Krumpal, 2013; Schill & Kirk, 2017). It remains a noticeably relatable phenomenon in almost every field of social research.

Stecklov et al. (2015) conducted a fascinating and provocative study. They explored contingencies at the high sterilization level reported in the Dominican Republic (DR) in 2010. They observed a high correlation between the level of pre-existing familiarity, respondent and interviewer, and high reported sterilization use. They suspected that the high sterilization use correlates with respondents' propensity to present themselves positively to interviewers; in the DR, sterilization has long been cherished as a go-to contraceptive method. They provided ample evidence supporting their findings. They found that a high reported sterilization level is, in fact, a result of the respondent's tendency to demonstrate a socially approved behavior. From the above studies, one may immediately notice the high likelihood of the prevalence of desirability bias, especially in social survey research focusing on the dynamics of stigmatized behaviors. Thereby, developing a capable framework for identifying the bias in the collected information and simultaneously providing the legitimate contamination-free aggregates remains desirable, especially for the research circles involved in social survey research. This chapter is primarily devoted to gaining the above-reported objectives by addressing the issue of SDB in relation to contraceptive usage behavior. A two-layered strategy was proposed to investigate the potential factors affecting the propensity of contraceptive use in a population, given that the SDB remains active. Abstractly, a multi-level regression model capable of explaining masked (contaminated) binary responses is suggested resulting from the investigation of tabooed conducts through large-scale household survey research. The degree of prevalence of the masking is entertained by involving a masking parameter at the methodological level. For the proposition of a hybrid approach, the rationale of randomized response technique (RRTs) has been exploited – well-celebrated methods to generate masked data when the main concern lies in the privacy protection of the respondent.

Methods and Materials

The Data

The focus of this work is to study Pakistan Social and Living Standards Measurement (PSLM) 2013-14 survey data, collected and assembled by the Pakistan Bureau of Statistics (PBS). The PSLM is a major national-level data collection exercise employed by PBS to monitor the population's living conditions and assist the government in formulating optimal policies. It provides rich information at the household level about several socio-economic variables, such as health conditions, expenditure, education level, and housing conditions, women's decision-making. It is noteworthy that Pakistan has more than 210 million persons according to the 2018 census and stays the seventh most populous country in the world. The reported propensity for contraceptive usage remains noticeably lower than its neighboring countries and among most of the Muslim-majority countries (Saleem & Bobak, 2005).

To meet the objectives of the study, ever-married female participants of the PSLM sample aged 15-49 years are considered. Thus, we examine a national representative sample of responses of 17,446 female participants fitting the above profiles, responding to the question, *"Did you ever use a contraceptive?"* (PSLM questionnaire provides a list of 10 means of contraceptives, including modern methods). A *"yes"* response to the above-reported question is coded as "1" and "0". Moreover, we consider five literature-driven explanatory variables to explain the differences between individuals at the micro-level. Micro variables include, *age of respondent in years (Age), education level (Edu), women decision making (WDM), number of male children currently alive (Boys)* and *region*. The notion behind the use of well-established covariates remains consistent with the fair evaluation of the proposed procedure in the light of existing literature. The education level of respondents is determined by placing the responses into five categories based on years of formal education. As such, "0" implies five years of education at most, whereas "1" indicates the maximum of ten years' education. The code "2" proxies twelve years of education (diploma holders are also included in this category). The category code "3" represents fourteen years of formal education, and "4" represents graduates with eighteen years of education. In the category with code "5", we gathered post-graduation qualification (PhD) information and participants with professional degrees (doctor, engineers, lawyers, etc.). The variable WDM quantifies the extent of direct female involvement in the household decision-making, spanning issues from groceries to the next birth. A code "1" is assigned if her consent is asked for and "0" if she is not being consulted. The variable *region* indicates the locality of the participant of the study; "1" is urban, and "0" is given to the rural participant. Below are some of the existing studies that emphasize the significance of the above-mentioned determinants.

- Age: (i) Fikree et al. (2001), in the context of Pakistan. (ii) Worku et al. (2014), in the context of Ethopia. (iii) World Family Planning (2017), globally.

- Edu: (i) Wong and Masson (1985), comparative study of fifteen countries. (ii) Castro (1995), a comparative study of 26 demographic surveys. (iii) Saleem and Bobak (2005), in the context of Pakistan.

- Boys: (i) Arokiasamy (2002), in the context of India. (ii) Saleem and Bobak (2005), in the context of Pakistan. (iii) Ding and Hesketh (2006), in the context of China.

- WDM: (i) Mason (1997), in the context of Asia. (ii) Jejeebhoy and Sathar (2001), in the context of Pakistan and India. (iii) Thapa and Bajracharya (2017), in the context of Nepal.

- Region: (i) Fikree et al. (2001), in the context of Pakistan. (ii) Jejeebhoy and Sathar (2001), in the context of Pakistan and India. (iii) Fotso et al. (2013), in the context of Nairobi.

Table 7.1: Descriptive of micro and macro variables at national and divisional level

	[1]Pc.	[2]Age	[3]Edu.	[4]Boys	[5]WDM	[6]Region
National	0.3773	31	0	0,8	0.6309	0.3275
Divisional						
Malakand	0.6502	28	0	0,7	0.6801	0.169051
Hazara	0.3360	32	0	0,8	0.5312	0.173666
Mardan	0.4965	32	0	0,7	0.9388	0.418824
Peshawar	0.4995	30	0	0,5	0.9251	0.669095
Kohat	0.4275	30	0	0,5	0.8667	0.317647
Banu	0.5769	30.5	0	0,7	0.9615	0.211538
DI Khan	0.3080	33	0	0,1	0.8137	0.262357
Rawalpindi	0.5812	32.5	1	0,4	0.7029	0.407468
Sarghoda	0.3698	31	0	0,2	0.5925	0.35368
Faisalabad	0.6154	33	1	0,2	0.7822	0.447337
Gujranwala	0.5592	32	1	0,3	0.6249	0.395567
Lahore	0.5145	32	1	0,3	0.7932	0.615385
Sahiwal	0.3876	32	0	0,2	0.7416	0.303828
Multan	0.4706	32	0	0,4	0.6765	0.397059
DG Khan	0.4260	30	0	0,4	0.6000	0.235772
Bahawalpur	0.1838	32	0	0,5	0.4824	0.314865
Larkhana	0.1976	30	0	0,6	0.4834	0.128035
Sukhar	0.2572	30	0	0,6	0.5666	0.125632
Haiderabad	0.2086	30	0	0,4	0.5158	0.165512
Mirpur Khas	0.1476	30	0	0,5	0.4036	0.084337
Karachi	0.4523	32	1	0,4	0.5776	0.735084
Quetta	0.2005	30	0	0,8	0.5013	0.324873
Zhob	0.0964	30	0	0,4	0.3522	0.163522
Sibi	0.1737	30	0	**0,0**	0.5842	0.289474
Naseerabad	0.1857	31	0	0,6	0.7048	0.166667
Kalat	0.2174	30	0	**0,0**	0.3217	0.26087
Islamabad	0.5341	32	2	**0,0**	0.7045	0.761364

[1]Proportion of respondents ever used contraceptives. [2]Median age of respondents. [3]Median education level. [4]Minimum and maximum number of male children for any respondent. [5]Proportion of respondents, involved in decision making process of household. [6]Proportion of urban respondents.

Table 7.1 gives the descriptives of the micro attributes, at the national and divisional levels of the country, based on the responses of participants of the survey. It is noteworthy that divisions are administrative stratifications of the country based on geographical access and cultural similarities and therefore provide a good proxy of various active social streams existent in the country. The PSLM 2013-14 surveys offer data for 27 divisions from four provinces of the country, namely, Baluchistan, Khyber Pakhtunkhwa, Punjab and Sindh.

Existing Techniques and Account of Related Complications–Usual Logistic Model

A single logistic regression is run, including all participants in the survey for national estimates. It is then disaggregated at the divisional level by employing a separate logistic model for every division. In this regression, $Y_i (i = 1,2, ..., n)$ is the outcome variable being the response to the inquiry *"have you ever used any contraceptive method?"*. Every realization follows a Bernoulli distribution which takes on the value 1 (yes response) with probability θ_i and 0 otherwise with $(1 - \theta_i)$ probability. Thus, in general,

$$Y_i \sim Bernoulli(\theta_i)$$

and

$$\theta_i = \frac{1}{1+e^{-x_i\beta}}, \qquad\qquad ...(1)$$

where, x_i is $(k + 1) \times 1$ vector of covariates including a constant and β is $(k + 1) \times 1$ vector of unknown parameters. The results of a usual logistic regression analysis are in Table 7.2.

At the national level, all five covariates play a significant role in explaining contraceptive use behavior; one may notice that the findings are consistent with the reported literature. Separate logistic regressions for each division, however, show varying results. It was found that the intercept coefficients, Age and WDM, remain highly significant across the divisions. The estimated effects of age and WDM have positive signs. It indicates that controlling for other variables, a higher level of female involvement in household matters is associated with a higher likelihood of contraceptive use and aged couples are more likely to use contraceptives. However, alarmingly, the estimates of education and the number of male children, the region show a varying degree of heterogeneity, not only restricted to the extent of significance but in the direction of association with contraceptive practice; this is altering. Moreover, we observe an explosion of the standard errors of the estimates, quantifying the impact of the number of male children on contraceptive use in three divisions, *DI Khan, Sargodha* and

Zhob. These contradictory findings raise legitimate concerns about the validity of results based on usual logistic regression.

Table 7.2: Estimates of logistic regression – national and divisional level

	Intercept	Age	Edu	WDM	Boys	Region
National	-4.7826 ***	0.0784 ***	0.1874 ***	1.9548 ***	0.4626 ***	0.4589***
	(0.0929)	(0.0023)	(0.0175)	(0.0439)	(0.0335)	(0.0401)
Divisional						
Malakand	-3.8400***	0.0722***	-0.0195	2.0655***	0.7492***	1.0541***
	(0.46804)	(0.0150)	(0.1106)	(0.2126)	(0.1067)	(0.2911)
Hazara	-3.8087***	0.0506***	0.1559	2.0234***	0.0465	0.3218
	(0.3951)	(0.0104)	(0.0935)	(0.2014)	(0.0861)	(0.2242)
Mardan	-5.8050***	0.1313***	0.0134	1.6218**	-0.0094	0.0862
	(0.8075)	(0.0154)	(0.1105)	(0.5895)	(0.1336)	(0.2325)
Peshawar	-6.8698***	0.1520***	-0.0370	2.1559***	0.3192	0.2134
	(0.5718)	(0.0110)	(0.0632)	(0.3962)	(0.2087)	(0.1688)
Kohat	-5.4631***	0.1013***	-0.0886	2.0696***	0.1731	0.5589
	(0.8837)	(0.0191)	(0.1295)	(0.5833)	(0.3177)	(0.3126)
Banu	-4.761***	0.0622***	0.2308	2.9549***	-0.1763	0.9678*
	(1.3538)	(0.0194)	(0.1519)	(1.1134)	(0.1785)	(0.4075)
DI Khan	-4.6007***	0.0674***	0.4080**	1.4727***	-13.1227	0.3088
	(0.8538)	(0.0193)	(0.1493)	(0.4627)	**(882.7434)**	(0.3443)
Rawalpindi	-3.7975***	0.0824***	-0.1301	2.0500***	1.1376	0.3748
	(0.5223)	(0.0134)	(0.0785)	(0.2167)	(0.8221)	(0.1969)
Sargodha	-4.3849***	0.0727***	-0.0062	2.1029***	6.6635	0.1357
	(0.5013)	(0.0128)	(0.0989)	(0.2432)	**(267.7056)**	(0.2231)
Faisalabad	-3.0932***	0.0742***	0.0693	1.2557***	-0.6122	0.2217
	(0.3944)	(0.0100)	(0.0749)	(0.1836)	(0.6895)	(0.1674)
Gujranwala	-2.7797***	0.0459***	0.0451	2.2501***	0.1070	0.1417
	(0.3622)	(0.0091)	(0.0688)	(0.1431)	(0.7692)	(0.1458)
Lahore	-3.7532***	0.0658***	0.0401	1.7163***	0.0810	0.3033*
	(0.3903)	(0.0091)	(0.0606)	(0.1907)	(0.2350)	(0.1505)
Sahiwal	-3.7018***	0.0504***	0.1447	1.7119***	0.2181	0.3123
	(0.5709)	(0.0137)	(0.1081)	(0.3063)	(0.6893)	(0.2414)
Multan	-6.6226***	0.1195***	-0.0947	3.1824***	1.1621*	0.7331***

	(0.5642)	(0.0135)	(0.0933)	(0.2746)	(0.5788)	(0.2191)
DG Khan	-4.2288***	0.0679***	-0.1213	2.5733***	0.4315	0.3143
	(0.4809)	(0.0122)	(0.1068)	(0.2357)	(0.5127)	(0.2371)
Bahawalpur	-5.1207***	0.0560***	0.1019	2.3227***	0.2328	0.3326
	(0.5389)	(0.0131)	(0.1160)	(0.2762)	(0.2995)	(0.2395)
Larkhana	-5.6659***	0.0861***	0.3425*	1.9758***	1.4797	0.7104***
	(0.4830)	(0.0119)	(0.1380)	(0.2187)	(0.9973)	(0.2713)
Sukhar	-5.9682***	0.1086***	0.1026	1.7805***	-0.1904	0.7385***
	(0.4084)	(0.0100)	(0.0912)	(0.1790)	(0.2875)	(0.2156)
Haiderabad	-5.1571***	0.0912***	0.0531	1.1569***	0.6039	0.4583*
	(0.3745)	(0.0099)	(0.0958)	(0.1616)	(0.4681)	(0.1990)
Mirpur Khas	-5.8732***	0.1038***	0.3428*	0.9970***	0.1178	0.1637
	(0.5984)	(0.0155)	(0.1466)	(0.2391)	(0.2817)	(0.3973)
Karachi	-4.5639***	0.0728***	0.1964***	2.2779***	-0.0136	0.4216*
	(0.4526)	(0.0113)	(0.0723)	(0.1808)	(0.2172)	(0.2011)
Quetta	-4.8858***	0.0748***	0.2234***	1.1919***	0.0016	0.6297***
	(0.4658)	(0.0123)	(0.0811)	(0.2076)	(0.1367)	(0.2025)
Zhob	-5.8731***	0.0598***	0.2878	2.6539***	-12.3108	-0.0222
	(0.8230)	(0.0208)	(0.1676)	(0.4557)	**(809.6243)**	(0.4247)
Sibi	-5.8422***	0.0862***	0.347	1.8538***	----	-0.2841
	(1.0699)	(0.0256)	(0.2276)	(0.5732)		(0.4892)
Naseerabad	-6.9777***	0.0979***	1.0829***	2.2734***	-0.2097	0.8397*
	(0.8901)	(0.0187)	(0.2734)	(0.5125)	(0.2478)	(0.3471)
Kalat	-3.1594***	0.0111	0.4917	2.5479***	----	0.6885
	(1.2016)	(0.0342)	(0.4690)	(0.5550)		(0.5876)
Islamabad	-6.9926***	0.1721***	-0.0195	2.0498***	----	0.0968
	(1.8782)	(0.0449)	(0.2240)	(0.6779)		(0.6199)

***p-value <0.000, **p-value <0.001, *p-value <0.05. Standard errors of estimates are in parenthesis.

Realizations and Hypothesis

There are three vivid realizations in afore-documented outcomes.

1. The propensity of contraceptive usages varies noticeably across divisions (Table 7.1).

2. Aggregate level estimates (national level) confront with dis-aggregations (divisions).

3. The estimates are inconsistent with the well-establish facts in existing literature.

The heterogeneity in the reported proportions of contraceptives' practices across divisions can be associated with the varying extent of acceptability of contraceptives embedded in varying social streams approximated by the use of divisions as strata. But, fragmented, un-interpretable and spurious estimates of the determinants are an indication of the existence of masked data (Zimbalist, 2021). These jointly pose a rather serious threat to the validity of the usual modeling strategies not weighing the deteriorating nature of above-nominated contaminations.

At this stage, as a hypothesis, it is re-emphasized that the data are likely to be masked with group structure (defining the variability at a higher or macro-level) where the individual's behaviors are embedded within higher contextual levels. In the next section, a new methodology to deal with this complexity has been proposed.

Hybrid Approach

The incorporation of a multi-level probabilistic mechanism has been proposed, especially designed to handle masked data. Under the study design, let Y_{ij} represent the reported binary response to the question *"have you ever used any contraceptive method?"*, for i'th respondent (1 if "yes" and 0 if "no") in the j'th division. In case of a masked response, instead of modeling the probability of reported status of the respondent (as we demonstrated in equation (1) by employing usual logistic regression), we suggest to model the probability of actual status. Note that, when social desirability bias is not involved, reported and actual responses become equivalent. Let π_{ij} be the true probability that the respondent is actually practicing contraceptives and $1 - \pi_{ij}$ is the probability in case of actual "no". This notion implies that $P(Y_{ij} = 1) = \pi_{ij}$ and $P(Y_{ij} = 0) = 1 - \pi_{ij}$. Due to SDB, we believe response is masked, thus the proportion of actual status of respondents and that of reported masked status is related to each other by the following equation,

$$\theta_{ij} = c\pi_{ij} + d. \qquad \qquad \text{... (2)}$$

Where, c and d are functions of masking parameter(s) highlighting the extent of masking in the reported responses and determined by the investigator. Our claim is, instead of θ_{ij} (reported probability of contraceptives use), π_{ij} (actual probability) is a function of the covariates, such that,

$$\pi_{ij} = f_{\beta_j}(X_{ij}),$$

where, for modeling binary response, $f_{\beta_j}(X_{ij}) = \left(1/1 + e^{-x^T_{ij}\beta}\right)$.

So,

$$\theta_{ij} = cf_{\beta_j}(X_{ij}) + d,$$

which, then implies that,

$$\widehat{\pi}_{ij} = \frac{\hat{\theta}_{ij}-d}{c}.$$

Thus, when we assume the logistic regression for $f_{\beta_j}(X_{ij})$, we have,

$$g(\pi_{ij}) = \log\left(\frac{\theta_{ij}-d}{c+d-\theta_{ij}}\right) = \beta_j X_{ij}, \qquad \qquad ...(3)$$

where $g(.)$ is a monotonic and differentiable link function over the domain equal to $(d, c + d)$. Furthermore, X_{ij} is a $(k + 1) \times 1$ vector of observations on the micro-level variable (including the intercept) for the i'th individual in the j'th division, and β_j consists of $(k + 1)$ unknown micro coefficients, specific to the j'th division.

A popular choice of constants, "c" and "d", in the randomized response literature is based on the seminal work of Warner (1965) by restricting $c = 2p - 1$ and $d = 1 - p$. In our setting, p is the masking parameter approximating the extent of masking in the response, caused by SDB. It can take values over the range of (0,1). A value of "1" indicates the absence of masking that is when true status and reported status are equivalent. As we move away from the value "1" towards the value "0", the extent of masking becomes stronger. For instance, p = 0.95 implies that a 5% degree of masking is prevalent in the reported responses. The equation (2) is then rewritten as,

$$\theta_{ij} = (2p - 1)\pi_{ij} + (1 - p) \qquad \qquad ... (4)$$

An unbiased estimator of the true probability of contraceptives user, is then given by,

$$\pi_{ij} = \frac{\theta_{ij} + p - 1}{2p - 1}$$

Using the above specifications and equation (3), it is now straightforward to write a general form of the logit model for masked binary responses, as follows,

$$g(\pi_{ij}) = \log\left(\frac{\theta_{ij}+p-1}{p-\theta_{ij}}\right) = \beta_j X_{ij} \qquad \ldots(5)$$

$$\text{where } g(\pi_{ij}) = \log(\pi_{ij}/1 - \pi_{ij})$$

In the second phase, it was addressed the issue of the heterogeneous nature of responses at the divisional level. The variability in contraceptives practice across divisions is captured by introducing two macro-level variables to further elaborate the group structure active at a higher contextual level. We consider *female's standardized share in household income (Inc)* and the proportion of elected members in the national assembly representing right-wing or religious parties and thus quantifying the *voting behaviors within each division (VB)*. This is achieved by regressing "J" micro coefficients $(\beta_{1k}, \beta_{2k}, \ldots\ldots, \beta_{jk})$ pertaining to the k'th micro variable, related to macro-level variables. The general model is given by,

$$\beta_{jk} = G^T_{jk}\gamma_k + \alpha_{jk}, \qquad \ldots(6)$$

where, $\alpha_{jk} \sim N(0, \sigma_{kk})$. Moreover, G_{jk} provides the measurements on l_k macro variable with γ_k as a vector of unknown coefficients. It is assumed that, for $k \neq k^*$, $\text{cov}(\alpha_{jk}, \alpha_{j^*k^*}) = \sigma_{kk^*}$ if $j = j^*$ and "0" otherwise.

Simplified Model for PSLM 2013-14 Data

The general structure provided in equations (5 and 6), can now be specified for the PSLM 2013-14 data, as

$$g(\pi_{ij}) = \beta_{oj} + \beta_{1j}(Age)_{ij} + \beta_{2j}(Edu)_{ij} + \beta_{3j}(WDM)_{ij} + \beta_{4j}(Boys)_{ij} + \beta_{5j}(Region)_{ij},$$
$$\ldots(7)$$

where $i = 1,2,\ldots,n_j$, such that, n_j is number of individuals in the sample from the j'th division with $j = 1,2,\ldots,27$. Adding in, female average income share in the household in a standardized form (Inc) and the proportion of elected members representing right-wing or religious parties in national assembly from a given division (VB), as macro-level variables, the β's are regressed as,

$$\beta_{oj} = \gamma_{oo} + \gamma_{o1}(\text{Inc})_j + \gamma_{o2}(\text{VB})_j + \alpha_{oj}$$

$$\beta_{1j} = \gamma_{1o} + \gamma_{11}(\text{Inc})_j + \gamma_{12}(\text{VB})_j + \alpha_{1j}$$

$$\beta_{2j} = \gamma_{2o} + \gamma_{21}(\text{Inc})_j + \gamma_{22}(\text{VB})_j + \alpha_{2j}$$

$$\beta_{3j} = \gamma_{3o} + \gamma_{31}(\text{Inc})_j + \gamma_{32}(\text{VB})_j + \alpha_{3j}$$

$$\beta_{4j} = \gamma_{4o} + \gamma_{41}(\text{Inc})_j + \gamma_{42}(\text{VB})_j + \alpha_{4j}$$

$$\beta_{5j} = \gamma_{5o} + \gamma_{51}(\text{Inc})_j + \gamma_{52}(\text{VB})_j + \alpha_{5j}, \qquad \qquad \dots (8)$$

where, the α's are normally distributed macro errors.

Finally, the multi-level logistic regression model for masked binary responses which offers the information about contraceptive practice in Pakistan, is deduced by combing the models given by equations (7) and (8), as follows,

$$g(\pi_{ij}) = \gamma_{oo} + \gamma_{o1}(\text{Inc})_j + \gamma_{o2}(\text{VB})_j + \left[\gamma_{1o} + \gamma_{11}(\text{Inc})_j + \gamma_{12}(\text{VB})_j + \alpha_{1j}\right](\text{Age})_{ij}$$

$$+\left[\gamma_{2o} + \gamma_{21}(\text{Inc})_j + \gamma_{22}(\text{VB})_j + \alpha_{2j}\right](\text{Edu})_{ij} + \left[\gamma_{3o} + \gamma_{31}(\text{Inc})_j + \gamma_{32}(\text{VB})_j + \alpha_{3j}\right](\text{WDM})_{ij} + \left[\gamma_{4o} + \gamma_{41}(\text{Inc})_j + \gamma_{42}(\text{VB})_j + \alpha_{4j}\right](\text{Boys})_{ij} + \left[\gamma_{5o} + \gamma_{51}(\text{Inc})_j + \gamma_{52} + \alpha_{5j}\right](\text{Region})_{ij} + \alpha_{oj}. \qquad \dots (9)$$

It needs to be highlighted that equation (9) can now recursively capture the fluctuations at the divisional level, while masking parameter is accounted for by the randomized response methodology. Moreover, when p = 1 that in case of in-active desirability bias and therefore no masking of the responses, our proposition converges toward the usual multi-level logistic model. This realization again emphasizes the generality of the devised technique.

Empirical Evaluation

This section demonstrates the applicability of the proposed mechanism using the PSLM 2013-14 data. At this stage, it is appropriate to document some hurdles during the study. No study to date is probably available in the literature dealing with modeling contraceptive use while also addressing the issue of masked data. Thus, *a priori*, the prevalent extent of masking in the data is not obtainable. This complication is met by considering the various masking parameter values guided by the multi-level logistic regression.

Moreover, the yardstick we use to deduce an appropriate model depends upon the literature-guided interpretability of results, combined with considerable statistical evidence (tests) highlighting the suitability of the model.

In Table 7.3, the results of seven more competitive models proposed to demonstrate the applicability of proposed methodology. Table 7.3, gives the estimation of fixed effects of the multi-level logistic regressions, based on various values of the masking parameter($p = 1.0, 0.9, 0.85, 0.8, 0.78, 0.77, 0.76$). Further, the results in Table 7.3 are aided by providing scaled residuals and goodness of fit measures for every level of "p" (Table 7.4).

Start by exploring the case of $p = 1.0$, when the masking effect is not entertained (reported status is considered to be the true status). A clear violation of the assumption of normal residuals imposed by the model (6) is seen through the behavior of the scaled residuals (Table 7.4). This residual pattern raises questions about the legitimacy of results for $p = 1.0$. With the inclusion of the masking parameter, the scaled residuals start behaving normally (Table 7.4). It is appropriate to conclude that the responses are not only masked but also pose severe threats to the usual modeling avenues. These findings leave us with the question of quantifying the more likely extent of masking that may have prevailed in the data.

Table 7.3: Estimates of fixed effects with respect to the varying extent of masking

	Estimates						
	$p = 1.0$	$p = 0.90$	$p = 0.85$	$p = 0.80$	$p = 0.78$	$p = 0.77$	$p = 0.76$
Intercept	-5.761 ***	**-9.140*****	-12.351***	-15.975***	-1.670 ***	-1.780 ***	-2.070***
	(0.262)	**(0.001)**	(0.920)	(1.470)	(0.002)	(0.001)	(0.007)
Age	0.103***	**0.156*****	0.194***	0.238***	0.256***	2.670***	0.299***
	(0.007)	**(0.001)**	(0.018)	(0.025)	(0.002)	(0.009)	(0.007)
IS	-0.042	**0.241*****	0.565	1.204*	1.210***	1.320***	1.080***
	(0.163)	**(0.001)**	(0.033)	(0.504)	(0.002)	(0.001)	(0.007)
VB	1.754***	**3.136*****	4.747***	5.391**	4.220***	4.810***	6.950***
	(0.384)	**(0.001)**	(1.198)	(1.189)	(0.002)	(0.001)	(0.007)
Edu	0.142*	**0.206*****	0.269*	0.246	0.307***	0.311***	0.450***
	(0.055)	**(0.001)**	(0.120)	(0.168)	(0.002)	(0.001)	(0.007)
WDM	1.712***	**3.123*****	4.958***	6.936***	6.910***	7.650***	9.460***
	(0.159)	**(0.001)**	(0.708)	(1.176)	(0.002)	(0.001)	(0.007)
Reg	0.492***	**0.764*****	0.979***	1.301***	1.440***	1.460***	1.820***
	(0.083)	**(0.001)**	(0.208)	(0.282)	(0.002)	(0.001)	(0.008)

Boys	0.129 (0.117)	**0.571***** **(0.001)**	0.633 (0.449)	0.406 (0.533)	0.875*** (0.002)	0.736*** (0.001)	0.559*** (0.004)
Age:IS	0.001 (0.004)	**-0.003***** **(0.001)**	-0.008 (0.010)	-0.019 (0.014)	-0.185*** (0.002)	-0.022*** (0.009)	-0.019*** (0.004)
Age:VB	-0.042 *** (0.010)	**-0.066***** **(0.001)**	-0.077** (0.025)	-0.075* (0.036)	-0.658*** (0.002)	-0.065*** (0.009)	-0.087*** (0.004)
IS:Edu	-0.014 (0.035)	**-0.027***** **(0.001)**	-0.036 (0.071)	-0.036 (0.095)	-0.307*** (0.002)	-0.053*** (0.001)	-0.047*** (0.007)
VB:Edu	-0.077 (0.079)	**-0.110***** **(0.001)**	-0.164 (0.165)	-0.108 (0.229)	-0.157*** (0.002)	-0.205*** (0.001)	-0.419*** (0.007)
IS:WDM	0.028 (0.099)	**-0.060***** **(0.001)**	-0.199 (0.274)	-0.527 (0.438)	-0.462*** (0.002)	-0.532*** (0.001)	-0.178*** (0.005)
VB:WDM	0.389 (0.236)	**0.113***** **(0.001)**	-0.866 (0.901)	-1.210 (1.475)	-0.117*** (0.002)	-0.574*** (0.001)	-1.890*** (0.004)
IS:Reg	0.054 (0.055)	**0.049***** **(0.001)**	0.035 (0.124)	0.054 (0.163)	0.036*** (0.002)	-0.009*** (0.001)	-0.048*** (0.007)
VB:Reg	-0.159 (0.117)	**-0.288***** **(0.001)**	-0.407 (0.293)	-0.646 (0.398)	-0.723*** (0.002)	-0.677*** (0.001)	-1.040*** (0.007)
IS:Boys	-0.062 (0.071)	**-0.222***** **(0.001)**	-0.314 (0.262)	-0.537 (0.317)	-0.601*** (0.002)	-0.686*** (0.001)	-0.677*** (0.004)
VB:Boys	0.119 (0.209)	**-0.218***** **(0.001)**	-0.067 (0.686)	1.031 (0.875)	0.587*** (0.002)	0.806*** (0.001)	1.230*** (0.004)

Table 7.4: Measures of model assessment

	Scaled Residuals					Goodness of Fit		
	Min	1st Q	Median	3rd Q	Max	AIC	BIC	Log-lik
p = 1.0	-14.603	-0.579	-0.258	0.649	6.499	17348	17534.4	-8650
p = 0.90	**-2.999**	**-0.548**	**-0.352**	**0.611**	**2.972**	**17479.2**	**17665.6**	**-8715.6**
p = 0.85	-2.381	-0.547	-0.423	0.592	2.379	17695.1	17881.5	-8823.6
p = 0.80	-2.000	-0.560	-0.500	0.584	2.000	18040	18226	-8996
p = 0.78	-1.883	-0.577	-0.531	0.592	1.883	18223.6	18410	-9087.8
p = 0.77	-1.829	-0.586	-0.547	0.598	1.829	18322.4	18508.8	-9137.2
p = 0.76	-1.779	-0.592	-0.562	0.602	1.779	18432.1	18618.5	-9192.1

Based on the residuals' behavior, all models incorporating the masking parameter ($p < 1$) are sound. Though, a varying degree of significance of the fixed effects and changing the direction of association with contraceptive practice is observed. For example, the multi-level model with $p = 0.85$, reveals that only Age, VB, Edu, WDM and region significantly explain contraceptive use, whereas, when $p = 0.80$, Age, Inc, VB, WDM and region are significant factors. The intercept remains significant in all cases of p. Other models with $p = 0.90, 0.78, 0.77$ and 0.76 show that all the covariates' fixed effects are significantly associated with proportions of contraceptive users. This complication is dealt with by taking clues from the literature along with statistical methods to assess the appropriateness of the models.

First, the cases of $p = 0.85$ and 0.80 were considered. For these models, the education level of female respondents and the number of alive male births remain insignificant in explaining contraceptive behavior. Many researchers have studied the impact of education, the number of alive male births, and associated family planning attitudes of couples. For example, Summers (1992) observed that educated women choose to have fewer children. Castro (1995), in a meta-analysis of 26 demographic surveys, agreed with the above findings. On the other hand, Arokiasamy (2002), in a study linking son preference with contraceptive use in India, noticed that the gender of children is an important determinant of family planning. Other than the theoretical un-interpretability of models with $p = 0.85$ and 0.80, further investigation uncovers the underlying statistical weaknesses of the models. The correlation matrices of both models expose the existence of a high correlation between the coefficients of the fixed effects. As such, when $p = 0.85$, nine pair-wise correlation coefficient values are higher than 0.75, for $p = 0.80$ the situation is no better with seven pairs correlated to an extent greater than 0.75. As is well understood, this high degree of correlation among explanatory variables can alter the true nature of statistical modeling. Moreover, on a cautious note, it is believed that excluding such determinants is not an appropriate course of action as they remain significant for other masking parameter scenarios.

In the light of the above discussion, the focus is on four more sensible models that accommodate the extent of masking with $p = 0.90, 0.78, 0.77$ and 0.76. Two features are immediately observable (i) estimates are interpretable in the light of literature (Table 7.3), and (ii) residuals are behaving normally (Table 7.4). Furthermore, the goodness of fit measures is comparable with the baseline model when $p = 1.0$ (Table 7.4). For instance, the increase in AIC criterion related to the model with $p = 0.90$ is 131.20 units compared to the base model. Similarly, this increase remains $875.60, 974.40$ and 1084.1 for $p = 0.78, 0.77$ and 0.76, respectively. Moreover, Table 7.5 displays the estimates of the standard errors of the intercept, boys, age, education, WDM and region, averaged over all divisions. The least heterogeneity is witnessed when the model with p = 0.90 is employed. The model with p=0.90 selected to explore the contraceptive usage behavior by looking at these facts. The results of the chosen model are bolded in Tables 7.3, 7.4 and 7.5.

Table 7.5: Estimated variability of the random effects averaged over all divisions

	Coefficients					
	Intercept	Boys	Age	Education	WDM	Region
p = 0.90	**0.706**	**0.703**	**0.026**	**0.183**	**0.562**	**0.226**
p = 0.78	0.459	1.727	0.057	0.378	0.945	0.574
p = 0.77	0.016	1.485	0.058	0.362	0.891	0.579
p = 0.76	0.415	1.773	0.063	0.451	0.856	0.692

Further Discussion of the Chosen Model with p = 0.90

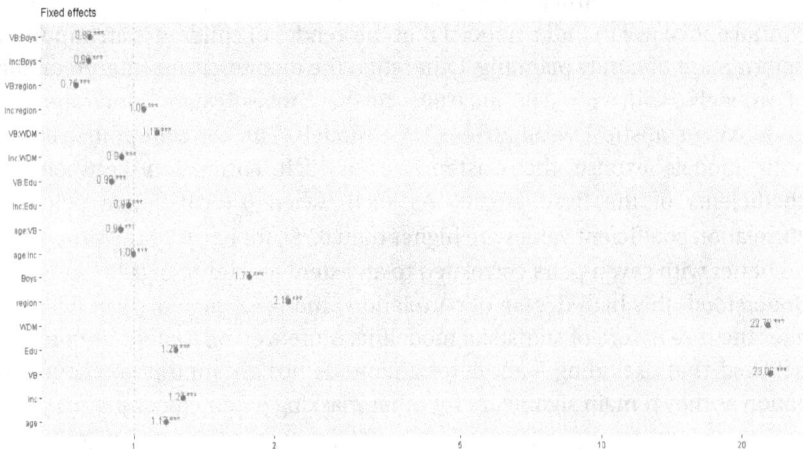

Figure 7.1: Odds of contraceptive use estimated through the multilevel logistic regression model with masking parameter **p = 0.90**

Now, we start reading the output of the corresponding fixed effects of the chosen model (Table 7.3). The rule of *dive by 4* was employed to interpret the upper bound of predictive difference corresponding to a unit difference in the explanatory variable while controlling for others. The overall coefficient for *Age* is 0.156, dividing by 4 yields that a year increase in Age is at most associated with a 3.75% increase in the likelihood of contraceptive use, given that other factors remain constant. Using the same rationale, the maximum predictive increase in contraceptive use associated with Inc, VB, Edu, WDM, Boys, and region is 6%, 78%, 5%, 78.2%, 14% and 19%, respectively. The small standard errors attached to interaction terms (capturing the group structure through micro and macro variables) of the model highlight that sample sizes within each division are large enough to estimate the division-specific coefficients (Table 7.3). All group-level interactions are significant; other than VB: WDM and Inc: Region, they are negatively associated with the proportions of contraceptive use when controlling for divisions. Figure 7.1 displays the estimated fixed effects (Table 7.4) in the form of odds of using contraceptive use.

Next, the results of the proposed multi-level logistic regression model, which handles masking in the data at each division level, have been reported. The gain of the proposed methodology is highlighted by comparing the results given in Table 7.6 with Table 7.2, where the latter is based on individual logistic regression for each division. Now, we compare the estimated effects of the determinants of contraceptive use via the multi-level model, which accommodates masking in the data and separate logistic regression effects at the division level.

- *Age:* A positive association of *age* is observed for each division regardless of the modeling strategy. When separate regression is employed, the minimum of the estimated effects is 0.010, whereas the maximum remains at 0.170. On the other hand, for the proposed model minimum and maximum estimated values are 0.125 and 0.204, respectively. Thus, the minimum predictive increase in contraceptive use is 3%, with respect to a one-year increase in age, which is captured in the *Zhob* division (Table 7.6). Similarly, the maximum increase is estimated for the *Peshawar* division, where one year increase in age is associated with an estimated 5% increase in contraceptive use.

- *Education:* The results for *Edu* further highlight the applicability of the proposed model. In the case of separate logistic regressions, it was observed that 8 divisions are projecting negative association (insignificant) and 21 divisions are positively associated with contraceptives use (only six of them are significant, Table 7.2). The minimum and maximum estimated effects of the *Edu* are -0.019 and 1.083, respectively. It is important to note that the effect of education is significantly positively associated when a single logistic regression was considered at the national level. The stability of estimates of the proposed model is evident in Table 7.6, in that only 2 divisions have a negative effect, whereas 25 divisions show that the female with an increased level of education is more likely to use contraceptives. These results are not only practically and theoretically more sensible but also exhibit more stability. The minimum of the estimated effect of *Edu* remains -0.054 for the *Peshawar* division and the maximum is estimated in the *Naseerabad* division, where a one-level increase in education of the females offers a 10% increase in the use of contraceptives.

Table 7.6: Estimates of multi-level logistic regression for all divisions – $p = 0.90$

	Coefficients					
	Intercept	Age	Edu	WDM	Boys	Region
Divisions						
Malakand	-8.82442	0.1773534	0.0761468	3.481044	1.876106	0.9157076
Hazara	-8.576194	0.1302449	0.3020363	3.267497	0.6539578	0.6757217
Mardan	-9.000866	0.1873098	0.041426	2.969746	0.6836167	0.5105225
Peshawar	-9.555789	0.2044868	**-0.0539573**	3.051113	0.6073923	0.5239734
Kohat	-8.731902	0.1599559	0.0271005	3.355053	0.3232741	0.7920392
Banu	-8.945785	0.1524775	0.3094666	3.358739	**-0.0443843**	0.8903796
DI Khan	-9.630549	0.1435023	0.4245153	2.796595	0.480328	0.8303401
Rawalpindi	-8.547831	0.1824293	**-0.0149695**	2.975471	0.8654718	0.7905064
Sarghoda	-8.979572	0.1551498	0.0679972	3.146995	0.7303301	0.6080222
Faisalabad	-8.381916	0.1870033	0.2001318	2.073047	0.2929635	0.7083176
Gujranwala	-8.183131	0.1594953	0.2078506	3.219052	0.5062538	0.5945775
Lahore	-8.806412	0.162283	0.1694495	2.619733	0.2566199	0.760716
Sahiwal	-9.087683	0.1395408	0.2750201	3.10317	0.5092187	0.7895514
Multan	-9.952899	0.1837182	0.0569525	3.639617	1.0844299	0.9181779
DG Khan	-9.349965	0.1632756	0.0587891	3.608492	0.6544836	0.7158997
Bahawalpur	-9.771951	0.1279384	0.2083883	3.366716	0.5723725	0.7432934
Larkhana	-9.324793	0.1368576	0.3568605	3.619368	1.0571589	0.9521182
Sukhar	-9.583849	0.1680215	0.237564	2.747868	0.1771553	0.8406989
Haiderabad	-8.623678	0.147448	0.1562353	2.304709	1.4079086	0.775954
Mirpur Khas	-9.574563	0.1535573	0.287702	2.462656	0.2278636	0.7214114
Karachi	-8.538582	0.1494921	0.2931874	3.762557	0.0463757	0.702659
Quetta	-9.142697	0.1334705	0.340738	2.784564	0.0476266	1.0021122
Zhob	-9.956053	0.1251288	0.312014	3.102834	0.4524781	0.7247004
Sibi	-9.450142	0.1352423	0.263021	3.09651	0.5711776	0.6960093
Naseerabad	-9.276462	0.1307421	0.5028095	3.251658	**-0.2676727**	0.8949096
Kalat	-9.076374	0.1397694	0.2828893	3.45924	0.5711776	0.7710355
Islamabad	-9.055335	0.1795441	0.1661251	2.905295	0.5711776	0.7474473

- **Women Decision Making (WDM):** Both strategies show that the direct involvement of females in household decisions increases the likelihood of contraceptives. The proposed model again outperforms the usual logistic model when the variability of the estimated effects between all divisions is compared. The separate logistic regressions produce a minimum estimated effect of 0.997 and a maximum of 3.182. In comparison, the proposed model provides 2.073 as a minimum value, obtained for the *Faisalabad* division, where a one-unit increase in the degree of women's involvement in decision-making is associated with a 50% rise in contraceptive usage. The maximum estimated effect is gained for the *Karachi* division, where the coefficient of *WDM* stays at 3.763.

- **Number of alive male children (Boys):** The usual logistic model again suffers from the issues of stability and interpretability. Out of 27 divisions, 7 exhibit a negative association, 17 a positive association, and for 3 divisions, we do not have data (Table 7.2). This "missingness" complication is seen to have an altering influence on the results of separate regressions. The minimum value of estimated effects is observed as -13.122, and the maximum of the coefficients is 6.663. The inherent variability between divisions is evident, along with the fact that data is likely to be masked, and the stability of the estimated effects of *Boys* on the use of contraceptives is noticeable and encouraging. In this case, only 2 divisions show a negative association out of 27. Moreover, the minimum effect estimate observed here is -0.267 (Naseerabad division), and the maximum value remains at 1.876 (Malakand division). Thus, in Naseerabad, a female with one additional male birth is at most 40% more likely to use contraceptives.

- **Region:** The separate regressions show that in 2 divisions, urban participants are less likely to use contraceptives, whereas, in 25 divisions, the urban locality is more likely to be associated with the contraceptive user. The minimum estimated effect is -0.284, and the maximum is 1.054. The chosen model with $p = 0.90$ yields a minimum value of 0.511 (Mardan), and the maximum locality effect is observed in *Quetta* with an estimated *Region* coefficient value of 1.002. Thus, participants from the Quetta division and an urban region are at most 20% more likely to use contraceptives than their rural female counterparts.

The homogeneous behavior of the estimated effects of the covariates obtained when masking is accommodated through the multi-level logistic model is further evident in Figure 7.2, which displays the side-by-side box plots of the estimated effects across all divisions.

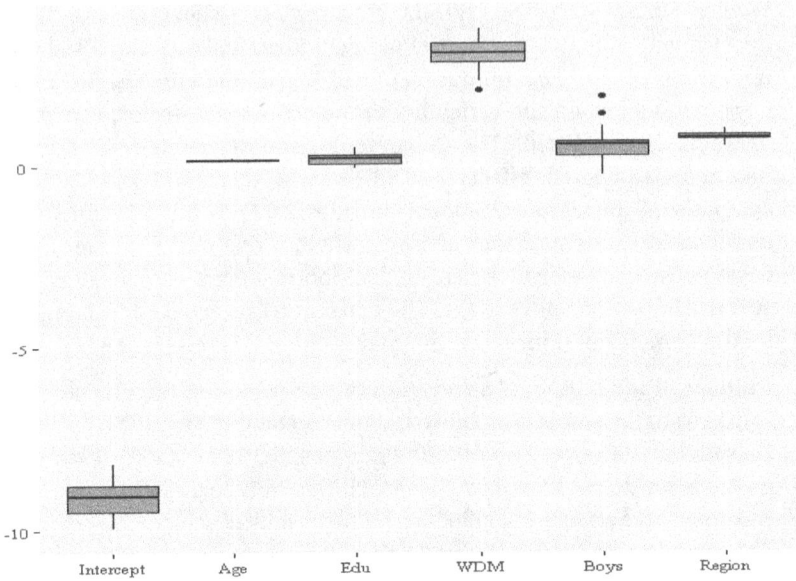

Figure 7.2: Estimated effects of determinants of contraceptives use, through the multi-level logistic regression model with **p** = **0.90**, across all divisions

Next, visuals of the behavior of the predicted probabilities are provided using contraceptives estimated through the proposed model (Figure 7.3). For demonstration purposes, we consider in detail the predicted probabilities with respect to education, women's decision making and region while controlling, first for age (panel a, b and c) and then for boys (panel d, e and f).

It can be seen that age is positively associated with predicted probabilities of the use of contraceptives across all other factors (Figure 7.3, a, b and c). Moreover, the different intercept levels and varying slopes of the predicted lines reveal informative patterns. For example, panel (a) highlights that those urban participants are more likely to use contraceptives than their identical age counterparts from rural localities. Additionally, the line corresponding to the urban region is steeper than rural, indicating that, as age increases, the likelihood of use of contraceptives rises in urban participants at a faster rate than in their rural counterparts. Similarly, women involved in decision-making are more likely to use contraceptives across all age groups. The rate of increase in predictive probabilities of use of contraceptives in aged participants with a higher level of empowerment is noticeable (panel b). The study of education levels and age also reveals an interpretable pattern: women with higher education are more likely to use contraceptives across all age groups. Similar behavior of the predicted probabilities is obvious when the above-mentioned factors are controlled for a number of alive male children (panels d, e and f). For example, for a given number of live male births, urban respondents are more likely to use contraceptives than their rural female counterparts. Similarly, autonomous females, for all numbers of live male births, reveal an elevated tendency to practice contraceptives compared to the rural participant. Likewise, more educated females exhibit a high propensity to use contraceptives, accounting for the number of live male births.

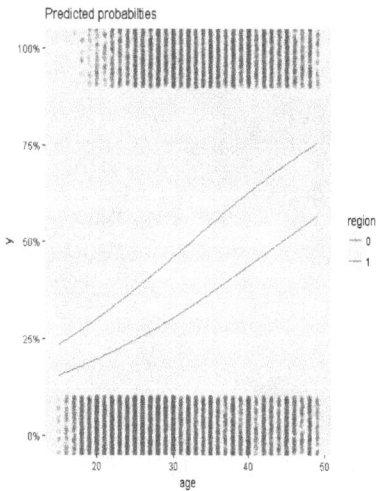

Panel – a

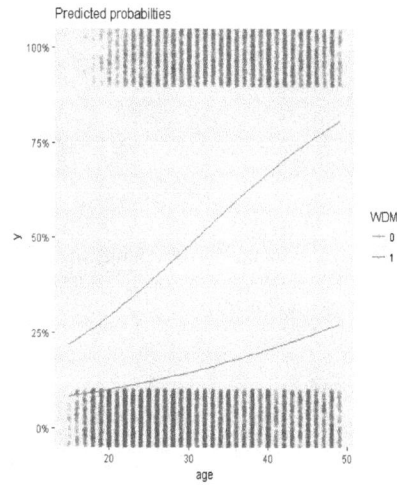

Panel – b

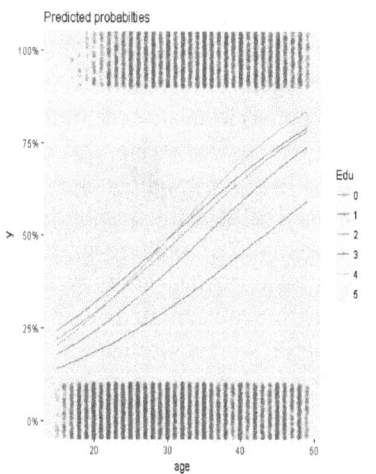

Panel – c

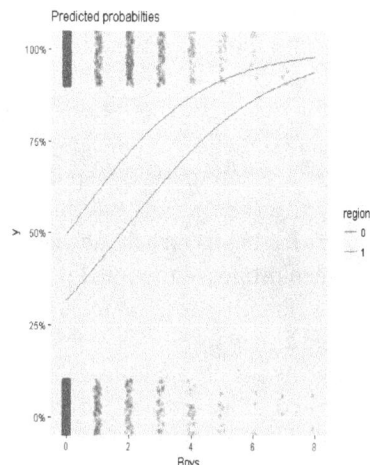

Panel – d

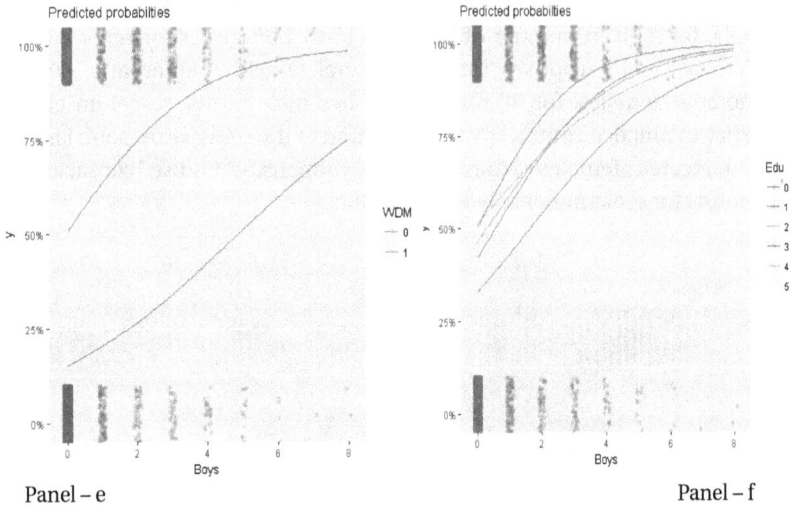

Panel – e   Panel – f

Figure 7.3: Display of predicted probabilities with respect to region Age and WDM controlling for age and boys, estimated through the multi-level logistic regression model with $p = 0.90$

Conclusion

The prevalence of SDB in survey research, especially when dealing with sensitive demographic and reproductive health issues, is well documented. Few methodological remedial measures have been devised to avoid the bias's pervasive effects, such as using latent variable models (Bollen et al., 2001) and multi-level modeling (Sana & Weinreb, 2008). Notably, the proposed schemes handling the desirability bias emphasized modeling perspectives while ignoring the psychological origin of the bias. Whereas in this research, it has delineated the discrepancies in suggested methods to tackle the SDB, especially when masked responses are attached to group-level confounders. Distinctive nature of the bias while connecting it with respondents' tendencies being socially desirable. A multi-level hybrid modeling approach has been proposed to model the masked binary response. The study provides a suite of methodological tools which are inherently proficient in dealing with masked binary responses at the group level, especially in reproductive health-related issues. A multi-level analysis of contraceptive use in Pakistan is advocated. The novelty of this research is based on two aspects: (i) identification and proximity of group structure and (ii) providing an avenue to resolve the issue of masked responses.

The most appropriate model for explaining the propensity to use contraceptives is a model with five micro-level variables. Furthermore, to accommodate the group structure revealed through exploratory data analysis, micro-level coefficients are regressed at two macro-level variables. The notion of involving higher-level variables remains consistent in determining the micro behavior at the aggregate contextual level. The final model is then supported to handle the masking effect while incorporating the masking parameter by taking clues from randomized response techniques. These efforts allow securing estimates of within-group (divisions) relationships and embodying in the modeling process the cross-level (overall) relationships while considering the extent of masking in reported data.

Limitations

At this stage, it is important to notify a few limitations of the proposed scheme along with possible rectification as future research potential. In the discussion, it is important to document that the proposed model, in its nature, is a post-hoc remedial measure and handles the effects of SDB at a methodological level, not a design level. This study dealt with the situation where data has already been collected, and an initial analysis reveals the patterns pointing to the existence of SDB. The proposition allows investigators to work with the same data while considering the presence of SDB by incorporating a masking parameter in the model. Given the working mandate of the approach, however, recommended that the design of future surveys, in order to inform policy decisions accurately, should take masking and recall bias into account. Using a randomization device at survey design level would ensure the respondent's privacy and thus make it impossible to attribute a given response to a particular individual. A privacy protection mechanism is believed to enhance the likelihood of reporting a valid response. Secondly, the permissible range of the masking parameter, p is given as (0-1), but the p = 0.5 value is not advisable. At this value, the model will not be estimable as the equation (4) always results in a constant value of 0.5. The applicability of more flexible formations, such as two-stage designs or non-linear functional, can be persuaded to handle this complication. However, this domain is left as a future research venue. Lastly, in this research, *a priori* did not use for the degree of masking (due to the limited available literature); however, nowadays, most survey exercises gave the interviewers to assess the extent of cooperation of respondents over the Likert scale. It will be interesting to explore and derive parallels between the degree of cooperation and the tendency to mask the data.

Reference

Arokiasamy, A. (2002). Gender preferences, contraceptive use and fertility in India: Regional and development influences. *International Journal of Population Geography, 8*(1), 49-67. https://doi.org/10.1002/ijpg.236

Bollen, K. A., Glanville, J. L., & Stecklov, G. (2001). Economic status proxies in studies of fertility in developing countries. *Population Studies, 56*(1), 81-96.

Castro, T. M. (1995). Women's education and fertility: Results from 26 demographic and health surveys. *Studies in Family Planning, 26*(4), 187-202. https://doi.org/10.2307/2137845

Ding, J. O., & Hesketh, T. (2006). Family size, fertility preferences, and sex ratio in China in the era of the one child family policy: results from national family planning and reproductive health survey. *BMJ (Clinical research ed.), 333*(7564), 371–373. https://doi.org/10.1136/bmj.38775.672662.80

Fikree, F. F., Khan, A., Kadir, M. M., Sajan, F., & Rahbar, M. H. (2001). What influences contraceptive use among young women in urban squatter settlements of Karachi, Pakistan? *International Family Planning Perspectives, 27*(3), 130-136. https://doi.org/10.2307/2673834

Fotso, J. C., Cleland, J., Mberu, B., Mutua, M., & Elungata, P. (2013). Birth spacing and child mortality: an analysis of prospective data from the Nairobi urban health and demographic surveillance system. *Journal of biosocial science, 45*(6), 779–798. https://doi.org/10.1017/S0021932012000570

Groves, R. M., Floyd, J. Fowler, Jr., Mick, P., Couper, J. M., Lepkowski, E. S. & Tourangeau, R. (2009). *Survey Methodology.* John Wiley and Sons.

Gill, G. J. O.K. (1993). The data's lousy, but it's all we've got (being a critique of conventional methods. London: *Gatekeeper Series.* Report No. 38.

Hussain, Z., Cheema, S. A., & Hussain, I. (2019). An improved two-stage stratified randomized response model for estimating sensitive proportion. *Sociological Research and Methods, 51*(3), 1413–1441. https://doi.org/10.1177/0049124119875963

Jejeebhoy, S. J. & Sathar, Z. A. (2001). Women's autonomy in India and Pakistan: The influence of religion and region. *Population & Development Review, 27*(4), 687-712. https://doi.org/10.1111/j.1728-4457.2001.00687.x

Karmali, D. B., Pednekar, G., Valaulikar, R., & Kamat, U. S. (2017). A descriptive study of gender preference and its relation to willingness for sterilization in pregnant women in a tertiary hospital in Goa. *International journal of reproduction, contraception, obstetrics and gynecology, 5*(3). http://dx.doi.org/10.18203/2320-1770.ijrcog20160605

Kellogg, S. S., Rosenbaum, T. Y., Dweck, A., Millheiser, L., Pillai-Friedman, S., & Krychman, M. (2014). Sexual health and religion: a primer for the sexual health clinician. *Journal of Sexual Medicine, 11*(7), 1606-1619.

Kelly, C. A., Soler-Hampejsek E., Mensch B. S., & Hewett P. C. (2013). Social desirability bias in sexual behavior reporting: Evidence from an interview mode experiment in rural Malawi. *International Perspectives on the Sexual and Reproductive Health, 39*(1), 14-21. https://doi.org/10.1363/3901413

Krumpal, I. (2013). Determinants of social desirability bias in sensitive surveys: A literature review. *Quality & Quantity, 47*, 2025–2047. https://doi.org/10.1007/s11135-011-9640-9

Mason, K. O. (1997). How family position influence married women's autonomy and power in five Asian countries. Revision of a paper prepared for the *CICRED Seminar on Women and the Family*, Paris.

Meisters, J. Hoffmann, A. & Musch, J. (2020). Controlling social desirability bias: An experimental investigation of the extended crosswise model. *PLoS ONE, 15*(12). https://doi.org/10.1371/journal.pone.0243384

Mneimneh, Z. M. Tourangeau, R. Pennell, B. E., Heeringa, S. G., & Elliott, M. R. (2015). Cultural variations in the effect of interview privacy and the need for social conformity on reporting sensitive information. *Journal of Official Statistics, 31*(4), 673-697.

Rosenfeld, B., Imai, K. & Shapiro, J. N. (2015). An empirical validation study of popular survey methodologies for sensitive questions. *American Journal of Political Science, 60*(3), 783–802.

Saleem, S. & Bobak, M. (2005). Women's autonomy, education and contraception use in Pakistan: a national study. *Reproductive Health, 2*(8), https://doi.org/10.1186/1742-4755-2-8

Sana, M. & Weinreb, A. A. (2008). Insiders, outsiders, and the editing of inconsistent survey data. *Sociological Methods & Research, 36*(4), 515–541. https://doi.org/10.1177/0049124107313857

Schaeffer, N. C. (2000). Asking questions about threatening topics: A selective overview. In *The Science of Self-Report: Implications for Research and Practice*, edited by Arthur A. Stone, Jaylan S. Turkkan, Christine A. Bachrach, Jared B. Jobe, Howard S. Kurtzman, and Virginia S. Cain. Mahwah, NJ: Erlbaum, 105-121.

Schill, D. & Kirk, R. (2017). Angry, passionate, and divided: Undecided voters and the 2016 presidential election. *American Behavioral Scientist, 61*(9), 1056-1076.

Schröder, J. & Schmiedeberg, C. (2020). Effects of partner presence during the interview on survey responses: The example of questions concerning the division of household labor. *Sociological Methods & Research.* https://doi.org/10.1177/0049124120914938

Stecklov, G., Weinreb, A. A., & Sana M. (2015). Family planning for strangers: an experiment on the validity of reported contraceptive use. *PloS one, 10*(8).

Summers, L. H. (1992). Investing in *all* the people. *World Bank Policy Research Working Paper* no. 905, World Bank, Washington, DC.

Thapa, M. & Bajracharya, J. (2017). Gender preference in current pregnancy among primigravidae. *Nepal Journal of Obstetrics and Gynecology.* https://doi.org/10.3126/njog.v12i1.18979

Vesely, S. & Klöckner, C. A. (2020). Social desirability in environmental psychology research: Three meta-analyses. *Frontier in Psychol, 11*(1395). https://doi.org/10.3389/fpsyg.2020.01395

Warner, S.L. (1965). Randomized response: A survey technique for eliminating evasive answer bias. *Journal of the American Statistical Association, 60*(309), 63-69.

Wong, G. Y. & Mason, W. M. (1985). The hierarchical logistic regression model for multilevel analysis. *Journal of the American Statistical Association, 80*(391), 513-524. https://doi.org/10.2307/2288464

Worku, G. A., Tessema, A. G., & Zeleke, A. A. (2014). Trends and determinants of contraceptive use among young married women (Age 15-24) based on the 2000, 2005, and 2011 Ethiopia Demographic and Health Surveys: A multivariate decomposition analysis. *Demographic and Health Surveys.* Working paper #103. https://dhsprogram.com/pubs/pdf/WP103/WP103.pdf

World Family Planning Highlights (2017). Department of Economic and Social Affairs. United Nations. (ST/ESA/SER.A/414).

Zimbalist, A. (2021). Bystanders and response bias in face-to-face surveys in Africa. *International Journal of Social Research Methodology, 25*(3), 361-377. https://doi.org/10.1080/13645579.2021.1886397

Important Terminologies

- **Social Desirability:** The person(s) tendencies to stay socially acceptable.

- **Social Desirability Bias:** The avoidance of reporting socially undesirable responses while replacing them with desirable ones.

- **Stigmatized Behavior:** Discrimination against someone based on distinguished characteristics or attributes.

- **Data Masking:** The assembly of data with prime objective of hiding the identity of respondent(s) to resolve the issue of privacy protection.

- **Masking Effect:** Privacy protection, Loss of testing accuracy, Loss of generality, and Increased level of noise in the available information.

Chapter 8

The Use and Method of Psychodrama as a Research Method in Cultural and Intercultural Psychology

Ezgi Gül Ceyhan
Muğla Sıtkı Koçman University, Turkey

Chandan Maheshkar
Department of Management, CDGI, Indore, India
East Nimar Society for Education (ENSE), Indore, Indore

Abstract: Psychodrama is a technique of emotion transmission and reflection developed by Jacob Levy Moreno in the 1920s. It evaluates the unity of actions, emotions, and thoughts with consciousness in context and experience. Specifically, psychodrama is a method for uncovering and reflecting an awareness of cultural and psychological areas within a group and identifying problems. It is a convenient method for psychological analysis of self-reflection, creativity, and role-based psychological revitalization (enacting). Culturally specific psychological situations are critical to community-specific emotionally charged domains' unique dynamics and contexts. It is essential to focus on the technique of psychodrama and sociodrama as individual and intra-group evaluation and research methods of cultural and social emotions such as transfer-reflection (perception), personality, behavior, and emotion. Can the participant observation technique be used as a data-providing tool in psychodrama? This study, which emerged with the question, includes discussions on psychodrama as a methodology. In this chapter, the participant observation technique offers a way to qualitative research data. Therefore it is based on a literature review from qualitative research methodology.

Keywords: Psychodrama, Sociodrama, Cross/Cultural Psychology, Intercultural Psychology, Research Methodology, Participant Observation, Emotions, Self-reflection

***

Introduction

Psychodrama is a blend of mechanisms, including dramatics, role-play, observations, and group dynamics (Lim et al., 2021; Skar, 2020; Karp et al., 1998). Scientometric visualization made psychodrama a complex but essential method to execute research in the social sciences. There is a dire need for excellent transparency while conducting research through psychodrama. Researchers in psychodrama-based research need a rigorous understanding of human psychology, research methods, dramatics, and psychodrama processes to gain more complete results. However, psychodrama has lost its theatrical roots in many countries (Baim, 2018). If its roots in socio-psychological studies and academics as a pedagogical instrument are discovered, it will benefit from many insights and practical approaches.

Notably, this chapter introduces psychodrama and sociodrama in cultural and cross-cultural studies. It is essential to have comprehensive knowledge of the dynamics of a culture and to define individual emotions and behaviors. There are patterns of transference in emotional-behavioral communication within the culture. Common feelings and thoughts have a communicative and interpretive function between individuals. Does this show that individuals have these emotions and behaviors? Or should it be explored within existential psychology with a sociocultural perspective? How do people think, how do they feel, how do they exist in a culture, and how do they behave? Do they act with cultural/psychological reflexes embedded in our emotions and behaviors, or do they shape their emotions, thoughts, and behaviors in the "I-other" relationship by being aware of cultural phenomena?

The most prevalent literature is individualistic and collectivistic cultural studies. The prevalence of these studies is because the two cultural domains are comparable. The differentiated structures of the emotional and mind domains are explained in terms of these cultural differences. But in this case, it seems important for cultural studies to do more research on psychology. In the functioning of certain stereotypes and a sense of belonging, the existence of psychological fields shaped by the cultural field in the relations between the psychological, mental attachment and the "I" are revealed. Determining harmony and incompatibility of cultural diversity is considered necessary in psychology, sociology, and political science. Culture can be said to exist primarily where the individual-society domains are synthesized: Individuals define themselves around certain cultural norms in interpersonal situations such as school, marriage, groups, customs, and traditions. Emotional indicators, behaviors, and definitions are important.

The psychological processes of recognizing people's existence and becoming aware of it in a realm outside daily life are quite different from the proposition that they are sociocultural beings in experience in daily life. The concept of culture is not independent of the ongoing, habitual patterns of emotion-behavior and the existence of conditioned individualities that are their bearers. The subject carries a part of the other within the self as a characteristic of sociability. It is a feature of projection in which certain expressions of mood arise in the relation of creative subjects to one another. First of all, cultural-social projections should be considered as the map of this study. This study aims to activate multidisciplinary thinking tools. Human beings are carriers and creators of expressions. These expressions emerge in the relationship of the determinations between emotion and reason to each other.

This work is designed to be flexible because the dynamics of any cultural work are different. In the social sciences, research-based differences and variations of psychodrama and sociodrama application domains may emerge in multidisciplinary fields that study emotions and behaviors in particular contexts and perspectives. How can psychodrama use in emotional and cultural states as a methodology? Based on this question, it emerged from considering and testing the methodology of participant observation and observation technique as well as the psychodrama technique as a research methodology. The focus is on the difficulty of defining the existential states of the individual in a culturally independent manner. A discussion of psychodrama and sociodrama as a methodology in cultural and cross-cultural psychology is presented. This discussion includes the benefits, challenges, and limitations of its use. In the methodological design of this section, literature review, one of the qualitative research methods, was used. This chapter has emerged from the multidisciplinary focus on emotional aestheticization and collective selves.

Cultural and Cross-cultural Psychology

Experiential knowledge, which provides important information for psychodrama, is provided by culture. It is important to determine emotional and behavioral resilience to pressure and reflect internalized pressure on action (Thompson, 2005, p. 223, 232). Particular perspectives determine the way perceive the world. The impact of our beliefs can be functional in the context of the 'self-other' relationship in situations where socio-cultural domains differ (Feyerabend et al., as cited in Dach-Gruschow et al., 2011). Cultural values contain linkages of emotion-behaviors. The most important feature of shared cultural representations is the belief that other members share these representations. There is a relationship between collective representations and cultural values (Wan & Chiu, 2011, pp. 40, 42, 45, 47-48). The functionality of emotions in a socio-cultural context is that they can be easily integrated into specific cultural meanings and practices. Emotions and behaviors can be adapted, transformed and integrate. This situation expresses the essence of our socio-cultural relationships (Ekman et al., as cited in Mesquita & Lev, 2007, p. 734). Actions motivated by culturally determined psychosocial threats and risks have two consequences: avoidance of emotional behavior and triggering of emotional behavior (Mesquita & Lev, 2007, p.736-737).

Emotion-behavior models have become concrete in culture. Different cultural models and emotional perceptions effectively change reality (Mesquita & Lev, 2007, p. 737-738). Meaning is linked to emotional experience. Cultural perspectives are evaluated relationally and contextually. The cultural model includes action-behavior and adaptation (Mesquita & Lev, 2007, p. 742). Cultural models seem to influence the goals of emotional regulation. In cultures, individuals have different representations of desirable or normative feelings. It seems important to include ideal emotions derived from culturally sanctioned emotional states in the measurement (Mesquita & Lev, 2007, p. 752). Lewin's 'living space (Lebensraum)', culture's spatialized meaning stated that the psychological environment functions the performed or anticipated actions. Culture can offer opportunities for action that an individual is unaware of (Boesch, 1991, p. 31). Cultural theory holds unnoticed potentials because they don't have to be hidden even though they are not perceived. In addition to subjective action tendencies, there are objective situational pressures to consider. The coordination of the subjective and objective has to consider the external situation's conditions. The experientialism of aesthetic emotion and spiritual symbolism is not limited to religious domains. Cultural aestheticism is an expression of practices embodying certain spiritual fields: 'values embodying the ideal of order that inspires hope, trust, and consolation' (Boesch, 1991). Projective identification, a psycho-cultural mechanism, is located between the self and the other. Projective identification involves the psychology of defining the other. Thus, 'individuals in groups exhibit social roles determined depending on their demographic characteristics' (McRae & Short, 2005, p. 141). In the psycho-creative process, improvisation and spontaneity are essential in psycho-cultural reflections (Moreno, 1934).

Cross-cultural research has many difficulties. It is related to the fact that inferences are difficult to translate into data due to variations in the subjective psychological interpretation of individuals. Researchers need to understand the intricacies of each culture (Beins, 2011). The emotional states of one culture can be considered pathological in another culture (Rothbaum et al., as cited in Beins, 2011, p. 41). If a cross-cultural study includes differences in measurement results ("category and scoring"), it shows bias (Van de Rijver & Leung, 2011, p.18). It is necessary to briefly mention the differences between psychodrama and sociodrama and cultural data collection analyses—the two main approaches to data collection in psychology and social sciences:

interview and observation. Subjective experiences may require a preliminary interview. The interview method is more accessible than observation. Therefore, it is a method often used in psychology (Karasz, 2011, pp. 219-220). The experiential interaction between the self and the other in psychodrama makes the observation technique more important.

The psychological meanings of cultural differences may differ across subsets of a culture. In psychodrama, emotional flow can be observed within the experience. There are two types of observation in psychodrama and sociodrama. Introspection, which is a first, to be a participant in psychodrama and sociodrama, to share the feelings of a close relationship, trust and harmony with other participants, and second, external observation as Psychodramatist/director. Particularly, the second type of observation is effective in separating psychological modes, recognizing certain emotions, and working on identified emotions. As Karasz (2011, p. 225) states, 'the choice of what to observe: in modern societies, where individuals move fluidly between social settings and contexts, it is not always clear which social settings will shed light on relevant psychological phenomena'. Therefore, observations are most accessible in environments where the activity is relatively repetitive and structured (Karasz, 2011, pp. 226-229).

Cultural creativity takes reference from the culture it is in and is effective in bringing a synthesis to innovations with these references. The relationship between existential concerns and cultural adaptation works bidirectionally in emotional and behavioral performances. Performance may be encouraged or inhibited. The synthesis of these two fields is the cultural learning of the processes of integrating the self into the collective field. Culture coordinates behavior and emotions. The complementarity of culture on selves is possible with certain cultural modes and styles. The fields that become routinized through repetition regulate the reactivity of cultural conditioning. The established concepts of each culture include structured and often routinized responses to the environment (Leung et al., 2011, pp. 264-265, 267). Individual behavior and psychology can be affected by cultural meaning and experience (Delle-Fave et al., 2011, p. 29). The role of culture, the acquisition of behavioral rules and social roles are important in influencing the psychological development of individuals (Herskovitz as cited in Delle-Fave et al., 2011, p. 129). In collectivist societies, members change their behavior to adapt to group and context characteristics (Diaz-Guerrero et al., as cited in Delle-Fave et al., 2011, p. 132).

The other is the possibility of the revelation of the "I". The opposite is also possible, the role of others in forming the subjectiveness. I will take the *psycho-aesthetics* (my emphasis) concept as a means of adaptation. *Psycho-aesthetics* is the point where its subjectivity intersects with the universal. Salgado (2007, pp. 56-57, 62-63) states that meaning is formed as a result of the coordination of at least two people in its 'dialogic adaptation'. In the observation methodology, one may use cultural mediation tools within his/her cultural background. Self-reflexive emotions regulate our emotions interpersonally. Emotions such as 'sympathy, empathy, pride, shame, generosity and guilt, anger, moral goodness and evil include the other' (Traverthen as cited in Salgado 2007, pp. 64-66). Dominant modes can interrupt some emotional experiences. In a dialogical framework, it can be said that the potential and a different I-position remain dormant. The *psycho-aesthetics* state is formed when others call us to the material world. At the meta-psychological level, 'our existence in the world, the face of otherness in the self-other relationship appears in the sense of belonging and its search' (Matias & Valsiner, 2007, p. 400). The relationship between social networks and life satisfaction is important. With the differentiation of roles in socio-cultural contexts, areas of experience can change. Life satisfaction both affects and is affected by sociability. Cultural and psychological differences are parallel (Stadler et al. 2016, pp. 84-85, 93, 96).

Psychodrama and Sociodrama

Psychodrama is an action-based mechanism that purposefully presents a situation's intricacies and critical aspects towards a safe exploration of strong emotions and other behaviors. It can offer opportunities to clarify past events and envision the future with broader perspectives on individual and social phenomena. According to Chimera and Baim (2010), "psychodrama can, for example, help people to better understand themselves and their history, resolve loss and trauma, overcome fears, improve their intimate and social relationships, express and integrate blocked thoughts and emotions, practice new skills or prepare for the future." Because of its versatility and equal prominence for body, mind, and thoughts, it can be used in a wide array of social and business situations to help people in self-management, managing relationships, dealing with and regulating behaviors, and handling personality disorders or stress. Creativity and spontaneity are core principles of psychodrama that stimulate cognitive responses and help to gain new insights about life, other individuals, and the way to consider challenges.

Sociodrama is a psychodrama method that addresses or explores issues/conflicts in any social context. In this, a group explores various social roles and how a particular social situation/issue influences them. There is considerable scope for sociodrama in societal, organizational and educational settings. Beliefs, values, and ideas on how life should be are the core of almost every culture. These socio-cultural forces significantly influence people's everyday actions in almost every role and situation. According to Skar (2020), "a tendency in psychodrama research is the focus on proving effectiveness."

From an academic perspective, sociodrama is a strong pedagogy that uses the case study method with role-playing to demonstrate critical issues. Through principles of adult learning and effective communication skills, psychodrama enables learners to actively participate in the learning process and take past experiences as resources for teaching-learning and reflective practices (Jones, 2001, Maheshkar, 2019).

Psychodrama and Sociodrama in Cultural Psychology

Cultural meaning includes psychological pressures and resistance. An individual in a culture is a sociocultural data acceptor of moods and behaviors. This acceptance is psychologically inseparable from defining the self-concept within existential sociability. Culture does not impose its values on the individual as pure and homogeneous. In particular, the individual interprets these values with a subjective perspective and adapts them socio-culturally. A culture determines its hierarchies/authorities. A designated area creates its emotional state. Cultural authority systems can have a psychological effect on individuals, and with the compulsion to maintain this, the individual can act. The individual may create a sense of worthlessness in the sociocultural sense. And revealing it can be difficult. Psychodrama and sociodrama are helpful in such sociocultural moods. In addition, academic knowledge, experience, and studies gain importance in measuring emotions and thoughts in sociocultural studies. Dealing with the emotions and thought processes through participatory observation in the group means taking responsibility in the case of dominating the qualitative field and qualifying the observations and comments. Observation and interpretation need to get rid of subjectivity. Psychodrama aims to raise the person's awareness, especially in the process of emotion and thought. The concepts of play-role (acting), spontaneity, and creativity provide information about the interpretation of psycho-cultural projections.

In psychodrama, experience is important. Choosing the person suitable for the role is a valuable result of the preliminary interview. Sociometric measurements are essential in psychodrama and sociodrama. The most common psychodrama techniques are– 'Role changing (reversal)', which allows the protagonist to see the world from the other person's perspective, and encourage objective awareness of himself in interaction with others, and 'Mirroring' (Wilkins, 1999, pp. 34-36). The need for good qualitative research reports is increasing day by day in psychodrama (Reason & Rowan, as cited in Wilkins, 1999, p. 126). The emotional backgrounds are difficult to trace due to the reciprocal determinations between the self and the other. The mutually observable expressions in this relationship are explanatory in the field, such as clarity about the cultural past, inhibitions, and cultural feelings.

The integration of the individual with the action can affect the expressions of the meaning of the action (Blatner as cited in Wilkins, 1999, p. 130). As a result of internal tensions, the unconscious can be triggered. If reenactment is to cause any anxiety, it elicits psychological maneuvers. The presence of emotional concentrations between role and action gives an idea about the psychological infrastructure. Reenaction (role) as a means of change may reflect 'cultural taboos'. Intense fragile emotions, behaviors, and extreme psychologies require therapeutic intervention (Wilkins, 1999, pp. 131-132, 134-135). Integration of differences in the group is gained through experience. The importance of experience rests on the vague and unpredictable phenomenon of emotion-behavior and ideas outside of experience. One of the points that the psychodrama trainer and director should pay attention to is that psychodrama and sociodrama cannot work in all psychological and emotional states.

Examining thoughts, feelings, and behavior as a whole in action is important in terms of the internal representation of the self- and inter-subjective modes of representation. In particular, the 'spontaneity, creativity and role, animation' feature of psychodrama and sociodrama can be explanatory in emotional states such as 'anxiety-stress-ocd' of cultural meaning (Schacht, 2009, p. 48, 65, 165). Psychodrama and sociodrama can be used as effective methods for interacting with different cultures and any culture with subcultures. It is influenced by the differences between cultural groups and the core value commonalities. According to other standard methodologies, in analyzing a particular phenomenon through action, desired answers or carelessly given answers are not found in psychodrama and sociodrama. It is important to observe emotions and emotional management methods. Therefore, the differences between the subjects in the experience and the determination of their ideas in action are pretty convenient in psychodrama/sociodrama (Butcher et al., 1998, pp. 64-65).

Differences within a nation can coexist between collectivist and individualistic values. It is very important to position these values between group selection and group formation culturally and to observe and interpret the interaction of differences. It is influential in determining cultural meaning and action. In this respect, role theory states the relationship between stereotyped behavior and emotions and roles (Moreno as cited in Fox, 1987, p. 20, 61). Role theory emphasizes the importance of action and social categories in daily activities. The self is linked to the role that embodies individual and collective syntheses. 'The symbolic representation of this functioning form is shaped by the cultural patterns found in it and is called the perceived role between the individual and the other' (Fox, 1987, p. 62). In psychodrama and sociodrama, internalized roles and the self-connection of roles are experienced culturally and socially in the presence of the other. The constant interaction of ego and role shows a 'cognitive structure' and activates the use of 'stereotyped responses' (Fox, 1987, p. 63).

With the concept of spontaneity, creativity emerges in 'disharmony and tension' (Schacht, 2008). Strategies to cope with the variable factors and uncertainties that the individual is in make psychological adaptations possible. Calculating psychological costs and performing psychological maneuvers determine the direction in which adaptation and integration will take place. Role formation in psychodrama and sociodrama includes the whole identity stage, the collective-social dimension. The collective and social dimension expresses the realization of the behavior with the roles in the action. In particular, individuals can convey and reflect on the areas they belong to and attach emotional meaning to culture-specific role models. The presence of the 'other' can make the participant stand in the background, behave differently, or convey emotionally different feelings. The visibility of role and emotional structures is determined within the framework of the relations between the inner and outer worlds. The tension and harmony between the ideal and the typical can be reflected on the stage and categorized (Stimmer, 2008, p. 120). The psychodrama and sociodrama trainer/director has the flexibility to shape the group with specific interventions and include specific participants to get the desired data. However, this situation is related to the group or individual situation in the process. In particular, how is ego functioning conveyed in social competence? The question is essential (Heln, 2008, p. 234).

In psychodrama, social and cultural analysts can use auxiliary egos to test and influence them as extensions of themselves. What is important here is to pay attention to the 'developmental blocks' that prevent the emergence of emotional and behavioral expression and to observe where the 'original flow of freedom is blocked' (Karp, 1994, Pp. 32, 35). The power behind the developmental process emphasizes the existential field (Verhofstadt-Deneve, 2007). The existential dialectic perspective explains moods (Mijuskovic & Yalom, as cited in Verhofstadt-Deneve, 2007, p. 118). 'The intense activation of I-Me reflection inevitably in psychodrama emphasizes this existential anxiety, loneliness and guilt' (Verhofstadt-Deneve, 2007, pp. 119-122).

E.g., the person can use emotional transformation mechanisms to avoid showing their weaknesses. These mechanisms can be designed within the framework of cultural patterns in the presence of "others". Such situations may reveal the person's emotion-behavior synthesis, making it visible under other forms, deflecting it, or reflecting it in other forms. The individual behaviors observed, especially in psychodrama groups, are related to the 'being me' process. Being self depends on the absence of a certain closeness in the group and the development of a certain closeness within the framework of a sense of trust over time. Therefore, the group is 'trainable and flexible'. Spontaneity education 'being self' is an effective mechanism for individuals exposed to unexpressed thoughts and feelings, such as sadness and anxiety, and social-cultural individually restrictive situations. The concepts of spontaneity and creativity provide effective analysis, especially in situations where the individual represses, resists and unconsciously encodes them. Creativity shows how tensions between ego and role (individual, social and cultural) are transformed. However, although the concepts of spontaneity and creativity feed each other, they differ from the concept of 'impulsive and automatic' spontaneity (Moreno as cited in Karp: 1994, p. 38).

The social and cultural atom are intertwined, and the role in social-culture is dynamic (Daniel, 2007, p. 80). Spontaneity is the authentic self within the moment. An appropriate response is important. The most diagnostic form of psychodrama is 'for a person to react in three possible ways, not responding, giving a new response to an old situation, and finally the possibilities of reacting to a new or adequate situation' (Karp, 1994, p. 39). When it is observed, information about the character's emotional state is obtained. The observation of the character in the experience and the moment of action are determined first by whether the person can take the role. In the presence of emotions and behaviors that need to be satisfied, the presentation of spontaneity is important. The ability to respond to a particular situation meets the hunger for action. Completing unexpressed emotions with unfinished emotions is vital, which is a psychological burden on the person. The actor/thinker character replaces 'known solutions with newly recognized behavioral possibilities'. It offers the opportunity to eliminate culturally preserved and determined roles and old attitudes. Changing feelings and thoughts is possible by trying new roles (Karp, 1994, pp. 42-43).

Social and cultural roles are within the field of Sociodrama. Psychodrama is individual-focused, and sociodrama is group-focused (as cited in Moreno, Von-Ameln & Kramer, 2020, p. 95). Sociodrama is effective in analysis for the analysis and change of social reality. There are various socio-dramatic methods. These methods are sensitive to socio-cultural contexts. Sociodrama deals with collective themes due to social effects, ethnic conflicts, and group changes in cultural and social perceptions, and the collective aspect is always important (Von-Ameln & Kramer, 2020, p. 96). Compared to psychodrama, the use of sociodrama, pattern and model scenarios is more common such as when a group plays a parliamentary session. However, by designing the group in the light of social and cultural contexts, the scenario process can be determined according to the study. In group and collective-oriented studies, intense topics should not be handled immediately. If an intense subject is covered in the early stages, there is a superficial concern with the methodology, and there are often disruptions in participation (Von-Ameln & Kramer, 2020, p. 97).

> Who took on which role and why? To what extent does each individual's role in the improvised play coincide with their role in the reality of everyday life? Which role behavior is useful and which is not? What roles were represented? Which roles were left vacant? How was the overall interaction of the roles?
>
> ~ Von-Ameln & Kramer (2020, p. 99).

The methodological design includes several possibilities. Potential processes within the group involve difficulties. Sociometric measurements of group members are important in this case. Two important steps are topic sampling and appropriate scenario selection (Von-Ameln & Kramer, 2020, pp. 101-109). Intercultural awareness, the identification of cultural perceptions and their interactions—cultural education, immigrants, and racism—can be treated in psychodrama and sociodrama. It has been seen to provide positive benefits in situations such as empathy and awareness. The group should be treated as the bearers of socio-cultural roles. The psychodramatic approach is unsuitable in situations such as 'aggression, violence, sexuality, emotional traumas'. In particular, 'shameful issues are taboo in a group setting'. Social and cultural norms can hinder the process of revealing participant weaknesses and failures of the participants (Von-Ameln & Kramer, 2020, pp. 110-111, 243-247).

Kellermann (2007, pp. 95-96), who deals with 'Diversity Sociodrama and Conflict Transformation', explains the diversity of sociodrama as dealing with how people feel ('stereotypes, prejudice, racism, xenophobia, intolerance'). Common examples include: immigrants, African-Americans, homosexuals, Japanese, Germans, Jews, Arabs, the poor, women, the elderly, the disabled, the unattractive, the obese, and many others. In heterogeneous populations, prejudices are based on cultural differences such as age, gender and marriage. Status, wealth, occupation, nationality, country of origin, socioeconomic status, sexual orientation, culture, religion, political affiliation and physical (height, weight, disability) and many other variables. Awareness of subjective judgments is important in sociodrama; negative internalized perceptions, projections, displacements, or representations and transfers of figures from the past onto a present person. The theme of sociodrama is based on the diversity of people. It is one reason why terms such as culture, race, nationality, and sex are used. These areas provide legitimacy to people's statements. Many types of differences, such as any change in cultures (language, traditions), ethnic group, socioeconomic status, religious beliefs, and socio-cultural positions create problems in communication. With deep nationalism and ethnocentric feelings, cultural reactions, or the traditionalization of the reactions, emerge. Mood states (such as loyalty, pride, and belonging) may differ within the group. It is helpful to have a deep knowledge of other cultures in the group. It should be taken into account that belief and meaning are inherent in culture (Kellermann, 2007, pp. 97-98, 100-101, 105, 112). According to Moreno (as cited in Kellermann, 2007, p. 113), too much diversity creates social tension. It is necessary to have certain definitions for research and the problem (Schützenberger, 2007, p. 158, 165). Awareness of emotional complexes (Jung, as cited in Gasseau & Scategni, 2007, p. 262) becomes visible in psychodrama. For emotional states that are difficult to express, the role (reversal) technique shows the part of the person's self that contains undesirable or rejected emotions, images and thoughts (Gasseau & Scategni, 2007, pp. 263-264, 271).

Discussion

Humans are sociocultural beings who normalize specific patterns of emotion and behaviors and are conditioned within this framework. In particular, the system labelled culture is not free from subjectivity and interpretation. Thus, general laws cannot be mentioned. Emotional meaning includes the concept of organized coordination. Sociocultural meaning includes shortcuts, modes and styles. However, the definition of emotional reality methodologically is experienced and revealed in the process. Therefore, as sociocultural beings, people are often unaware of the awareness of the emotional field, which is the latent force, even though people experience daily life as 'existence and escape'. This situation provides its reality with awareness in psychodrama and sociodrama.

One who works on emotions may find this field very productive. As a result of the application of participant observation technique in psychodrama, the question of how the relationship between sociocultural data and individual's self-presentation can be assessed, integrating the self-presentation in the sociocultural field between the self and the other provides important data. The individual performs his/her self-presentation aesthetically in a way that takes others as a reference. The concept of aesthetics here refers to the presentation of meaning and expressive arguments through psychological costs and maneuvers within the sociocultural space of one. Therefore, the field of psychodrama can facilitate understanding of this aesthetic structure with sociocultural dynamics in experience, spontaneity and role. Cultural studies and intercultural studies have their dynamics. Of course, this area will expand when group dynamics change. There are two important stages in psychodrama and sociodrama. First, it is getting to know the participants before the process, and second, in the process.

Conclusion

Psychodrama as a research method potentially gives a different understanding of performative actions and how things work performatively and effectively. The psychodramatic methodology is essentially an experimental setting that involves cognitive elements to a certain level to engage participants in a specific role and adequately stimulates characters' probable dimensions in every situation under consideration. Subjects may play various roles in various situations, depending on the type of psychodrama research. Psychodrama complements sociometry in a deeper exploration of interpersonal relations. The problem in any research is to get the subject's cooperation in providing the researcher with study material. Various methods can be used to activate the subject to various degrees. In the questionnaire method, the subject is asked to cooperate only to give some written statements or select one among a group submitted to him by the investigator, dealing with specific facts, events, attitudes, or relationships with other people. In the interview method, the subject gives a verbal report along the same lines. Through psychodrama, a different set of tests (behavior, projection, reaction) may elicit from the subject a more active response to a situation outlined by the researcher towards generating descriptions of how psychodrama actions generate experiences. It has been realized that psychodrama can be further developed as a research method. With various utilities, it is adaptable depending upon individuals' needs and situations, whether it is about business, society, academics, culture, and/or religion (Pramann, 2016).

References

Baim, C. (2018). Theatre, therapy and personal narrative. Doctoral Thesis. University of Exeter. Retrieved on May 16, 2022 from http://hdl.handle.net/10871/33997

Beins B. C. (2011). Methodological and conceptual Issues in Cross-cultural Research. In Keith K. D. (ed.), *Cross-cultural psychology: contemporaray themes and perspectives* (pp. 37-56). Wiley- Blackwelly.

Boesch E. E. (1991). *Symbolic action theory and cultural psychology.* Springer.

Butcher J. N., Nezami E., & Exner J. (1998). Psychological assassment of people in diverse cultures. In Kazarian S. S., & Evans D. R. (Eds.), *Cultural clinical Psychology: Theory, Research and Practice* (pp. 61-106). Oxford University Press.

Chimera, C. & Baim, C. (2010). Introduction of Psychodrama. Workshop for IASA Conference, Cambridge, 29th August 2010. Retrieved on April 10, 2022 from https://www.iasa-dmm.org/images/uploads/Chip%20Chimera%20and%20 Clark%20Baim%20Workshop% 20on%20Psychodrama.pdf

Dach-Gruschow, K., Au, E. W. M., & Liao, H.-Y. (2011). Culture as lay personal beliefs. In A. K.-y. Leung, C.-y. Chiu, & Y.-y. Hong (Eds.), *Cultural processes: A social psychological perspective.* (pp. 25–39). Cambridge University Press.

Daniel S. (2007). Psychodrama, Role Theory and cultural atom: New developments in role theory. In Baim C., Burmeister J.& Maciel M. (Eds.). *Psychodrama: advances in theory and practice.* (pp. 67-83). Routledge.

Delle-Fave A., Massimini F.& Bassi M. (2011). *Psychological selection and optimal experience across cultures: Social empowerment through personal growth.* Springer.

Fox J. (Ed.) (1987). *The essential Moreno: Writings on Psychodrama Group method and Spontaneity by J. L. Moreno.* Springer

Gasseau M.,& Scategni W. (2007). Jungian Psychodrama: From Theoretical to Creative Roots. In Baim C., Burmeister J.& Maciel M. (Eds.). *Psychodrama: advances in theory and practice.* (pp. 261-271). Routledge.

Heln J. (2008). Ich-Fonktion und soziales atom. In Gunkel S. (Hrsg.) *Psychodrama und Soziometrie. Erlebnisorientierte Aktionsmethoden in Psychotherapie und Pädagogik.* (s.231-243). Vs Verlag.

Jones C. (2001). Sociodrama: a teaching method for expanding the understanding of clinical issues. *Journal of palliative medicine, 4*(3), 386–390. https://doi.org/10.1089/109662101753124039

Karasz A. (2011). Qualitative and mixed methods research in cross-cultural psychology. In Van de Rijver F. J. R., Chasiotis A.& Breugelmans S. M. (Eds.) *Fundemental Questions in cross-cultural Psychology.* (pp. 214-235). Cambridge University Press.

Karp M. (1994). The River of freedom, Holmes P., Karp M.& Watson M. (Eds.) *Psychodrama since Moreno: Innovations in theory and practice.* (pp. 27-45). Routledge.

Karp, M., Holmes, P., & Tauvon, K. B. (1998). *The Handbook of Psychodrama.* London: Psychology Press.

Kellermann P. F. (2007). *Sociodrama and Collective Trauma.* Jessica Kingsley Publishing.

Leung A. K. Y., Chen J. & Chiu C. (2011). Multicultural experience fosters creative conceptual expansion. In Leung A. K. Y., Chiu C.& Hong Y. Y. (Eds.). *Cultural processes: a social psychological perspective.* (pp. 263-286). Cambridge Universiy Press.

Lim, M., Carollo, A., Chen, S., & Esposito, G. (2021). Surveying 80 Years of Psychodrama Research: A Scientometric Review. *Frontiers in psychiatry, 12,* 780542. https://doi.org/10.3389/fpsyt.2021.780542

Maheshkar, C. (2019). A study of evaluation of competency mapping scales in management education. *Doctoral Thesis.* University of Indore, India.

Matias L. & Valsiner J. (2007). General Conclusions, Mathias L. & Valsiner J. (Eds.) *Otherness in question: Laybyrinths of the self.* (pp. 393-407). Information Age.

McRae M. B. & Short E. L. (2005). Racial-Cultural Training for Group counselling and psychotherapy. In Carter R. T. (Ed.), *Handbook of racial-cultural Psychology and counseling: Training and Practice* (pp. 135-148) John Wiley & Sons.

Mesquita B.& Lev J. (2007). The cultural psychology of emotion. In Kıtıyama S., & Cohen D. (eds.), *Handbook of cultural Psychology* (pp.734-760). The Guilford Press.

Moreno J. L. (1934). *Who shall survive?: A new approach to the problem of human interrelations.* Nervous and Mental Disease Publishing.

Pramann R. (2016). Benefits, limitations, and potential harm in psychodrama (training). CCCU Training in Psychodrama, Sociometry, and Group Psychotherapy.

Salgado J. (2007). The feading of a diological self: Affectivity agency, and otherness. In Mathias L. & Valsiner J. (Eds.), *Otherness in question: Laybyrinths of the self* (pp. 53-73). Information Age Publishing.

Schacht M. (2008). Zwischen ordnung und chaos. Neue aspekte zur theoretischen und pratiktischen fundierung der konception von spontaneitat und kreativitat. Gunkel S. (Hrsg.) *Psychodrama und Soziometrie. Erlebnisorientierte Aktionsmethoden in Psychotherapie und Pädagogik* (s. 51-87). Vs Verlag.

Schacht M. (2009). *Das ziel ist im weg: Störungsverständnis und Therapieprozess im Psychodrama.* Springer.

Schützenberger A. A. (2007). Transgenerational Analysis and Psychodrama: Applying and Extending Moreno's Concepts of the Co-unconscious and the Social Atom to Transgenerational Links. In Baim C., Burmeister J., & Maciel M. (Eds.), *Psychodrama: advances in theory and practice* (pp. 155-175). Routledge.

Skar, S. (2020). A turn to arts-based research methodology in psychodrama research. *Z Psychodrama Soziom,* 19, 211–226. https://doi.org/10.1007/s116 20-020-00572-y

Stadler C., Pötscher-Gareiß, M., Wieser M., Otto, C., & Marlok, Z. (2016). Interkulturelle Netzwerkforschung. Kulturvergleichende Analyse sozialer Netzwerkcharakteristika und Lebenszufriedenheit. Stadler C., Wieser M., & Kirk K. (Eds.), *Psychodrama. Empirical Research and Science 2* (pp. 83-100). Springer. https://doi.org/10.1007/978-3-658-13015-2_8

Stimmer F. (2008). Spregelbilder: typen und, soziokulturelle atome narzisstischen verhaltens. Gunkel S. (Hrsg.) *Psychodrama und Soziometrie. Erlebnisorientierte Aktionsmethoden in Psychotherapie und Pädagogik.* (s. 113-131) Vs Verlag.

Thompson C. E. (2005). Psychological Theory and culture Practice implications. In Carter R. T. (Ed.), *Handbook of racial-cultural Psychology and counseling: Training and Practice* (pp. 221-235). John Wiley & Sons.

Toukmanian S. G. & Brouwers M. G. (1998). Cultural aspects of self disclosure and psychotherapy. In Kazarian S. S. & Evans D. R. (Eds.), *Cultural clinical Psychology: Theory, Research and Practice* (pp. 106-127). Oxford University Press.

Van de Rijver F. J. R., & Leung K. (2011). Equivalence and bias: a review of concepts, models and analytic procedures. In Matsumoto D., Van de Rijver F. J. R. (Eds.), *Cross-cultural methods in psychology* (pp. 17-46). Cambridge University Press.

Verhofstadt-Deneve L. (2007). Existential-dialec psychodrama: The Theory behind practice. In Baim C., Burmeister J., & Maciel M. (Eds.). *Psychodrama: advances in theory and practice* (pp. 111-127). Routledge.

Von-Ameln S., & Kramer J (2020). *Fundamentals of psychodrama.* Springer.

Wan C., & Chiu C. (2011). Culture as intersubjective representations of values. In Leung A. K. Y., Chiu C.& Hong Y. Y. (Eds.), *Cultural processes: a social psychological perspective* (pp.40-65). Cambridge University Press.

Wilkins P. (1999). *Psychodrama*. Sage.

Chapter 9

Cross-cultural Collectivistic and Individualistic Comparison between Vietnamese and Western Cultures

Tuan, V. V.

Hanoi Law University, Vietnam

Anh, H. B.

Hanoi Law University, Vietnam

Abstract: Theoretical constructs relating to Vietnamese and Western cultures are discussed at length first before specific individualistic and collectivistic constructs go into detail. The research design combines cross-sectional studies and a descriptive quantitative approach using the convenient sampling method. Although the impact of the global socio-economy has far-reaching consequences on all walks of life, the cultural identity and beliefs imprint each culture, which is not faded or harmonized completely by cultural exchanges taking place every day. Moreover, cross-cultural communication enriches and enhances cultural and spiritual understanding. In order to have diverse cultural backgrounds, long-lost or endangered cultural entities have to be preserved and developed before becoming disappeared. Therefore, knowing well the nature of cultural differences between Vietnamese and Western cultures avoids cultural shocks, embarrassment or being in a dilemma in communication. In reality, such a cultural understanding of Western cultures, significantly a rich, traditional Vietnamese culture would contribute greatly to the overall picture of the global cultural interferences.

Keywords: Cross-cultural Communication, Vertical and Horizontal Individualism and Collectivism, Cultural Identity, Cultural Exchange, Cultural and Spiritual Understanding

***

Introduction

The terms *individualism* and *collectivism* are commonly used by or referred to Western and Eastern people, which also yield various meanings. Many scholars (Triandis, 1995, 2002; Sinha, 2014; Gad et al., 2015; Boone et al., 2007; Brewer & Venaik, 2011) have made numerous attempts to highlight the meanings of individualism and collectivism regarding Westerners and Easterners. In doing so, they have discovered considerable complexity in what should be included in these cultures. They have even tried to know the causes and consequences of westerners and easterners in terms of individualistic and collectivistic behaviors. The concepts of individualism and collectivism are defined as general and multi-dimensional, encompassing many differences in attention, motivation definitions, emotional connections to in-groups, and belief system and behavioral patterns (Shavitt et al., 2011). Individualism is supposed to promote autonomy, whereas collectivism is thought to advocate interdependence. Furthermore, the constructs of individualism and collectivism have been mentioned frequently in different research fields, which indicate that essential studies on the disparity of individualism and collectivism constructs should be conducted intensively. They have prevalently emphasized the discourse on the psychological impacts of western and eastern cultures for ages. Hence, culture avails the overall framework wherein people learn to adapt their thoughts, behaviors, and emotions to acquaint themselves with their environment.

Communication refers to the exchange of ideas, information and feelings between two or more people. It involves two parties, one speaker or sender who delivers a message and a person to whom it is communicated (the receiver). Communication is examined from many disciplinary perspectives, it is often regarded as a discipline in its own right, and it is also a focus of sociolinguistics, psycholinguistics, and information theory (Schmidt & Richards, 2011). Communication is considered an interaction within a social context. It denotes the interlocutors exchanging signals in the forms of verbal or graphic, gestural or visual. In essence, communication manipulates codes yielded by body language or sounds made with the voice. Whichever way communication occurs, it involves a process in which someone desires to pass a meaning intent to the interlocutor (receiver) (Foluke, 2018). The complete circle of communication happens when the receiver returns feedback to the signal that the sender initiates in the information exchange. It mentions the process of exchanging ideas and interaction between at least two persons, commonly understood as a two-way process. This process implicates a mutual understanding of participants to encode and decode message exchanges as a means of human connectedness. Communication is something human beings employ in different means and everyday walk of life thanks to a basic level of its method, i.e. a language, which denotes verbal and non-verbal communication as long as passing meaning messages. Therefore, there would be chaos without communication, and human existence and civilization would not be as developed as today (Buarqoub, 2019). In general, communication generally involves sending and receiving ideas or information between persons. In other words, communication is how interlocutors employ shared verbal or non-verbal codes, systems and media to exchange ideas or thoughts in a specific cultural context.

Cross-cultural communication mentions an exchange of mutual information between one person and another or a group of people from different cultural backgrounds. Actually, more problems are reported in cross-cultural communication than in communication between persons who share the same cultural background. During the intercommunication, each person comprehends the other speakers' messages according to his or her cultural conventions and expectations. The more significantly different the cultural conventions of the speakers likely are, the more easily misinterpretations and misunderstandings might occur, which even leads to a complete breakdown of communication. Research into real-life situations, such as business transactions, international education exchanges, and workplaces at multinational companies, has been indicated. In practice, cross-cultural communication occurs in a situation where people from different cultures communicate with one another by initiating a transactional, symbolic process concerning the attribution of meaning between the sender and the receiver in one-way and two-way communication styles. Hurn and Tomalin (2013) define that cross-cultural communication deals with the way people from different cultures interact with each other, either face-to-face or at a distance. Thus, communication might take place in spoken or written language, body language, and the language of etiquette and protocol.

Intercultural communication includes an interdisciplinary field of research that investigates how people interact and comprehend each other across group boundaries or discourse systems of various sorts, including national, geographical, linguistic, ethnic, occupation, class or gender-related boundaries and how such boundaries influence language use. This may entail the study of corporate culture, a professional group, a gender discourse system, or a generational discourse system (Schmidt & Richards, 2011). Intercultural communication is possibly considered a particular form of human communication from different cultural backgrounds. This interaction occurs when two or more persons communicate simultaneously to promote mutual understanding between speakers, usually for the sake of maintaining relationships. As a profound impact of the global integration, communicators from different cultures attempt to interact with each other to exchange ideas, and information, which may encounter cultural barriers. People participating in intercultural interactions confront many challenges because of cultural diversities. Intercultural communication, therefore, has played an essential part in studying how it influences the quality of each communication in a multicultural environment. In reality, cultural communication studies merely emphasize differences in language structure and cultural principles for monitoring communicative exchanges and extra-linguistic or so-called non-verbal patterns of communication. By overviewing another angle, intercultural communication implicates a situation where people of diverse cultural identities interact with each other. Otherwise, it may refer to a study subject that cares about interactions among individuals of different cultural ethnic groups and comparative studies of communication patterns across cultures (Zhu, 2011, p. 422). Overall, intercultural communication is generally a form of communicative exchange between interlocutors who interact in different cultural diversities such as nationalities, regional boundaries, languages, and cultures for information-sharing and mutual understanding.

Although cross-cultural and intercultural communications are frequently used interchangeably, they are different in disciplines. Many researchers have recently pointed to the tendency to distinguish cross-cultural and intercultural communication (e.g., Kiesling, 2015; Jackson, 2019; Kecskes, 2017). To differentiate between two terms, i.e., "cross-cultural" and "intercultural", the combining forms, namely "cross" and "inter", disclose the apparent disparity. While "inter" implies being between, "cross" denotes a bridging from one side to the other. In other words, the difference would be understood that "intercultural" refers to somewhere in the middle, whereas "cross-cultural" signifies the span of two nodes. Hence, the distinction would suggest that cross-cultural communication appears when two cultures are compared; in contrast, intercultural communication refers to the situation when two cultures come in contact (Gudykunst, 2003, p. 175; Kiesling, 2015, p. 620). Intercultural communication recognizes the coexistence of multi-cultures in a single community, concentrating on the productive encounters between two cultures.

In contrast, the significant aspect of cross-cultural communication acknowledges the comparison between two (or more) cultures. This reflection indicates the difference between one culture within one country or one country with another, remarkably Western and Eastern cultures. Kecskes (2017) claims that intercultural and cross-cultural pragmatics are frequently used, but they refer to two different disciplines. Cross-cultural pragmatics compares and contrasts different cultural aspects of language use, such as speech acts, language behavior, or behavior patterns, whereas intercultural pragmatics concentrates on interlocutors' interaction from cultural diversity using different languages. In addition, cross-cultural pragmatics examines each language and culture separately, investigating the different and similar aspects between many entities, while intercultural pragmatics is concerned with the communicative process. It studies the speech production and comprehension of communicators who possess cultural diversities and languages, using a common language such as English, French or Chinese to exchange information. Overall, cross-cultural communication compares different cultures to investigate and lead to individual change, but not collective transformations. Concerning cross-cultural societies, one culture is supposed to be the dominant culture compared with other cultures. Meanwhile, intercultural communication recognizes a deep understanding and respect for all cultures. Among these communities, intercultural communication strengthens the mutual cultural exchange and the deep relationships among interlocutors.

When examining the differences and similarities between individualistic and collectivistic cultures, Rhee et al. (2020) suggest the contrastive analysis between two taxonomies that individualistic cultures strengthen the demands of the individual over the needs of the group as a whole. In this aspect, people are considered independent and autonomous. Besides, each individual's attitudes and progress are commonly influenced by social behavior. By contrast, collectivist cultures focus on the needs and goals of the group as a whole over the demands and desires of each individual. As a result, the relationship with other group members and the interconnectedness between people are valued as central determinants in each person's identity. Generally speaking, collectivistic cultures stress the community, while individualism concentrates on each person's sake and interests (Darwish & Huber, 2003; McConachy & Spencer-Oatey, 2021). Fatehi et al. (2020) differentiate these terms by proposing that individual cultures stress promoting self-interest, personal autonomy, or privacy of the individual.

Individual cultures concentrate on self-realization, individual initiative, independence, individual decision-making, and an understanding of personal identity as the individual's total attributes. However, they do not concern with the needs and interests of others. On the other hand, collective cultures highlight the loyal contribution to the group, emotional sacrifice to groups or organizations, and do not emphasize individual privacy. In these cultures, the harmony of group decisions is received higher respect than individual decisions. Besides, collectivistic societies seem to be interdependent and have an awareness of personal identity as understanding one's stance with the group and caring about the demands and concerns of others. It is rational to reckon that people with an individualistic cultural background are likely to have more personal self-recognition and fewer collective self-cognitions than people from a collective cultural background (Xia et al., 2019; Čeněk, 2020; Jayawickreme, 2013). In its essence, within cross-cultural and intercultural pragmatics, cultures might be seen as a proxy for one national boundary in the sense that "that linguistic patterns of a particular language prevalent within an individual nation are seen ipso facto as linked to national culture" (McConachy & Spencer-Oatey, 2021, p. 734).

Parting Line of Western and Eastern Cultures

It is hard to suggest one most widely accepted definition of what culture is. There has been a great concern about arriving at a sole and most generalized cultural definition for all walks of life. Culture cannot be defined as one unique definition because "each cultural world operates according to its internal dynamics, principles, and laws – written and unwritten. Even time and space are unique to each culture. There are, however, some common threads that run through all cultures" (Hall & Hall, 1990, p. 3). Similarly, Trompenaars and Hampden-Turner (2012) state that "a shared system of meanings. It dictates what we pay attention to, how we act and what we value" (p. 13). Later, Trompenaars and Woolliams (2020) propose that "culture is man-made, confirmed by others, conventionalized ... It provides people with a meaningful context in which to meet, to think about themselves and face the other world" (p. 3). Oxford Advanced Learner's Dictionary[1] supplies many definitions. The meaning concerning the way of life defines that culture refers to the customs and beliefs, art, way of life and social organization of a particular country or group. UNESCO (2001) defines "culture as the set of distinctive spiritual, material, intellectual and emotional features of society or a social group, that encompasses, not only art and literature, but lifestyles, ways of living together, value systems, traditions and beliefs" (p. 9). Western culture is "a term used to refer to a heritage of social norms, ethical values, traditional customs, belief systems, political systems, and specific artefacts and technologies that have some origin or association with Europe" (Sogari et al., 2019, p. 181). Culture can be viewed as the overall lifestyles of particular groups of people. It represents how a group of people behaves, interacts, and organizes their lives, how their customs, language, values and feelings compromise, and how material artefacts and shared systems of attitudes communicate. In essence, culture is learned, inherited, and taught from one generation to another according to the flow of time. It is one of the critical factors affecting how people experience their lives, reflecting national pride and identity. The diverse definitions of culture have emerged in different aspects of life. Cultural differences have a bearing on many aspects of

---

[1] Oxford Advanced Learner's Dictionary 10th edition © Oxford University Press, 2020

geographical identifications. This chapter deals with comparing a large body of Western cultures with a typical, rich, traditional Vietnamese as one of the denotations reflecting cultural diversity.

Western culture, possibly referred to as Western civilization, Western lifestyle, or European civilization is a term widely used to denote a heritage of social norms, ethical values, traditional customs, religious beliefs, political systems, and specific artifacts and technologies that result from European or American originality. Western culture is genealogized as a "European civilization that extends from *Plato to NATO*" (Birken, 1999, p. 17). This implicit ideology certifies that Western culture is likened to "the key human characteristic of rationality as the hallmark of occidental culture beginning with Greece" (Birken, 1999, p. 1). On the same side, Xu et al. (2018) claim that one of the primary sources of Western cultures is rooted in the Greek and Roman civilizations. They further claim that "Greece was the cradle of Western civilization" (p. 1). Pokhrel (2011) reflects the difference between Western culture and non-Western societies using Eurocentrism, which denotes the contrastive meaning. The author states that Eurocentrism is a cultural phenomenon that stems from the histories and cultures of non-Western societies according to a Western perspective. In this regard, Western Europe functions as a universal signifier in that it is assumed that European cultural values are supposed to be superior to those of non-European societies (Amin, 2010; Dussel, 1998; Lander, 2000; Quijano, 2000). In terms of its nature, Eurocentrism is regarded as an anti-universalist phenomenon and encourages imitating a "Western model based on 'Western values' - individuality, human rights, equality, democracy, free markets, secularism, and social justice" (Pokhrel, 2011, p. 321). The anti-universalist phenomenon is treated as a cure to many problems despite socially, culturally, and historically different societies. The distinction between the 'West' and 'non-West' may be divided under the view of cultural divisions. Similar to contemporary perspectives (e.g., Birden, 1999; Pokhrel, 2011; Xu et al., 2018), Browning (1997) also certifies that the foundation of Western culture is formulated by the ideas and values derived from ancient Greek philosophy, Roman law, and Christianity. He assumes that the 'West' refers to countries with cultural backgrounds evolving from European civilization, such as Western Europe, North America, Australia and New Zealand. On the contrary, the 'non-West' denotes countries that evolved from societies that did not share the West's ideas, values, and transformations.

Eastern culture generally implies the societal norms of Eastern countries like Vietnam, China, Japan, ... Fuller (2011) states that both regions and their crops heavily influence eastern cultures, especially rice harvesting. Nevertheless, the distinction between secular society and religious philosophy is not remarkable compared to Western cultures. Eastern cultures possibly refer to "a term used to refer to a heritage of social norms, ethical values, traditional customs, belief systems, political systems, and specific artefacts and technologies that have some origin or association with Asia" (Sogari et al., 2019, p. 181). Previously, Xu (2004) pointed out the different perspectives on contrasting cultural values and beliefs between the East and West. From the author's stance, Eastern cultures mainly refer to those Asian cultures dominated by Buddhism and Confucianism, such as China, Japan, Korea, Malaysia, and Vietnam. Whereas, Western cultures generally refer to those cultures predominant by Christianity, especially Protestantism, like the United States, Canada, the United Kingdom, Germany, France, and the Nordic countries. In search of Eastern information, there seem to be limited studies conducted to discover the classification of Eastern cultures.

Cross-Cultural Individualistic and Collectivistic Eastern and Western Reflections

Individualism and collectivism are commonly mentioned in cross-cultural communication. Many people in different parts of the world have defined *Individualism* and *Collectivism* in numerous ways. It is because the terms are ill-defined and sound difficult to measure explicitly. Social psychologists (e.g., Hofstede, 2011; Triandis, 1995; Shavitt et al., 2011) have made many efforts to measure the tendencies to understand the core nature of individualism and collectivism. Thanks to their attempts, they have proposed enormous complexity in what should be contributed to these constructs. They have examined and identified the causes and consequences of people's behaviors and attitudes toward individualistic and collectivistic ways and figured out that people typically exist as both individualists and collectivists inside themselves (e.g., Čeněk, 2020; Boone et al., 2007; Darwish & Huber, 2003).

Concerning the definitions of collectivism and individualism, various perspectives relate to these terms. Collectivism can be viewed as a social pattern comprising closely linked individuals who consider themselves as parts of or more collectives (e.g., colleagues, group, nation), who are bonded by responsibilities imposed by collectives, or who show their willingness to devote themselves to the goals of these collectives rather than their own goals, or even who underline their connectedness to a member of these collectives. By contrast, individualism is defined as a social pattern that denotes the loosely connected individuals who see themselves as independent of collectives or who are promoted by their preference, desire, rights, and their connectedness they have constituted with others or prioritize their objectives over the goals of others, or focus on rational analyses of the advantages and disadvantages to connect others (Triandis, 1995). In cross-cultural psychology, Čeněk (2020) postulates that individualism refers to a complicated behavior aroused by individual care for his or her benefit when socializing with other social groups. Whereas collectivism is initially defined as a behavior associated with the involvement of one individual with broader social surroundings and societal interests in traditions and values. Previously, similar to Čeněk's (2020) research, Shavitt et al. (2011) claim that individualistic and collectivistic constructs have prevailed in the discourse on the study of the psychological influences on cross-cultural research over the last 30 years. Someone labeled as individualistic is thought to be mysterious, autonomous, independent, and respectful of others' privacy. Such kind of people is described as abstract and universal entities. Their social status is not necessarily predetermined or attributed, but their actual achievements define whose surroundings the individualists belong to. Furthermore, their interpersonal relationship is settled down by rational principles. Otherwise, they are serious about the connectedness with other people in such an equal and equitable way. Individualistic people seemingly comply with rules or legal regulations to protect their rights. "In-groups are perceived as more heterogeneous than out-groups. Debate and confrontation are acceptable. Conflict with out-groups is accepted but not desired" (Gouveia et al., 2012, p. 225). On the other hand, collectivism promotes well-being and social harmony over individual concerns. Under the collectivistic perspective, all individuals are engaged in an interpersonal network, and they perceive themselves as members of the united associations. They highlight their roles or status in the mutual interests in which individuals are stimulated to prioritize the in-group interests over their own. In a collectivistic community, individual prestige is highly respected and harmfully influenced in the event of their failure to obey pre-described duties and obligations. "In-groups are perceived as more homogeneous than out-groups. In-group harmony is required, and conflict with out-groups is expected" (Gouveia et al., 2012, p. 225). In another individualistic and collectivistic outlook, Darwish and Huber (2003) state that individualism reflects how individuals participate in groups. It also refers to the loose link among people in a community. Therefore, people in individualistic cultures have owned the characteristics of self-actualization, individual initiatives, and achievements because of the concentration on their own identities. By contrast, collectivism involves societies with people engraving the feeling of togetherness in their heads, which lasts over their lifetime with total loyalty. Besides, the concept of the *face* also clings to these individualistic and collectivistic cultures. *Self* is associated with the representation of self-worth, self-presentation, and self-value in individualistic societies that emphasize the role of personal privacy. Meanwhile, people's attitudes on their worth and values are highly respected under their in-group and out-group circumstances rather than themselves.

The importance of *face* denotes one's pride, honor, dignity, insult, shame, disgrace, prestige, or humility. Compared with the differences between collectivism and individualism, Triandis et al. (1988) share the same self-attribute but differentiate the other features. They specify five major factors, i.e., the self, activities, attitudes, values, and behavior. These elements show the disparity between the individualistic and collectivistic constructs. The distinction between self-orientation and collectivity-orientation should be highlighted concerning the self-perspective. Self-orientation is inclined to pursue any dedicated interests to himself or even to a very small in-group, whereas collectivity-orientation is likely to refer to the pursuit of the common interests of all members in one society. This contrastive distinction can be said that self-oriented people do everything for their own sake or in a very "sub-collectivity" interest. By contrast, collectivity-oriented persons pursue the mutually equal interests of the collectivity. Similarly, the self is separated into two different dimensions to a certain extent. In particular, individualist cultures are remarkable with the independent *self* outlook, whereby people have characteristics of autonomy with personally specific qualities, while collectivist cultures are dominated by the interdependent self-construal, in which the self is a symbol of connectedness among group members within the surrounding social context (Saad et al., 2015). Thus, the core components of individualism include independence and uniqueness, whereas duty to in-group, interdependence, and preserving harmony contribute to the core factors of collectivism. The individualism-collectivism construct is thought to be resourceful as a mechanism for cultural differences that greatly impact the ways culture influences what and how people think.

In general, individualism-collectivism constructs within social science discourse have been imprinted in Hostede's (1980) footsteps, which recommended four major cultural dimensions: horizontal individualism, vertical individualism, horizontal collectivism, and vertical collectivism. There have emerged some summaries relating to these four attributes in different fields.

Horizontal individualists tend to desire to be unique and different from others. They totally prefer respecting their privacy, and the principles of social justice (high equality) and self-direction (high freedom) lead their lives. In these communities, the pecking order is highly appreciated; interpersonal relationships are built up based on the socially equivalent status, where people share the same equality, rights, and obligations. In this regard, an autonomous self is respected. However, people feel more or less equal to others in terms of social status even though they are aware of perceiving themselves as independent. Horizontal individualism exists through universalistic values and features that persons show their preferences for protecting or defending their independence from others. People think of themselves as unique among others who share equality with them. In reality, they develop a strong sense of self-reluctance, but they discourage becoming distinguished or having high status in their community.

Table 9.1: Attributes of cultural orientation of horizontal and vertical individualism and collectivism

Cultural Orientation	Dimension (Hierarchy)	
	Horizontal	Vertical
Individualism	Independent/autonomous self and similar to others, equality in status.	Independent/autonomous self and different from others, status differential expected and accepted → inequality, intra-group competition, submission to authority.
Collectivism	Interdependent self and similar to others, equality in status.	Independent self and different than others, status differential → inequality is accepted, self-sacrifice for in-group is essential, submission to authority.

Source: Fatehi et al., 2020

Vertical individualists are inclined to appreciate personal achievements and place the maximum importance. It is likely to consider these people as perfectionists as they wish to achieve glorious accomplishments. This vertical individualism is remarkably characterized by a mixed emphasis on value principles, particularly power (low equality) and self-direction (high freedom). Interpersonal affinities are established for a mutual benefit if personal status places a significant value on the degree of the association. Vertical individualists are treated as independent entities in a hierarchical world where societal members are fully aware of a must to compete with each other to demonstrate, promote, and outperform themselves to improve their status.

Horizontal collectivists have the characteristics of cooperation. The harmony within the in-group is highly acknowledged. It emphasizes the value principles of togetherness and social support (high equality) and plays down the important roles designated privacy and self-direction (low freedom). Interpersonal rapports are formulated in a communal relationship, focusing on cooperation, friendship, and affections. In other words, horizontal collectivism refers to the cultural orientation in which the self is an adhesive component of one member to an in-group where all participants show equality and loyalty. The self is considered codependent, and equality is highly appreciated in these communities. One of the most remarkable features of horizontal collectivism accounts for egalitarian norms which navigate the in-group objectives. That is why people in this pattern wish to promote connectedness, mutual interests, and similarities with one another despite caring about authority.

Table 9.2: Vertical/Horizontal individualism and collectivism

Theory	Dimension	Cultural Level	Individual Level	Transmission
Individualism/ collectivism (Hofstede)	Ind Col	Individualism	Not measured	Work-related values → IND/COL → (behavior and mental proc.)
Horizontal and vertical individualism and collectivism (Triandis, Singelis)	+ HC - + HI - + VC - + VI -	Individualism / Collectivism	Ori.allo- and idiocentrism, later horizontal and vertical IND / COL	IND / COL → allocentric / indiocentric tendencies → behavior and mental proc.
Interdependent and independent self (Markus, Kitayama)	+ INDS - + INTS -	Independent and interdependent social relations (≈ IND / COL)	Independent and interdependent self-construal	IND / INT social relations → INDS / INTS → behavior and mental proc.

Source: Čeněk, J. (2020)

Vertical collectivists possess the principal characteristics that reflect dutiful and responsible individuals. They show and respect the hierarchy, demonstrating a sense of compliance and conformity, indicating low equality. Personal choices and self-determined behaviors are not encouraged in these societies because of the discouragement of personal freedom. Interpersonal relationships are established by hierarchical principles, which means that vertical collectivism emphasizes respect for hierarchical positions, principally older and higher social status people. Spiritual socialization is considered a backbone, essence, or specialty in vertical collectivism because individuals become interdependent among members in this pattern without caring about differences in status. They tend to preserve the in-group integrity, sacrifice their interests, and submit to authority with no question of the reasons why they are required to participate. Love-giving and equality are strongly emphasized in this community.

Table 9.3: Characteristics of Vertical and Horizontal Individualism and Collectivism

	Vertical		Horizontal	
	Collectivism	*Individualism*	*Collectivism*	*Individualism*
Self	Interdependent	Independent	Interdependent	Independent
	Different from others	Different from others	Same as others	Same as others
Fiske orientation	Communal sharing	Marketing pricing	Communal sharing	Market pricing
	Authority ranking	Authority ranking	Equality matching	Equality matching
Rokeach values	Low equality	Low equality	High equality	High equality
	Low freedom	High freedom	Low freedom	High freedom
Political system	Communalism (e.g., rural village in India)	Market democracy (e.g., United States, France)	Communal living (e.g., Israeli kibbutz)	Democratic socialism (e.g., Sweden, British Labour Party)

Source: Singelis et al., 1995

Individualism and Collectivism in Vietnamese Culture

The reference mentioned above compares and contrasts the meaning of the terms: Western and Eastern cultures. This study, however, circumscribes to a representative of Eastern cultures, particularly only Vietnamese culture compared with Western cultures. Vietnamese culture has had a close long-term commitment to Chinese culture under a far-reaching, dominant influence of Confucian philosophy from ancient China – one of the most influential doctrines which laid the foundation for much of Chinese culture (Tran, 2020; Quynh, 2021). In its essence, Vietnam has a cultural identity of a collectivistic society. As such, Vietnamese culture in the form of collectivism under the cross-cultural influence plays a vital part in the formation and development of Vietnamese lifestyles and global socio-economic integration with other long-standing cultures of the world. It is worth noting that the most influential collectivistic characteristics of Vietnamese culture, which are widely acknowledged, reflect the "culture of villages" emanating from its wet rice civilization. In an agricultural culture like Vietnam, the spiritual connectedness is engraved in persons' minds and inner feelings. Villages embracing families, relatives, or tribes empower the strength of preserving and conserving traditional values again the process of domestic cultural dissolution by the invasion of foreign cultures. Customs and traditions denote a strong collectivistic tie among members in villages via a nearly immutable underlying established by the unquestionable consciousness implying that all familial and communal values must be sacred and regarded as utmost superior to individual values. Their *self* is voluntary to devote and sacrifice to the communal villages under the spiritual obsession of Confucian philosophy. In addition, the self has to lean on or immerse in the community because without attaching to the communal groups, an individual becomes meaningless and useless to his or her ancestry, which sheds light on the fact that a person's role and integration into a community is very tight – a typical characteristic of interdependence in collectivism. In general, cultural villages in Vietnam have been preserved and maintained a strong sense of cohesiveness within the family, representing a tight connectedness and interdependence regarding collectivism in Vietnamese society.

Vietnam is considered as a newly industrializing country since it practiced a market economy, *Doi Moi*, or market liberation from 1986, so it has implemented a fascinating, promising, and open-door policy to call for foreign direct investments, which led to a new wave of the far-reaching cross-cultural exchanges with foreign cultures. Together with the development of the fourth industrial revolution, commonly referred to as Industry 4.0 (Schwab, 2016), its impacts have been recognized on the economy, business, national and global scale, society, and the individual, which are all imprinted on Vietnamese society. The challenges posing for international joint ventures in such a developing economy like Vietnam into market-oriented economies are so significant that cross-cultural communication plays a vital part in breaking the ice in all relationships. Although Vietnam is known for an agricultural culture where collective work style is still remarkable, the country is converting to a market economy under the supervision and direct instructions of the central and local governmental organs. This transformation represents a case of striking differences in work values. In contrast, Western conglomerates from capitalistic markets have encountered severe challenges in harmonizing cultural differences to attain excellent and successful business relationships. Besides, the country is possibly divided its culture into the North and South regions with different modes of behaviors and lifestyles due to historical traits of foreign invaded rules in the twentieth century. The North people tend to conserve the national culture – a nostalgic Confucius philosophy while the South tends to be interfered with by Western influences owning to American domination. Despite cross-cultural assimilation between Western and Eastern cultures, Vietnamese people still preserve their traditional collectivistic culture because of their socialist regime with a sole communist party.

To determine the influence of adaptive behavior of high collectivistic performers in an individualistic societal culture, Nguyen et al. (2010) prove that there is no difference in the extent between high and low collectivism. In addition, the generation gaps and intergeneration values are also compared in some studies (e.g., Adam, 2020; Cox et al., 2014). They have investigated whether collectivism and individualism are somehow influenced in two central regions in Vietnam, namely a communist system in the north and a capitalist system in the south. Their research findings conclude that Vietnamese people are inclined to conserve their collectivistic construct more than individualistic values. For example, different generations may live together in a house. Residential care homes are not popular in Vietnamese society as people think from the bottom of their hearts that children must show their gratitude to their old parents or fulfill their filial duty. Additionally, legal and societal prejudice protects the elderly rights to share homes with their children, a symbol of collectivistic cultural traits, reflecting the spirit of cultural villages. Similarly, Hill (2016) claims that a greater level of collectivism has a strong and positive effect on the quality of the exchange between a supervisor and a subordinate, which results in better subordinate job satisfaction. This finding is very resourceful for domestic and international managers to understand their diverse workforce while dealing with workers in developing countries like Vietnam. The aforementioned results have something in common with that of the study conducted by Tran (2020) on the organizational culture of Vietnamese and Chinese corporations because of task and relationship orientations in the collectivistic organizational culture. They conclude that despite sharing the same collectivistic work patterns, Vietnamese workers are more task-oriented and relationship-oriented than Chinese ones. Vietnamese cultures are a significantly complicated, mixed, and blended structure spanning a long, traditional history. Many cultural characteristics and traits were impacted mainly by China, France, and the United States during the twentieth century. Despite being colonized for over a thousand years, Vietnamese culture still keeps its identity, rich and not faded by foreign cultures. Altogether, Vietnam is widely recognized for its high-context culture in which people are engulfed in various cultural features of long-term orientation, high collectivism and power distance.

Empirical Findings between Individualism and Collectivism in Western and Vietnamese Cultures

The Western cultures are chosen as representative cultures for comparison purposes because of their increasing economic cooperation, the cultural distinctiveness between Eastern communist and Western capitalist societies, and the continuing cultural exchanges between the two cultural values under various programs and international socio-economic cooperation. This cross-level conceptualization framework of collectivistic and individualistic values contributes to the incomplete panoramic picture of cross-cultural psychology, which is currently crucial for global integration.

Table 9.4 illustrates the contrastive analysis of Western cultures and Vietnamese culture conducted in the locale of Vietnam. The study adopted the revised research instrument developed by Triandis and Gelfand (1998), with 16 statements divided equally into four sub-constructs, particularly horizontal and vertical collectivism/individualism. Because of the uncertainty of the sample, Cochran's formula, combined with the convenience sampling of the non-probability method, was employed to select the respondents. In particular, 385 Westerners and 385 Vietnamese participants were chosen to function as the study subjects. Indeed, data mining and screening had been gone through a rigorously scientific process on account of the liability of the outcomes before using a statistics program for the data treatment. A descriptive qualitative approach was applied to find out the differences between the two cultures, thanks to the primary source, which had been exploited via the adapted questionnaire.

In terms of Western profiles, most of them were males (n=334; equivalent to 86.8%), whereas the modest participants (n=51; same as 13.2%) were females. Concerning the duration of time living in Vietnam, most Westerners spent under 5 years living here, particularly 286 respondents accounting for 69.6%. Following this rank, 64 participants (16.6%) claimed that they had lived in Vietnam for less than 1 year. 63 people representing 13.8%, said they had lived here for over 5 years. Concerning their occupation, most of the respondents (n=289; equal to 75.1%) did not prefer revealing their jobs. 61 travelers (15.8%) came here for their vacation, and finally, a small number, i.e., 35 respondents (9.1%), stated that they got temporary residence cards in Vietnam. For Vietnamese people, 225 male respondents participated in the study, making up 58.4%, compared with 160 females accounting for 41.6% of the sample. Regarding their ages, 35 respondents, equivalent to 9.1%, were in their 20s, 81 persons, same as 21.0%, were in their 30s, 110 participants, similar to 28.6%, were in the 40s, 106 people corresponding to 27.5% were in the 50s, and 53 respondents parallel to 13.8% were over the 60s. As for their occupations, 38 state officials same as 9.9%, took part in the study. The number of freelancers was 23, identical to 6.0%. 26 students, equal to 6.8%, were involved in this research. Additionally, 32 workers, much like 8.3%, participated in the study. 31 civil servants, similar to 8.1%, functioned as the respondents. 24 educators, equal to 6.2%, expressed their viewpoints. 42 travelers, equivalent to 10.9%, were willing to partake in the survey. Remarkably, 51 businessmen/women agreed to view their stances, and the majority of the respondents (n = 118; same as 30.6%) did not want to reveal their working positions. Regarding the frequency of conversing with Western contacts, 102 participants, similar to 26.5%, said they often talked to Westerners about 4 or 5 times per week. 164 people, the same as 42.6%, estimated that they sometimes had conversations with Western people in daily life about 4 or 5 times per month. Finally, 119 respondents making up 30.9% confessed that they rarely speak to Western people, about once a month.

Table 9.4 presents the contrastive analysis between the Western and Vietnamese cultural traits. As clearly shown in horizontal individualism, the degree of two cultural constructs is pointed out oppositely. Generally, the self is remarkably emphasized in Western cultures. In particular, the self-dependence (M = 4.46) and personal identity (M = 4.55) are assessed as very high, while the choice of whose reliance should be (M = 4.00) and one's action (M = 4.04) are also reported high. In contrast, horizontal individualism is considered low in Vietnamese culture. The results confirm that the considerable disparity in horizontal individualism between Westerners and Vietnamese is consistent with the other research (e.g., Čeněk, 2020; Hu et al., 2014; Pae, 2020a; Vu et al., 2017). Given the demonstrated viability of these constructs, it is easy to recognize that the culture of the village (Quynh, 2021) – a portrayal of Vietnamese collectivistic society – reflects a clear difference compared with that in Western cultures, where horizontal individualism is highly reflected, which are illuminated in many studies recently (e.g., Triandis & Gelfand, 2018; Hakim et al., 2017; Swaranjeet et al., 2018; Sinha, 2014). The autonomous self in this cultural pattern is postulated in Westerners with different inequality, promoting self-independence. In contrast, interdependence is highly adored in a united, equal Vietnamese horizontal collectivistic spirit. Thus, people with such a high extent of horizontal individualism would reinforce the essence of self-sufficiency, autonomy, and uniqueness.

The differences are somehow similar to vertical individualism with vertical individualism, and the differences are somehow similar to the previous horizontal collectivism. Mainly, Western vertical individualistic persons show high competition preferences with others (M = 4.41) and become tense and aroused if left behind (M = 4.43). They also feel that winning is everything (M = 4.06), and they take competition for granted (M = 4.03). On the contrary, Vietnamese individuals express low perspectives on vertical individualism. From the above data, it can be concluded that the dissimilarity of the two cultural families dates back to their geographical origins. Brewer & Venaik (2011) claimed that "people living in rich countries tend to be more individualistic in their outlook than those in poorer countries" (p. 441). This statement further implies that Westerners tend to embrace the idealism about their proneness to self-proclaim to be vertical individualistic people. Hence, the results confirm the persistent gap between the two cultures. Vertical individualism is primarily imprinted by competition and autonomy, similar to horizontal individualism. However, societies characterized by a high degree of vertical individualism show a propensity for personal differences and an intense state of competitive status. The core nature of vertical individualism promotes individual achievement and attainment, which concentrates on the group's external aspects, control and stability.

There is a reverse shift between two poles when comparing horizontal collectivism in two cultures. While Westerners consider it low, Vietnamese culture sees it high or very high. In particular, they have great pride in their colleagues' achievements (M = 3.97) and have highly positive co-operations with their coworkers (M = 4.02). In addition, they appreciate very high with their colleagues' well-being (M = 4.38), and they feel very highly relaxed at socializing with their workmates (M = 4.48). In Vietnamese culture, cultural identity is carved in the village's culture, where collaboration and cohesion among societal members are strongly emphasized. People are inclined to respect group unity and embrace spiritual values such as equality and universalism. The high or very high denotation of horizontal collectivistic traits in Vietnamese culture is symbolized by interdependence and teamwork, such as giving feasts or corporate cultures where people commonly share objectives with others, showing interdependence and sociability. As such, the results of Vietnamese culture displayed in Table 9.4 highlight the importance of the internal group or discretion and flexibility of the collaborator. The affinity revealed in this study is also in line with other studies (e.g., Solís & Leiva, 2018; Quynh, 2021; Tran, 2020; Xia et al., 2019).

The same situation as horizontal collectivism is presented in Table 9.4, in which people from Western cultures express low perspectives towards vertical collectivism, whereas Vietnamese people have high or very high viewpoints on this construct. Specially, familial togetherness is reported very high (M = 4.43). Following this rank, the stances on caring for families over other duties (M = 4.10), familial union (M = 3.92) and respecting decisions made by groups (M = 3.88) are also acknowledged as high in Vietnamese culture. Vertical collectivism, to a certain extent, does promote group unity. It supports hierarchies and the defense of authority, respect for rules and norms, especially hierarchical culture, which forms clear lines of authority and control over organizational processes (Sinha, 2014; Shavitt et al., 2011; Rhee et al., 2020).

Table 9.4: Comparison of collectivistic and individualistic degrees between Western cultures and Vietnamese culture

No.	Statement	Western cultures		Vietnamese culture	
		Mean	Std. Deviation	Mean	Std. Deviation
Horizontal individualism					
1	I'd rather depend on myself than others.	4.00	.580	2.12	.840
2	I rely on myself most of the time; I rarely rely on others.	4.46	.703	2.05	.923
3	I often do "my own thing."	4.04	.526	2.28	.820
4	My personal identity, independent of others, is very important to me.	4.54	.710	2.17	.642
Vertical individualism					
5	It is important that I do my job better than others.	4.41	.824	2.44	.782
6	Winning is everything.	4.06	.544	2.29	.824
7	Competition is the law of nature.	4.03	.520	2.40	.791
8	When another person does better than I do, I get tense and aroused.	4.43	.719	2.11	.864
Horizontal collectivism					
9	If a co-worker gets a prize, I would feel proud.	2.37	.974	3.97	.596
10	The well-being of my co-workers is important to me.	2.39	.835	4.38	.818
11	To me, pleasure is spending time with others.	2.41	.651	4.48	.813
12	I feel good when I cooperate with others.	2.34	.683	4.02	.829
Vertical collectivism					
13	Parents and children must stay together as much as possible.	2.17	.669	4.43	.689
14	It is my duty to take care of my family, even when I have to sacrifice what I want.	2.32	.643	4.10	.874
15	Family members should stick together, no matter what sacrifices are required.	2.29	.650	3.92	.923
16	It is important to me that I respect the decisions made by my groups.	2.43	.670	3.88	.605

Legend: 1.00 – 1.80 (very low); 1.81 – 2.60 (low); 2.61 – 3.40 (neutral); 3.41 – 4.20 (high); 4.21 – 5.0 (very high)

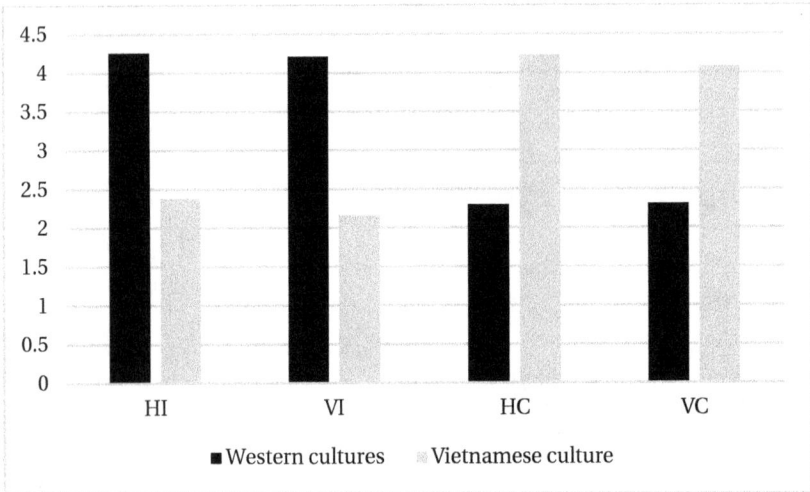

Figure 9.1: Contrastive differences of cultural constructs between two cultures according to average means

Figure 9.1 presents a meta-analysis of the four cultural constructs that clearly contrast the opposite cultural poles between Western cultures and Vietnamese. The results totalize each comparative weighted mean in each category.

The outcomes figure out the reconfirmation of the long-standing differences which formulate two separate cultural fields. Although global integration and cross-cultural communication have strong connection, as mentioned in many studies (e.g., Kecskes, 2017; Hurn & Tomalin, 2013; Kiesling, 2015), harmony cannot bridge the gap between two cultures. That is, the cultural identity does not lose its essence. Each cultural value and belief still preserve its original nature with a firm confirmation, such as "east is east, and west is west, and never the twain shall meet" (Xu, 2004; Regestein, 2012; Hu et al., 2014; Schroe¨n et al., 2014). No matter how global integration occurs, each cultural identity still keeps its values and beliefs.

Limitations and Scope for Future Research

This chapter deals with limited sources compared with a tip of a large iceberg of communication. Beside the obtained information from the secondary sources such as the aforementioned studies, it also used primary sources in the form of the surveyed questionnaire. It is advisable for the future research that the contrastive comparison between two cultural schools should be conducted largely among the easterners and easterners, not constrained to Vietnamese culture as a representative of the eastern cultures towards the western ones. For more liable outcomes, both qualitative and quantitative approaches should be carried out to formulate the overall research picture.

Conclusion

With global socio-economic development, most countries have been trying to understand and cooperate to create an equal, respectable, and collaborative environment. These countries have to promote their mutual understanding via cross-cultural activities to achieve this aim, which is an excellent obstacle to international diplomacy. The concern about the homogenization between Vietnamese and Western cultural bipolarization that can happen due to the effect of globalization upon the cultural identity is reflected by examining a contrastive analysis between Westerners and the Vietnamese. The results again prove that strongly ongoing global economic collaborations occur and two cultures simultaneously come in touch with one another. However, each cultural identity and essence are not harmonized, and a clear line between the two cultures is remarkably recognizable. It can be said that these two cultures help to promote the mutual understanding of Western and Vietnamese people in all aspects. The development of one cultural entity causes no harm to another; adversely, these two cultures exist, develop, and maintain their cultural values during diversifying and conserving their traditional cultural identities. Grasping the cultural differences thoroughly, dismal relationships resulting from cultural misunderstanding would be easily put aside to replace with successful connectedness to pave the path to establishing mutual understanding and developments among people worldwide.

References

Adam, H. (2020). Socioeconomic effects of collectivist and individualist education: A comparison between North and South Vietnam. *TVSEP Working Paper, No. WP-020, Leibniz Universita¨t Hannover, Thailand Vietnam Socio Economic Panel (TVSEP), Hannover.* http://hdl.handle.net/10419/222615

Amin, S. (2010). *Eurocentrism: Modernity, religion, and democracy: a critique of Eurocentrism and culturalism.* Monthly Review Press.

Birken, L. (1999). Chaos Theory and "Western Civilization". *Review (Fernand Braudel Center), 22*(1), 17-30.

Boone, C., Meng, C., & Velden, R. (2007). Individualism and collectivism. In J. Allen, Y. Inenaga, R. Velden, & K. Yoshimoto (Eds.), *Competencies, Higher Education and Career in Japan and the Netherlands. Higher education dynamics, 21.* Springer, Dordrecht. https://doi.org/10.1007/978-1-4020-6044-1_10

Brewer, P., & Venaik, S. (2011). Individualism-Collectivism in Hofstede and GLOBE. *Journal of International Business Studies, 42,* 436-445. https://doi.org/10.1057/jibs.2010.62

Browning, S. A. (1997). Understanding Non-Western Cultures: A Strategic Intelligence Perspective. *Strategy Research Project.* https://apps.dtic.mil/sti/pdfs/ADA326929.pdf

Buarqoub, I. A. S. (2019). Language Barriers to Effective Communication. *Utopía y Praxis Latinoamericana, 24*(6), 64-77.

Čeněk, J. (2020). Cultural dimension of individualism and collectivism and its perceptual and cognitive correlates in cross-cultural research. *Journal of Education Culture and Society, 6*(2), 210-225. https://doi.org/10.15503/jecs20152.210.225

Cox, A., Hannif, Z., & Rowley, C. (2014). Leadership styles and generational effects: examples of US companies in Vietnam. *The International Journal of Human Resource Management, (25)*1, 1-22. https://doi.org/10.1080/09585192.2013.778311

Dang, N. T. (2018). *The human rights-based-approach to development: a case study of a development project in the Central Highlands of Vietnam* [Doctoral dissertation, The University of Western Sydney]. http://hdl.handle.net/1959.7/uws:48764

Darwish, A. E., & Huber, G. L. (2003). Individualism vs Collectivism in Different Cultures: A cross-cultural study. *Intercultural Education, 14*(1), 47-56. https://doi.org/10.1080/1467598032000044647

Dussel, E. (1998). Beyond Eurocentrism: The World-System and the Limits of Modernity. In F. Jameson & M. Miyoshi (Eds.), *The Cultures of Globalization,* (pp. 3-31). Duke University Press. https://doi.org/10.1515/9780822378426-003

Fatehi, K., Priestley, J. L., & Taasoobshirazi, G. (2020). The expanded view of individualism and collectivism: One, two, or four dimensions? *International Journal of Cross Cultural Management, 20*(1), 7-24. https://doi.org/10.1177/1470595820913077

Foluke, F. (2018). What is Communication?. In Daniel, I. O. A. (Ed.), *Communication and Language Skills* (pp. 21-41). Cambridge Scholars Publishing.

Fuller, D. Q. (2011). Pathways to Asian Civilizations: Tracing the Origins and Spread of Rice and Rice Cultures. *Rice 4*, 78-92. https://doi.org/10.1007/s12284-011-9078-7

Gad, S., Mark, C., & Louis, H. (2015). Individualism-collectivism and the quantity versus quality dimensions of individual and group creative performance. *Journal of Business Research, 68*(3), 578-586. https://doi.org/10.1016/j.jbusres.2014.09.004

Gennady, G. K., Valeriya, B. K., Alexander, N. S., & Elena, A. D. (2017). Does collectivism act as a protective factor for depression in Russia?. *Personality and Individual Differences, 108*, 26-31. https://doi.org/10.1016/j.paid.2016.11.066

Gouveia, V. V., Milfont, T. L., Martinez, M. C., & Paterna, C. (2012). Individualism-collectivism as predictors of prejudice toward Gypsies in Spain. *Revista Interamericana De Psicología/Interamerican Journal of Psychology, 45*(2), 223-234.

Gudykunst, W. (2003). *Cross-cultural and Intercultural Communication.* Thousand Oaks: Sage.

Hall, E. T., & Hall, M. R. (1990). Understanding cultural differences. Yarmouth, Me: Intercultural Press.

Hakim, N., Simons, D. J., Zhao, H., & Wan, X. (2017). Do easterners and westerners differ in visual cognition? A preregistered examination of three visual cognition tasks. *Social Psychological and Personality Science, 8*(2), 142-152. https://doi.org/10.1177/1948550616667613

Hill, U. (2016). The Influence of Culture on Leader-Member Exchange and Job Satisfaction of Subordinates: A Vietnamese Study. In A. Arora & S. Bacouel-Jentjens (Eds.), *International Fragmentation. International Marketing and Management Research* (pp. 37-62). Palgrave Macmillan, Cham. https://doi.org/10.1007/978-3-319-33846-0_3

Hiroshi, Y., & Norhayati, Z. (2019). Explanations for cultural differences in thinking: Easterners' dialectical thinking and Westerners' linear thinking. *Journal of Cognitive Psychology, 31*(4), 487-506. https://doi.org/10.1080/2044 5911.2019.1626862

Hofstede, G. (1980). *Culture's Consequences: International Differences in Work-Related Values.* Beverly Hills: SAGE.

Hofstede, G. (2011). Dimensionalizing Cultures: The Hofstede Model in Context. *Online Readings in Psychology and Culture, 2*(1), 1-26. https://doi.org/10.9707/2307-0919.1014

Hu, Q., Schaufeli, W. B., Taris, T., Hessen, D. J., Hakanen, J., Salanova, M., & Shimazu, A. (2014). East is East and West is West and never the twain shall meet: Work Engagement and Workaholism across Eastern and Western Cultures. *Journal of Behavioral and Social Sciences, 1*, 6-24.

Hurn, B. J., & Tomalin, B. (2013) What is Cross-Cultural Communication?. In *Cross-Cultural Communication* (pp. 1-19). Palgrave Macmillan, London. https://doi.org/10.1057/9780230391147_1

Jackson, J. (2019). *Introducing Language and Intercultural Communication* (2nd ed.). Routledge. https://doi.org/10.4324/9781351059275

Jayawickreme, N., Jayawickreme, E., & Foa, E. B. (2013). Using the individualism-collectivism construct to understand cultural differences in PTSD. In K. Gow & M. Celinski (Eds.), *Mass trauma: Impact and recovery issues* (pp. 55–76). Nova Science Publishers.

Jung-Soo, Y. (2021). Revisiting Hofstede's Uncertainty-Avoidance Dimension: A Cross-Cultural Comparison of Organizational Employees in Four Countries. *Journal of Intercultural Communication, 21*(1), 46-61.

Kececi, M., (2017). The impact of collectivism on the relationship between leadership styles and organizational citizenship behavior. *Research Journal of Business and Management (RJBM), 4*(4), 465-484. http://doi.org/10.17261/Pressacademia.2017.755

Kecskes, I. (2017). Cross-cultural and intercultural pragmatics. In Y. Huang (Ed.), *The Oxford Handbook of Pragmatics* (pp. 234-268). Oxford: Oxford University Press. https://doi.org/10.1093/oxfordhb/9780199697960.013.29

Ki-Seok, K., & Sung, S. K. (2013). A historical comparison of intellectual renaissance in the East and the West. *Comparative Education, 49*(1), 16-27. https://doi.org/10.1080/03050068.2012.740217

Kiesling, S. F. (2015). Cross-cultural and Intercultural Communication and Discourse Analysis. In D. Tannen, H. E. Hamilton, & D. Schiffrin (Eds.), *The*

Handbook of Discourse Analysis (pp. 620-638). John Wiley & Sons, Inc. https://doi.org/10.1002/9781118584194.ch29

Lander, E. (2000). Eurocentrism and Colonialism in Latin American Social Thought. *Nepantla: Views from South 1*(3), 519-532.

LeFebvre, R., & Franke, V. (2013). Culture Matters: Individualism vs. Collectivism in Conflict Decision-Making. *Societies, 3*(1), 128-146. https://doi.org/10.3390/soc3010128

Lubis, B. N. A., & Sagala, R. W. (2020). The Comparative of Indonesian and Western Culture in Live Action: A Study of Cross-Culture. *English Teaching and Linguistics Journal, 1*(2), 56-59.

Mai, P. N, Cees, T., & Albert, P. (2012). Cooperative Learning in Vietnam and the West-East educational transfer. *Asia Pacific Journal of Education, 32*(2), 137-152. https://doi.org/10.1080/02188791.2012.685233

McConachy, T., & Spencer-Oatey, H. (2021). Cross-Cultural and Intercultural Pragmatics. In M. Haugh, D. Kádár, & M. Terkourafi (Eds.), McConachy, T., & Spencer-Oatey, H. (2021) *The Cambridge Handbook of Sociopragmatics* (Cambridge Handbooks in Language and Linguistics, pp. 733-757). Cambridge: Cambridge University Press. https://doi.org/10.1017/9781108954105.037

Neuliep, J. W. (2009). *Intercultural communication: A contextual approach*. Los Angeles: Sage.

Nguyen, H. D. N., Le, H., & Terry, B. (2010). Co-operation: A Cross-Society and Cross-Level Examination. *Negotiation and Conflict Management Research, 3*(3), 179-204. https://doi.org/10.1111/j.1750-4716.2010.00057.xC

Nima, G., Mark, N. B., Watson, P. J., Kristl, H. D., & Daniel, L. L. (2003). Individualist and collectivist values: evidence of compatibility in Iran and the United States. *Personality and Individual Differences, 35*(2), 431-447. https://doi.org/10.1016/S0191-8869(02)00205-2

Pae, H. K. (2020a). The East and the West. In: *Script Effects as the Hidden Drive of the Mind, Cognition, and Culture. Literacy Studies (Perspectives from Cognitive Neurosciences, Linguistics, Psychology and Education), 21*. Springer, Cham. https://doi.org/10.1007/978-3-030-55152-0_6

Petrić, B. (2009). 'I Thought I was an Easterner; it Turns Out I am a Westerner!': EIL Migrant Teacher Identities. In F. Sharifian (Ed.), *English as an International Language: Perspectives and Pedagogical Issues* (pp. 135-150). Bristol, Blue Ridge Summit: Multilingual Matters. https://doi.org/10.21832/9781847691231-010

Pokluel, A. K. (2011). Eurocentrism. In D. K. Chatterjee (Ed.), *Encyclopedia of Global Justice*. Springer, Dordrecht (pp. 321-325). https://doi.org/10.1007/978-1-4020-9160-5_25

Pollock, J. E., Chun, H. W., & Kim, C. A. (2008, July 18). *Teaching Western Literature to Non-Western Students*. [Paper presentation]. Advanced Placement Annual Conference, Seattle, WA, United States. https://files.eric.ed.gov/fulltext/ED502671.pdf

Quijano, A. (2000). Coloniality of Power and Eurocentrism in Latin America. *International Sociology, 15*(2), 215-232. https://doi.org/10.1177/0268580900015002005

Qiushuang, Z., & Qianni, L. (2020). A Study of the Differences between Chinese and Western Cultures from the Perspective of Hofstede's Cultural Dimension Theory. *East African Scholars Journal of Education, Humanities and Literature, 3*(4), 125-128. https://doi.org/10.36349/EASJEHL.2020.v03i04. 006

Quynh, L. H. C. (2021). The Influences of Collectivism on Vietnamese Communication Style. *International Journal of Research in Engineering, Science and Management, 4*(7), 10-14.

Ralston, D., Thang, N., & Napier, N. (1999). A Comparative Study of the Work Values of North and South Vietnamese Managers. *Journal of International Business Studies, 30*, 655-672. https://doi.org/10.1057/palgrave.jibs.8490889

Regestein, Q. R. MD. (2012). "Oh, East is East and West is West, and never the twain shall meet" - Rudyard Kipling. *Menopause: The Journal of The North American Menopause Society, 19*(12), 1291-1293. https://doi.org/10.1097/ gme.0b013e3182752f1b

Rhee, M., Alexandra, V., & Powell, K. S. (2020). Individualism-collectivism cultural differences in performance feedback theory. *Cross Cultural & Strategic Management, 27*(3), 343-364. https://doi.org/10.1108/CCSM-05-2019-0100

Saad, G., Cleveland, M., & Ho, L. (2015). Individualism-collectivism and the quantity versus quality dimensions of individual and group creative performance. *Journal of Business Research, 68*(3), 578-586. https://doi.org/10 .1016/j.jbusres.2014.09.004

Schmidt, R. W., & Richards, J. C. (2011). *Longman Dictionary of Language Teaching and Applied Linguistics* (4th ed.). Routledge. https://doi.org/10.432 4/9781315833835

Schroën, Y., Wietmarschen, H. A. V., Wang, Wijk, M., E. P. V., Hankemeier, T., Xu, G., & Greef, J. V. D. (2014). East is East and West is West, and never the twain shall meet?. *Science, 346*(6216), S10-S12. https://www.chi.is/wp-content/ uploads/2017/03/TCM-Dec-19-issue_Schroen_S10-12.pdf

Schwab, K. (2016). *The Fourth Industrial Revolution.* Geneva: World Economic Forum.

Shavitt, S., Torelli, C. J., & Riemer, H. (2011). Horizontal and vertical individualism and collectivism: Implications for understanding psychological processes. In M. J. Gelfand, C.-y. Chiu, & Y.-y. Hong (Eds.), *Advances in culture and psychology* (pp. 309-350). Oxford University Press. https://doi.org/10.1093 /acprof:oso/9780195380392.003.0007

Singelis, T. M., Triandis, H. C., Bhawuk, D., & Gelfand, M. J. (1995). Horizontal and vertical dimensions of individualism and collectivism: A theoretical and measurement refinement. *Cross-Cultural Research: The Journal of Comparative Social Science, 29*(3), 240-275. https://doi.org/10.1177/1069397 19502900302

Sinha, J. B. P. (2014). Collectivism and Individualism. In: *Psycho-Social Analysis of the Indian Mindset.* Springer, New Delhi. https://doi.org/10.1007/ 978-81-322-1804-3_2

Sogari, G., Liu, A., & Li, J. (2019). Understanding Edible Insects as Food in Western and Eastern Societies. In D. Bogueva, D. Marinova, T. Raphaely, & K. Schmidinger (Eds.), *Environmental, Health, and Business Opportunities in the New Meat Alternatives Market* (pp. 166-181). IGI Global. http://doi:10.40 18/978-1-5225-7350-0.ch009

Solís, M., & Leiva, B. G. (2018). Adjustment between collectivist/individualist attributes of a person with the perceived culture of the work unit: An analysis of its influence on organizational citizenship behavior. *Accounting & Management, 64*(2), 1-18. http://dx.doi.org/10.22201/fca.24488410e.2018.1514

Swaranjeet, A., Manisha, S., & Shakuntala, J. (2018). Factors Affecting Individualism-Collectivism: An Empirical Study. *AIMS Journal of Management, 4*(1), 79-101.

Taras, V., Sarala, R., Muchinsky, P., Kemmelmeier, M., Singelis, T. M., Avsec, A., Coon, H. M., Dinnel, D. L., Gardner, W., Grace, S., Hardin, E. E., Hsu, S., Johnson, J., Karakitapoğlu, Z., Kashima, E. S., Kolstad, A., Milfont, T. L., Oetzel, J., Okazaki, S., ... Sinclair, H. C. (2014). Opposite Ends of the Same Stick? Multi-Method Test of the Dimensionality of Individualism and Collectivism. *Journal of Cross-Cultural Psychology, 45*(2), 213–245. https://doi.org/10.1177/0022022113509132

Tran, Q. H. N. (2020). The Organizational Culture of Vietnamese and Chinese Corporations: Do Age and Gender Make a Difference? *Public Organization Review volume, 20*, 549-562. https://doi.org/10.1007/s11115-019-00458-0

Tri, T. M. (2016). *Employee motivation in public sector: Evidence from Ho Chi Minh City* [Master's thesis, University of Tampere]. http://urn.fi/URN:NBN: fi:uta-201608022105

Triandis, H. C., & Gelfand, M. J. (1998). Converging measurement of horizontal and vertical individualism and collectivism. *Journal of Personality and Social Psychology, 74*(1), 118-128. https://doi.org/10.1037/0022-3514.74.1.118

Triandis, H. C., Brislin, R., & Hui, C. H. (1988). Cross-cultural training across the individualism-collectivism divide. *International Journal of Intercultural Relations, 12*(3), 269-289. https://doi.org/10.1016/0147-1767(88)90019-3

Triandis, H. C. (1995). *Individualism and Collectivism* (1e). Routledge. https://doi.org/10.4324/9780429499845

Triandis, H. C. (2002). Individualism-collectivism and personality. *Journal of Personality, 69*(6), 907-924. https://doi.org/10.1111/1467-6494.696169

Trompenaars, F., & Hampden-Turner, C. (2012*). Riding the waves of culture: Understanding cultural diversity in business.* London: Nicholas Brealey Publishing.

Trompenaars, F., & Woolliams, P. (2020). *Riding the Waves of Culture*, Fourth Edition. New York: McGraw-Hill Education.

UNESCO (2001). *UNESCO Universal Declaration on Cultural Diversity.* Paris: UNESCO.

Vu, T-V., Finkenauer, C., Huizinga, M., Novin, S., & Krabbendam, L. (2017). Do individualism and collectivism on three levels (country, individual, and situation) influence theory-of-mind efficiency? A cross-country study. *PLoS ONE 12*(8). e0183011. https://doi.org/10.1371/journal. pone.0183011

Wang, Z., Wang, Y., Li, K., Shi, J., & Wang, F. (2021). The comparison of the wisdom view in Chinese and Western cultures. *Current Psychology.* https:// doi.org/10.1007/s12144-020-01226-w

Xia, F., Gerben, A. V. K., & Disa, A. S. (2019). Revisiting cultural differences in emotion perception between easterners and westerners: Chinese perceivers are accurate, but see additional non-intended emotions in negative facial expressions. *Journal of Experimental Social Psychology, 82*, 152-159. https://doi.org/10.1016/j.jesp.2019.02.003

Xie, Q. (2007). Cultural Difference between the East and the West. *Canadian Social Science, 3*(5). Retrieved from https://core.ac.uk/download/pdf/236294259.pdf

Xu, G., Chen, Y., & Xu, L. (2018). A Concise History of Western Cultures. In G. Xu, Y. Chen & L. Xu (Eds.), *Introduction to Western Culture*, (pp. 1-24). Palgrave Macmillan, Singapore. https://doi.org/10.1007/978-981-10-8153-8_1

Xu, Y. (2004). When East and West Meet: Cultural Values and Beliefs and Health Behaviors. *Home Health Care Management & Practice, 16*(5), 433-435. https://doi.org/10.1177/1084822304264659

Yaling, L. (2018). The Comparison between the Eastern and Western Management Ideas. *Advances in Social Science, Education and Humanities Research, 233*, 1307-1310. https://doi.org/10.2991/iccessh-18.2018.288

Yang, L., Li, J., Wilkinson, A., Spaniol, J., & Hasher, L. (2018). East-West cultural differences in encoding objects in imagined social contexts. *PLoS ONE 13*(11): e0207515. https://doi.org/10.1371/journal.pone.0207515

Yiend, J., Andre, J., Smith, L., Chen, L. H., Toulopoulou, T., Chen, E., Sham, P., & Parkinson, B. (2019). Biased cognition in East Asian and Western cultures. *PLoS ONE 14*(10): e0223358. https://doi.org/10.1371/journal.pone.0223358

Yoon-Na, C., Anastasia, T., Molly, I. R., Seong-Yeon, P., & Hyun, J. L. (2013). To be or not to be green: Exploring individualism and collectivism as antecedents of environmental behavior. *Journal of Business Research, 66*(8), 1052-1059. https://doi.org/10.1016/j.jbusres.2012.08.020

Zhu, H. (2011). Glossary. In H. Zhu (Ed.), *The Language and Intercultural Communication Reader* (pp. 418-425). Routledge.

Chapter 10

The Psychology of Acculturation: Losing My Religion

Janelle Christine Simmons

AmeriCorps VISTA – AARP Foundation, New York, USA

Abstract: The chapter discusses terminologies such as acculturation, culture, multicultural education, and the like. It will also discuss acculturation through the lens of balance. Part of this balance is often giving up certain aspects of one's cultural mores and beliefs, such as one's firmly held religious beliefs. How does a person acculturate without losing himself/herself? Does becoming a citizen of another country require rejecting one's religious/cultural beliefs? How much can one impose another culture, and how much does that culture impose his/her strongly held beliefs on the "foreigner"? And various psychological and cultural aspects regarding assimilation and acculturation have been explored.

Keywords: Acculturation, Assimilation, Religion, Culture, Multiculturalism, Language Barriers, Religious/Culture Beliefs,

***

Introduction

"Also thou shalt not oppress a stranger: for ye know the heart of a stranger, seeing ye were strangers in the land of Egypt."

– Exodus 23:9 (KJV)

Many years ago (i.e., in the late 1990s), I was an undergraduate student at Michigan State University. A graduate student by the last name of Nguyen was completing research on the Vietnamese population and acculturation. I applied to be her research assistant, and I was accepted. While assisting her in collecting, coding and analyzing data, one thing became clear to me as a young adult, the topic of acculturation is not easy, nor is the process of acculturation.

Since I was a small child, many of my closest friends had been non-Green card-holding individuals and non-United States citizens. I often watched them struggle with their beliefs and longing to fit in and "be an American." I also often attended religious services with them. I brought them to church, and they brought me to the Buddhist or Hindu temples, etc. Through this exchange, I began to see the differences in our religions. Ironically, my faith in Christ was strengthened. Perhaps, this was because I was born in the United States, I spoke English, and it was not my second language. My family had been established within this country for centuries on one side and many decades on the other. I realized, however, that there is a conundrum in the term acculturation. In effect, the receiving country often expects their new visitor, asylum seeker, new Green Card holder or new citizen to change and adapt to their ways. As we know, the famous proverbial saying goes:

"When in Rome, do what the Romans do."

– St. Ambrose.

Approximately 20 years later, I completed my dissertation titled "Multicultural Leadership Characteristics of a School Director in an Educational Setting in South Korea: A Case Study" (Simmons, 2016). While examining an educational program/school in a country that is not known to be the most embracing when it comes to non-White foreigners; it became clear that South Korea would much rather have an acculturated society rather than a multicultural one (Simmons, 2016). That begs the question, what is acculturation?

In this book chapter, the reader will be further introduced to defined terms, the process of acculturation, an examination of psychological and cultural theories, language barriers, the concept of losing one's religion, etc. Then the totality of the chapter will be discussed. Finally, there will be a conclusion. This chapter will end with further recommendations. However, before we reach the end, let's consider what acculturation means? What does religion mean? And what do the two have to do with one another?

Conceptual Declarations

While the Encyclopedia Britannica, Inc. (2022) defines acculturation as being "the processes of change in artifacts, customs, and beliefs that result from the contact of two or more cultures" (p. 1); the author would like to emphasize that for this chapter, people will be the focus. According to Sam & Berry (2010), acculturation is defined as follows: "the process of cultural and psychological change that results following meeting between cultures" (p. 472). Another term that Berry coined in 2003 is psychological acculturation

(Sam & Berry, 2010). Psychological acculturation describes the process by which the individual in a new or adoptive society/country works through psychologically adjusting to the main culture and the stress (i.e., acculturative stress)[1] they may experience (Sam & Berry, 2010). A consequence of acculturation is a term known as adaptation (Sam & Berry, 2010). Adaptation refers to how people manage socioculturally and their psychological well-being. Thus, one could say that adaptation measures how well one acculturates.

Assimilation is another term that is almost the antithesis of acculturation. While acculturation involves first-hand contact and two-way interaction, assimilation does not as it is uni-dimensional (Ozer, 2017; Safak-Ayvazoglu et al., 2020; Sam & Berry, 2010). What is assimilation? Assimilation is the process by which newcomers are expected to adapt to the mainstream culture of a locale or country by learning their language, eating their foods and "Doing What the Romans Do" (Brown & Bean, 2006; Sam & Berry, 2010; Simmons, 2016). Assimilation is a reality that occurs in many nations, even those that claim to be "multicultural," e.g., South Korea (Simmons, 2016). According to the Migration Policy Institute, assimilation is the process of "integration or incorporation" (p. 1). Other terms that may come up are biculturalism, globalization, integration, and multiculturalism.

Biculturalism describes the phenomenon of one blending one's cultural heritage and even their "lived experiences" with the dominant culture (Huberty, n.d.). However, they are not forced to assimilate. They are not forced to deny themselves. Therefore, this process makes one less depressed, less anxious, more confident and maintains healthy familial relationships (Huberty, n.d.). In contrast, assimilation would have led to one denying themselves and hiding aspects of their culture or hiding their culture altogether to reduce "cultural conflict" (Huberty, n.d.). Globalization is defined as (Simmons, 2016). Integration is an integral term in acculturation theory. It means that one has decided to be a social participant in a host country in order to be accepted as an equal in said country (Sam & Berry, 2010).

Multiculturalism is a "theoretical, practical, and political framework that values cultural diversity" (Simmons, 2016, p. 15). In fact, in certain European countries, multiculturalism is [to] be defined as "an intersection where different ethnic groups maintain a distinct culture and identity (Power, 2011)" (Simmons, 2015, p. 16). In other words, while biculturalism looks at how one person tries to integrate their culture with another culture (Sam & Berry,

---

[1] Acculturative stress is defined as the changes that one goes through while moving between cultures A & B. It describes their simple shifts in behavior such as dressing, eating, listening for understanding, speaking, etc., which sometimes produces stress that is specifically related to the process of acculturation.

2010), multiculturalism can be a theory or a practice (Simmons, 2016). Within the theoretical component and/or framework, it is the concept that one or more cultures come together where various cultures learn about the host country and acquire language skills, education, etc. The host country also adapts to said cultures by learning about them (Simmons, 2016).

This chapter focuses on acculturating people and whether that process leads one to lose faith. While there is no proper definition of religion, there are definitions at one's disposal (Conroy, 2010). Religion focuses on having faith. While atheism describes one with no belief in God or any supernatural power, religion is the juxtaposition of that rendering (Oppy, 2021). According to Oppy (2021), "religion is the feelings, acts, and experiences of individual men in their solitude, so far as they apprehend themselves to stand in relation to whatever they may consider 'godlike' (p. 519)."

Acculturation

Portrayal of Acculturation

Acculturation is a term with many parts. It describes how the "other" (Simmons, 2016), i.e., persons such as asylum seekers, expatriates, immigrants, the indigenous population, other minority groups and sojourners, try to interact with the "main culture" and how the "main culture" interacts with them (Sam & Berry, 2010). It involves various components that could address cognitive activities, ethnic identities, integrating one's identity with the culture or addressing cultural expectations, etc. (Matera et al., 2020; Sam & Berry, 2010). Acculturation always involves at least two identities (Encyclopedia Britannica, 2020; Sam & Berry, 2010), but multiculturalism always examines two or more identities, usually many more (Simmons, 2016).

The Process of Acculturation

The process of acculturation takes a different direction than that of assimilation. Initially, assimilation was in fashion. Most European nations imposed their Anglo-Saxon values and expected conformity from minority groups as well as immigrant populations (Brown & Bean, 2006). As immigrants "emigrate" to European countries, myriad political and social implications ensued/ensue (Matera et al., 2020). However, assimilation involves integration where the immigrant population starts to resemble the population of the host societies (Brown & Bean, 2006). The immigrant population of the 1st generation tries to conform to the expectations of the "majority" (Brown & Bean, 2006). The second and third generations further conform, and by the third to fourth generation, the immigrant group or family is most likely fully assimilated (Brown & Bean, 2006).

How does this process of assimilation and parts of acculturation take place? One must learn the host country's language (Brown & Bean, 2006; Ozer, 2017; Simmons, 2016). For example, when the author received a scholarship from the Korea Society in 2022, she left the United States, moved to South Korea, and studied Korean. Through that language acquisition, the author could adapt to the host country's expectations. However, the difference in the process of assimilation and acculturation would be through the former; the author would have tried to be like the Koreans; in the former, the author was able to adjust herself without losing herself or her identity.

The next one tends to need to acquire some form of education. There tends to be a lag in earning even after immigrant groups and populations acquire education in the host country (Brown & Bean, 2006). There are also entry policies that when an abundance of immigrants is accepted into the host country, and most may be uneducated or unskilled, the competition for jobs becomes intensive, therefore offering less jobs (Brown & Bean, 2006). In addition, assimilation or certain forms thereof may be blocked (Brown & Bean, 2006). According to Brown & Bean (2006), "immigrants who become 'racialized' and are trusted as disadvantaged racial or ethnic minorities may find their pathways to economic mobility and assimilation blocked because of racial or ethnic discrimination" (p. 2). Regardless, several theories specifically discuss acculturation.

Assimilation Theories

First, there is "Classic Assimilation" (Brown & Bean, 2006). This term was coined in the 1920s by the Chicago School (Brown & Bean, 2006). This form of assimilation requires conformity (Brown & Bean, 2006). Thus, one will become more similar to the majority group rather than their immigrant group/population (Brown & Bean, 2006). There is also "First" Structural Assimilation, which requires close relationships with people from the host country (Brown & Bean, 2006). It also leads to intermarriage and ethnic identity with the host country (Brown & Bean, 2006). This acceptance leads to the immigrant being in a position of not facing prejudice or discrimination since they are considered to be with the "us"-es and not with the "thems" (Brown & Bean, 2006). Finally, there is New Assimilation. New Assimilation refers to groups, like religious groups, using their power and unity to force the host country to acquiesce (Brown & Bean, 2006).

The Racial/Ethnic Disadvantage Model describes assimilation as an unlikely segmented process. In other words, there is no straight line to assimilation (Brown & Bean, 2006). The first two to three generations may be very ethnic, and then one realizes the next generation is fully assimilated (Brown & Bean, 2006). Why? Probably because the language was learned automatically, they grew up in the host country and may have light ties to their original immigrant group. Nonetheless, assimilation has finally occurred within that family unit (Brown & Bean, 2006).

The Racial/Ethnic Disadvantage Model indicates that the process of complete assimilation cannot even be accomplished (Brown & Bean, 2006). Many times, the path to assimilation is blocked by the majority within the host country (Brown & Bean, 2006). Brown & Bean (2006) stated the following: "But in general, this literature, especially its more recent versions, argues that language and cultural familiarity may often not lead to increased assimilation. Lingering discrimination and institutional barriers to employment and other opportunities block complete assimilation" (p. 4). Regardless of how one assimilates, many immigrant groups who choose to do so lose something of themselves. This is not the case when one chooses or naturally evolves via the path of acculturation.

Acculturation Theories

When it comes to assimilation, three main theories may resemble some aspects of acculturation but do not. In contrast, one leading theory discussed is the Acculturation Theory based on the Acculturation Model (Ozer, 2017; Sam & Berry, 2010; University of Lincoln, 2022). This theory discusses the main components during the process of acculturating. Unlike assimilation, the person remains who they are but also adjusts to the host country for a healthier transition.

The Acculturation Model by Berry is a four-fold theory (Safak-Ayvazoglu et al., 2020; University of Lincoln, 2022). Berry created it (Sam & Berry, 2010; University of Lincoln, 2022). It contains four components that are utilized to explain acculturation (Ozer, 2017; University of Lincoln, 2022). These four components are as follows: assimilation (Brown & Bean, 2006; Huberty, n.d.; Ozer, 2017; Sam & Berry, 2010; Simmons, 2016; University of Lincoln, 2022), integration (Ozer, 2017; Sam & Berry, 2010; University of Lincoln, 2022), marginalization (Sam & Berry, 2010; University of Lincoln, 2011) and separation (Ozer, 2017; Sam & Berry, 2010; University of Lincoln, 2022). Assimilation describes one ability to conform to the majority culture (Sam & Berry, 2010; Simmons, 2016).

Integration is the process by which a social participant in a host country is accepted as an equal in said country (Ozer, 2017; Sam & Berry, 2010; University of Lincoln, 2022). Choosing one's culture and separating is juxtaposed with the concept of assimilation, where one's chooses the host country's culture as their new culture (Ozer, 2017). Marginalization is the process by which one cannot choose or act within the cultural heritage, assimilation, and is also not able to integrate (Ozer, 2017). Separation is also known as heritage culture or choosing one's heritage culture (Ozer, 2017). It is the act of living in one's space with people of one's culture (Ozer, 2017) (e.g., Chinatown, Little Italy).

There is also something called the ABCs of acculturation (Ozer, 2017; Sam & Berry, 2010). The ABCs of acculturation are as follows; 1) Affect, 2) Behavior, and 3) Cognition (Ozer, 2017). In this way, the person who acculturates has learned how to manage their emotions and emotional responses and how to adapt their behavior and think through problems, languages, etc. (Ozer, 2017; Sam & Berry, 2010; Simmons, 2016). Thus, factors such as age, educational background, ability to learn languages, ability to adapt to a new diet, etc., all affect the propensity to acculturate and how fully they acculturate (Ozer, 2017).

During the process of being a new immigrant, "international immigrants bring cultural traditions, languages, and values differing from those found in the cultural context of reception in their new home country" (Ozer, 2017, p. 1). The process of acculturating includes 'cultural shedding', where one starts to remove parts of their culture or not operate in them as fully (Ozer, 2017). There is cultural learning where they must learn about the new culture, its language and the nuisances associated with it (Ozer, 2017). There is also cultural conflict (Ozer, 2017), which often leads to stress (Brown & Bean, 2006; Ozer, 2017; Sam & Berry, 2010). The more intense the cultural stress is, the more the person undergoes both physiological and psychological stress (Ozer, 2017). Cultural distancing also occurs due to a lack of social support, prejudice, racism, et al. (Ozer, 2017).

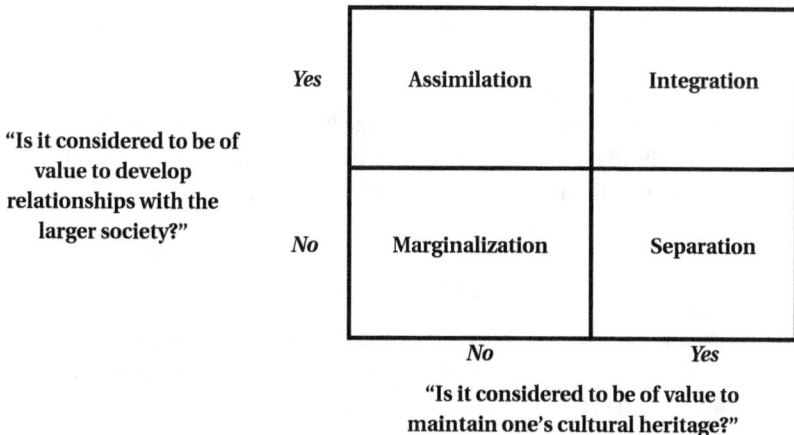

		No	*Yes*
"Is it considered to be of value to develop relationships with the larger society?"	*Yes*	Assimilation	Integration
	No	Marginalization	Separation

"Is it considered to be of value to maintain one's cultural heritage?"

Figure 10.1: Berry's Acculturation Model

The *Culture Learning Approach* (CLA) refers to the fact that new immigrants may lack the necessary skills to assimilate or acculturate (Sam & Berry, 2010). The CLA has two directions which include the following: "(a) an inquiry into socio-psychological aspects of intercultural encounters with a focus on communication styles and communication competence [...], and (b) an inquiry into cultural differences in communication styles, norms, and values in an effort to predict sociocultural adaptation" (p. 475). The main aspect of the process that must be overcome is language deficiencies (Sam & Berry, 2010). Thus, adequate social skills lead to or can at least assist with adequate or positive social interactions (Sam & Berry, 2010). Once acceptable social interactions occur, the person(s) will have an easier time acculturating to the host country (Sam & Berry, 2010). Regardless, these theories call for some form of adaptation (Sam & Berry, 2010). Immigrants and the host country must change how they interact with immigrant populations in order for all parties to live harmoniously. Language deficiencies are among the most significant barriers to acculturation or even assimilation.

Language Barriers

An issue that has been repeatedly addressed regarding immigrant populations is language acquisition or language barriers (Brown & Bean, 2006; Matera et al., 2020; Safak-Ayvazoglu et al., 2020; Sam & Berry, 2010; Simmons, 2016). Language barriers may also be barriers to formal education and/or skills training (Brown & Bean, 2006) outside of one's cultural group, etc. In fact, in reference to the CLA, immigrants who are trying to adapt to a society (Sam & Berry, 2010), lack the necessary skills to do so (Brown & Bean, 2006). Thus, language acquisition as well as learning about one's surroundings and the culture, are necessary to thrive and survive (Simmons, 2016). If not, they will not be able to engage in the new culture, making ordinary day-to-day interactions difficult (Sam & Berry, 2010). In fact, there is a direct relationship between one who has attained language fluency and being able to adapt socioculturally (Sam & Berry, 2010). Regardless, one area of the immigrant groups' personal life that is challenged is almost always their religion or the expression of their religion.

Losing My Religion

R.E.M. is a music group/band that published and sang a famous song titled "Losing My Religion." They published and performed this song live from Night on BBC Radio 1 in 1991 (AZ Lyrics.com, 2022). In part of the song, the words are as follows:

Consider this
Consider this, the hint of the century
Consider this, the slip
That brought me to my knees, failed
What if all these fantasies come
Flailing around
Now I've said too much

I thought that I heard you laughing
I thought that I heard you sing
I think I thought I saw you try

Perhaps, they are singing of a love relationship. However, I like to think that they are singing of a relationship that never transcends, which can be one's relationship with God or man. At some point, R.E.M. realizes that somewhere, a mistake occurs, and one must fall on their knees whether they are praying or crying. Nonetheless, the imagery in the author's head is always a person who is struggling to try to connect with the Creator.

The question the author poses is this – Is it necessary for those who are acculturating to give up their religion? In the process of assimilation, at least forced assimilation; this reality would be expected. However, when it comes to acculturating to a new country, how often do people lose their faith?

It has been shown that: "Continuing large-scale immigration from majority Muslim countries has transformed the religious landscape of historically Christian and increasingly secularized European societies" (Gungor et al., 2013, p. 203). One religious minority group that still struggles with assimilating and/or acculturating within Europe is Muslims (Celeste et al., 2016). It may be the case since Muslims and their religious faith, known as Islam, is incompatible with most Western values (Gungor et al., 2013). Unfortunately, for a long time, European psychologists have failed to research acculturation regarding religious dimensions and religions overall (Gungor et al., 2013). They often choose cultural heritage (Gungor et al., 2013; Sam & Berry, 2010; University of Lincoln, 2022).

According to Celeste et al. (2016), "[...] problems of some minority adolescents to *fit in* with their ethnically diverse peer groups may trigger peer rejection, with long-term consequences for their future development" (p. 544). These adolescents are easily identifiable because they are Muslims. They tend to be more resistant to changing their religion (Gungor et al., 2013). However, they also tend to be exposed to more diverse populations than their parents and/or grandparents (Celeste et al., 2016). They may often feel and experience 'public hostility' because they are Muslims in Europe, and specific to these adolescents' experiences, they may feel pressured to conform (Celeste et al., 2016).

Specific to this study, the Muslim students were Turkish and Moroccan (Celeste et al., 2016; Gungor et al., 2013). Within Flanders, Belgium, Muslims are "the most disadvantaged and devalued immigrant population" (p. 548). Due to Belgium's 'super-diversity', the threat that many Muslims face vanishes once they adopt the mainstream culture (Celeste et al., 2016). In most cases, this adoption leads to acculturation rather than assimilation, as Muslims are a distinct population. For Muslims in Flanders, the reaction is usually to choose cultural heritage (University of Lincoln, 2022) which follows the path of separate or assimilation (Celeste et al., 2016). Those who choose to reject the imposition of concepts and realities like the New Atheism (Lynch & Dahanayake, 2018) most likely separate Celeste et al., 2016; Lynch & Dahanayake, 2018; Sam & Berry, 2010. In fact, among researchers, the issue of Turkish Muslims and other types of Muslims has been that one the immigrants were identified as being Muslim and continued to worship Allah as their God; they were rejected by the majority group (i.e., the Dutch), according to Verkuyten & Yildiz (2007).

For Muslims who have moved to the Netherlands from Syria, other factors exist to consider (Safak-Ayvazoglu et al., 2020). Civil war continues to brew within Syria, forcing approximately 5.6 million Syrians to flee from 2011-2017 (Safak-Ayvazoglu et al., 2020). 937,718 applied for asylum throughout Europe, and only 590/2956 were granted refugee status (Safak-Ayvazoglu et al., 2020). 3.5 million in Turkey and 2 million in Lebanon (Safak-Ayvazoglu et al., 2020). Many of them suffer as they are newly exhausted in their host country, they have and continue to experience trauma, there is overcrowding at refugee camps, and they are unable to study or work while they wait for the asylum process to end, which usually lasts two (2) years (Safak-Ayvazoglu et al., 2020).

Safak-Ayvazoglu et al. (2020) stated the following: "Among all the immigrant groups, they found that legally disadvantaged immigrants diverge from the mainstream the most" (p. 558). Many of these immigrants from Syria felt rejected while they were socially distanced through this process. They also acculturated less (Safak-Ayvazoglu et al., 2020). Due to the perceived distance between their culture and the Netherlands, the refugee's acculturation process was negatively affected (Safak-Ayvazoglu et al., 2020). Regarding acculturative stress, these Muslims face the most stress from their religious identity (Safak-Ayvazoglu et al., 2020). In addition, they still felt stressed from trying to maintain a communal way of life like in Syria, language acquisition and cultural adaptation (Safak-Ayvazoglu et al., 2020).

In their study, Group 1 had one Syrian Christian and 14 Muslims (Safak-Ayvazoglu et al., 2020). By the end of the study, 3/15 had rejected their religion to fit in (Safak-Ayvazoglu et al., 2020). In group 2, the participants of the study increased their social interactions with the host country, promoted cultural exchange as a solution and learned Dutch (Safak-Ayvazoglu et al., 2020). In Group 3, the participants actively sought recognition (Safak-Ayvazoglu et al., 2020). They worked at actively sharing who they were and emphasizing similarities rather than differences (Safak-Ayvazoglu et al., 2020). It appeared that Group 2 and Group 3 did better at acculturating to the Netherlands and finding some form of acceptance by the Dutch (Safak-Ayvazoglu et al., 2020).

Like Safak-Ayvazoglu et al. (2020), the acculturation process of Muslims in Italy was compared to those in Sweden (Matera et al., 2020). It was found that Italians found Muslims to be less threatening if they went along and became more like the majority group in their host country (Matera et al., 2020). In 2015, Swedish-Italian immigrants were much more accepting or Muslim immigrants than full-blooded Italian (Matera et al., 2020). Indeed, 25% of Italian Muslims were discriminated against because they were Muslim, as opposed to 16% of Muslims who resided in Sweden (Matera et al., 2020). Ironically, while Muslim immigrants were appreciated for assimilating, Arab Christians were not (Matera et al., 2020).

Discussion

It is clear that assimilation and acculturation are two sides of the same coin. On the head of that coin, one is asked to just "become" like us. On the tail of that coin, one is asked to consider becoming a bit like "us", so it is easier for us to understand who you are and grow together. According to the author, acculturation and/or multiculturalism is the preferred method of receiving immigrant populations and maintaining the mainstream culture (Simmons, 2016). For example, Muslim populations that enter the United States of America should be embraced, allowed to worship freely, build mosques, etc. However, Sharia law, as was attempted in Texas (CBN News, 2017), should never be a reality or America would cease to exist.

Regarding losing one's religion, the author would like to point out that Celeste et al. (2016) may have confused the term assimilation with acculturation. Moreover, it should be noted as a side note that often, those labeled as Muslim terrorists may have been terrorized by the majority group or host country and then chose cultural heritage and some form of recompense rather than losing their identity. It has been noted that the "New Atheism" does not just proscribe that Atheists should continue not to believe in God but that people who believe in God, such as Jews, Christians, and

Muslims (i.e., monotheists), must be rid of their foolish beliefs in God (Lynch & Dahanayake, 2018).

Unfortunately, refugees and asylum seekers are sometimes advertently or inadvertently asked to change who they are, live in safer surroundings, or find a better way of life. It is time that academicians, government officials and non-profit leaders truly examine what the process of immigration and acculturation should look like. To merely ask someone to give up who they are to become a citizen when many of these nations, for instance, the United States of America, fought to be able to worship freely and not be constricted by the Church of England is laudable and laughable. The one thing people should be able to have outside of the freedom to speak their mind is the freedom to worship the Creator according to their religious beliefs as long as they are not committing a crime based on the principle of just laws. Alternatively, else we will all be losing "our" religion.

Conclusion

In conclusion, immigrants continue to move to new countries of origin. In the case of the war in Ukraine, the world continues to watch Ukrainians being moved to countries like Poland, Britain, etc., as asylum seekers. As they report the human rights offences that have occurred and their needs to organizations such as Chosen People's Ministries (https://www.chosenpeople.com/), the author wonders if anyone checks to see if they are emotionally and socially and intellectually ready to adapt to the new country and culture they have found themselves placed within or forced to live within. Wars search for new work and environments often find various immigrant communities represented as the minority in their new host country and a struggling minority at that (Pflum, 2022).

Further Recommendations

Further research needs to be completed regarding the effects of assimilation and acculturation on one's faith system. It would be interesting for someone to complete a longitudinal study with cross-sections of cultures and faith representations (e.g., Judaism, Christianity, Islam, etc.). In addition, it would be interesting to see the results of a quantitative or mixed-methods research design. As previously noted, religious dimensions have mostly been left out of the discussion(s) of assimilation and acculturation.

Moreover, while the focus of the last decade to two decades is overwhelmingly colored on studying Muslims who have moved to a new host country, the author suggests examining other groups. For example, due to the war in Ukraine, which has many Christians, it would be a good idea to study how they acculturate to countries like America, Israel, Poland, etc. Is their experience different because of their religious identification as Christians?[2] Are they more accepted into countries that are majority Jewish or Christian? These are questions that need to be answered in the future. If there is a huge difference, then host countries must consider how they treat Muslims and how they believe a "stranger" should be treated once they meet a strange land.

References

AZ Lyrics (2022). *Losing my religion.* Retrieved on May 24, 2022 from https:// www.azlyrics.com/lyrics/rem/losingmyreligion.html

Brown, S.K. & Bean, F.D. (2006, October 1). *Assimilation models, old and new: Explaining in long-term process.* Retrieved on May 24, 2022 from https://www. migrationpolicy.org/article/assimilation-models-old-and-new-explaining-long-term-process/#:~:text=Assimilation%20Models%2C%20Old%20and%20 New%3A%20Explaining%20a%20Long-Term,and%20host%20societies%20 come%20to%20resemble%20one%20another/

CBN News. (2017). *Texas gov signs off on bill to keep sharia law out of courts.* Retrieved on May 25, 2022 from https://www1.cbn.com/cbnnews/us/2017/ june/texas-gov-signs-off-on-bill-to-keep-sharia-law-out-of-courts

Celeste, L., Meeussen, C., Verschueren, K. & Phalet, K. (2016). Minority acculturation and peer rejection: Costs of acculturation misfit with peer-group norms. *British Journal of Social Psychology, 55,* 544-563.

Conroy, M. (2010). Defining religion. *Teaching theology and religion. 13*(2), 137.

Encyclopedia Britannica, Inc. (2022). *Acculturation.* Retrieved on May 23, 2022 from https://academic-eb-com.ezproxy.liberty.edu/levels/collegiate/article/ acculturation/3494.

Gungor, P., Fleischmann, F., Phalet, K., & Maliepaard, M. (2013). Contextualizing religious acculturation: Cross-cultural perspectives on Muslim minorities in Western Europe. *European Psychologist, 18*(3), 203-214. https://doi.org/10.102 7/1016-9040/a000162

Huberty, E.S. (n.d.). *What is cultural assimilation?* Retrieved on May 24, 2022 from https://www.humanrightscareers.com/issues/what-is-cultural-assimilation

Lynch, T. & Dahanayake, N. (2018). Guilt, enculturation and religion: Response to Cordner. *Philosophical Investigations, 41*(1), 104-108. https://doi.org/10.111 1/phin.12176

Matera, C., Picchiarini, A., Olsson, M., & Brown, R. (2020). Does religion matter? Italians' responses towards Muslim and Christian Arab immigrants as a function of their acculturative preferences. *International Journal of Intercultural Relations, 75,* 1-9.

Oppy, G. (2021). Defining 'religion' and 'atheism.' *Sophia, 60,* 517-529. https://doi .org/10.1007/s11841-021-00543-2

---

[2] 100,000 Ukrainians can resettle in the United States under the Department of Homeland's Security program (Pflum, 2022).

Ozer, S. (2017). Psychological theories of acculturation. *The International Encyclopedia of Intercultural Communications*, 1-14. https://doi.org/10.100 2/9781118783665

Pflum, M. (2022). *Americans hosting Ukrainian encounter 'unbelievably difficult' process.* Retrieved on May 25, 2022 from https://www.nbcnews.com/ news/world/americans-hosting-ukrainian-refugees-encounter-unbelievably -difficult-rcna29580

Safak-Ayvazoglu, A., Kunuroglu, F., Van De Vijver, F. & Yagmur, K. (2020). Acculturation of Syrian refugees in the Netherlands: Religion as social identity and boundary marker. *Journal of Refugee Studies, 34*(1), 555-578. https://doi. org/10.1093/jrs/feaa020

Sam, D. L., & Berry, J. W. (2010). Acculturation: When Individuals and Groups of Different Cultural Backgrounds Meet. *Perspectives on Psychological Science: A Journal of the Association for Psychological Science, 5*(4), 472–481. https://doi. org/10.1177/1745691610373075

Simmons, J.C. (2016). Multicultural leadership characteristics of a school director in an educational setting in South Korea: A case study. *Doctoral Dissertation.* Available from ProQuest Dissertations and Theses (UMI No. 1292).

University of Lincoln. (2022). *Working in a cross cultural team.* Retrieved on May 24, 2022 from https://crossculturalteamsatdublinbus.blogs.lincoln.ac. uk/berrys-model-of-acculturation/

Chapter 11

Culture and Its Influence on Peoples' Behavior towards Education of Persons with Disabilities in Nigeria

Odirin Omiegbe
University of Delta, Agbor, Nigeria

Abstract: Persons with disabilities require special (adapted, modified) education to learn with ease and develop their innate abilities and potentials. Unfortunately, some cultural and religious practices hinder them from benefitting from special education. This chapter found out that some of these cultural and religious practices are deeply rooted in superstition in Nigeria. They make persons with disabilities more vulnerable, not enrolling in school, not attending school, or dropping out of school. Such cultural and religious practices include killing some of them for rituals, sending them to beg for alms, initiation from childhood to adulthood, circumcision, and early marriage. The chapter suggests that to put a stop to such barbaric cultural and religious practices which impede the education of persons with disabilities; awareness should be made among the citizens on the need to put a stop to such practices, laws should be passed, and violators of such laws should be prosecuted and sentenced accordingly amongst others.

Keywords: Culture, Religion, Superstition, Influence, Behavior, Persons with disabilities, Nigeria

***

Introduction

Government, governmental agencies, non-governmental agencies, and educational institutions worldwide devote massive sums of money to provide educational infrastructure, equipment, teaching aids, and manpower, train teachers, and conduct research to improve teaching competence. In addition, they ensure that all citizens are given access to the conventional educational provision. Unfortunately, some groups of persons cannot benefit from such conventional educational provisions. They require special education, which is "formal special education training given to people (children and adults) with special needs" (Federal Republic of Nigeria, 2014). This group of persons includes the hearing, speech, visual, physical and health impaired, intellectually retarded, emotionally disturbed, learning disabled, gifted and talented. Using related statistics of the WHO (2011) that 15% of any given population has a disability, then (given its estimated population of about 185 million) one may suppose that the total figure of persons with disabilities in Nigeria should be around 27 million (Etieyibo & Omiegbe, 2017). The Nigerian Government came up with educational policies, built and equipped schools to cater to the needs of persons with special needs and signed into law the Discrimination against Persons with Disabilities (Prohibition) ACT in January 2019 to cater for the rights and welfare of persons with disabilities. Its effort at ensuring the education of persons with disabilities through formal special education training is indeed laudable. However, one may rightly ask: Are these policies being met? Are all persons with disabilities enrolled in schools? Are there factors that hinder these policies from being achieved? These questions provide the basis for examining patterns of behaviors, and how culture influences those behaviors towards their education. Therefore, this chapter aims to succinctly peruse cultural practice as an impediment to the education of persons with disabilities and as a conceptual framework for the practical improvement of special education in Nigeria. Following the completion of this chapter, the reader will be able to (a) explain the conceptual background of the effect of cultural beliefs on the education of persons with disabilities, (b) identify some cultural beliefs that impede special education in Nigeria, (c) tell how these impediments of special education for persons with disabilities can be eliminated to make them benefit from education in Nigeria.

Cultural Beliefs and Conceptual Frameworks

Culture, Religion and Superstition

The term *'culture'* has various meanings; however, for this topic, it will be taken to mean a set of shared attitudes, beliefs, values, goals and practices that characterize an institution, an organization, or a group (Uwagie-Ero et al., 1998). Culture is shared and passed from parents to children or from one generation to another (Eboh & Ukpong, 1995). *'Religion'* can be said to be part of the culture and may be defined as a belief in the existence of a deity or a supernatural power, a being that created and controls the universe and who is worshipped based on such belief. *'Superstition'* can be taken to mean a belief or way of behaving based on fear of the unknown or the belief that certain events or things will bring good or bad luck. This understanding of 'superstition' takes superstition as an aspect of culture (Etieyibo & Omiegbe, 2016). *Attitude* is defined as "the opinions and feelings somebody has about something or someone shown in behavior" (Longman, 2009). It is the way someone behaves towards others which could be good, bad, positive, negative, friendly, or aggressive (hostile) (Hornby, 2015).

Conceptual Frameworks

Framework 1

No matter how *civilized;* every society has some beliefs handed down from generation to generation. They affect their attitude toward certain persons or things or even their philosophy of life. For instance, some Americans strongly believe that the number 13 (thirteen) is associated with bad luck, so is the black cat in Britain and they avoid them in each case. Thus in America, it can be noticed in the lifts (elevators) in some high-rise apartment buildings that floor 13 is deliberately omitted. One can see floor 12, and the next, floor 13, will have the floor 14 written on it. Sometimes, some Britons will return to their homes if a black cat crosses the road in front of their cars in the morning. This belief of avoiding whatever is associated with evil has, from history, affected people's attitude toward persons with disabilities simply because handicapping conditions were associated with evil. In the past, children with disabilities were thrown away to avoid them. Many a time, these children died, but at other times, they survived and roamed the forest like wild animals. An example of this is the wild boy of Aveyron, who was picked up in the forest by hunters in Aveyron, France, in 1798. Jean-Marc Gaspard Itard tried unsuccessfully to educate the boy but found out that he was severely retarded and could not be educated. Even though he failed, his attempt laid the foundation for the education of the intellectually retarded. In the old testament of the Bible, persons with disabilities were considered an abomination, and they were prohibited from becoming priests or even coming near the altar of God. In medieval times, persons with disabilities, when they were not destroyed or isolated, were used as jesters or "fools" to entertain in the courts of kings. The above examples show that out of ignorance or fear, people tend to avoid anything associated with evil, including persons with disabilities. The same belief is prevalent in this country (Nigeria). Even though they are no longer destroyed, the birth of a child with disabilities in the family brings with it depression, sadness and often a sense of guilt. In Nigeria today, the mystery surrounding the birth of a child with disabilities has been attributed to many factors such as punishment for sin committed (Abosi & Ozoji, 1985), the will of God and supernatural powers (Obani, 1984). Because of these beliefs, the birth of a child with disabilities into a family brings mixed feelings. This feeling may lead to rejection of the child or over-protection. When the latter prevails, the parents are reluctant to send the child to a special school or seek an educational program; instead, they prefer keeping him at home (Ekeleme, 1987).

Framework 2

A proper understanding of blindness can only be achieved by critically examining the dynamic forces that interlace the traditional Nigerian community. This community constitutes the unit base of the people who mass return to the community from urban centers and at times, from overseas during major traditional, Christian or Muslim festivals, such as New Yam festivals, Christmas, and Sallah, respectively. They demonstrate their unshakable attachment to the ideals of the community life, norms, folklores, local language, and beliefs which are binding on all irrespective of their acquired Western education or religious sophistication. These forces constitute the lifeblood of the community, and in this important dimension, customs die hard. It is actually because, despite the effects of civilization and scientific and technological breakthroughs, the average Nigerian treasures in his subconscious mind the rich gems of traditional norms and beliefs, which by stealth control his perception of a blind person. No matter what literature is available in the field of visual handicaps, he glibly accepts its "gospel" (teaching), but down in his intrinsic being, the traditional beliefs about blindness enjoy an unchallenged spell that unwittingly impinges on the acquired knowledge about visual handicaps (Abosi & Ozoji, 1985).

This analysis pattern comes close to Sigmund Freud's (1856-1939) psychoanalysis of 'consciousness' and 'unconsciousness' where the latter imperiously and insidiously determine how the former is to express itself. Just as Freud and, to some extent, neo-Freudians believe that the conscious cannot be fully understood except a thorough x-ray of the unconscious is undertaken, so also must we examine the tenets of traditional life and its attitudes if we are to understand and appreciate our people's (Nigerians) conceptualization of the visually impaired. However, being helplessly caught in such an unfortunate dilemma does not prevent Nigerians from taking and maintaining a positive and definite stand in conceptualizing blindness. The traditional religion appears to be the source of those forces held dear because, as Mbiti (1975) rightly points out:

> African Traditional Religion, apart from being the richest part of the African heritage, is also closely bound up with the traditional way of life. This way of life became primordially articulated in personal idioms, folklores, myths, and beliefs as our forefathers responded to

the inexplicable interventions in their lives. Such views thus became sacred sanctions which were religiously preserved and even furthered to enhance their sanctity as they passed down through the memories from one generation to another (Abosi & Ozoji, 1985).

As handed down to us in their totality, these views constitute the tenets of the traditional systems of thought that some scholars have aptly labelled *magico-religions*. This point aims to examine these systems of thought vis-à-vis their explanation of blindness in Nigeria. Therefore, blindness represents one of those examples of a typical physique that Nigerians have as a traditional means of explaining away beliefs. Such explanations do not consider the white man's views. The differential tenets of both western and traditional systems of thought have been noted by Nduka (1974) that "... African society does not have this reflective and critical thinking (when compared with the open and scientifically oriented societies of the West). It developed a wide variety of philosophies, but failed to develop critical philosophy. Deviation from norms based on these philosophies is severely frowned at." He emphasized the differentiating role of generating alternatives which the traditional system lacks, when he asserts that:

> Science is the knowledge obtained through observation and experimentation and subjected to epistemological refinement. Because Africans frown at questioning what is traditional, they have operated a system of thoughts whose epistemological underpinning has been largely religious and mystical for centuries. In such a system, knowledge is obtained from insight into reality directed by the sanctions of religion and custom. The paucity of such knowledge vis-a-vis a discourse and analytic knowledge is as evident as the technological difference between traditional and industrial society.

This exposition has undoubtedly dual advantages. Firstly, it shall attempt to lay bare the sources of our people's (Africans) conception and explanation of blindness. Secondly, its analysis shall also identify those sources that are indeed spurious in the sense of having no logical foundation which qualifies them to be tagged superstitions. It shall be observed shortly that most of these beliefs hinge essentially on the illogical principles of causation that connect issues also on their illogical implications (Nduka, 1974). A mind that has cultivated a wealth of scientific and empirical investigation tools will undoubtedly find most of them as a bunch of nonsensical thought of the *primitive* mind that stand in sharp contrast to the Western System of mechanically oriented thoughts. However, traditional explanations on disabilities are as follows (Abosi & Ozoji, 1985):

1. God-mediated beliefs: Among the Nupe and Hausa communities, it is strongly believed that God blinds some people out of likeness so that they do not see any evil thing.

2. Supersensible forces:

   - Evil spirits: Among the Tivs, blindness is caused by *Mbatsav*, i.e., the unseen evil spirits who use their power to reward the parents for their evil deeds by giving birth to a blind child.

   - Magic: In Kagoro (Kaduna), if a beautiful woman consistently gives birth to blind children, then an ugly woman has spoiled the eggs in her womb.

   - Witchcraft: The belief in witchcraft is focused on the assumption that "spirits of living human beings can be sent out of the body on errands to do havoc to other persons in body, mind or estate" (Idowu, 1976).

   - Juju: In some parts of Kaduna state, for instance, if a pregnant woman sees a masquerade and refuses to confess or offer sacrifice, she would give birth to a blind child.

3. Socio-cultural Explanation

   - Destiny: Some Nigerians have been found to believe strongly that a blind person is destined to be so right from the foundation of the world.

   - Mockery: Practically all over Nigeria, it is strongly believed that a blind man should never be laughed at or mocked. The belief is that the condition could be reversed. In Benin, it was once told that one 'Agbedo' caused a ten-year-old boy to continue laughing because the boy laughed at his disability.

   - Rudeness: Rudeness to elders is believed to cause blindness. It is also believed that a pregnant woman who refuses kindness to an old man could be visited when the old man dies as a sign of punishment.

4. Sex-linked Factors: Among the Ibos, it is believed that having sex with a cow is punishable by the gods of the land, with a type of disability by "Ala", the goddess of virginity and truthfulness. However, if anyone sees them and conceals the incidence, he/she will be blind instantly.

5. Prophylactic: " It is believed that a person is blinded to save the whole community from her nefarious activities through divine providence. This belief is common among the Tivs.

6. Environmental Causations: Among some tribes in Nigeria, notably Nupe, Margi (Bornu State) and Tivs, it is believed that hot smoke from

urine is hazardous to the eyes. The practice among these people is to look away when they are urinating to avoid being blind.

7. **Folklores and Myths:** Among the Manpun (Plateau State), if a visually impaired walks about freely, it is generally believed that he exchanged his own eyes with those of evil spirits.

8. In Nigeria, studies on beliefs about disabilities include: a curse from God, ancestral violations of societal norms, offenses against the gods of the land, breaking laws, family sin, adultery, misfortune, witches and wizards, among others (Eskay et al., 2012).

It is pertinent to state that most of these explanations on traditional causes of disabilities have no scientific basis to hold on to and in spite of that; some Nigerians use them as focal point for evaluating persons with disabilities. No wonder then that most of these attitudes are either neutral or negative in context (Abosi & Ozoji, 1985).

Cultural and Religious Practices that Impede the Education of Persons with Disabilities in Nigeria

Cultural and religious practices which have been identified to affect school enrolment and regular school attendance of children with disabilities in Nigeria are as follows:

Killing of Persons with Disabilities

Some groups of persons with disabilities (*Mental Illness, Emotional Disturbance and Intellectual Retardation*) are killed due to superstitious beliefs, thereby interfering with their school enrolment and attendance. Persons with mental illness, emotional disturbance and intellectual retardation are sometimes killed for ritual purposes, and others are labelled as witches or wizards and are lynched to death (Omiegbe, 1998, 2001; Houreld, 2009; Oko, 2003) **and children with disabilities are significantly affected** (CIMPRIC & UNICEF, 2010) [Emphasis mine]. Persons with disability and their families have often suffered social isolation, discrimination and, in the most extreme cases, violence and death due to such widely-held folk beliefs (Groce, 2005; Betterbe et al., 2010; Human Rights Watch, 2012). The exact number of victims of such abuses is unknown and is widely believed to be underreported (McVeigh, 2014; Evans, 2015). Children with physical disability or deformity, mental disability and recurring illnesses are often believed to be agents of evil spirits and are accused of witchcraft (Omunukuma, 2010; Isioma, 2019). Foxcraft (2009) reports that in Nigeria, "Children who have some forms of disabilities or unique character traits such as erratic behavior, bedwetting or epilepsy are especially vulnerable to witchcraft accusations". Those most vulnerable, including children with autism and people with mental illness, are targets, and reports of witchcraft accusations, particularly against individuals with mental illnesses, are increasing (Sleap, 2011).

Oculocutaneous Albinism (Coloring [Pigmentation] of the Skin, Hair and Eyes)

In some African countries, it is believed that body parts of persons with albinism make potent charms that can make people rich and successful (Thuku, 2011). The Independent Expert on the enjoyment of human rights by persons with albinism has received hundreds of reports of persons with albinism who have been targeted or attacked in many parts of Africa, under the belief that certain body parts of a person with albinism can be used, through rituals or traditional medicine, to *induce various benefits, commonly wealth, good luck and political success.* Ntinda (2011) posits that "many beliefs and superstitions surround albinism. In some other parts of Africa, people with albinism are killed for their parts to be used in making fetish potions which the witchdoctors allegedly advise their clients to drink to obtain wealth". Okoro (1975) also noted that:

> Albino children are seldom treasured as other children because the inherent delicacy of albinos is well known. It is gathered that some Nigerians, especially the Yoruba ethnic group, think that body parts of persons living with albinism make potent love portions and charms that can make people rich and successful. Albinism is associated with a lot of myths and beliefs in some Nigerian societies, especially in the Yoruba ethnic group. These beliefs have led to **negative behavior** towards people living with albinism. An investigation by Leadership reveals that Nigerians living with albinism suffer discrimination from their families, schoolmates and peers. **Many people with albinism drop out from school** partly because of uncorrected refractory errors and partly because of discouragement. [Emphasis Mine]

Some families even commit infanticide on babies born with albinism (Adenekan, 2019). In Tanzania, miners use the bones of persons with albinism as amulets or bury them where they are drilling for gold (Human Rights Council, 2011) for luck and protection, while fishers weave the hair of persons with albinism into their nets to improve their catches. These beliefs expose persons with albinism to violent physical attacks and mutilation. It was adumbrated in the Human Rights Report that the superstitions, erroneous beliefs, and myths put the security and lives of persons with albinism at constant risk. Other frequent myths that threaten the life and physical integrity of persons with albinism include: that sexual intercourse with a woman or a girl with albinism can cure HIV/AIDS—'such a myth has led to some women with the condition being raped' (Setume, 2016); that the sacrifice of persons with albinism can appease "the god of the mountain" when a volcano starts to erupt; or that pulling out the hair of a person with albinism brings good luck. The effect of these beliefs on persons with albinism is constant violent attacks on them, such as ritual attacks, trafficking in persons and sale of children, infanticide, and abandonment of children (Adelakun & Ajayi, 2020). Adenekan (2019), in a study on albinos among the Yoruba ethnic group in Nigeria, asserts that:

> The result of this study corroborates with the report of New Telegraph in an interview of the highest-ranking chief in the town, Chief Isaac Olawale Adegboye, the Oluoye of Ibule-Soro, who said that the people are generally hospitable but not to albinos because of Jooro River which usually kills albino who comes into the town. It is also in line with the report of the Priest of the River, Chief James Jayeoba, who said that the present residents of the town should not be blamed for the taboo as the history of the town predates many of them. They both claimed that the presence of an albino in the town would infuriate the river goddess who would flood the entire town, destroy lives and property until the albino is killed. According to the Priest, their forefathers told them that if they brought an albino near the town, the river would turn into an ocean and wash away all the inhabitants of the town.

OHCHR (2013) [Office of the United Nations High Commissioner for Human Rights], in a preliminary report on the attacks and discrimination against persons with albinism submitted under Human Rights Council Resolution 23/13 of 13 June 2013, asserts that:

- In some communities, erroneous beliefs and myths influenced by superstition put the security and life of persons with albinism at risk.

- OHCHR has received information from various countries on cases of killings and dismembering of persons with albinism for ritual purposes.

- It has also collected information on the multiple and intersecting forms of discrimination against persons with albinism face worldwide.

The report recorded over 200 cases of ritual attacks against persons with albinism in 15 countries between 2000 and 2013. It is not to say that all the cases of ritual attacks were reported. It was reported that ritual killings were always on the rise shortly before and during elections, so persons with albinism were at greater risk during this period. The killing, attacks, mutilation, trafficking, and exclusion of persons with albinism violate their right to life, dignity, security, and freedom from discrimination, to mention just a few, as enshrined in the constitutions of most countries and most international Human Rights Instruments. The attacks on persons with albinism seem to be on the rise due to the high demand for the body parts of persons with albinism, which appears to be sustained by the high prices that some are willing to pay to obtain them. In its resolution 23/13, the Human Rights Council expressed concern about the impunity associated with attacks against persons with albinism; access by persons with albinism to justice, remedies and redress are extremely limited in that persons with albinism face significant difficulties in having their cases brought to justice for the following reasons: the fear of further attacks, reprisals or further stigmatization; difficulties in finding witnesses owing to the seclusion they face within their community and frequently, the involvement of family and community members in the hostilities; the ignorance of legal rights; poverty; the inadequate capacity of the judicial system to address such cases; the lack of legal aid and adequate legal representation; and the lack of knowledge of or confidence in the law enforcement agencies and the judiciary (Adelakun & Ajayi, 2020).

Cases of Violent Attack on Albinos in Nigeria

United Nations (28 July 2021) in a report with the heading "Witchcraft killings of People with Albinism Rose During Pandemic – UN Expert" notes that "killings of people with albinism have increased during the COVID-19 pandemic, as some people who were plunged into poverty due to the pandemic; turned to witchcraft with the hope of gaining quick wealth". However, the following are reported cases of the violent attack on albinos in Nigeria: Two cases of killing an albino came to limelight in South-South Nigeria. In Ugbogui village, a remote farm settlement in the Edo State of Nigeria, a person with albinism was beheaded while working on the farm. Similarly, another person was killed while working on his farm in Abraka Urhuoka Quarter in the Abraka community in Delta State, Nigeria. When he was found, some parts of his body were missing (Nigerian Tribune, 2011). Also, ANSA (2020), an online blog with the heading "*Joy, a Refugee with Albinism Fights against Discrimination*", narrates the case of Joy as follows:

> I was kidnapped because I'm albino. I wasn't the one who decided to leave my country; I was kidnapped. In Nigeria, there are people who believe that sacrificing a person with albinism can bring wealth. There has always been this discrimination against people with albinism; they are considered people who bring bad luck. I think people don't understand albinism, and they exclude and discriminate people with albinism. Due to superstition, I was kidnapped and taken from my

home in Nigeria, but then I managed to escape from the kidnappers, and I ended up with human traffickers, men who sell women. These people took me to Libya and sold me to other groups of human traffickers. I was with them for two months, together with other women, and then they decided to let us all go one day. I stayed there for a week, and then I was transferred to Trento, where I received accommodation and requested asylum. It is **difficult** for people with albinism to **attend university in Nigeria** without protection from their parents or siblings; there's always the fear of not knowing what can happen to them [Emphasis Mine].

Angular Kyphosis (Disjointed Spinal Cord; Hunchback)

People with angular kyphosis (disjointed spinal cord; hunchback) are mostly killed for rituals (Omiegbe, 2001). It is believed that body parts of persons with spina bifida (protruded or disjointed spinal cord) make potent charms that can make people rich and successful (Thuku, 2011). There are reports in the local media which suggest that the trafficking of people with this condition is not uncommon.

Cases of Violent Attack on People with Angular Kyphosis in Nigeria

The following are reported cases of violent attacks on people with angular kyphosis in Nigeria: the killing of a famous herbalist, a male angular kyphosis sufferer, in Benin City, Edo State, Nigeria (Omiegbe 2001); the killing of a 22-year-old female angular kyphosis sufferer, Taibat Oseni, in Osun State, implicated a Nigerian senator. According to the Osun State Police Command, Oseni was kidnapped from her home and then taken to a 15-year-old abandoned building owned by a senator, where she was killed and her protrusion removed (Dike 2009; Kolawole 2009); and in 2002, the Nigeria police arrested a man in Ikot-Akpan Abia, Akwa-Ibom State, who mainly traded in parts of people with angular kyphosis and had been in the business for more than a decade. In his confession, he claimed that he sold the parts to herbalists and medical practitioners for rituals and that the kidnapping of people with angular kyphosis is widespread. A person with angular kyphosis attracts the sum of N400 000 (US$2100) (Nkanga, 2002). In the heading '*Ritual Killing and Hunchback in Nigeria*', Igwe (2012) of Sahara Reporters cited a case of the killing of a woman with angular kyphosis in Nigeria and report that "a court in Southern Nigeria remanded in custody four persons for allegedly killing a hunchback woman, Mrs Ifeoma Angela Igwe, for ritual purposes. The hoodlums went to the woman's house, kidnapped and took her to a nearby bush where they beheaded and butchered her, and later removed the hunch.

The hunch is believed to contain a 'magical substance or mercury' that can make people rich".

Akinloye (December 21, 2014) in Sunday Punch Nigerian Newspaper with the heading "Nigerian Hunchbacks: 'People See us as Money Making Machines' notes that *The fear of being kidnapped for money rituals is greater than the shame of being a hunchback. Hunchbacks have become endangered species in Nigeria and reports that* "Mr Adeoye Dowo, 22 years old, was lured by his female friend into a bush at Ago Alaye, a village in Odigbo Local Government Area in Ondo State, Nigeria, strangulated and his hump removed by three men". Ebegbulem (February 18, 2017) in Vanguard Nigerian Newspaper with the headline "Horror: 62-year-old Man with Hunchback Murdered in Edo" reports that "It was a tragic end for 62-year-old farmer identified as Mr Olomu, from Orhue community in the Owan West Local Government Area of Edo State, who was murdered last week, after which his hunchback was severed from his body. The deceased reportedly hired some people to work on his farm, but unknown to him, the labourers had been planning for three months earlier to kill him so they can severe his hunchback and use it for money making rituals". Jannah (April 23, 2019) in Daily Post Nigerian Newspaper with the heading *Ritualists kill Hunchback Woman, Pay Son N7 M* reported that:

> Detectives from Ondo State Police Command are on the trail of suspected ritualists who killed a 60-year-old woman with a hunchback. The police are also on the trail of the woman's son, who colluded with the kidnappers after being paid N7 million Naira Naira (US $ 2,800,000,000). The woman, identified as Mrs. Rukayat Abodunde, was abducted and killed by two shooters who came to her home in Ayetoro Street in Ondo town, pretending to have come to buy fish from her. The abduction happened around 10 P.M.

Okezie-Okeh (December 21, 2019) in Sun News online categories cover story feature with the heading 'Hunchback Hunters' reported a *chilling story of how a prison warden, moviemaker and herbalist abducted,* Olusegun Fasakin from his home at Igangan-Ijesa, Atakunmosa East Local Government Area of Osun State, Nigeria and butchered him. Okoli (October 26, 2015) in Vanguard Nigerian Newspaper with the headline *Murder of Hunchback: Police Nab Suspected Ritualist* in Abia reported that:

> Abia State police command has arrested a suspected ritualist of Dikeukwu autonomous community in Umuahia North Local Government Area of Abia State, for allegedly killing a hunchback, Mr. Ukata Iheme, for money

making purposes. The suspect, who was said to have committed the crime with another suspect, now at large, allegedly killed and buried the victim.

Ikeji (December 12, 2020) with the heading *Missing Hunchback Man Found Dead Two Weeks after Kidnapped (Graphic Photos)* in an online blog reports that a man with hunchback who was declared missing two weeks ago has been found dead in a suspected case of ritual killing. Mr Suberu Dada, of Obeiba Ihima, Okehi LGA, Kogi State, Nigeria, was kidnapped on Nov 22, 2020. Unfortunately, his decaying body was found today, Dec 8, 2020, at Iruvochinomi, Ege, Adavi LGA in Kogi State, Nigeria.

Alms-Begging

Alms-begging is an act of soliciting money from a passerby in public places by evoking pity. Culture and religion encourage alms begging. In some cultures, it is believed that persons with disabilities are imbued with supernatural powers, which has resulted in people giving alms to them, believing that they would be rewarded in return for the alms giving (Ekelemeke, 1987). Many parents who send their children with disabilities to beg for alms do so for economic reason (Omiegbe, 1995). However, Dunapo (2002) notes that there are also cultural and religious aspects to the practice of using children with disabilities for alms-begging". He further states, "Begging is also a human problem involving not only persons with disabilities but also refugees from war-ravaged countries. It has religious and cultural connotations." Islamic religion and the Almajiri/culture sustain the practice of using children with disabilities to beg for alms in the context of the Islamic injunction and the Almajiri system, where alms-begging is justified and legitimized (Etieyibo & Omiegbe, 2016), which thus prevent them from enrolling in school and attending school regularly. Kehinde (14 February 2020) in Guardian Nigerian Newspaper, with the heading "Street Beggars: Begging in Coat of Many Colours", depicts how parents and guardians send their children and wards (children with disabilities inclusive) to beg for alms for financial gain instead of enrolling them in school. Nikoro (19 January 2021), in her article titled "Children with Disabilities in Nigeria: Their Right to Education and the Legality of Street Begging" decried the attitude of parents sending their children with disabilities to beg for alms thereby denying them their **rights to basic education"** [Emphasis Mine].

Cultural Traditions and Practice of Parents

In Zamfara State, Nigeria, like many other parts of the world, inaccessibility, low participation, withdrawal and dropping out of the girl-child (including children with disabilities) from school are attributed to many factors of cultural tradition and practices of the parents toward the education of their daughters, prominent among these factors are socio-cultural beliefs, customs, early marriage, pregnancy (UNESCO, 2002). It is pertinent to note that Nigeria is a multi-religious society with three major religions–Islam (53.5%), Christianity (45.9%), adherents of Nigeria's indigenous religions and others (6.0%) (CIA, 2018), and religious beliefs have significant role in shaping gender-related behaviors and practices. Interestingly, Nigeria's geo-political zones are characterized by the interplay of religion and cultural values. Religion may be associated with the socio-cultural framing of gender norms and the girl-child marriage practices (Wall, 1998). More than a third of girls in Nigeria end up in child marriages, with 22 million married before the age of 18; and the nation has the highest number of child brides in Africa (UNICEF, 2019; Girls, not brides, 2019a; Girls, not brides, 2019b). Even though early marriage is prevalent in Nigeria it is not limited to one religious group. Available evidence reveals that child marriage is more prevalent in Muslim communities (Ayiga & Rampagane, 2013), and Northern Nigeria has some of the highest rates of early marriages in the world where 39% of girls are married off before the age of 18, and 16% are married before they turn 15 years old. However, the number of Nigerian girls that are married before their 18th birthday is as high as 58.2%, and the prevalence of child marriage varies widely across the country, but figures are as high as 76% in the North West region, compared with 10% in the South-East" (Save the Children, 2021).

This is associated with the belief among the conservative Muslims that Quran allows girls to marry at any age, and Prophet Muhammad's wife was nine years at marriage. It is also believed among Muslims in most parts of Northern Nigeria that it is permissible for a man to marry a child as young as 9 years, as long as sexual relations with her are postponed until she has attained puberty. Moreover, Islamic law condones child (early) marriage and supports men's rights over their female counterparts. Also, Islamic scholars assert that Islam fixes no age limit for marriage, and children of the youngest age may be married or betrothed even though they insist that a girl should not be allowed to get married until she is ready for marital sexual relations. Perhaps this accounts for the prevalence of child marriages in Northern Nigeria, where young girls between 12 and 14 are **withdrawn from primary schools** to marry husbands who are often significantly older than them (Research Cyber, 2021) [Emphasis Mine].

However, in the Northern parts of Nigeria, child brides are usually forced to have sexual intercourse with their spouses as soon as they are married, and many get pregnant in their first year of marriage. These early pregnancies often lead to Vesico Vaginal Fistula (VVF), Rector Vaginal Fistula or Obstetric

Fistula as these young girls are giving birth at a very tender age when their bodies are not physically able to deliver a fetus. The pregnancy also puts them at a greater risk of sexually transmitted diseases, HIV/AIDS, Human Papilloma Virus (HPV) and domestic violence. This practice is detrimental to the well-being of the girl-child (Nigeria Health Watch, 2021) in terms of health and education, whereby they become pregnant, sick and enmeshed in household chores which prevent them from attending school or dropping out of school. Moreover, Mobolaji et al. (2020), in a study aimed at addressing the existing research gap by explicitly examining the influence of ethnic and religious affiliations on girl-child marriage based on a nationally representative sample of female adolescents in Nigeria, found out that ethnicity and religion have independent associations with girl-child marriage in Nigeria.

In various parts of the world, different practices mark transitioning from one phase of life to another. It could be as simple as handing over the car keys to a younger teenager showing that he is now an adult and responsible for his or her own decision, or as elaborate as throwing rituals or spiritual events that welcome the person to a new phase. In Nigeria, most of these rights are typically celebrated through music, dance and ceremony. These rites may be similar to one or more tribes, bearing a different name somewhere else with slight alteration. Many of them used to be barbaric, with female genital mutilation being one of the most well-known. While the number of tribes practicing these barbaric rites is reduced and more tribes are adopting new practices that are less harmful, there are still some groups in the country that celebrate these today (Ugobude, 2019). However, some of these different initiation 'practices that mark transitioning from one phase of life to another' prevent the girl-child from attending school or dropping out of school, and they include the following:

Childhood to Adulthood Rite of Passage Initiation Ceremony

Childhood to adulthood rite of passage, which hinges on cultural traditions and practices, is another contributing factor influencing girl–child education with the initiation ceremony, which still marks the transition from childhood to adulthood among communities in sub-Saharan Africa, Zamfara State, Nigeria, inclusive. When the schedule of such ceremonies overlaps with the school calendar, it leads to school absenteeism and dropout. Traditionally, initiated girls may also find it difficult to continue schooling after passage to adulthood as the next step is expected to be marriage (UNESCO, 2002). An example of a childhood to adulthood rite of passage is the 'Iria Ritual', popular with various tribes in the Niger Delta, with some forms of the ritual being harsher than the others. It typically involves young girls between 14 and 16 years undergoing rituals that prepare them for marriage. In some places, these girls must be bare-breasted before the crowd for inspection. The goal of this is to ensure that their virginity is intact. The young girls also visit the fattening room, where they are well-fed with nourishing body meals, especially pounded yam mixed with pounded plantain. In the fattening room, the ladies are pampered and groomed to dance half-naked at the market square. At the end of their stay in the fattening room, their physique changes and they look more beautiful. Their bodies are then painted in different colors for the dance. In times past, it was believed that if one did not go through the 'Iria ritual', it would be tough for her to give birth to a child. One of the common beliefs among the people is that young women going through puberty have attachments to water spirits, so they gather at the stream at dawn to chase the spirits away. After this, a senior male member of the tribe strikes the girls with sticks and sends them back to the village (Ugobude, 2019), signaling the end of the initiation ceremony.

Female Circumcision Initiation Ceremony

Female circumcision, also known as female genital mutilation (FGM), is defined by the WHO (1998) as all procedures which involve partial or total removal of the external female genitalia and/or injury to the female genital organs, whether for cultural or any other non-therapeutic reasons. In Nigeria, the subjection of girls and women to obscure traditional practices is legendary (UNICEF, 2001). Female genital mutilation is an unhealthy traditional practice inflicted on girls and women worldwide. It is widely recognized as a violation of human rights, deeply rooted in cultural beliefs and perceptions over decades and generations, with no easy task for change (Okeke et al., 2012). Though female genital mutilation (FGM) is practiced in more than 28 countries in Africa and a few scattered communities worldwide, its burden is seen in Nigeria, Egypt, Mali, Eritrea, Sudan, the Central African Republic, and the northern part of Ghana, where it has been an old traditional and cultural practice of various ethnic groups (WHO, 1998; Odoi, 2005). The highest prevalence rates are in Somalia and Djibouti, where female genital mutilation (FGM) is virtually universal. Female genital mutilation (FGM) is widely practiced in Nigeria, and with its large population, Nigeria has the highest absolute number of cases of female genital mutilation (FGM) worldwide, accounting for about one-quarter of the estimated 115–130 million circumcised women worldwide (UNICEF, 2001). In Nigeria, female genital mutilation (FGM) has the highest prevalence in the south-south (77%) (among adult women), followed by the south-east (68%) and south-west (65%), but practiced on a smaller scale in the north, paradoxically tending to in a more extreme form (UNICEF, 2001; Adegoke, 2005). Nigeria has a population of 150 million, with the women population forming 52% (Adegoke, 2005). The national prevalence rate of FGM is 41% among adult women. Prevalence rates progressively decline in the young age groups, and 37% of circumcised women do not want female genital mutilation (FGM) to continue. 61% of women who do not want female genital mutilation (FGM) said it was a bad, harmful tradition, and 22% said it was against religion. Other reasons cited were medical complications (22%), painful personal experiences (10%), and the view that FGM is against the dignity of women (10%). However, there is still considerable support for the practice in areas deeply rooted in local tradition (UNICEF, 2001).

Reasons abound on why female genital mutilation (FGM) is practiced in Nigeria. In a study by Okeke et al. (2012) on female genital mutilation (FGM), the respondents gave reasons for female genital mutilation (FGM): They regarded female genital mutilation (FGM) as a tribal traditional practice (our custom is a good tradition and has to be protected), as a superstitious belief practiced for the preservation of chastity and purification, (Verzin, 1975) family honor, hygiene, esthetic reasons, protection of virginity and prevention of promiscuity, modification of socio-sexual attitudes (countering failure of a woman to attain orgasm), increasing the sexual pleasure of husband, enhancing fertility and increasing matrimonial opportunities. Other reasons are to prevent mother and child from dying during childbirth and for legal reasons "[one cannot inherit property if not circumcised] (Worsley, 1938).

In some parts of Nigeria, the cut edges of the external genitalia are smeared with secretions from a snail footpad with the belief that the snail being a slow animal would influence the circumcised girl to 'go slowly' during sexual activities in future (Akpuaka, 1991). Also, female genital mutilation (FGM) is often routinely performed as an integral part of social conformity and in line with community identity (Odoi, 2005).

However, it is pertinent to state that FGM (Female circumcision) initiation ceremony, due to its side effect, is among the other cultural constraints on girl-child education that create similar dilemmas to those who pass through initiation ceremonies. Normally, circumcised girls—the girl child negatively influences their uncircumcised peers. They perceive themselves as adults and, as a result of this, become rude to teachers and often reject schools as an institution for "children" by exhibiting abnormal behaviors of **frequent school absenteeism and reduced performance**, which leads them to **drop out of school** and eventually marry (Ghaghara, 1993) at such a tender age. In addition, the initiation practice of female genital mutilation is also detrimental to the well-being of the girl-child in terms of health and education, whereby they become sick, which prevents them from attending school or dropping out of school [Emphasis Mine].

Conclusion

Children with disabilities require the best form of education to minimize the effects of disability and develop adequate powers and potentials (Abosi & Ozoji, 1985). However, this chapter has shown that cultural and religious practices affect, to a large extent, the education of persons with disabilities. They are confronted with violent attacks, maimed, killed, girls are given out in marriage at an early age, sent to beg for alms and hidden at home by their parents from public glare due to societal stigmatization and fear of their safety from human predators thereby depriving them of attending school.

Unlike traditional beliefs about disability reported mainly among people with little or no education in remote rural areas, these beliefs are increasingly reported among educated urban populations. It is unclear whether traditional beliefs about disability have been brought from rural to urban areas with urban migrants, whether these beliefs reflect new urban myths (Brunvand, 1981) or some combination. However, at their most extreme, the well-being and, in some cases, the very lives of persons with disabilities are at risk. These beliefs also appear to present unacknowledged barriers as children with disabilities are **kept from school** and adults with a disability are **hidden in their homes** by families who fear they will be branded witches and accused of selling their family member's health or intellect for wealth or social advancement (McGeown, 2012) [Emphasis mine].

Some research findings indicate that such traditional beliefs are receding in the face of significant efforts in many countries by disability advocates, and government and civil society dispelling such negative attitudes and practices. Education, exposure to the mass media and a rapidly urbanizing population have all been cited as contributing to changing ideas and attitudes (Scheer & Groce, 1988; Mallory, 1993; Officer & Groce, 2009). It is believed that new legislation, including ratification of the United Nations Convention on the Rights of Persons with Disabilities and progressive national disability policies in many sub-Saharan countries, have made further inroads against stigmatizing beliefs. A range of actions is beginning to address witchcraft practices in general and allegations of witchcraft against persons with disabilities in particular. Disabled people's organizations (advocacy groups run by and on behalf of persons with disabilities) have brought together communities, politicians, the media and civil society working in conjunction with United Nations agencies such as UNICEF to confront issues of witchcraft and disability head-on, particularly when it comes to ritual killing and mutilation of persons with disabilities (Batterbee et al., 2010). Larger human rights organizations, such as Human Rights Watch, are involved. But, smaller NGOs (non-governmental organizations) have also shown strong leadership in advocacy against accusations of witchcraft. Of particular note is the Nigerian NGO (non-governmental organizations) "Stepping Stones Nigeria", working with abandoned street children accused of witchcraft, has brought the issue of children with disabilities and witchcraft to the United Nations Committee on the Rights of the Child (Batterbee et al., 2010) and dedicated their 2012 Day of the African Child to children with disabilities. Declaring 'Disability is not Witchcraft', Stepping Stones Nigeria and Stepping Stones Nigeria Child Empowerment Foundation called upon the Nigerian government "to take action to demystify the common ailments that are associated with witchcraft and prevent the labeling of children with disabilities as *witches*" (Stepping Stones Nigeria, 2012). However, more action is needed. Public information campaigns and discussions are needed in those countries affected by witchcraft to raise awareness about the causes of disabilities and the rights of persons with disabilities. Community volunteers, health professionals and social workers must be informed and trained to **identify children with disabilities or adults hidden away by families** and provide support and counseling to address issues of witchcraft. Disabled Peoples Organizations can and must play an essential role in raising these issues—and should be key partners in working with government and civil society to address the issue of witchcraft and disability at local and national levels (Groce & McGeown, 2013) [Emphasis mine].

Be that as it may, these suggestions are indeed laudable. However, to change peoples' negative disposition and behavior towards persons with disabilities and their education due to cultural beliefs and practices, put a stop to these barbaric cultural beliefs and practices that endanger the lives of persons with disabilities in Nigeria, and make them attend school and benefit maximally from special education; the following suggestions are made:

1. Laws should be promulgated on those cultural and religious practices that negatively affect the education of persons with disabilities.

2. When such laws are enacted, awareness should be created to educate the citizens in the following ways:

    a. Organization of Seminars and symposiums for the governors, legislators, council chairmen, councilors, and traditional and religious leaders who will, in turn, pass on such information to their subjects or followers in the urban and rural areas of the country.

    b. Regularly writing newspaper articles and editorials by electronic and print media to point out how some cultural and religious practices impede the education of persons with disabilities.

    c. Production and broadcast of radio and television jingles and drama on scenes depicting how cultural and religious practices impede the education of persons with disabilities with the intent of changing the attitude of those persons involved in these barbaric cultural and religious practices which hinder the education of persons with disabilities in line with Albert Bandura's theory of social learning defined by Secord and Bechman (1964) as "an interactive process whereby a person's behavior is modified to conform to expectations held by members of the group to which he/she belongs."

d.   Maintaining synergy between ministries/agencies, non-governmental organizations (NGOs) disabilities people's organizations (DPOs) and media organizations in creating awareness on educating the citizens on harmful cultural and religious practices which hinder the education of persons with disabilities.

3.   Persons with disabilities should be allowed to showcase their talents on December 10th of every year, a day set aside by the United Nations to recognize their self-worth and dignity, which will thus make the society have positive attitude towards them and their education.

4.   Cultural and religious practices which negatively impact the education of persons with disabilities should be included in the curriculum of tertiary, secondary, and primary institutions and taught to the students to make them familiar with such practices and avoid practicing them.

5.   Parents and guardians should report promptly to the appropriate governmental law enforcement agencies when it is observed that some persons or group of persons are hampering the education of their children and wards with disabilities through some cultural and religious practices that violate the law for appropriate action to be taken to enable their children and wards access education.

6.   Violators of cultural and religious laws that impede the education of persons with disabilities should be sentenced appropriately. Publicizing such convictions should be made in the electronic and print media to deter others.

It is hoped that the Nigerian Government and the citizens would cooperate and work assiduously and harmoniously to put a stop to these despicable cultural and religious practices which impede the education of persons with disabilities so that they would be properly educated like the 'able-bodied' persons, contribute meaningfully to the development of themselves and that of the society in which they reside.

References

Abosi, O. C. & Ozoji E. D. (1985). *Educating the Blind* (A Descriptive Approach). Spectrum Books.

Adegoke, P. (2005). *Female Genital Mutilation: An African Humanist view.* Ibadan University Humanist Society.

Adelakun, O. S, & Ajayi, M. A. O. (2020). Eliminating discrimination and enhancing equality: A case for inclusive basic education rights of children with Albinism in Africa. *Nigerian Journal of Medicine, 29*(2), 244-251.

Adenekan, T. E. (2019). Information Needs of Albinos in the Yoruba Ethnic Group. *Nigeria International Journal of Technology and Inclusive Education, 8*(1), 1385-93.

Akinloye, B. (2014, December 21). Nigerian Hunchbacks people see us as money making machines. *Sunday Punch Nigerian Newspaper*. https://punchng .com/nigerian-hunchbacks-people-see-us-money-making-machines/

Akpuaka, F. C. (1991). Vulval adhesions following females circumcision in Nigeria. *Postgrad Doct Afr,13*, 98-99.

ANSA (2020, June 23). Joy, a refugee with albinism fights against discrimination. *Info Migrants Blog*. https://www.infomigrants.net/en/post/25554/joy-a-refugee-with-albinism-fights-against-discrimination

Ayiga, N. & Rampagane, V. (2013). Determinants of age at first marriage in sub-Saharan Africa: a comparative study of Uganda and South Africa. *Journal of Social Development in Africa, 28*(1), 9-34.

Batterbee, L. Foxcroft, G., & Secker, E. (2010). *Witchcraft stigmatization and Children's Rights in Nigeria, Stepping Stones Nigeria report*. 54th session of the UN committee on the Rights of the Child in Geneva.

Brunvand, J. (1981). *The Vanishing Hitchhiker: American Urban legends and Their Meanings*. W. W. Norton & Company.

CIA (2018) *The World Fact book*. https://www.cia.gov/library/publications/the -world-factbook/geos/xx.html

CIMPRIC, A. & UNICEF (2010). *Children accused of witchcraft: An anthropological study of contemporary practices in Africa*. UNICEF WCARO.

Dike, G. (2009, October 11). Murder of hunchback: Senator Ogunwale moved to Abuja. *The Sun News*.

Dunapo O. S. (2002). Causative and Sustaining Factors to Street Hawking in Nigeria: Implications for all Development. In R.U. Okonkwo & R.O. Okoye (Eds.), *The Learning Environment of the Nigerian Child* (pp. 36-49). NISEP.

Ebegbulem, S. (2017, February 18). Horror: 62 year-old man with hunchback murdered in Edo. *Vanguard Nigerian Newspaper*. https://www.vanguardngr. com/2017/02/horror-62-year-old-man-hunchback-murdered-edo/

Eboh, O. & Ukpong D. E. (1995). *Social Studies Education for Nigerian Universities*. Whyte and Whyte Publishers.

Ekelemeke, R. (1987). Introduction and Concepts of Special Education. In Ogbue R.M., Obani T.C., & Abosi O.C. (Eds.), *Special Education: A Reading Text*. Heinemann Educational Books.

Eskay M., Onu V.C., Igbo J.N., Obiyo N., & Ugwuanyi L. (2012). Disability within the African Culture. *US-China Education Review, B 4*, 473-484.

Etieyibo, E. & Omiegbe, O. (2017). *Disabilities in Nigeria: Attitudes, Reactions and Remediation*. Hamilton Books.

Etieyibo, E., & Omiegbe, O. (2016). Religion, culture, and discrimination against persons with disabilities in Nigeria. *African journal of disability, 5*(1), 192. https://doi.org/10.4102/ajod.v5i1.192

Evans, R. (2015, Oct 11). Witchcraft abuse cases on the rise. *BBC News*. http://www.bbc.com/news/uk-34475424

Federal Republic of Nigeria (2014). *National Policy on Education 14th Edition*. NERDC Press.

Foxcraft, G. (2009). Witchcraft Accusations: A protection concern for UNHCR and the Wider Humanitarian Community? Stepping Stones Nigeria NGO, UNHCR.

Ghaghara, L (1993). Cited in Kainuwa, A. & Yesuf, N. B. M. (2003), Cultural Traditions and Practices of the Parents Barriers to Girl-Child Education in Zamfara State, Nigeria. *International Journal of Scientific and Research Publications*, 3(11).

Girls not brides (2019a). Child marriage and the SDGs. https://www.girlsnotbrides.org/themes/sustainable-development-goals-sdgs/

Girls not brides (2019b). Nigeria - Child Marriage Around The World. https://www.girlsnotbrides.org/child-marriage/nigeria/#stats-references

Groce, N. & McGeown, J. (2013). Witchcraft, Wealth and Disability: Reinterpretation of a folk belief in contemporary urban Africa. *Working Paper 30*. Leonard Cheshire Disability and Inclusive Development Centre, University College London, UK.

Groce, N.E. (2005). Violence against disabled children: UN Secretary General's report on violence against children thematic group on violence against disabled children: findings and recommendations. UNICEF: New York, US.

Hornby, A. S. (2015). *Oxford Advanced Learner's Dictionary*. Oxford University Press.

Houreld, K. (2009, October 18). African Children denounced as "Witches" by Christian Pastors. *The Huffington Post*. http://www.huffpost.com/2009/10/18/African-children-denounce-n--324943.html

Human Rights Council (2011). Report of the Office of the United Nations High Commissioner for Human Rights of Persons with Albinism; 12 September, 2011.

Human Rights Watch (2012). "Like a Death Sentence": Abuses against Persons with Mental Disabilities in Ghana. http://www.hrw.org/sites/default/files/reports/ghana1012webwcover.pdf

Idowu, C. (1976). In Abosi O.C. & Ozoji E.D. (1985). *Educating the Blind a Descriptive Approach Ibadan* (p. 32). Spectrum Book.

Igwe, L. (2012, July 03). Ritual Killing and Hunchbacks in Nigeria. *Sahara Reporters* http://saharareporters.com/2012/07/03/ritual-killing-and-hunchbacks-nigeria

Ikeji, L. (2020, December 08). Missing hunchback man found dead two weeks after Kidnapped (graphic photos). https://www.lindaikejisblog.com/2020/12/missing-hunchback-man-found-dead-two-weeks-after-he-was-kidnapped-graphic-photos.html

Isioma, C. L. (2019). Witchcraft stigmatization and abuse of children in Akwa-Ibom state, Nigeria. *International Journal of Sociology and Anthropology*, 11(4), 43-53.

Jannah, C. (2019, April 23). Ritualists kill hunchback woman, pay son N7m. *Daily Post Nigerian Newspaper*. https://dailypost.ng/2019/04/23/ritualists-kill-hunchback-woman-pay-son-n7m/

Kehinde, S. (2020, February 14). Street beggars: Begging in coat of many colours. *Guardian Nigerian Newspaper.* https://guardian.ng/opinion/street-beggars-begging-in-coat-of-many-colours/

Kolawole, Y. (2009, October 7). Senator quizzed over alleged murder. *Thisday News Paper.*

Longaman, P. (2009). *Longman Dictionary of Contemporary English.* Pearson.

Mallory, B. L. (1993). Changing beliefs about disability in developing countries: Historical factors and sociocultural variables In D.Woods (Ed.), *Traditional and changing views of disability in developing societies.* World Rehabilitation Fund.

Mbiti, J. (1975). *An Introduction to African Religion.* Heinemann Educational Books.

McGeown J. (2012). Out of the Shadows: Qualitative study of Parents' and Professionals' attitudes and beliefs about children with Communication Disability in Uganda and how best to help them Master's Thesis. Centre for International Health and Development. UCL

McVeigh, K. (2014, October 08). Child witchcraft claims increasing as 'hidden crime' is investigated. *The Guardian.* https://www.theguardian.com/uk-news/2014/oct/08/child-witchcraft-claims-hidden-crime-met-police-under-reported

Mobolaji, J. W, Fatusi, A.O, & Adedini, S. A (2020). Ethnicity, religious affiliation and girl-child marriage: a cross-sectional study of nationally representative sample of female adolescents in Nigeria BMC Public Health. https://bmcpublichealth.biomedcentral.com/articles/10.1186/s12889-020-08714-5

Nduka, D. (1974). African Traditional Systems of Thought and their Implications for Nigerian Education. *West African Journal of Education, 18*(2), 153-165.

Nigeria Health Watch (2021). Reclaiming Girlhood: Early Marriage a Challenging Public Health Dilemma in Nigeria Thought Leadership Series April 2021. https://nigeriahealthwatch.com/reclaiming-girlhood-early-marriage-a-challenging-public-health-dilemma-in-nigeria/

Nigerian Tribune (2011, March 23). Albinos as endangered species.

Nikoro, J. (2021, January 19). Children with Disabilities in Nigeria: Their Right to Education and the Legality of Street Begging. https://dnllegalandstyle.com/2021/36046/

Nkanga, E. (2002, 5 May). Police kill seven robbers, arrest 30 others. *Thisday Newspaper.*

Ntinda, R. N. (2011). Customary Practices and Children with Albinism in Namibia. https://www.kas.de/c/document_library/get_file?uuid=b6dc0797-15b0-962e-f1bc-46a19ab239f7&groupId=252038

Obani, T.C. (1984). Adolescent Understanding and Judgment of Handicap: A Cross cultural Study. *Ph.D. Thesis.* University of Birmingham.

Odoi, A. T. (2005). Female genital mutilation. In Kwawukume, E. Y, & Emuveyan, E. E., (Eds.), *Comprehensive Gynecology in the Tropics,* 1e (pp. 268–78). Graphic Packaging.

Officer, A., & Groce, N. E. (2009). Key concepts in disability. *Lancet (London, England), 374*(9704), 1795–1796. https://doi.org/10.1016/S0140-6736(09)61527-0

OHCHR (2013). Persons with albinism Report of the Office of the United Nations High Commissioner for Human Rights, United Nations GeneralAssembly (A/HRC/24/57) https://www.ohchr.org/Documents/Issues/Albinism/CN-Witchcraft_EN.docx

Okeke, T. C., Anyaehie, U.S.B., & Ezenyeaku, C.C.K (2012). An Overview of Female Genital Mutilation in Nigeria. *Annals of Medical and Health Sciences, 2*(1), 70–73. https://doi.org/10.4103/2141-9248

Okezie-Okeh, C. (2019, December 21). Hunchback haunters. *Sun News Online* https://www.sunnewsonline.com/hunchback-hunters/

Oko, E.O. (2003). Extra –Judicial Killings in Nigeria: The Case of Afikpo Town. Paper presented at the 17th International Conference of International Society for the Reform of Criminal Law, 24-28 August, The Hague, Netherlands.

Okoli, A. (2015, October 26). Murder of hunchback: Police nab suspected ritualist in Abia. *Vanguard Nigerian Newspaper.* https://www.vanguardngr.com/2015/10/murder-of-hunchback-police-nab-suspected-ritualist-in-abia/

Okoro, A. (1975). Albinism in Nigeria. *British Journal of Dermatology, 92*(5), 485-492. https://doi.org/10.1111/j.1365-2133.1975.tb03116.x

Omiegbe, O. (1995). The Handicapped and Begging. Paper Presented at the Fifth National Conference National Council For Exceptional Children at the Department of Special Education, University of Ibadan, Ibadan,Nigeria 28-31st August.

Omiegbe, O. (1998). *An Introduction to Special Education.* Bellco Publishers.

Omiegbe, O. (2001). Superstitious beliefs associated with the handicapped in Africa. In A.O. Orubu (Ed.), *African traditional religion: A book of selected readings* (pp. 26-28), Institute of Education, University of Benin, Benin Nigeria.

Omunukuma, O. (2010). Defending the existence of and solidarizing with alleged childwitches: Significations on the Nigerian witchcraft phenomenon (pp. 27-35). In Ademowo, A. Foxcroft, G. & Oladipo, T. (Eds.), *Suffereth not a witch to live.* Muffy Prints.

Research Cyber, (2021) Early Marriage in Nigeria: Causes and Solution https://www.researchcyber.com/early-marriage-in-nigeria-causes-and-solutions

Save the Children (2021). Changing the Story of the Nigerian Girl Child https://nigeria.savethechildren.net/sites/nigeria.savethechildren.net.files/library/changing-the-story-of-the-nigerian-girl-child.pdf

Scheer, J. & Groce N. (1988). Impairment as a Human Constant: Cross-Cultural and Historical Perspectives on Variation. *Journal of Social Issues, 44*(1), 23-37. https://doi.org/10.1111/j.1540-4560.1988.tb02046.x

Secord, P. F. & Bechman, C. N (1964). *Social Psychology.* McGraw Hill Book.

Setume, D. S. (2016). Myths and Beliefs about Disabilities: Implications for Educators and Counselors. *Journal of Disability & Religion, 20*(1-2), 62-76. https://doi.org/10.1080/23312521.2016.1152938

Sleap, B. (2011). Using the Law to tackle Accusations of Witchcraft: Help Age International's position. Help Age International, London.

Thuku, M. (2011). Myths, discrimination, and the call for special rights for persons with albinism in Sub-Saharan Africa. *In Amnesty International Editorial Review on Special Programme on Africa.*

Ugobude, F. (2019, June 30). Unique Cultural Rites Passage in Nigeria. *Guardian.* https://guardian.ng/life/unique-cultural-rites-of-passage-in-nigeria/

UNESCO (2002). Strategy for the Acceleration of Girls Education in Nigeria. Abuja: Federal Republic of Nigeria.

UNICEF (2001). Children's and Women's right in Nigeria: A wake up call, Situation Assessment and Analysis (pp. 195–200). *Harmful Traditional Practice (FGM) Abuja NPC and UNICEF Nigeria.*

UNICEF (2019). A Profile of Child Marriage in Africa. UNICEF. https://data. unicef.org/resources/a-profile-of-child-marriage-in-africa/

United Nations (2020). Concept Note & Preliminary Data - Elimination of Harmful Practices: Accusations of Witchcraft and Ritual Attacks. https://www. ohchr.org/sites/default/files/Documents/Issues/Albinism/CN-Witchcraft_EN .docx

United Nations (2021, July 21). Witchcraft killings of people with albinism rose during pandemic – UN expert. https://www.ohchr.org/en/press-releases/20 21/07/witchcraft-killings-people-albinism-rose-during-pandemic-un-expert ?LangID=E&NewsID=27346

Uwagie-Ero, T.O., Iseye, B. O., & Omiegbe O. (1998). *Citizenship Education.* Avwega Productions.

Verzin, J. A. (1975). Sequelae of female circumcision. *Tropical Doctor, 5*(4), 163-169.

Wall, L. L. (1998). Dead mothers and injured wives: the social context of maternal morbidity and mortality among the Hausa of northern Nigeria. *Studies in family planning, 29*(4), 341–359.

WHO (1998). Female Genital Mutilation: An overview. World Health Organization, Geneva.

WHO (2011). International Classification of Functioning, Disability and Health. World Health Organization, Geneva.

Worsley A. (1938). Infibulation and female circumcision: a study of a little-known custom. *The Journal of obstetrics and gynaecology of the British Empire, 45*, 686–691. https://doi.org/10.1111/j.1471-0528.1938.tb11160.x

Chapter 12

Native Country and Its Influence on Social Support and Cultural Shock among Foreign Students

Feba Thomas

Xavier Institute of Management & Entrepreneurship,
Kalamassery, Kochi, India

Abstract: The students face culture shock and social support when they go for their studies from one country to another. This research emphasizes social support as a coping strategy in reducing the cultural shock that international students face in the assimilation process from their home country to another for education. The sample collected for the study includes Indian and international students. This research indicates that cultural shock can be reduced if social support is received from the families. The study also proves that social support from families reduces stress when they are in a new environment, thereby improving their well-being. There are scarce studies on social support and cultural shock among international students.

Keywords: Cultural Shock, Social Support, Cultural Diversity, Homesickness, Foreign Students, Indian Students, International students

***

Introduction

Culture shock is triggered when an individual learns and lives in a new environment. Berry (1997) has defined Cultural shock as "*the reduction in the individual's health status, who has struggled to adjust to a new culture, psychologically and socially.*" Particularly, students studying in foreign institutions usually experience cultural stress. It is because of differences in the beliefs, norms, and customs that a particular national/native culture holds. A culture transmits different values and beliefs, and the way they manage stress also differs. Cultural shock is otherwise known as acculturative stress (Sedikides et al., 2009).

Culture shock is negative, while stress is negative (dis-stress) and positive (eustress). The reports have shown that about 95% of the people have homesickness as they stay away from their homes, they are miles apart from their home country and the host country, and the students are not aware of the distance of the new environment. Stress can be minimized to a larger extent once there is copying. The term *'Acculturative stress' is a substitute for 'culture shock', which was first started by the Institute of International Education in Chicago in 1951 in the event of the arrival of the first Indian student in Germany to study (Oberg, 1954).*

Berry (2003) explained acculturation as an individual's process that comprises a continuous interaction between groups of persons from diverse cultures. The different modes of acculturation include assimilation, integration, marginalization, and separation related to acculturative stress and social support (Sullivan & Kashubeck-West, 2015). *Social support is a comfort and well-being that an individual receives from formal and informal sources with the societal organization and people. It acts as a coping mechanism to reduce stress* (Sabouripour & Roslan, 2015). Social support (family, significant others, and friends) reduces international students' stress levels. Homesickness is one of the key factors seen among international students when they come to another environment (Kegel, 2015). The study has addressed homesickness or being sick of home as a factor that causes culture shock among the students studying abroad (Fanari et al., 2021).

Social support is a form of help that comes from others, including parents, friends, and others, while resilience is a characteristic that an individual possesses for oneself. It will help the students to reduce the acculturative stress, the stress and loneliness that foreign students face (Lin & Kingminghae, 2014).

International students examine unique challenges, and coping strategies help overcome the challenges that the students face. In 2020, there was a massive dip in the foreign students arriving in India. In 2021, there is an increase of about 14% of foreign students arriving in India. The majority of international students coming to India are from Nepal, followed by Afghanistan, Bangladesh, Bhutan and Saudan in the AY 2021.

The foreign students need to adjust to the new environment, culture, and education system. Nowadays, many students are going abroad for their studies. It is observed that there are various issues they face, like homesickness and other problems relatively because they leave their family members and come for their academic opportunities in a different country (Lee, 2021; Kegel, 2009). In the real-world social support can reduce depression. Social support can provide emotional support for international students by reducing culture shock (Li et al., 2021).

The current research helps measure the level of stress that an international student faces as soon as they move from one country to another. Students tend to face stress when they cannot cope with the culture. The objective of the current research is (a) to find out the measures of culture shock that the foreign students face and (b) To find out the native country and its influence on culture shock and social support among foreign students.

Theoretical Background and Literature Review

The acculturation theory consists of four modes: assimilation, integration, marginalization, and separation. Assimilation is a mode when an individual adapts to the cultural setting of the host culture and rejects the home culture. Integration is a mode when an individual adapts to the cultural setting of the host culture while maintaining their home culture. Marginalization is a mode in which an individual rejects his or her host culture as well as home culture. Separation is when an individual rejects the host culture and adapts to the home culture (Berry, 1997). The different modes of acculturation include assimilation, integration, marginalization, and separation related to acculturative stress and social support (Sullivan & Kashubeck-West, 2015). Social support theory is associated with social support helping reduce the intensity of the individual's stress when they undergo adverse events (Uchino, 2004). Perceived institution support theory will help the individuals improve performance and decrease the stress they undergo (Creswell, 2008).

The acculturation process includes changes in attitude, identities, values, and beliefs. There are circumstances where the minority groups will face psychological, physical, and social consequences. One of the significant consequences of acculturation is acculturative stress. Acculturation consists of a two-dimensional approach where the individual adapts to his or her culture (home culture) and adapts to the host country's culture (Cabassa, 2003).

The cultural shocks the foreign students have when they assimilate into another country for their studies and the social support and how they adapt to the new culture have been discussed. The more the support received, the lesser the culture shock levels among foreign students. Culture shocks and coping mechanisms have been observed among Korean students (Mcleod et al., 2021). The Chinese students have depression when they are in a new location. It will eventually lead to cultural shock among these students when they need to adjust to another environment (Wei et al., 2007). The support from the families reduces the culture shock that the individuals face, thereby reducing the stress to a greater extent (Mallinckrodt & Leong, 1992). Culture shock has become common because there are people from diverse cultures, and they need to minimize the amount of stress they are facing because of the adaption to the new environment (Xia, 2009; Murwantono & Rinawati, 2021).

Foreign students face adjustment difficulties and cultural shock in the host countries (Bertram, 2014). Cultural shock among international students is associated with depression and anxiety. It has been observed that the international student's peer support has reduced the stress (Crockett et al., 2007). The support among the foreign students reduces their loneliness (Lin & Kingminghae, 2014). It is noted that the Koran immigrants have overcome the cultural shock with social support (Thomas & Choi, 2006). The coping strategy and the social support reduce the cultural shock that the students face (Bai, 2016). The foreign students in Europe experience less culture shock than in Asia, Lain America, and Africa (Yeh & Inose, 2003). The cultural shock is related to students' cultural background, communication skills, and academic progress. It was observed that students from Asian and African countries have greater levels of cultural stress while relating to students from other countries. The language issue is another critical reason for cultural stress among foreign students (Thomson et al., 2006).

Social support helps adjust and reduces an individual's stress (Solberg et al., 1994). Social support is the comfort and well-being that an individual receives from informal and formal sources with other people or societal organizations. It plays a crucial role when the individual comes in contact with an individual from another culture by helping them to cope with the host culture (Bochner, 2003). It is included as it is an integral part of the current research among international students as it helps in the adjustment process of the individuals. It is a mechanism by which interpersonal relationships would protect individuals from the deleterious effects of stress. In the research, it has been considered that social support is a protective factor that gives good health. It is a mechanism in which there is an interpersonal relationship to protect individuals from the harmful effects of stress (Kessler et al., 1985). It also enhances the adjustment levels of the individuals by creating a positive effect and self-confidence or a sense of personal satisfaction (Meehan et al., 1993).

There are two kinds of social support- instrumental and emotional support. Emotional support expresses love, care, sympathy, social companionship, and concern. Instrumental support mentions the various types of tangible support an individual receives. It is otherwise called informational support (Finfgeld-Connett, 2005). Another study has examined perceived social support in three forms: tangible support, emotional support, and informational support (Schaefer et al., 1981).

Sullivan and Kashubeck-West (2015) identified the relationship between social support, acculturation modes and the culture shock among the undergraduate and graduate foreign students in the United States who study in the public university. The students face a less cultural shock when they have greater social support. There was a relationship between social support and the level of acculturative stress. Kim et al. (2012) investigated the coping strategies that can manage cultural shock in Korean immigrant adolescents in the United States. The study examined the strategies involved in engaging in some valuable activities and having social support to have positive emotions. When adolescents can cope with acculturative stress, they have psychological well-being and a sense of happiness. The social support from the family members and friends played a significant part in the coping mechanism to manage culture shock.

Social support is a powerful coping mechanism for stress (Lazarus & Folkman, 1984). Social support acts as a mediator and moderator in between stress, thereby reducing stress and improving physical health (Finch & Vega, 2003). Social support has a vital role in helping an individual adjust to a new environment. Social support from a particular person (friend and family member) helps in the adjustment process. The adjusting capability of the students from another country when they arrive in a new place is only based on academic achievement. They are able to adjust to the new place, or else there will be acculturative stress that the students need to face (Yusoff & Othman, 2011). The Asian and American individuals reported stress because of the cultural changes, and there is a relation between the cultural shock and social support from friends and families (Singh et al., 2015). The Chinese students in host countries face cultural shock and cross-cultural problems (Ng et al., 2013). These students reported increased emotional problems such as depression and emotional well-being (Li et al., 2021). Wang et al. (2012) had empirically tested another study which focuses on the patterns of acculturative adjustment and its profiles among the students from China studying in the United States. The students reported higher self-esteem and a better adjustment process. The new students studying in the first semester reported that social support was a coping mechanism for better cross-cultural transition.

One of the common problems contributing to stress is Homesickness, which is observed among the international students who come and study when they have to leave their families and try to adjust to the new culture. It is one of the common problems these students undergo (Kegel, 2009). The students have issues with the English Language, which is one of the reasons for stress when they come to a new culture. Not knowing the language of the place where the students reside is one of the primary causes of their depression and anxiety (Parray et al., 2020; Wu et al., 2015). Depression is observed among university students who have to leave their families and come to a new place for their education. Suicide attempts are observed among students of diverse backgrounds due to cultural shock (Gomez et al., 2011). Paukert et al. (2006) examined the relation between acculturative stress and the attributional style among culturally diverse students. It was observed that men had higher acculturative stress compared to women. Social support also played a vital part in the reduction of culture shock.

Culture shock is a significant problem faced by African students when adjusting to another country (Boafo-Arthur, 2014). Acculturative stress is negatively related to social support (Franco et al., 2019). The Chinese students face a lower amount of stress and racial discrimination in the USA. Cultural shock mediated the relationship between the home culture and depression (Rajab et al., 2014; Falavarjani et al., 2019). The study reported that about 75% of the students had problems associated with depression, and about 25% had suicidal concerns and homicidal thoughts. The students often experience cultural shock when they come from one country to another country (Hamboyan & Bryan, 1995).

Methodology

Sample

The current study measures the cultural shock and social support among foreign students when they come for studies from one country to another. A descriptive research design is followed in the current research because the sample consists of foreign students in various countries. The quantitative descriptive study analyzes foreign students' cultural shock and social support levels. The sampling technique is purposive. The data is primarily collected through an online questionnaire on social support and culture shock. The international students (n=100) from several universities in Zambia, India, Uganda, Zimbabwe, Tanzania and China were considered as a sample.

The demographic part of the assessment has questions relating to age, gender, length of stay, and country of origin. The origin consists of Students studying abroad from India and students studying in India from Foreign countries. The sample size consisted of 100 international students studying in India and abroad.

Perceived Social Support

Zimet et al. (1988) developed a multidimensional social support scale on three factors, i.e., significant others, friends, and family. The study participants were given a 7-point Likert scale to measure them on each given item—the reliability of the *Perceived Social Support* scale was 0.84.

Culture Shock

Sandhu and Asrabadi (1994) developed the scale ASSIS to measure the culture shock or acculturative stress that foreign students face. ASSIS (Acculturative stress for International students) has 36 items on a 5-point Likert scale. Culture shock consists of Seven factors, homesickness (4 items), perceived discrimination (8 items), fear (4 items), guilt (2 items), perceived hate (5 items), culture shock (3 items), and miscellaneous (10 items). The reliability of the ASSIS is 0.96.

Hypotheses

From the literature review performed, the following hypotheses are proposed:

H1: There is a positive association between culture shock and social support.

H2: The native country has an association with culture shock.

Analysis and Interpretation

Descriptive Analysis

The present study investigates the association between social support and culture shock with a demographic variable native country. The sample consists of 100 foreign students, of which 47% consist of male students, and 53% consist of female students. The foreign students' age group ranges from 20-23 years. Few students completed the questionnaire through an online survey, whereas few completed it through a questionnaire. The total mean score of the culture shock scale is 3.15. The social support scale has a total mean score of 5.46.

Table 12.1: Participants Demographic Profile (N=100)

Demographic Variable	Categories	Foreign students (n=100)
Gender	Male	47
	Female	53
Age	20-23	56
	24-27	41
	27 and above	3
Origin	Indian Students studying Abroad	42
	Foreign students studying in India	58
Length of stay	2 Years	31
	3 Years	26
	4 Years	41
	4 Years and above	2

Table 12.1 represents the demographic profile of the participants the gender male (n=47) and female (n=53), age 20-23 (n=56), 24-27 (n=41), and 27 years and above (n=3). The origin Indian students studying abroad (n=42) and foreign students studying in India (n=58). The length of stay 2 years (n=31), 3 years (n=26), 4 years (n=41) and 4 years and above (n=2).

Table 12.2: Descriptive Statistics, Reliability (Cronbach's Alpha) and Correlation Matrix

Measures	M	SD	A	1	2	3	4	5	6	7	8	9	10	11	12
Discrimination	3.00	0.87	0.89	1											
Homesickness	3.69	0.67	0.67	.43**	1										
Perceived Hate	3.04	0.90	0.80	.82**	.33**	1									
Fear	2.82	0.95	0.79	.84**	.41**	.84**	1								
Cultural Shock	3.52	0.74	0.75	.65**	.41**	.62**	.53**	1							
Guilt	2.99	1.12	0.63	.69**	.39**	.72**	.73**	.41**	1						
Miscellaneous	3.13	0.84	0.87	.91**	.43**	.88**	.91**	.64**	.76**	1					
Support from Significant Others	5.06	1.26	0.80	.21**		.13	.15	.04	.04	.13	1				
Support from Friends	5.62	1.02	0.75	.05	-.07	-.03	.07	-.09	-.03	.06		1			
Support from Family	5.69	0.91	0.78	.19	.07	.20**	.18	.10	.37**	.26**			1		
Total Culture shock	3.15	0.75	0.96	.95**		.91**	.92**	.70**	.79**	.96**	.15	.02	.24**	1	
Total Social Support	5.46	0.87	0.84	.02	.18	.09	.13	16	.02	.18	.20*	.87	.84**	.74**	1

** Correlation is significant at the 0.1 level (2-tailed)

Table 12.2 represents the Standard deviation (SD) and Mean in the correlation matrix for the variables comprised in the research, the reliability value ranges from 0.63 to 0.96. The significant correlation ranges from -.03 to .96. The highest factor with the mean score in culture shock is homesickness (Mean=3.69), and social support from family (Mean=5.69) has the highest mean score.

Table 12.3 represents the SD, Mean, and ANOVA for the native country on culture shock among students. It is observed in India, China, Uganda, Zimbabwe, Tanzania and Zambia. The highest amount of culture shock is observed in China (Mean= 3.64), followed by Zambia (Mean=3.52), Tanzania

(Mean=3.19), and Zimbabwe (Mean=3.07). The F value is 5.85 with a 5% level of significance.

Table 12.3: Mean, Standard Deviation, & Anova between Native Country on Culture shock (N=100)

Native Country on Culture Shock					
Native Country	N	Mean	SD	f-value	Sig(2-tailed)
India	41	2.82	0.69		
China	28	3.64	0.60		
Uganda	9	2.79	0.69		
Zimbabwe	7	3.07	0.70	5.85	0.000
Tanzania	8	3.19	0.86		
Zambia	7	3.52	0.47		

Table 12.4: Regression Coefficient of Social Support and Culture Shock

Variable	B	B	SE
(Constant)	3.324		.589
SS1	.035	.071	.055
SS2	- .001	- .003	.056
SS3**	- .183	- .327	.067
SS4***	.269	.504	.067
SS5	.024	.057	.053
SS6	- .051	- .077	.085
SS7	.091	.206	.061
SS8	.076	.166	.049
SS9	- .061	- .098	.074
SS10	.093	.168	.065
SS11	- .146	- .176	.083
SS12	- .123	- .183	.077
R^2		0.36	

**p<0.001; *p<0.005

The above table represents the impact of social support predicators on cultural shock among international students. The R^2 value of .36 revealed that social support's predictor variable explained the 36% significance of the cultural shock outcome variable. The T statistics value of SS3 & SS4 representing family support is -2.75 and 4.01, respectively.

Discussion and Implication

From the current study, it is evident that there is an association between cultural shock and social support among foreign students. They often face adjustment difficulties when they come to a new country and face cultural shock. Chinese students faced a considerable amount of culture shock and adjustment difficulties (Bertram et al., 2014). Social support from family members helps reduce the stress that the students face when they come to another country for their studies.

The impact of predicators is social support on culture shock among international students. It is found that two factors from the social support scale significantly impact the outcome variable culture shock among international students. Foreign students have to adapt to the new cultural norms of the host country. The result shows the hypothesized country of origin and its association with the culture shock. There is an association with the native country and cultural shock foreign students face, i.e., India, China, Uganda, Zimbabwe, Tanzania and Zambia. The results also indicate that foreign students from China and Zambia stated greater stress levels than students from India, Uganda, Zimbabwe and Tanzania. A similar study (Nasirudeen et al., 2014) has reported that the country of origin has an association and impact on cultural shock. Foreign students in China had more culture shock than the other countries. Social support from the family reduces the cultural shock to a greater extent among the foreign students. Social support has a significant association with cultural shock among foreign students (Li et al., 2021).

The study also utilized the social support theory to lessen the stress that the students face. The existing social support theory consists of the three important perspectives: coping and stress, the perspective of the relationship and the social constructionist (Lakey & Cohen, 2000). The theory of social support helps in reducing stress levels among individuals by providing psychological well-being (Cohen, 1996). The native country influences culture shock, whereas the native country does not influence social support. Studies have reported that demographics like the length of stay (Ayoob et al., 2011) and gender (Akhtar & Kröner-Herwig, 2015) influence acculturative stress among international students.

The study results offer significant insights to the practitioners seeking to help the international students studying in another country. The measures to reduce the stress among the international students should be practiced in the universities and the institutions that admit foreign students. The institutions should ensure they provide facilities to help international students feel comfortable. International students' relations and their affairs in the universities should take active involvement in catering to the needs of these students. The university counseling centers should also take explicit care of the well-being of these students.

The present research findings show that the students from Zambia and China had more cultural shock than the other students from India, Uganda, Zimbabwe, and Tanzania. These students should be given proper care and proper support. There should be social support and perceived institutional support provided by the institutions. The international students should have a better connection with the domestic students and have resilience; this can aid them in coping better in a new country. The international students should have the ability to develop meaningful and interpersonal relationships with domestic students and peers in the institutions.

Conclusion

The study concludes and suggests practical implications for both educators and administrators. The acculturation requirements and the host country's culture should be appreciated to avoid the stress that the foreign students face. The institutions with an intake of international students must ensure that there are proper strategies implemented to facilitate them to overcome the issues caused due to cultural diversity. While understanding the culture shock levels, the institutions can provide better social and financial support to foreign students. They face much stress as soon as they arrive from their native nation to another. Homesickness is one of the critical factors that will lead to cultural shock to them. Social support is a coping mechanism for reducing the stress that the students face. However, from the study, it could benefit the families and friends by reducing the cultural shock levels faced by their dear ones. This research will help the *office of student affairs* in the institutions to take proper actions to help international students face cultural shock and mental health issues, thereby reducing their academic performance. The international students often face homesickness and discrimination leading to acculturative stress. The international students face poor academic performance because of the various stressors they face when they cannot adjust to the host country due to their acculturation process as they come for their studies. The study has concluded that international students face many problems in the process of acculturation, affecting their academic performance. The support received from friends and families helps them adjust to the new place by reducing acculturative stress. Future research could focus on the other factors that could influence cultural shock and the other external sources of coping strategies in providing social support to foreign students.

References

Akhtar, M., & Kröner-Herwig, B. (2015). Acculturative stress among international students in context of socio-demographic variables and coping styles. *Current psychology, 34*(4), 803-815. https://doi.org/10.1007/s12144-015-9303-4

Ayoob, M., Singh, T., & Jan, M. (2011). Length of stay, acculturative stress, and health among Kashmiri students in Central India. *Pakistan Journal of Social and Clinical Psychology, 9*, 11–15.

Bai, J. (2016). Perceived Support as a Predictor of Acculturative Stress among International Students in the United States. *Journal of International Students, 6*(1), 93-106. https://doi.org/10.32674/jis.v6i1.483

Berry, J. W. (2003). Conceptual approaches to acculturation. In K. M. Chun, P. Balls Organista, & G. Marín (Eds.), *Acculturation: Advances in theory, measurement, and applied research* (pp. 17–37). American Psychological Association. https://doi.org/10.1037/10472-004

Berry, J.W. (1997). Immigration, Acculturation, and Adaptation. *Applied Psychology, 46*(1), 05-34. https://doi.org/10.1111/j.1464-0597.1997.tb01087.x

Bertram, D. M., Poulakis, M., Elsasser, B. S., & Kumar, E. (2014). Social support and acculturation in Chinese international students. *Journal of Multicultural Counseling and Development, 42*(2), 107-124. https://doi.org/10.1002/j.2161-1912.2014.00048.x

Boafo-Arthur, S. (2014). Acculturative experiences of Black-African international students. *International Journal for the Advancement of Counselling, 36*(2), 115-124. https://doi.org/10.1007/s10447-013-9194-8

Bochner, S. (2003). Culture shock due to contact with unfamiliar cultures. *Online readings in psychology and culture, 8*(1), 1-12. https://doi.org/10.9707/2307-0919.1073

Cabassa, J. L. (2003). Measuring Acculturation: Where we are and where we need to go. *Hispanic Journal of Behavioral Sciences, 25*(2), 127-146. https://doi.org/10.1177/0739986303025002001

Creswell, J.W. (2008). *Educational research: Planning, conducting, and evaluating quantitative and qualitative research*. Prentice Hall India.

Crockett, L. J., Iturbide, M. I., Torres Stone, R. A., McGinley, M., Raffaelli, M., & Carlo, G. (2007). Acculturative stress, social support, and coping: relations to psychological adjustment among Mexican American college students. *Cultural Diversity and Ethnic Minority Psychology, 13*(4), 347.

Falavarjani, M. F., Yeh, C. J., & Brouwers, S. A. (2019). Exploring the Effects of Acculturative Stress and Social Support on the Acculturation-Depression Relationship in Two Countries of Similar Social Status. *Journal of International Migration and Integration, 21*, 509-528. https://doi.org/10.100 7/s12134-019-00662-3

Fanari, A., Liu, R. W., & Foerster, T. (2021). Homesick or sick-of-home? Examining the effects of self-disclosure on students' reverse culture shock after studying abroad: A mixed-method study. *Journal of Intercultural Communication Research, 50*(3), 273-303.

Finch, B. K., & Vega, W. A. (2003). Acculturation stress, social support, and self-rated health among Latinos in California. *Journal of immigrant health, 5*(3), 109-117.

Finfgeld-Connett, D. (2005), Clarification of social support. *Journal of Nursing Scholarship, 37*(1), 4-9.

Franco, M., Hsiao, Y. S., Gnilka, P. B., & Ashby, J. S. (2019). Acculturative stress, social support, and career outcome expectations among international students. *International Journal for Educational and Vocational Guidance, 19*(2), 275-291. https://doi.org/10.1007/s10775-018-9380-7

Gomez, J., Miranda, R., & Polanco, L. (2011). Acculturative stress, perceived discrimination, and vulnerability to suicide attempts among emerging adults. *Journal of youth and adolescence, 40*(11), 1465-1474. https://doi.org/10.1007/s10964-011-9688-9

Hamboyan, H., & Bryan, A. K. (1995). International students. Culture shock can affect the health of students from abroad. *Canadian Family Physician, 41,* 1713-1716.

Kegel, K. (2009). Homesickness in international college students. In Walz, G. R., Bleuer, J. C., & Yep R. K. (Eds.), *Compelling Counseling Interventions: VISTAS 2009* (pp. 67-76). American Counseling Association.

Kegel, K. (2015). Homesickness and Psychological Distress in Asian International Students: The Potential Mediating Roles of Social Connectedness and Universal-Diverse Orientation. *PhD Thesis.* Lehigh University.

Kessler, R.C., Price, R.H., & Wortman, C.B. (1985). Social factors in psychopathology: Stress, social support, and coping processes. *Annual Review of Psychology, 36*(1), 531-572.

Kim, J., Suh, W., Kim, S., & Gopalan, H. (2012). Coping strategies to manage acculturative stress: Meaningful activity participation, social support, and positive emotion among Korean immigrant adolescents in the USA. *International Journal of Qualitative Studies on Health and Well-being, 7*(1). https://doi.org/10.3402/qhw.v7i0.18870

Lakey, B., & Cohen, S. (2000). Social support theory and measurement. In Cohen, S., Underwood, L. G., & Gottlieb, B. H. (Eds.), *Social support measurement and intervention: A guide for health and social scientists* (pp. 29-52). Oxford University Press. https://doi.org/10.1093/med:psych/9780195126709.003.0002

Lazarus, R.S., & Folkman, S. (1984). *Stress, appraisal, and coping.* Springer.

Lee, J. (2021). *Unique challenges and opportunities for supporting mental health and promoting the well-being of international graduate students.* Council of Graduate Schools.

Li, Y., Liang, F., Xu, Q., Gu, S., Wang, Y., Li, Y., & Zeng, Z. (2021). Social support, attachment closeness, and self-esteem affect depression in international students in China. *Frontiers in Psychology, 12,* 618105. https://doi.org/10.3389/fpsyg.2021.618105

Lin, Y. & Kingminghae, W. (2014). Social Support and Loneliness of Chinese International Students in Thailand. *Journal of Population and Social Studies, 22*(2), 141-157.

Mallinckrodt, B., & Leong, F. T. (1992). International graduate students, stress, and social support. *Journal of College Student Development, 33*(1), 71-78.

McLeod, K. D., Eslami, Z. R., & Graham, K. M. (2021). Culture Shock and Coping Mechanisms of International Korean Students: A Qualitative Study. *International Journal of TESOL Studies, 3*(1), 14-28.

Meehan, M.P., Durlak, J.A., & Bryant, F.B. (1993). The relationship of social support to perceived control and subjective mental health in adolescents. *Journal of Community Psychology, 21*(1), 49-55.

Murwantono, D., & Rinawati, R. (2021). Culture Shock and Campus Program in ELT for Thai Undergraduate Students at University of Islam Sultan Agung and University of Ahmad Dahlan. *English Review: Journal of English Education, 9*(2), 437-444.

Nasirudeen, A.M.A., Josephine, K.W.N., Adeline, L.L.C., Seng, L.L. & Ling, H.A. (2014). Acculturative stress among Asian international students in Singapore. *Journal of International Students, 4*(4), 363-373.

Ng, T. K., Tsang, K. K., & Lian, Y. (2013). Acculturation strategies, social support, and cross-cultural adaptation: a mediation analysis. *Asia Pacific Education Review, 14*(4), 593-601.

Oberg, K. (1954). *Culture shock* (p. 1). Bobbs-Merrill.

Parray, A. A., Sohely, S., Mallick, S., Zahura, F. T., Mistry, B., Sharkar, P., Nahar, J., Sumi, K., Islam, A. & Khan, M. S. (2020). Acculturation and adaptation issues among International students: Experiences from the largest Public University of Bangladesh. https://doi.org/10.21203/rs.3.rs-51527/v1

Paukert, A.L., Pettit, J.W., Perez, M., & Walker, R.L. (2006). Affective and attributional features of acculturative stress among ethnic minority college students. *The Journal of Psychology, 140*(5), 405-419.

Rajab, A., Rahman, H. A., Panatik, S. A., & Mansor, N. S. (2014). Acculturative stress among international students. *Journal of Economics, Business and Management, 2*(4), 262-265. https://doi.org/10.7763/JOEBM.2014.V2.136

Sabouripour, F., & Roslan, S. B. (2015). Resilience, optimism and social support among international students. *Asian Social Science, 11*(15), 159-170. http://dx.doi.org/10.5539/ass.v11n15p159

Sandhu, D. S., & Asrabadi, B. R. (1994). Development of an Acculturative Stress Scale for International Students: Preliminary Findings. *Psychological Reports, 75*(1), 435–448. https://doi.org/10.2466/pr0.1994.75.1.435

Schaefer, C., Coyne, J.C., & Lazarus, R.S. (1981). The health-related functions of social support. *Journal of Behavioral Medicine, 4*(4), 381-406.

Sedikides, C., Wildschut, T., Routledge, C., Arndt, J., & Zhou, X. (2009). Buffering acculturative stress and facilitating cultural adaptation: Nostalgia as a psychological resource. In Wyer, R. S., Chiu, C.-y., & Hong, Y.-y. (Eds.), *Understanding culture: Theory, research, and application* (pp. 361–378). Psychology Press.

Singh, S., McBride, K., & Kak, V. (2015). Role of Social Support in Examining Acculturative Stress and Psychological Distress among Asian American

Immigrants and Three Sub-groups: Results from NLAAS. *Journal of Immigrant and Minority Health, 17*(6), 1597-1606.

Solberg, V. S., Valdez, J., & Villarreal, P. (1994). Social support, stress, and Hispanic college adjustment: Test of a diathesis-stress model. *Hispanic Journal of Behavioral Sciences, 16*(3), 230-239.

Sullivan, C., & Kashubeck-West, S. (2015). The interplay of international students' acculturative stress, social support, and acculturation modes. *Journal of International Students, 5*(1), 1-11.

Thomas, M., & Choi, J. B. (2006). Acculturative Stress and Social Support among Korean and Indian Immigrant Adolescents in the United States. *Journal of Sociology and Social Welfare, 33*(2), 123–143.

Thomson, G., Rosenthal, D., & Russell, J. (2006, October). *Cultural stress among international students at an Australian university.* Australian International Education Conference 2006.

Uchino, B.N. (2004). *Social support and physical health: Understanding the health consequences of relationships.* Yale University Press.

Wang, K.T., Heppner, P.P., Fu, C.C., Zhao, R., Li, F., & Chuang, C.C. (2012). Profiles of acculturative adjustment patterns among Chinese international students. *Journal of Counseling Psychology, 59*(3), 424-436. https://doi.org/10.1037/a0028532

Wei, M., Heppner, P. P., Mallen, M. J., Ku, T.-Y., Liao, K. Y.-H., & Wu, T.-F. (2007). Acculturative stress, perfectionism, years in the United States, and depression among Chinese international students. *Journal of counseling psychology, 54*(4), 385-394. https://doi.org/10.1037/0022-0167.54.4.385

Wu, H. P., Garza, E., & Guzman, N. (2015). International student's challenge and adjustment to college. *Education Research International.* https://doi.org/10.1155/2015/202753

Xia, J. (2009). Analysis of impact of culture shock on individual psychology. *International Journal of Psychological Studies, 1*(2), 97-101. https://doi.org/10.5539/ijps.v1n2p97

Yeh, C. J., & Inose, M. (2003). International students' reported English fluency, social support satisfaction, and social connectedness as predictors of acculturative stress. *Counselling Psychology Quarterly, 16*(1), 15-28.

Yusoff, Y. M., & Othman, A. K. (2011). An early study on perceived social support and psychological adjustment among international students: The case of a higher learning institution in Malaysia. *International Journal of Business and Society, 12*(2), 1-15.

Zimet, G. D., Dahlem, N. W., Zimet, S. G., & Farley, G. K. (1988). The Multidimensional Scale of Perceived Social Support. *Journal of Personality Assessment, 52*(1), 30–41. https://doi.org/10.1207/s15327752jpa5201_2

Chapter 13

African Culture and Traditions Matter: Managing Psychological Wellbeing During and After a Crisis

Wandile Fundo Tsabedze

Department of Psychology, University of South Africa, South Africa

Siboniso Collin Gumedze

Department of Psychology, University of South Africa, South Africa

Mpho Maotoana

University of Limpopo, Department of Psychology, Sovenga, Limpopo, South Africa

Mokoena, Patronella Maepa

Sefako Makgatho Health Sciences University, South Africa

Abstract: The Swati culture is rich and diverse with different practices and beliefs such as mourning '*Kufukama*' and the reed dance '*Umhlanga*'. Emaswati believes that sharing traditional beer '*Umcombotsi*' and tobacco snuff brings unity. With the COVID-19 pandemic, the Emaswati nation got a culture shock when it was announced that the cultural and traditional events had to come to a standstill, stealing from rich cultural activities. COVID-19 pandemic impacted the psychosocial welling of African people, which prime to a gap in how they have to adjust to the rules and regulations of the pandemic self-quarantine, which led to the most prolonged lockdown. Psychological well-being and African perspectives were examined among Emaswati. People must be aware of such pandemics, which are always unpredictable, and awareness to prevent mental health illnesses for future pandemics. Therefore, integrating traditional and modern ways of dealing with such pandemics is essential when planning for the future.

Keywords: African Culture, Psychosocial well-being, Cultural Values, Emaswati Traditions, Pandemic, Cultural Shock

***

Introduction

In March 2020, the world came to a stand-in all spheres of life due to the COVID-19, which World Health Organisation (WHO) declared a pandemic (WHO, 2020). This pandemic escalated stress, depression, anxiety, gender-based violence, and increased mental health illnesses. Preventive action was comprehensively upgraded worldwide in order to deal with this pandemic. Many countries immediately announced a national lockdown to curb the spread of the virus. The underestimation of the severity of COVID-19 by the Eswatini or Swaziland government resulted in delayed action against the pandemic. However, later the Eswatini authorities were forced to implement physical distancing, self-isolation, closure of non-essential services, schools, social gatherings (funerals, weddings, and cultural events), traveling restrictions and recursive national lockdowns to mitigate the impact of COVID-19.

The pandemic not only did it affect the economic system of the country, but it also affected the culture of Emaswati, psychologically and socially. Most of the cultural practices of the Amarula Festival '*Buganu*' (this is where the whole nation comes together to feast and interact with others to form a new relationship which later becomes their social support). The reed dance '*Umhlanga*' (where young girls come together to socialise and dance for the royalties, and the whole national community watch these young girls dancing), which has significant therapeutic benefits, was put on hold due to COVID-19. Eliminating these traditional practices has led to minimal social interaction. According to Brody (2020), psychologists have enunciated concerns that the loss of access to social connections will fast-track the already rising rates of loneliness among individuals.

Eswatini has faced other infectious illnesses, such as HIV/AIDS, tuberculosis (T.B.) and Ebola hemorrhagic fever, which impacted their cultural psychology and dealt with post-pandemic effects (Buseh et al., 2002). Though other illnesses challenged the Emaswati nation, nothing took away their cultural and traditional practices, which are therapeutic. COVID-19 affected how the Swati people lived their daily lives and dictated cultural activities.

Despite COVID-19 being a medical condition, its effects affect the psychosocial well-being of people in general (Kumar & Nayar, 2021). Together with their families, those infected with the virus suffer medically and present with psychological sequelae (Yao et al., 2020). In this chapter, we looked at how COVID-19 affected the psychosocial well-being of Emaswati. Emaswati takes pride in their rich African culture and is rooted in their customs even though they have adopted Western practices (Debly, 2014).

It is also important to highlight that COVID-19 did affect the Swati nation regardless much culture and traditions matter to Emaswati. For example, the reed dance *(Umhlanga)* was affected by COVID-19, boys initiating *(Kubutseka)* during the gathering of young regiments *(Lusekwane)* and Swati prayer *(Incwala)*.

Africans are known for their "Ubuntu" ('I am because we are'); it resembles unity and collectivism other than individualism, and Emaswati believes in unity and humanity that brings harmony and sharing. On the contrary, the novel pandemic coronavirus prohibits Ubuntu because of the restrictions on no sharing of objects. People must quarantine and keep social distancing. Quarantine brings confusion to the space of the people's psychological and social well-being and culture shock/dilute. It is also recommended that more studies be carried out in Africa on how the COVID-19 pandemic affected African people's culture and traditions to adjust to the new normal of life.

Methodology

Study Design

The study used a case-series research design, precisely multiple cases which focus on an issue and then select several bounded cases to illustrate that issue. The sample was/is exposed to the COVID-19 pandemic hence the multiple case study design. The sample was based on exposure to the COVID-19 pandemic, which resulted in the culture and traditions of the Emaswati being affected by the COVID-19 pandemic. The case-series design was used to gain more insight from different researchers on how they viewed COVID-19's affected culture of Emaswati. The outcome of the COVID-19 pandemic with new rules and regulations resulted in the psychological well-being population being affected by the COVID-19 pandemic.

Description of Population

The study population is Emaswati, who are geographically based at Eswatini and upholds the Swati culture. The population is known for being rurally dominated, still preserves the culture and traditions as a solid common binding characteristic/trait. Plecher (2020) projected that between the years 2015 to 2025, the population of Emaswati would range from 1.08 to 1.19 million. However, with the high death rate in 2020 and 2021 due to COVID-19, the population is unpredictable. Therefore, the assumption is that it will be less, and based on the projection population at risk in 2021 is 1.14 million.

Case in Context, Analysis and Discussion

Disruption in Traditional Therapeutic Methods: A Case of COVID-19

The lockdown brought many restrictions, such as a limited number to attend social gatherings and social distancing. As people battled to cope with the pandemic, their usual coping methods/resources (the traditional acts) were not available to help them do so. Perceived double stressors were also every day among Emaswati. Under the different lockdown measures, the country's government had to apply the new usual way of living among Emaswati. The first level of lockdown was the hardest alert of COVID-19, which was announced on 27 March 2020. This lockdown level became a shock to the country, and none of the Emaswati was prepared for this kind of lockdown. The pandemic affected the psychosocial pathways (culture, traditions, religion, mental health, education and spirituality) of Emaswati; they had to prepare for the new ecological context brought by COVID-19. The government implemented that everyone had to self-quarantine in their different homes. It was a culture shock for all citizens in the country since they were not used to spending most of the time with families the whole day. Families were indirectly introduced to individualism since no extended families were allowed to visit. More chaos in the homesteads, such as the Gender-Based Violence (GBV) rate, escalated, and more GBV cases were reported to the police stations.

The government introduced the soft lockdown, allowing some community activities only if the COVID-19 rules and regulations were implemented. For example, funerals were allowed with a limited number of people to 50 attendees only. No extended families and community workers were allowed to attend the funerals. Funerals were only allowed due to the high mortality rate caused by COVID-19. In the implementation process, many cultural and traditional activities were burned, which affected the psychosocial well-being of Emaswati.

In addition, to date, Emaswati are under the most extended lockdown they have ever experienced, the most prolonged lockdown which has affected the family, culture, tradition, religion and mental health of the people. Since the lockdown started in other countries when the World Health Organization (WHO) announced the medical and psychological war which was declared by the COVID-19 pandemic on 31 December 2019 in Wuhan (Hubei province in China), the ecological context of Emaswati has never been the same, where there are restrictions such as no shaking of hands and hugging, keep social distancing and wearing of a mask and that is the new normal of the people. COVID-19 restrictions still apply in this most extended lockdown. For instance, most cultural activities can resume. However, there should be health precautions and guidelines.

Furthermore, plans to stop the rising number of infections included social distancing, wearing masks, self-quarantine and regular hand washing or sanitising. Touching and shaking hands with the next person, and keeping contact with the next person, were regarded as one way of spreading the virus (Nyabadza, Chirove, Chukwu, & Visaya, 2020). It is challenging among the Emaswati, as they shake hands when greeting a person, show love, and welcome them in their own space. People from collectivist cultures may have more concrete and interdependent self-concepts than people from individualist cultures (Hofstede, 1980), and African cultures are considered collectivist (Triandis, 1989). These two theories maintain that African culture is all about collectivism. However, all this changed when COVID-19 was learned in the African continent. Most cultures had to be introduced to individualism due to the lockdown restrictions foreign to the African people. The Swati culture is also about collectivism. It is the strong social support of the Swati people. When COVID-19 was discovered, most of them had to adapt to the new rules, the new normal among the Swati people. For instance, there was no visit from extended families, which are the closest social support the families have. Muris et al. (2002) reported that African people are more likely to have a high level of separation anxiety than Western people (used to individualism). This shows that during COVID-19, more African people, including the Swati people, were affected by the rules and regulations of COVID-19 since no visitors were not allowed to visit their extended families and perhaps to induce separation anxiety. A study conducted by Kim, Nyengerai and Mendenhall (2020) in South Africa which is a neighbouring country to Eswatini, reported that most people showed symptoms of depression and trauma when COVID-19 was announced for the first time in South Africa because they had to be in quarantine for 21 days without any social life and being physical contact with our extended families. Therefore, it is more likely that most of the Swati people had mental health issues due to being exposed to the COVID-19 pandemic.

Moreover, the spiritual being of the Swati people was also affected by the fact that churches were shut down. The Swati people are known for their solid spiritual practices, such as attending Good Friday, known as Easter collectively. This is whereby churches gather together at the royal church and share the world of good from different religions and churches. The king and his family came to listen to what the churches wanted to share with him. Conversely, since COVID-19 was announced in March 2020, such events never took place and did affect the well-being of the people spiritually.

Churches are considered among the vast population in the country, and they are a faster spread of the virus.

During level 5 of lockdown, most families were locked in their homes and houses, with nowhere to go except in the surroundings of their homes, this exposed this culture to individualism and depression of being home and not working, and lack of social support from families, friends and work colleagues was a significant challenge. In addition, Mbunge (2020) reported that the prolonged effects of lockdown resulted in the outbursts of uncertainties, acute panic, fear, depression, obsessive behaviors, social unrest, stigmatization, anxiety, and increased gender-based violence cases and discrimination in the distribution of relief food aid.

Social Challenges Associated with COVID-19

WHO regulated no visiting the hospitals or medical centers where the COVID-19 patients were being hospitalized. For instance, once doctors declare that the individual is positive, no relatives can visit the individual in the hospital until tested negative or is free from the virus. The healing process of the individuals diagnosed with the virus was not easy because there was no social support from the families and community. Nyashanu et al. (2020) reported that in South Africa, the collectivist community, such as those living in informal settlements, were more affected during the COVID-19 pandemic because of overcrowding. This challenge led to no space for social distancing and no access to a good hospital. Therefore the community experience depression, anxiety, and hunger (there were no jobs). Such results imply to Eswatini whereby the country's health system is not to the standard to accommodate its community; hence, the pandemic impacts the lives of the public. Moreover, Bernardo and Mendoza (2020) reported that in the collectivist cultures, hope is brought when they are socially supporting each other during the hardship times, which is not the case during the COVID-19 pandemic when an individual is sick and has to survive alone after visiting hours at hospitals were canceled. This did not only affect those who were hospitalized but also their loved ones at home.

The Use of Traditional Medicine during COVID-19

Traditional healing is a healthcare delivery system in the Swati culture. Many plants are being used in traditional medicine. Emaswati relies on traditional medicine for their health care needs, including some who attend modern or Western health institutions because traditional medicine is anchored in the culture and religious beliefs of the people. The occurrence of traditional healing is believed to be spiritually related (Amusan et al., 2002). However, WHO (2020) discouraged people from using traditional medicine, which created stress for Emaswati as this is their traditional way of coping. The reliance on herbal medicine continued to rise during the second wave of the COVID-19 pandemic because, historically, most Emaswati believed in traditional healing. Plants such as '*Umhlonyane*,' a commonly used traditional medicine for treating flue, were being drunk and used for steaming by the majority of the people to heal themselves from coronaviruses. Another plant is the gum tree, or eucalyptus leaves called '*Gomu.*' Fever tea leaves called '*Umsutane*' were used for steaming to kill the virus in the body. WHO (2020) reported that the virus is transmitted from one person to the other via respiratory droplets and in contact with the other person. Hence Emaswati finds that the traditional route of curing the virus will work and be of great use among victims. In Addition, Bhuda and Marumo (2020) stated that during the pandemic, most South Africans preferred to use traditional medicine over Western medicine because it is accessible, cheaper and does not have side effects.

As traditional medicine became more common, the World Health Organisation (WHO) warned against the use of traditional herbs that are not laboratory tested in treating COVID-19. As a result, African governments struggled to contain the coronavirus pandemic (Muhammad, 2020). Resulting in a negative impact psychologically among Emaswati due to that they believed the traditional medicine was working well. On the other hand, a modern vaccine was underway to find the treatment of COVID-19; however, observationally so, the response was not well taken by most Emaswati because they strongly felt that their way of killing the virus was working for them, it was cheap and convenient to use, and it was not going to be foreign on their body. However, despite firing the warning shot, people were more comfortable with their traditional medicine because it has many benefits and has a long history of traditional medicine use. In Tanzania, President John Magufuli was also pushing for the use of traditional herbs rather than COVID-19 testing kits. He further ordered an investigation into the National Laboratory Services, accusing it of carrying out nonhuman tests that turned out to be positive for coronavirus (Mugabi, 2020). This elaborates on how much traditional medicine is trusted and used among African people. Muhammad (2020) acknowledges traditional medicines in Africa and Asia, which have been used to heal flu-related sicknesses. For example, Artemisia is regarded as one of the traditional medicine which can be used to treat medicine.

The Impact of COVID-19 on Mourning Rituals

The state of bereavement is not easy to go experience while isolated from loved ones who can give social support (Endomba et al. 2020). During COVID-19 families had to go through challenging bereavement period ever experienced. For instance, in family bereavement, where the family had lost their close relative, it was not allowed to attend the funeral due to several restrictions related to funerals serving as spreader events. According to Bear et al. (2020), the pandemic denied people to bury their loved ones, so than they usually do.

These dynamics were precipitated because psychologists were at increased risk due to their circumstances. They identified some families: single-parent households, multigenerational Black and Minority Ethnic groups, men without degrees in lone households and precarious work, small family business owners in their 50s and elderly households. Hypothetically, such regulation affected the families and initiated depression, stress, incomplete grieving process of the individuals, prolonged grief disorder, post-traumatic stress, poor bereavement outcomes among relatives, and moral injury and distress for the community since they were not allowed to attend funerals. Selman et al. (2020) reported that most families had post-traumatic stress disorder (PTSD) because 'goodbyes' were not allowed during the pandemic, nor were they allowed to visit their loved ones in hospitals to prevent contact with them the person having the virus. In addition, there are Swati traditional practices which help the individuals to heal, for instance, dressing the deceased while at the mortuary and also making sure that the deceased has well prepared by taking some of the clothes to the casket and supporting the corpse, all these were burned, and this had emotional distress to the family and relatives since such traditions cannot take place any more.

In addition, grieving was not easy for them during the COVID-19, according to Kubler-Ross (1970) stages of grief, the grieving individual experiences denial, anger, bargaining, depression and acceptance; however, this was not experienced by the Swati people, there were rules which affected the grieving process other never got the chance to accept the death of their loved one due to rate of deaths from immediate and extended families. Such practices (burring the deceased within three days, wearing the black robe '*Kuzila*,' sharing the Swati traditional beer '*Umcomotsi*,' Snuff '*Indlelo*' and after seven days blowing of the cuddle '*Kucima Likhandlela*') are generally done during the caused most of the community never to understand death because of the psychological distress the individuals were experiencing. Moreover, Makgahlela et al. (2019) indicated that ritual performance is associated with myriad psychosocial benefits, including preventing a culture-specific bereavement illness. Essentially, ritual performance is for healing in that it lessens bereavement from becoming disabling. However, no rituals such as the cleansing ritual '*Kuzila*' occurred during lockdown because no one was allowed to go outside their homes. In addition, the rituals needed an elder to get herbs from the forest, yet everyone was in quarantine.

Roles of Elders during a Funeral

Funerals are respected in all cultures worldwide. It is essential to know that elders taught us to respect the deceased and prepare funerals, including the rituals and practices (Jindra & Noret, 2011). However, due to COVID-19, the elders were not allowed to attend funerals or gatherings since they were regarded as one of the high-risk populations. There are traditional rituals when a person dies in the Swati funerals, for instance, wearing the black robe '*Kuzila*' and widowhood, which facilitate the morning and grief response and are facilitated by the elders. However, such practices were not well performed in families due to the COVID-19 restrictions. In addition, '*Kugeza*' (to cleanse) the family after the funeral was prohibited as per the COVID-19 regulations.

Swati women play a central role in the care and disposal of the dead and managing bereavement. Mortuary rituals provide members of the society with adaptive means of the morning of the dead, and the expressions of grief ensure a periodic adjustment to human loss. Funerals and morning rites involve music and poems recited by the elders, capturing many aspects of Swati culture. After elders were barred from attending funerals, funerals are no longer perfect mediums for understanding Swati traditional and popular culture and appreciating the impact of social support on Swati society. To interrupt and control coronavirus during community transmission, trained teams with appropriate protective equipment and essential now handle the roles of elders during funerals. For anyone involved in the management of burial has to use COVID-19 regulations. It is the new normal, which society has to embrace and adapt. Before taking the corpse, the burial team should fully inform the bereaved family about the burial process as much as possible. The immediate management of the dead is done by none specialists, such as local organizations and communities. These disruptions to traditional practice can result in feelings of resentment, anger or fear (for example, beliefs about misfortune when not paying respect to the deceased) (Lee, 2009). Loss of support from elders during funerals further limits the ability to cope and increases distress.

Morning "Kufukama" during COVID-19

There is a custom called '*Kufukama*,' whereby relatives (older women) of a deceased come together to psychologically and emotionally support the deceased's family by guarding the body a day before the funeral, a whole night. It is a solid support system for the family who has a loss. According to Awolalu and Awolalu (1979), the funeral morning '*Kufukama*' is an essential rite of passage in many societies. While there are differences among those aspects peculiar to each culture, there are specific motifs common to morning in all cultures. The custom is practiced because women comfort the deceased's family, ensuring that they provide counseling and emotional support. It also happens during the week before the funeral, whereby the community and relatives from far come and comfort the family. To some extent, they offer food and money and do chaos while preparing for the funeral. However, the custom was burned as it was regarded as a super spreader of the pandemic.

With major or minor variations among the various ethnic groups, the principal stages in the morning of an aged person are an announcement of the death, preparation of the corpse for burial, the lying in state, the internment, and the rituals, feasting and ceremonies of the days following the burial. According to Ademiluka (2009), among the Nupe people in Nigeria, the mourners continue in this sorrowful mood for eight days. During this period, the relatives of the deceased may not wash, dress their hair or change their clothes. Furthermore, neither the older people nor the women may leave their huts except to relieve themselves (Awolalu & Awolalu, 1979). It is also customary for the deceased's blood relatives to continue with '*kufukama*' after the burial among the Swati people. It is when the family gets psychosocial and emotional support.

Nonetheless, such practices were not allowed during COVID-19 as the relatives of the deceased were only allowed to mourn for only three days which left unfinished grieving and morning among the families. It was foreign to Emaswati because they are used to funeral preparations of seven days while going through the *Kufukama* process. Additionally, it affected their psychological well-being emotionally and not being able to grieve.

Among other factors, '*Kufukama*' offers a venue for the culturally accepted expression of loss-related emotions and marks a transition in which the irreversibility of death is emphasized. Simultaneously, it provides a starting point for recovery and renewal. This custom can become vehicles in the transformation, transition and continuity processes forming the basis of adjustment and recovery following bereavement. With the closure of '*Kufukama*' during the COVID-19 pandemic, individuals experience the most intense emotions during and after the funeral. Bereaved individuals cannot get social support and mourn the death of their loved ones, which may help them cope with the loss. Not performing the ritual may not lead to the externalization of feelings and fostering the expression of emotions and may not help gain control over the changes and uncertainties brought about by the loss. An absence of morning rituals is a risk factor for psychological reactions and complicated grief (Beristain et al., 2000). Morning rituals and activities of collective remembering may benefit the individual and serve essential social functions.

The Loss of Cultural Practices and Diminished Cultural Identity

Swati culture is the way of life in which Emaswati live every day. As the tribe is known for its collectivism, this is how they live their lives. All this changed COVID-19 and disorganized the life of Emaswati. There is no event without the Swati beer '*Umcombotsi*' and tobacco/snuff (*Sinefu*). During a social or a funeral gathering, *Umcombotsi* and *Sinefu* bring the community together; *Umcombotsi*, a drink from one calabash, '*Luziwo*,' *and Sinefu* is shared in a tiny tube called '*Indlelo*.' They share beer and tobacco while having chats among themselves; this is a therapeutic session for both males and females where they share their life experiences. There is a Swati idiom which says "*injobo ikhungelwa ebandla*." It means that when you have issues and a problem, you must open up to those you are socializing with. COVID-19 never allowed such gatherings because when they drink or smoke, they share in one calabash, '*Luziwo*' and '*Indlelo*,' which is a faster spread of coronavirus. Law enforcement was applied. For instance, if police officers and soldiers find a cultural practice will spill and confiscate the beer and the *Indlelo*. This law enforcement brought fear and trauma among the Swati people. Kim et al. (2006) advocated that people have to be allowed to practice their cultural beliefs because this is how they function in their familial, social, cultural and ecological contexts. In addition, traditional weddings were placed on hold during this pandemic which left most Swati people under stress and in dysfunctional families. In the Swati tradition, an individual cannot stay with someone dating without being married in a traditional wedding '*Umtsimba or Kuteka*.' Swati cultures and traditions were diminished by COVID-19.

Mid-week, during the Day, Funerals and the Second Wave of COVID-19

Grief is a normal response to losing someone important to you. When a loved one dies, friends and family need to be able to share stories and memories of the person and how they influenced their lives. The COVID-19 pandemic has affected the ability of friends and family to come together in person and grieve in typical ways and introduced mid-week funerals, regardless of whether the person's death was due to COVID-19 or other causes. Given the COVID-19 pandemic, hosting gatherings now could be dangerous to those who want to participate. As a result, family and friends find alternative ways to connect, support each other, and grieve after the loss.

COVID-19 has stopped the community's traditional rites and brought social changes, which resulted in psychological impacts on the livelihoods of societies in Swati culture. Burials were delayed after the death of an individual, but due to high death rates from the pandemic, mid-week burials had to be introduced. In Africa, death and dying rituals center on becoming ancestors and the way one passes and funeral rituals. Before burial, the home is prepared by covering the mirrors, removing the deceased individual's bed, and holding a vigil. They removed the body feet first from home and took a confusing path toward the burial so the deceased could become an ancestor and not wander back home. During the COVID-19 pandemic, it was introduced that burial should take place within three days of the death of an individual, and mid-week burials were introduced to the high number of deaths. Death was not familiar, it only occurred occasionally among communities, but burials had to occur every day due to the influx of the COVID-19 deaths. As a result, families could not perform the rituals they had to perform for burials. If no proper burial is administered for the deceased, they can wreak havoc as a ghost to the family and the community.

Moreover, in the Swati culture, funerals usually take place during the weekend. In the Swati beliefs, a funeral proceeding for a commoner starts at 4 AM from viewing the corpse in the graveyard. For royals, the funeral proceedings start at 00:00hrs. This is how the Swati people have been conducting funerals. In both the two funerals (commoner and royal), the aim is that they should be done from the graveyard when the sunrise rises. However, during COVID-19, there was a cultural diminish whereby mid-week funerals were introduced to the people. It resulted in cultural shock because the Swati people were not used to these funeral proceedings. Furthermore, regardless of the person's status (commoner or royal), funerals were conducted during the day. Due to that, more funerals were taking place, and the rate of deaths increased day by day.

Normalizing death has been the new normal in the COVID-19 era; the pandemic introduced social media to attend virtual funerals, live-streamed on Facebook, Twitter, YouTube and Instagram since a limited number can attend funerals. In both urban and rural Eswatini seeing a funeral is taboo; however, in this pandemic, death was an everyday event that affected the people's psychosocial well-being of the people. Preteens having access to social media has also impacted how death has been perceived among Emaswati. For instance, preteens login the live streaming of funerals, seeing graveyards and such practices causes trauma among preteens, and in Emaswati culture, children or preteens are not allowed to observe or experience preceding funerals due to that, it is conjectured that it might cause emotional trauma, on contrary COVID-19 modernized traditional funerals and practices by introducing broadcasting of funerals into social media. Winther-Lindqvist and Larsen (2019) maintain that losing a loved one is among the most common and stressful traumatic events that a child or an adolescent can experience and can be associated with mental health and somatic disorders among adolescents as well as a range of life issues and potential adverse outcomes that may impact longitudinal development.

COVID-19 caused complicated grief, a disorder that exists only in adults. However, it has been increasing among preteens due to the pandemic.

Grief is a fundamental reaction to loss. Morning rituals, funerals and commemorations were intended to allow open expression of grief through ritual. The massive loss and sudden deaths and the absence of morning rituals are risk factors for chronic grief symptoms (Walter, 1996). Many survivors of the COVID-19 virus cannot bury their relatives, and they do not know where they were buried.

Implications

Practically COVID-19 is still affecting the psychosocial well-being of individuals. It is the new normal that different cultures have to live with. For instance, social distancing, wearing of masks, restrictions of movements, burning of social gatherings, quarantine, and isolation were all precautions to stop the spread of the coronavirus. It impacted the African traditions and cultures and their practices. The WHO had to make sure that everyone was safe, considering the traditions and cultures of African people being impacted negatively. People's psychological well-being in a crisis is paramount; therefore, psychological coping strategies (problem-solving skills, emotionally supportive relationships, finding meaning in life, and religious coping) should be implemented to how individuals can cope during such a crisis (COVID-19). Theoretically, the study comprehended self and social behavior in differing cultural contexts theories in the research literature. Additionally, the study revealed the models which highlighted the importance of indigenous and cultural psychology in the psychosocial well-being among African people.

Limitations

The study used the case-series study design, which is not affected by analysis. Therefore, the sample was based on exposure to the pandemic. It solely concentrated on managing psychological well-being during and after a crisis and how traditions and culture get affected by COVID-19. The study generalized its observation based on how the population is responding to COVID-19 and how it affected the traditions and cultures of the Swati people. The study's observation was based on the exposure to the pandemic and the basis striking association between exposure and the outcome of COVID-19.

Future Research

Forthcoming studies should expand upon the pandemic's psychosocial pathways (mental health, adjustment, and adaptation). Studies could also involve the post-COVID-19 psychosocial pathways (depression and post-traumatic stress-related issues among individuals. Other research designs, such as explanatory and exploratory approaches, can be used in future studies to explore people's experiences and perceptions of COVID-19 pandemic issues.

Conclusion

It is clear that COVID-19 was sudden to every culture and tradition globally, and people had to adjust and cope with pandemic restrictions. On the other hand, well-being was being affected. The African cultures and traditions were also pretentious by the pandemic. It implies that more modern ways of doing had to be adapted, and COVID-19 has proven that acculturation is essential so that cultures be able to learn and incorporate the values, beliefs, norms and customs of other cultures, which are playing an important role (modernizing and blending of cultures which brings a better way of practicing the original culture and traditions, however still preserve culture and traditions) in the daily lives of the people. It is also indicated that COVID-19 affects the medical health of people and distresses the psychosocial sphere of individuals; therefore, it is also essential that all professions work multidisciplinary to have one goal when it comes to COVID-19-related future pandemics.

References

Ademiluka, S. O. (2009). The sociological functions of funeral mourning: Illustrations from the Old Testament and Africa. *Old Testament Essays, 22*(1), 9-20.

Amusan, O. O., Dlamini, P. S., Msonthi, J. D., & Makhubu, L. P. (2002). Some herbal remedies from the Manzini region of Swaziland. *Journal of Ethnopharmacology, 79*(1), 109-112.

Awolalu, J. O., & Awolalu, J. O. (1979). *Yoruba beliefs and sacrificial rites.* Longman.

Bear, L., Simpson, N., Angland, M., Bhogal, J. K., Bowers, R., Cannell, F., Gardner, K., Lohiya, A., James, D., & Jivraj, N. (2020). 'A good death during the Covid-19 pandemic in the U.K.: a report on key findings and recommendations.

Beristain, C. M., Paez, D., & González, J. L. (2000). Rituals, social sharing, silence, emotions and collective memory claims in the case of the Guatemalan genocide. *Psicothema, 12*(Sul), 117-130.

Bernardo, A. B., & Mendoza, N. B. (2020). Measuring hope during the COVID-19 outbreak in the Philippines: development and validation of the state locus-of-Hope scale short form in Filipino. *Current Psychology*, 1-10.

Bhuda, M. T., & Marumo, P. (2020). African Traditional Medicine and Healing in South Africa: Challenges and Prospects Before and During COVID-19. *Gender & Behavioural, cognitive psychopathy, 18*(4), 16718-16732.

Brody, J. (2020). Take Steps to Counter the Loneliness of Social Distancing. *The New York Times.* https://www.NYTimes.com//03/23/well/family/coronavirus-loneliness-isolation-social-distancing-elderly. HTML. Published 23 March.

Buseh, A. G., Glass, L. K., & McElmurry, B. J. (2002). Cultural and gender issues related to HIV/AIDS prevention in rural Swaziland: a focus group analysis. *Health care for women international, 23*(2), 173-184.

Debly, T. (2014). Culture and resistance in Swaziland. *Journal of Contemporary African Studies, 32*(3), 284-301.

Endomba, F. T., Wafeu, G. S., Efon-Ekangouo, A., Djune-Yemeli, L., Donfo-Azafack, C., Nana-Djeunga, H. C., & Kamgno, J. (2020). Support for families of isolated or deceased COVID-19 patients in sub-Saharan Africa. *Health Psychology Open, 7*(2), 2055102920975293.

Jindra, M., & Noret, J. (2011). Funerals in Africa. *Funerals in Africa: Explorations of a Social Phenomenon, 1.*

Kim, A. W., Nyengerai, T., & Mendenhall, E. (2020). Evaluating the mental health impacts of the COVID-19 pandemic in urban South Africa: Perceived risk of COVID-19 infection and childhood trauma predict adult depressive symptoms. *medRxiv.*

Kim, U., Yang, K.-S., & Hwang, K.-K. (2006). *Indigenous and cultural psychology: Understanding people in context.* Springer Science & Business Media.

Kubler-Ross, E. (1970). The Care of the Dying—Whose Job is it? *Psychiatry in medicine, 1*(2), 103-107.

Kumar, A., & Nayar, K. R. (2021). COVID 19 and its mental health consequences. *Journal of mental health (Abingdon, England), 30*(1), 1–2. https://doi.org/10.10 80/09638237.2020.1757052

Lee, K. (2009). Rituals, Roles, and Responsibilities Included in a Hmong Funeral: A Guidebook for Teachers to Better Understand the Process Their Hmong Students Experience in a Time of Family Loss.

Makgahlela, M., Sodi, T., Nkoana, S., & Mokwena, J. (2019). Bereavement rituals and their related psychosocial functions in a Northern Sotho community of South Africa. *Death Studies*, 1-10.

Mbunge, E. (2020). COVID-19's Effects of COVID-19 in South African health system and society: A descriptive study. *Diabetes Metabolic Syndrome: Clinical Research Reviews, 14*(6), 1809-1814.

Mugabi, I. (2020, 5 May). *COVID-19: WHO cautions against the use of traditional herbs in Africa*: https://www.dw.com/en/covid-19-who-cautions-against-the-use-of-traditional-herbs-in-africa/a-53341901.

Muhammad, F. (2020). COVID-19 Pandemic: The Role of Traditional Medicine. *International Journal of Infection, 7*(3).

Muris, P., Schmidt, H., Engelbrecht, P., & Perold, M. (2002). DSM-IV–defined anxiety disorder symptoms in South African children. *Journal of the American Academy of Child Adolescent Psychiatry, 41*(11), 1360-1368.

Nyabadza, F., Chirove, F., Chukwu, C., & Visaya, M. V. (2020). I am modelling the potential impact of social distancing on the COVID-19 epidemic in South Africa. *Computational mathematical methods in medicine, 2020.*

Nyashanu, M., Simbanegavi, P., & Gibson, L. (2020). Exploring the impact of COVID-19 pandemic lockdown on informal settlements in Tshwane Gauteng Province, South Africa. *Global Public Health, 15*(10), 1443-1453.

Plecher, H. (2020). Total population of the Kingdom of Eswatini 2025: (in a million inhabitants).

Selman, L. E., Chao, D., Sowden, R., Marshall, S., Chamberlain, C., & Koffman, J. (2020). Bereavement support on the frontline of COVID-19: recommendations for hospital clinicians. *Journal of pain symptom management, 60*(2), e81-e86.

Triandis, H. C. (1989). The self and social behaviour in differing cultural contexts. *Psychological Review, 96*(3), 506.

Walter, T. (1996). A new model of grief: Bereavement and biography. *Mortality, 1*(1), 7-25.

WHO. (2020). *Modes of transmission of virus causing COVID-19: implications for IPC precaution recommendations: scientific brief, 27 March 2020.*

Winther-Lindqvist, D. A., & Larsen, I. O. (2019). Grief and Best Friendship Among Adolescent Girls. *OMEGA-Journal of Death Dying,* 0030222819856146.

Yao, H., Chen, J.-H., & Xu, Y.-F. (2020). Patients with mental health disorders in the COVID-19 epidemic.

Chapter 14

Cultural Influences on Motivation Theories and their Application

Bhawna Tushir

Christ (Deemed to be) University, Delhi NCR, India

Garima Joshi

All India Institute of Medical Sciences (AIIMS), New Delhi, India

Vatsal Priyadarshi Pandey

Department of Psychology, Lakshmibai College Delhi University, New Delhi, India

Abstract: The tremendous measures of examination that have been made from achievement motivation speculations are examined in this chapter, emphasizing recent advancements. Some of the most notable contributions that have evolved from each of the ideas are discussed in this section. There is a discussion on the degree to which there are shared characteristics among hypotheses. Cultural influences have primarily been highlighted in cross-cultural psychology and psychology in general. These cultural influences on motivational strategies and their use have also been discussed. Finally, there is a review of how well current motivation theory aligns with present educational policy and practice. Researchers studying motivation look into some crucial contemporary practice and policy challenges; nevertheless, this exploration has not been deliberate across speculations.

Keywords: Cross-culture, Psychology, Motivation Theories, Self-determination Theory, Trans-conceptual Model

***

Introduction

Evolutionary theory has made its way from the margins to the center of social theory, providing insights into social change. In addition, while their ideas appear to be worried about full-scale degrees of progress right away, they explicitly suggest that miniature-level examples of progress drive more broad examples of progress. If subcultural variations are disregarded, it is possible to make incorrect generalizations about cultural effects (Lam & Ryan, 2022). Because motivation is complex and multifaceted, numerous elements that influence motivation should be considered. Many psychological studies of behavior place a premium on motivation. As a result, recognizing the elements that underline reasons for giving care, investigating the interrelationships across thought processes, and considering the effect of these inspirations on parental figure conduct and results will help endeavors to keep up with and support caring connections (Zarzycki et al., 2022).

Values assume a considerable part in the perspectives, investigations, and conversations of governmental issues, religion, instruction, and day-to-day life. Notwithstanding all of the consideration values get in the ordinary discussion, a deliberate report in standard psychology did not start until the 1990s. The idea of Values looks at the most famous present-day esteem speculations, emphasizing the thought of fundamental individual qualities. Travel inspiration regularly involves weighing apparent advantages against apparent 'costs' of a travel experience as a feature of a complex dynamic cycle. Personal well-being is one of the perceived benefits, whereas 'costs' relate to anything that could jeopardize the desired outcomes. In this regard, perceived risk is important in the trip decision-making process since it captures the uncertainty and potential adverse outcomes.

The major problem of creativity study is to "weave together many characteristics in isolation or even in antagonism to each other," as creativity scientists recently declared in the "Socio-Cultural Manifesto." Considering the interaction between individual, societal, and cultural aspects, the socio-cultural way to deal with inventiveness stresses the multi-faceted nature of innovativeness. Cross-public imagination research, specifically, assists with illustrating the socio-person relationship (Zhang et al., 2021). A special issue on motivation theory was published in Contemporary Educational Psychology two decades ago, and it continues to be significant both inside and outside the discipline. Experience sampling and other related methodologies, as well as "in-the-moment" reporting of motivation, are significant advancements. Extra psychological dimensions related to racist and discriminatory experiences should be included in some of the hypotheses (Wigfield & Koenka, 2020).

The social climate assumes a crucial part in inspiration, learning, and self-guideline, as indicated by the social cognitive hypothesis. This theory has a wide range of applications in psychology as well as other domains like education, business, and health. The theory's predictions have been put to the test in a variety of research investigations. Expected good outcomes for completing modeling activities were a major motivator for taking action (Schunk & DiBenedetto, 2020). Self-determination theory (SDT) is a broad paradigm for researching aspects in educational settings that encourage or hinder intrinsic drive, autonomous extrinsic reward, and psychological well-being. Both intrinsic motivation and well-internalized forms of extrinsic motivation predict various favorable outcomes across various educational levels and cultural settings. In the last two decades, SDT research and applications have exploded. Motivational processes can also be closely tied to specific instructional methods (Ryan & Deci, 2020).

In a situative viewpoint on human activity, people are viewed as parts of different, to some extent covering, and socially made frameworks. Individual and gathering exercises add to the social advancement of nearby or worldwide significance frameworks. The situative viewpoint has been utilized to research people and gatherings' development, character, inspiration, and learning. The situative methodology was created by formative analysts, social anthropologists, and, more recently, learning researchers (Nolen, 2020). During the 1970s and mid-1980s, another age of social-mental speculations of accomplishment inspiration arose, including the expectancy-value hypothesis, attribution hypothesis, and social learning hypothesis. Intra-individual elements eclipse key cultural, social, and relevant effects on inspiration. The four designers of the achievement objective hypothesis were joined by the conviction that achievement can be characterized in an assortment of courses in every accomplishment circumstance (Urdan & Kaplan, 2020).

Motivation is the intent behind any action, and the prime reason people commence, preserve and stop an activity (Deci & Ryan, 2012; Markus, 2016). It is a psycho-physiological process that drives all organisms towards goals. Due to its physiological nature, motivation is also considered a universal process exhibited by every human in almost a similar way. Traditional theories explain motivation as a physiological construct independent of external forces (Engin & McKeown, 2012). The focus of these theories was aimed at exploring motivation as an independent construct that is primarily shaped by internal processes. Research stated that these theories could be easily transferred and applied across cultures (McInerney et al., 2004). Despite the certain universal behaviors that humans have constantly displayed across cultures (i.e., hunger, safety and belonging), the applicability of these theories has been constantly questioned due to various contextual factors like societal norms, ethnicity, class and race responsible for shaping human behaviors and also contributing to individual differences.

Need-Based Theories of Motivation

Maslow's Hierarchy of Needs

Human motivations have been studied for as long as people are able to reflect on one another's actions. The Hierarchy of Needs, developed by Abraham Maslow, was the first attempt to arrange all motivations, from the most basic to the loftiest. Since then, Maslow's requirements scale has been frequently applied in business. The most basic motivator, according to him, is survival, followed by a need for security, then a want to belong or be liked. Self-esteem, self-actualization, and peak experience are "higher wants," according to him (Zohar, 2022). Maslow's "hierarchy of needs" is a notable inspiration hypothesis that groups individuals' needs arranged by apparent importance. It is addressed as a pyramid, with the main requirements at the base and the most unsignificant at the top. Even though Maslow later underscored that there might be exemptions in light of external conditions or individual changes, he contended that people regularly meet their principal prerequisites before fulfilling their higher human needs. He further said that failing to meet the pyramidal model's needs could result in bodily and mental sickness (Shoib et al., 2022).

The most basic of Maslow's Hierarchy needs are:

- The 'physiological' needs. Physiological drives are regularly utilized as a beginning stage for the inspiration hypothesis.

- The safety needs. When physiological necessities are met to a healthy degree, another arrangement of needs arises, which we could freely portray as the need might arise. All that has been referenced about physiological necessities additionally applies to these cravings, though less significantly.

- The social requirements. These necessities allude to the need to associate with others, be preferred, and construct long-haul connections.

- The esteem needs. Everyone in contemporary culture has a need or longing for a stable, immovably settled high self-assessment, confidence, as well as the regard of others.

- The "self-actualization" needs. It refers to the process of achieving one's needs. Even if these demands are met, it is common to anticipate a new wave of discontent and unrest. A man must be everything he can be. Self-actualization is the term for this need (Abulof, 2017).

Alderfer's ERG Theory

The ERG speculation stretches out Maslow's hierarchy of needs. Alderfer recommended that requirements might be partitioned into three rather than five classifications. Presence, relatedness, and development are the three classifications of necessities. The ERG hypothesis is not equivalent to the hierarchy of needs speculation. It does not suggest that lower-level needs should be met totally before more elevated-level requests can be met. According to ERG theory, if an individual cannot meet upper-level requirements consistently, lower-level needs become the primary determinants of motivation (Ahmad et al., 2022).

These different types of needs are described below -

- **Existence Need**: Existence necessitates the acquisition of basic materials. It refers to a person's physiological and physical safety requirements.

- **Relatedness Need**: Individuals seek public renown and recognition, and they require meaningful relationships (with family, classmates, or superiors), love, and belonging. This category includes Maslow's social demands as well as the external component of esteem requirements.

- **Growth Need**: Self-development, personal improvement, and advancement are all examples of growth demands. This category of needs includes Maslow's self-actualization demands as well as an intrinsic component of esteem needs (Acquah et al., 2021).

Crooks emphasizes that, like Maslow's Hierarchy of Needs theory, the ERG theory fails to address several concerns, the most important of which are the following two. For starters, human motivation is subjective; what one person considers to be a gratifying need may not be so for another. Second, as a result of unmet or met wants, human needs change, and so do human behaviors. As a result, employee behavior may result from met or unmet demands at work (Shikalepo, 2020). Obtaining monetary needs, sustaining interpersonal relationships with significant others and pursuing opportunities for personal development and improvement are among the ERG's requirements. Within the theoretical underpinning of SDT, previous research has revealed a relationship between psychological demands fulfillment and emotional adjustment. ERG requirements are strong indicators of emotional, behavioral, hyperactivity, and peer problems. This demand demonstrates the application of ERG theory to education, as well as its position as a supplement to Self-Determination Theory in the study of teenage needs (Poulou & Norwich, 2020).

Herzberg's Two-Factor Theory

Herzberg proposed the two-factor theory to describe worker motivation and identify the elements involved in the various stages. Worker motivation can be influenced by two sorts of elements, according to Herzberg: hygiene factors and motivation factors. The contextual elements of organizations that support workers are referred to as hygiene factors. Employees may harbor grievances against organizations if these are not provided. The content elements of the task and the immediate reward earned via satisfactory job performance are examples of motivation factors (LaBombard, 2022).

The two-factor theory of Herzberg's includes:

- Hygiene Factors: Company policy, supervision & relationships, working conditions, salaries, and security.

- Motivators: achievement, recognition, interesting work, increased responsibility, and advancement & growth.

Motivational variables might increase a person's desire to achieve self-actualization through work. Job discontent and satisfaction are linked to things including hygiene and motivation. Hygiene considerations are important, but they aren't enough to guarantee happiness. The two-factor approach has been widely used to identify the variables that motivate people to do their jobs (Al Khasawneh et al., 2022).

Recent positive psychology research has been able to link Herzberg's motivation-hygiene theory's basic principles with traits like optimism, grit, resilience, creativity, flow, and interest. Positive psychology is the study of the characteristics mentioned above. Some researchers stated that when they compared their findings, they found similarities with Herzberg's theory. In the sense that happiness does not simply entail the absence of unhappiness but that several underlying factors play a significant role in mediating such a relationship (Mitsakis & Galanakis, 2022). Herzberg's findings are not universally recognized. It is also not easy to categorize the factors as hygiene or incentive. Despite its defects, the thought can be a helpful instrument for supervisors since it underscores that improving the workplace goes a long way in moving representatives. Context-oriented components are unquestionably significant since their nonappearance prompts discontent. Supervisors should improve occupations by offering representatives chances to request work, expanding liability, development possibilities, and a task where their subordinates can feel effective (Thant & Chang 2021).

McClelland's Acquired Needs Theory

The most popular of the need-based motivation theories is David McClelland's acquired-needs theory. According to this idea, people develop three different desires due to their life experiences. Achievement, connection, and power are the three needs. Everyone has a combination of these wants, and it is considered that these needs influence employee behavior. All of these factors are on a scale, and everyone experiences them to varying degrees, but McClelland's hypothesis suggests that everyone possesses these requirements to varying degrees (Kirmani et al., 2019).

Based on the fulfillment of these three needs includes:

- Need of achievement: Achievement must be founded on demanding goals, willingness to take risks (if necessary) to attain goals, a desire to succeed, and a tendency to work independently.

- Need for power: A need for power stems from a desire to dominate and influence people, to win fights, to be competitive, and to enjoy prestige and recognition.

- Need of affiliation: Affiliation requires group collaboration rather than competition, dislikes risk and uncertainty, prefers group decisions, and wishes to be liked.

Multitasking traits focus on succeeding at completing tasks, competitive traits may take on more hard employment, and independent traits may try to be entrepreneurs. Most of the necessities for achievement are not learned and acquired from our life experiences. Based on the acquired needs self-assessment, each employee (independent of generation type) will have a dominant motivation. Develop a strategy that combines each employee's abilities and may be applied to teams and the business based on the type of motivator each person has (Cote, 2019). McClelland's obtained necessities hypothesis has enormous ramifications for representative inspiration. People with a solid requirement for accomplishment might be driven by objectives, while those with a significant requirement for power might endeavor to apply impact over those with whom they work, and those with a strict requirement for association might be persuaded to acquire endorsement from their friends and managers. At long last, people with a powerful urge for accomplishment might battle in administration positions, and being mindful of average errors could assist them in being more successful (Wangechi, 2019).

Adams' Equity Theory of Motivation

Equity theory depicts human motivation as a result of how people view their inputs and outcomes in contrast to others. When a person's perceived inputs and outcomes are comparable to those of the reference, feelings of equity are maintained. When the person's and their referent's perceived inputs and outcomes diverge, injustice feelings emerge. In such cases, equity theory predicts that the individual may try to change the inputs, outputs, or comparison to another (referent), which has clear consequences for workplace behavior (Davlembayeva et al., 2021). J. Stacy Adams created equity theory. While various theorists contributed to equity theory, it has always stood out because it assumes that "a large portion of motivated conduct is based on the perceived situation rather than the real set of conditions." Researchers have identified the employee counseling interview as a business communication event in which attitudes can be modified using rhetoric. According to the core argument of equity theory, employees seek a fair or equitable transaction, a balance between what they contribute and what they receive (Gates & Reinsch, 2022).

- Inputs & outputs: People's perceptions of their contributions to the environment are called inputs. The imagined benefits obtained from a circumstance are known as outcomes.

- Referent: The referent other could be a single individual or a group of people.

- Reaction to unfairness: The theory suggests several possible responses to perceived unfairness. Changing views of own or the referent's inputs and outcomes can help deal with the issue perceptually. Increase referent inputs, decrease own input, increase own outcomes, replace the referent, remove yourself from the situation and seek legal help.

- Individual reactions to inequity: The theory is more beneficial in understanding the conduct of equity-sensitive individuals, and businesses must pay close attention to how people perceive their relationships.

- Procedural and Interactional Justice, Beyond Equity: Equity theory considers perceived justice a motivator. Equity theory is a distributive justice theory since it deals with result fairness. The degree to which the organization's outcomes are regarded as fair is known as distributive justice. Procedural justice and interactional justice are other types of fairness recognized (Watters, 2021).

Role of Motivation in Different Aspects of Humans Endeavors

Ethics and Motivation

Although determining the reasons for human motivation is complex, Maslow's hierarchy of needs was a first step in the process, incorporating a broad view of motivation. Motivation is the force that propels a person toward achieving a specific goal. Employee motivation is not solely dependent on the need for a monetary stimulus; non-financial stimuli are also significant. The importance of activities for capitalizing on numerous chances lost in human resource management Motivation is linked to taking on challenges and appreciating the activity at hand (Loor-Zambrano et al., 2022). Motivation theories have been used to understand this fascinating and vital topic. One hypothesis that has been particularly successful in analyzing ethical behavior is reinforcement theory. Ethical behavior, like any other type of behavior, such as performance or cooperation, is learned due to one's activities. Individuals may engage in immoral behavior but receive positive repercussions, such as promotions for hitting sales quotas, in a variety of organizational circumstances (Slote, 2020).

The unethical behavior will persist as long as the person's unethical action is met with good effects. Thus, studying the rewards and penalties that follow unethical behavior and eliminating rewards while increasing the severity and likelihood of punishment is essential to limit unethical action (and, in some situations, legal concerns). The likelihood of punishment, as well as the severity of the punishment, has a substantial impact on ethical behavior (Slote, 2020). Motivation and ethics borrow arguments and notions from philosophical ethics theory. Character ethics and quandary ethics are frequently distinguished in philosophical research. There is a system of norms "by which appropriate behavior can be determined or judged" in quandary ethics. These authoritative orders encourage ethical results by emphasizing the consequences of a decision or enforcing a self-justifying rule. According to these views, a collection of identifying features must be acquired and cultivated, including a proclivity for ethical behavior, which must be acquired and cultivated (Ripoll, 2019).

Motivational Imbalance

The idea of motivational imbalance is that one need takes precedence over other fundamental considerations. Moderation, on the other hand, is the consequence of a motivational balance in which different people's needs are met equally. Notably, the various requirements constrain individuals' activities in moderation by banning actions that support some needs while undermining others. When there is a motivational imbalance, the dominant need drives out other needs. As a result, the behavioral limits imposed by the latter are removed, allowing previously avoided actions to occur (Hassan et al., 2021).

Motivation and Socio-psychological State

Motivation is the key to a company's success since it encourages employees to perform at their best. Employers rely on their employees' performance to meet their organization's goals. Despite their competence, employees who aren't appropriately motivated perform poorly. Employers want fully committed employees to their jobs rather than simply showing up. Work motivation is still an important aspect of organizational psychology since it helps to explain why people behave the way they do. Individuals and actual social conditions can benefit from actors who promote motivation (Mamun & Khan, 2020). The amount of motivation has long been linked to physiological reactions and behavioral implications (pain, hunger, fear, and rage). Increased motivation for behavioral involvement has also been linked to improved cardiovascular performance. As a result, studying motivational processes might help us better understand goal-oriented behavior and human health and physical function. Multidimensional classifications reflect the degree of motivation and the qualitatively diverse reasons that motivate people to participate in goal-directed activities. Various people have different motivations (Steel et al., 2021).

Individual motivational differences have been explained by concentrating on underlying psychological needs. Psychological needs are defined as natural psychological nutrition and humans' primary resources. They have a strong explicit impact on work performance and are closely linked to individual behavior. They are key drivers of individual performance because they provide satisfaction from dealing with various challenges. In addition to individual-level antecedents, the social context has been thought to impact motivation. Individual connection and social interchange emphasize the relevance of job motivation (Olafsen et al., 2018). Because these activities jeopardize common concerns, most people avoid them, making them "extreme." Motivational, cognitive, behavioral, affective, and social implications result from a situation of need imbalance. Extreme diets, extreme sports, extreme obsessions, various addictions, and violent extremism are all instances of extremisms that share a psychological core. Evidence from numerous categories of psychological processes, degrees of behavioral investigation, and phylogeny support the paradigm. Few models suggest that more research be done to understand better the tradeoffs between extremism and moderation (Kruglanski et al., 2021).

Traditional & Innovative Motivation

Because of the different expectations that people have about conventional motivational methods, defining them is difficult. It was decided to consider traditional motivation techniques like promotion, pay-for-performance, holidays, and personal achievement, which are linked to the reward system. Managers face difficult decisions when trying to find ways to motivate a larger audience. One explanation for this is that, in addition to culture, motivation is influenced by the individuals who live in that society and their current living situations (Anh Vu et al., 2022). Specific motivational methods may work for some people but may not work for others due to changing circumstances. Employee motivation has always relied on monetary incentives and vacations. Some executives even believe that employing fear as a motivator helps them succeed. Other classic ideas for motivating employees include a corporate automobile, a subsidized gym membership, and management comments (Ingrams, 2020).

Traditional motivating techniques have not always been successful in achieving their goals; as a result, new approaches have been developed. These novel methods can bring several advantages, including:

- Providing a stable foundation for an individual to be productive throughout the working day

- Providing the ability to save costs by reducing the number of health insurance premiums

- Recruiting high-potential individuals

- Contributing to the answer for raising the retirement age

- Allowing employees to sleep during the day has been shown to increase their daily work effectiveness as well as their health (Lewis et al., 2022).

Innovators are encouraged to build on the work of others in innovation networks. This generative user creativity necessitates new theorization to understand better the interaction between source innovation features and collective community motivation. Motivation is a big challenge in communities where contributors often choose which topics to work on. The study adds to our knowledge of how community incentives influence remixing and influence characteristics of remix depth (improvement and differentness). Source innovation quality mitigates the effects of learning and use-value (Stanko & Allen, 2022).

Descriptive Investigation

Motivational Theories & Applications

Four kinds of goal-directed motivation have emerged from a conceptual investigation of the relationship between values, goals, motives, and behavior. Egoism (improving one's well-being), altruism (improving the well-being of others), collectivism (improving the well-being of a group), and principlism (improving the well-being of a group) are all examples of prosocial activity (upholding some moral principle ideal). There are advantages and disadvantages to each type of prosocial drive. When prosocial impulses are combined, one's talents can compensate for another's shortcomings (Batson, 2022). Researchers have recently attempted to use SDT to create a more sophisticated understanding of motivation. According to SDT, behavioral reasons span a spectrum from feeling dominated to feeling independent. Intrinsic motivation is the most self-sufficient type of motivation. It entails behaving based on the behavior's inherent pleasure and delight. Extrinsic motives are used when people lack an intrinsic drive for a behavior. External, introjected, recognized, and integrated extrinsic motivation is the four types of extrinsic motivation (Hardy et al., 2022).

The self-determination theory (SDT) provides a framework for understanding this dynamic relationship and the importance of autonomy in physician development. Autonomy is a psychological desire associated with learning motivation, self-regulation, and having an internal center of control in SDT. Supporting learner autonomy allows students to internalize the principles and standards of the profession, resulting in integrated behavior and activity regulation. SDT's application to the autonomy concept opens many doors for educational interventions and future research on supervision and autonomy (Sawatsky et al., 2022). Based on theorized links between motivational and social cognition theories, the trans-contextual model (TCM) promises directed prediction, which predicts autonomous motivation in another context. It suggests that TCM designs should take into account changes throughout time. The advantage of value modeling is that it allows researchers to make more confident claims about how changing one variable would affect others. It is rarely done in testing motivational and social cognition models, such as the TCM (Kalajas-Tilga et al., 2022).

Effective self-regulation requires persistence and timely disengagement from personal goals, which is critical to well-being and performance. Throughout the history of motivation psychology, persistence has always been emphasized. As seen by the scarcity of relevant studies, researchers have recently been interested in goal disengagement. Classic expectancy-value components are combined with contemporary volitional self-regulation principles in the theories. Many theoretical approaches have made their way into applied disciplines (e.g., education, work, health) (Brandstätter & Bernecker, 2022). At various levels, several psychological models attempt to explain motivated behavior. Many of these hypotheses accept that motivation activity emerges from the foundation of a goal to participate in a particular task. These motivational psychological models have focused on different parts of the inspirational framework (Eccles & Wigfield, 2020). It includes subjective task values and ability judgments on domain-specific attainment decisions and performance. Then there is the task-specific relationship between attitudes and intentions and actual behavior. Finally, self-regulation impact goal pursuit and the function of emotions in achievement contexts (Umarji et al., 2021).

Even though motivation researchers regularly emphasize the necessity to synthesize theories, few attempts have been made. They noted in their meta-analysis of motivation therapies that there had been virtually no research that attempts to combine motivation theories and constructs, supporting this fact. They likewise noticed that mass population accept inspiration as either characteristic or extraneous. Surprisingly, a meta-analysis found that motivating interventions have large impact sizes (Anderman, 2020). Protection motivation theory (PMT) is a practical social psychology theoretical framework that has been acknowledged as one of the most successful explanatory theories for predicting an individual's protective intentions and behaviors. PMT analyses the cognitive processes that humans go through when confronted with threats by drawing on expectancy-value theories. It assumes that people have reasons to protect themselves when they are threatened in dangerous situations. According to PMT, protection motivation stems from threat assessment and coping assessment (Wu et al., 2020).

Cultural Influences on Motivation

Individual motivation, goals, decisions, and emotions are all influenced by culture. According to empirical research, East Asians and European Americans have different approaches to approach and avoidance motivation. When the goal is to obtain a good result, approach motivation is used, but avoidance motivation is used when the goal is to avoid an undesirable result. Asian cultures are more concerned with avoidance and prevention, while North American cultures are more concerned with approach and promotion. Culture is defined as a group's beliefs, attitudes, and behaviors shaped by shared values, norms, feelings, and ways of thinking that are learned and passed down through generations. Health beliefs, the meaning of illness, presenting symptoms, and overall health are all influenced and shaped by culture. People's minds, morals, norms, health choices, and overall way of life are all influenced by culture. As a result, cultural beliefs and practices play a significant role in motivating people (Osokpo et al., 2021).

One of the most important criteria for successful second language learning is motivation, which is a better predictor of success than many other characteristics. Persistence, strategy utilization, and attitudes are all examples of mechanisms that can influence language acquisition and accomplishment. Practical reasons, a desire to understand more about or connect with individuals of a different culture, or a desire for social status and prestige can motivate someone to learn a language (Peng & Patterson, 2022). In diverse languages, motivational mechanisms, including children's academic self-concept, task value, curiosity, and task-focused behavior, have been proven to play a key role in literacy learning. Despite evidence that culture and writing systems influence the cognitive foundations of reading development, little study has been done to see if culture influences motivation and reading skills. Concurrently assessed motivational processes and investigations of motivational processes in reading development are relatively uncommon (Inoue et al., 2021).

Culture refers to a group's or nation's shared way of perceiving and thinking, as well as its shared assumptions, beliefs, and behaviors. A person's psychological well-being, goal orientation, motivation, and study strategy can be influenced by culture, a set of shared attitudes, feelings, and activities among community members. Culture has an impact on people's perspectives and motivation for academic studies. During cultural adaptation, social learning influences individual differences in personality, motivation, and cognition (Boyle et al., 2020). Organizational culture, according to Schein, is a "pattern of shared basic beliefs that a group has learned as it has handled its issues of outward adaptation and internal integration." Wallach categorizes cultures into bureaucratic, inventive, and supporting cultures. A strong organizational culture typically results in motivated employees, indicating that the organization has an impact on employee motivation and performance, as well as a significant contribution to the achievement of organizational goals (Al-Sada et al., 2017).

Cross-cultural approaches are a powerful and complementary way of investigating the impact of social factors on the formation and evolution of prosocial behavior. According to cross-cultural research, relational socio-cultural environments reflect interpersonal relatedness tendencies, whereas autonomous socio-cultural circumstances stress self-centered orientations and promote individual segregation. If socialization and cultural experiences are crucial in the origin and development of prosocial conduct, infants raised in relational environments should be more likely to act prosocially than toddlers rose in autonomous environments (Torréns & Kärtner, 2017). According to the self-determination theory, human conduct is motivated by motivations that one wishes to satisfy. Intrinsic motivation (IM) refers to when someone engages in a behavior or activity for internal reasons (enjoyment, pleasure). Second, extrinsic motivation (EM) occurs when a person engages in behavior for reasons outside themselves. Motivation is the final component. It appears when a person cannot make the connection between his or her actions and the outcomes that have occurred (Tóth-Király et al., 2017).

Motivation in Cultural/cross-cultural Psychology and Psychology in General

According to basic psychological needs theory (BPNT), there are three innate wants, a sub-theory of self-determination theory. The degree to which an individual believes his or her objectives, activities, and behaviors are entirely self-directed and choice. The extent to which a person believes he/she can perform effectively and accomplish his/her objectives and interpersonal relatedness is concerned with how much a person feels loved and linked to other people's understanding (Walker et al., 2020). Cultural psychologists have extensively studied the relationship between culture and subjective well-being (SWB). Self-construal is an important concept in this context, according to studies. Self-construal studies how people perceive themselves about others, how these perceptions alter across cultures, and how this influences several psychological processes. In different cultures, social bonds have varying effects on SWB. Different cultural predictors of SWB appear to exist, all linked to self-construal (Ito et al., 2017).

The locus of motivation impacts how people initiate and regulate their behaviors as well as how good they are at it. Motivation, extrinsic motivation, and intrinsic motivation are the three main categories of self-determined behavioral processes. The closer someone comes to the intrinsic motivation end of the self-determination continuum, the more they believe they behave freely, guided by the internal values they give to their activities (Román et al., 2021). The self-determined end of this continuum is intrinsic motivation, which indicates behavioral engagement resulting from enjoyment and personal interest in the behavior. On the other hand, extrinsic motivation consists of a wide range of regulation styles with varying degrees of autonomy. Integrated and identified regulations, in particular, are highly self-determined regulatory techniques, notwithstanding their external purposes. The reasons for one's behavior that are consistent with one's identity and fundamental beliefs are integrated regulation. Identified regulation refers to personal values-based motivation (Ntoumanis et al., 2021).

Modeling, social comparisons, and relatedness are examples of social components of motivation. "People try to learn the modeled acts that they feel will lead to desired outcomes and help them achieve their objectives. People build expectations based on their observations of models and other experiences regarding the expected outcomes of various activities." Self-regulation, or "self-generated ideas, feelings, and behaviors that are consistently oriented toward the achievement of one's goals," is one of the cognitive aspects of motivation (Hattie et al., 2020). SDT's leading theory is BPNT. It defines psychological requirements fulfillment as the provision of innate psychological "nutrients" essential for long-term psychological growth and well-being. Autonomy, competence, and relatedness have been established as the three essential psychological criteria. The need for personal autonomy in making decisions and feeling responsible for one's actions is referred to as the demand for autonomy (Tang et al., 2020).

Because of cultural differences in the significance of personal control versus social accommodation, it appears that in Eastern cultures, disclosing issues and sharing personal things with others to cope with stress is considered less suitable than in Western cultures. Such admission implies a request for assistance from others, which may cause a peaceful relationship to be disrupted. It is impossible to rule out the notion that self-esteem and relationship concerns motivate people to pursue influence and adjustment goals (Ishii et al., 2017). Culture influences perception, motivation, learning and memory, group influence, socioeconomic class, female/male roles, attitudes, and decision-making, to name a few aspects of consumer behavior. As a result, a complex collection of variables must be understood when it comes to customer behavior. Consumer attitudes and desires differ greatly among countries, influencing behavior in various ways (AlMarshedi et al., 2017). Culture is defined as a set of shared behaviors and meanings that are interpreted in a particular setting. Cultural models and dimensions have been described previously to explore cross-cultural variances in various applications. Furthermore, behavioral biases may influence decision-making (AlMarshedi et al., 2017).

Conclusion

Over a decade, numerous studies have attempted to develop a universalistic view of human motivation. Most theories of human motivation are developed in the West, and their applicability to Eastern and Middle Eastern cultures has been constantly questioned. These theories have tried to explain motivation in an elementary form while ignoring that humans are complex beings and all the psychological processes result from their constant interaction with the socio-cultural environment. Also, most theories of motivation view motivation as an internal process and assume that humans are internally driven by personal motives, interests and mindsets (Markus, 2016) and ignore the role of culture. Hofstede (2001) stated that culture is like mental software that programs and dictates all the internal processes. Culture acts as software responsible for the collective programming of individuals belonging to the same group or clan (Hofstede, 2001). He stated that socio-cultural factors are responsible for creating and transmitting the content, ideas, value patterns and other symbolic meaningful systems that shape human behavior. Also, to develop a global understanding of the motivation process, it is important to take both the individual and contextual processes into account because motivation is not a fixed trait. It is a process that is constantly affected by various internal processes that are inherited and socio-environmental processes. Thus, an individual's state of motivation at a point in time is a result of the interaction between three factors. First, internal universal processes that are entirely inherited and contain genetic information common to entire species; second, individual tendencies that determine the uniqueness of an individual like their abilities and temperament; and finally, collective external processes shared by a group of individuals living nearby and it contribute most to this equation. It includes values, attitudes, goals and behavioral patterns learned after birth (Hofstede, 2001). Therefore, it is important to consider cultural components while working in the area of motivation, especially while applying theories developed in Western and individualistic societies to collectivist societies because the societal frameworks of East and West are poles apart. Western societies are more loosely knit where the emphasis is on personal values, goals and aspirations, while the Eastern societies are tightly knit where the emphasis is on the shared and social goals and welfare of one's clan and caste (Hofstede, 2003).

Overall, the data painted a positive picture of the relationship between cultural responsiveness and motivational factors, which corroborated past theories and empirical research that suggested supportive social situations can motivate people. Perhaps most importantly, it was able to find a positive, direct relationship between physiological responsiveness and motivational elements across all of the countries tested, proving the theory. Across countries, the correlations between physiological reaction and motivational factors or creative accomplishment were consistent (Zhang et al., 2021). Cluster membership was shown to differ significantly between activities, showing that the motivational system of values and emotions differs significantly. The expectancy-value theory correlates well with motivational and emotional profiles predicting task expectations and completion. Prior EVT research has focused chiefly on intentions and achievement, with the intention of the behavior gap being overlooked. The findings add to the understanding of how motivational characteristics influence task expectations and completion (Umarji et al., 2021). External events' impact on the supporting and thwarting intrinsic motivation is explored mainly in cognitive evaluation theory, and this mini-theory is widely utilized in studying or working situations.

References

Abulof, U. (2017). Introduction: Why we need Maslow in the twenty-first century. *Society, 54*(6), 508-509.

Acquah, A., Nsiah, T. K., Antie, E. N. A., & Otoo, B. (2021). literature review on theories of motivation. *EPRA International Journal of Economic and Business Review (JEBR), 9*(5), 1-6.

Ahmad, N., Rashid, N. R. A., Abdullah, N. A. T., Yean, C. P., Sharif, S., & Rahmat, N. H. (2022). Exploring Learners' Motivations for Studying From Home.

Al Khasawneh, M., Al Hadeed, O. A., Abdrabbo, T., Hashesh, M. Y. A., & Al-Abdullah, M. (2022). An Investigation of the Factors That Motivate Users to Participate in Online Communities. In *Research Anthology on Fandoms, Online Social Communities, and Pop Culture* (pp. 20-36). IGI Global.

AlMarshedi, A., Wanick, V., Wills, G. B., & Ranchhod, A. (2017). Gamification and behaviour. In *Gamification* (pp. 19-29). Springer, Cham.

Al-Sada, M., Al-Esmael, B., & Faisal, M. N. (2017). Influence of organizational culture and leadership style on employee satisfaction, commitment and motivation in the educational sector in Qatar. *EuroMed Journal of Business.*

Anderman, E. M. (2020). Achievement motivation theory: Balancing precision and utility. *Contemporary Educational Psychology, 61,* 101864.

Anh Vu, T., Plimmer, G., Berman, E., & Ha, P. N. (2022). Performance management in the Vietnam public sector: The role of institution, traditional culture and leadership. *International Journal of Public Administration, 45*(1), 49-63.

Batson, C. D. (2022). Prosocial motivation: A Lewinian approach. *Motivation Science, 8*(1),

Boyle, G. J., Wongsri, N., Bahr, M., Macayan, J. V., & Bentler, P. M. (2020). Cross-cultural differences in personality, motivation and cognition in Asian vs. Western societies. *Personality and Individual Differences, 159,* 109834.

Brandstätter, V., & Bernecker, K. (2022). Persistence and disengagement in personal goal pursuit. *Annual review of psychology, 73,* 271-299.

Cote, R. (2019). Motivating Multigenerational Employees: Is There a Difference?. *Journal of Leadership, Accountability & Ethics, 16*(2).

Davlembayeva, D., Papagiannidis, S., & Alamanos, E. (2021). Sharing economy platforms: An equity theory perspective on reciprocity and commitment. *Journal of Business Research, 127,* 151-166.

Deci, E.L & Ryan, R.M. (2012). Motivation, personality, and development within embedded social contexts: An overview of self-determination theory. In R.M. Ryan (Ed.), Oxford Handbook of Human Motivation (pp. 85-90). UK: Oxford University Press.

Engin, M., & McKeown, K. (2012). Cultural influences on motivational issues in students and their goals for studying at university. Learning and Teaching in Higher Education: Gulf Perspectives, 9(1). http://lthe.zu.ac.ae

Eccles, J. S., & Wigfield, A. (2020). From expectancy-value theory to situated expectancy-value theory: A developmental, social cognitive, and sociocultural perspective on motivation. *Contemporary Educational Psychology, 61,* 101859.

Gates, V. J., & Reinsch Jr, N. L. (2022). Commentary: Employee Counseling, Equity Theory, and Research Opportunities. *International Journal of Business Communication, 59*(1), 148-157.

Hardy, S. A., Nelson, J. M., Frandsen, S. B., Cazzell, A. R., & Goodman, M. A. (2022). Adolescent religious motivation: A self-determination theory approach. *The International Journal for the Psychology of Religion, 32*(1), 16-30.

Hassan, R., Poole, K. L., Lahat, A., Willoughby, T., & Schmidt, L. A. (2021). Approach-avoidance conflict and shyness: A developmental investigation. *Developmental Psychology, 57*(5), 814.

Hattie, J., Hodis, F. A., & Kang, S. H. (2020). Theories of motivation: Integration and ways forward. *Contemporary Educational Psychology, 61,* 101865.

Hofstede, G. (2001). Culture's Consequences: Comparing Values, Behaviors, Institutions, and Organizations Across Nations. (2nd Ed.). Sage.

Hofstede, G. (2003). Culture's Consequences: Comparing Values, Behaviors. Thousand Oaks CA: paperback.

Ingrams, A. (2020). Organizational citizenship behavior in the public and private sectors: A multilevel test of public service motivation and traditional antecedents. *Review of Public Personnel Administration, 40*(2), 222-244.

Inoue, T., Georgiou, G. K., Maekawa, H., & Parrila, R. (2021). Cultural influences on the relationship between self-concept, interest, task-focused behavior, and reading skills. *Journal of Cultural Cognitive Science, 5*(2), 311-323.

Ishii, K., Mojaverian, T., Masuno, K., & Kim, H. S. (2017). Cultural differences in motivation for seeking social support and the emotional consequences of receiving support: The role of influence and adjustment goals. *Journal of Cross-Cultural Psychology, 48*(9), 1442-1456.

Ito, E., Walker, G. J., Liu, H., & Mitas, O. (2017). A cross-cultural/national study of Canadian, Chinese, and Japanese university students' leisure satisfaction and subjective well-being. *Leisure Sciences, 39*(2), 186-204.

Kalajas-Tilga, H., Hein, V., Koka, A., Tilga, H., Raudsepp, L., & Hagger, M. S. (2022). Application of the trans-contextual model to predict change in leisure time physical activity. *Psychology & health, 37*(1), 62-86.

Kirmani, S. S., Attiq, S., Bakari, H., & Irfan, M. (2019). Role of core self evaluation and acquired motivations in employee task performance. *Pakistan Journal of Psychological Research*, 401-418.

Kruglanski, A. W., Szumowska, E., Kopetz, C. H., Vallerand, R. J., & Pierro, A. (2021). On the psychology of extremism: How motivational imbalance breeds intemperance. *Psychological Review, 128*(2), 264.

LaBombard, N. X. (2022). understanding employees of business operations at a university using herzberg's theory of motivation.

Lam, I. K. V., & Ryan, C. (2022). Intra-cultural variation among tourists of the same cultural background–does it matter?. *Tourism Recreation Research, 47*(1), 17-30.

Lewis, O. A., Teets, J. C., & Hasmath, R. (2022). Exploring political personalities: The micro-foundation of local policy innovation in China. *Governance, 35*(1), 103-122.

Loor-Zambrano, H. Y., Santos-Roldán, L., & Palacios-Florencio, B. (2022). Relationship CSR and employee commitment: Mediating effects of internal motivation and trust. *European Research on Management and Business Economics, 28*(2), 100185.

Mamun, M. Z. A., & Khan, M. Y. H. (2020). A Theoretical Study On Factors Influencing Employees Performance, Rewards And Motivation Within Organisation.

Markus, H.R. (2016). What moves people to action? Culture and motivation. *Current Opinion in Psychology.* 8.161-166. https://doi.org/10.1016/j.copsyc.2015.10.028

McInerney, Dennis & Maehr, M.L. & Dowson, M. (2004). Motivation and Culture. *Encyclopaedia of Applied Psychology.* 2. https://doi.org/ 10.1016/B9 78-0-12-809324-5.05634-0

Mitsakis, M., & Galanakis, M. (2022). An Empirical Examination of Herzberg's Theory in the 21st Century Workplace. Organizational Psychology Re-Examined. *Psychology, 13*(2), 264-272.

Nolen, S. B. (2020). A situative turn in the conversation on motivation theories. *Contemporary Educational Psychology, 61,* 101866.

Ntoumanis, N., Ng, J. Y., Prestwich, A., Quested, E., Hancox, J. E., Thøgersen-Ntoumani, C., ... & Williams, G. C. (2021). A meta-analysis of self-determination theory-informed intervention studies in the health domain: effects on motivation, health behavior, physical, and psychological health. *Health Psychology Review, 15*(2), 214-244.

Olafsen, A. H., Deci, E. L., & Halvari, H. (2018). Basic psychological needs and work motivation: A longitudinal test of directionality. *Motivation and emotion, 42*(2), 178-189.

Osokpo, H. O., James, R., & Riegel, B. (2021). Maintaining cultural identity: A systematic mixed studies review of cultural influences on the self-care of African immigrants living with non-communicable disease. *Journal of Advanced Nursing, 77*(9), 3600-3617.

Peng, A., & Patterson, M. M. (2022). Relations among cultural identity, motivation for language learning, and perceived English language proficiency for international students in the United States. *Language, Culture and Curriculum, 35*(1), 67-82.

Poulou, M., & Norwich, B. (2020). Psychological needs, mixed self-perceptions, well-being and emotional, and behavioural difficulties: Adolescent students' perceptions. *European Journal of Psychology of Education, 35*(4), 775-793.

Ripoll, G. (2019). Disentangling the relationship between public service motivation and ethics: An interdisciplinary approach. *Perspectives on Public Management and Governance, 2*(1), 21-37.

Román, N., Rigó, A., Kato, Y., Horváth, Z., & Urbán, R. (2021). Cross-cultural comparison of the motivations for healthy eating: Investigating the validity and invariance of the motivation for healthy eating scale. *Psychology & Health, 36*(3), 367-383.

Ryan, R. M., & Deci, E. L. (2020). Intrinsic and extrinsic motivation from a self-determination theory perspective: Definitions, theory, practices, and future directions. *Contemporary educational psychology, 61,* 101860.

Sawatsky, A. P., O'Brien, B. C., & Hafferty, F. W. (2022). Autonomy and developing physicians: Reimagining supervision using self-determination theory. *Medical Education, 56*(1), 56-63.

Schunk, D. H., & DiBenedetto, M. K. (2020). Motivation and social cognitive theory. *Contemporary Educational Psychology, 60,* 101832.

Shikalepo, E. E. (2020). The Role of Motivational Theories in Shaping Teacher Motivation and Performance: A Review of Related Literature. *International Journal of Research and Innovation in Social Science (IJRISS), 4.*

Shoib, S., Amanda, T. W., Menon, V., Ransing, R., Kar, S. K., Ojeahere, M. I., ... & Saleem, S. M. (2022). Is Maslow's Hierarchy of Needs Applicable During the COVID-19 Pandemic?. *Indian Journal of Psychological Medicine,* 025371762110 60435.

Slote, M. (2020). Agent-based virtue ethics. *Handbuch Tugend und Tugendethik,* 1-10.

Stanko, M. A., & Allen, B. J. (2022). Disentangling the collective motivation for user innovation in a 3D printing community. *Technovation, 111,* 102387.

Steel, R. P., Bishop, N. C., & Taylor, I. M. (2021). The relationship between multidimensional motivation and endocrine-related responses: A systematic review. *Perspectives on Psychological Science, 16*(3), 614-638.

Tang, M., Wang, D., & Guerrien, A. (2020). A systematic review and meta-analysis on basic psychological need satisfaction, motivation, and well-being in later life: Contributions of self-determination theory. *PsyCh journal, 9*(1), 5-33.

Thant, Z. M., & Chang, Y. (2021). Determinants of public employee job satisfaction in Myanmar: Focus on Herzberg's two factor theory. *Public Organization Review, 21*(1), 157-175.

Torréns, G. M., & Kärtner, J. (2017). The influence of socialization on early helping from a cross-cultural perspective. *Journal of Cross-Cultural Psychology, 48*(3), 353-368.

Tóth-Király, I., Orosz, G., Dombi, E., Jagodics, B., Farkas, D., & Amoura, C. (2017). Cross-cultural comparative examination of the Academic Motivation Scale using exploratory structural equation modeling. *Personality and Individual Differences, 106*, 130-135.

Umarji, O., McPartlan, P., Moeller, J., Li, Q., Shaffer, J., & Eccles, J. (2021). The motivational system of task values and anticipated emotions in daily academic behavior. *Motivation and Emotion, 45*(5), 599-616.

Urdan, T., & Kaplan, A. (2020). The origins, evolution, and future directions of achievement goal theory. *Contemporary Educational Psychology, 61*, 101862.

Walker, G. J., Yan, N., & Kono, S. (2020). Basic psychological need satisfaction and intrinsic motivation during leisure: A cross-cultural comparison. *Journal of Leisure Research, 51*(4), 489-510.

Wangechi, n. l. (2019). Effect of change management strategies on the performance of commercial banks in Kenya. *International Journal of Social Sciences Management and Entrepreneurship (IJSSME), 3*(1).

Watters, E. R. (2021). Factors in Employee Motivation: Expectancy and Equity Theories. *Journal of Colorado Policing, 970*, 4.

Wigfield, A., & Koenka, A. C. (2020). Where do we go from here in academic motivation theory and research? Some reflections and recommendations for future work. *Contemporary Educational Psychology, 61*, 101872.

Wu, D. (2020). Empirical study of knowledge withholding in cyberspace: Integrating protection motivation theory and theory of reasoned behavior. *Computers in Human Behavior, 105*, 106229.

Zarzycki, M., Morrison, V., Bei, E., & Seddon, D. (2022). Cultural and societal motivations for being informal caregivers: A qualitative systematic review and meta-synthesis. *Health Psychology Review*, 1-30. https://doi.org/10.108 0/17437199.2022.2032259

Zhang, Z. S., Hoxha, L., Aljughaiman, A., Arënliu, A., Gomez-Arizaga, M. P., Gucyeter, S., ... & Ziegler, A. (2021). Social environmental factors and personal motivational factors associated with creative achievement: A cross-cultural perspective. *The Journal of Creative Behavior, 55*(2), 410-432.

Zohar, D. (2022). The Motivations That Drive Me. In *Zero Distance* (pp. 111-124). Palgrave Macmillan. https://doi.org/10.1007/978-981-16-7849-3_11

About the Contributors

Akbar Husain is retired as a Professor from the Department of Psychology, Aligarh Muslim University, Aligarh. He was Chairman, Department of Psychology, and Dean, Faculty of Social Sciences, at the Aligarh Muslim University, Aligarh. He is the author, co-author, and editor of 45 books and 286 research papers, theoretical articles, and chapters in edited books. His attempt to rediscover the domains of spirituality in the field of Spiritual Psychology is worth appreciating. Professor Husain has standardized scales for the psycho-social and spiritual assessment of diverse populations. He has organized a number of national and international conferences and seminars in India and Malaysia. His main fields of study are: Spiritual & Positive Psychology, Health Psychology, Islamic Psychology & Counselling, and Psychological Testing.

Alankrita Kumar, Co-Director of mental healthcare organisation Sulhaa, is a dynamic entrepreneur who has brought mental health awareness to the forefront in India. With a psychology degree from Delhi University, she swiftly scaled her business and excelled academically through research work. Her commitment to destigmatizing mental health and providing accessible solutions has made her a prominent figure in the field. Alankrita continues to inspire and empower individuals through her incredible work in academia and commitment toward promoting psychological literacy.

Anh Hoai Be is a devoted teacher at Hanoi Law University, Vietnam. She has been a qualified teacher and has earned her reputation for teaching Marriage and Family Law for over 10 years so far. She is also interested in arming herself with profound knowledge of cross-cultural communication as this field has a great impact on her current position. She is actively contributing to many activities relating to Anti-violence Against Women and Their Children Act as well as the Mothers and Child Protection Law. Until now, she has conducted many research papers and attended international conferences on Marriage and Family Law.

Arslan Khan – Quaid-i-Azam University Islamabad, Pakistan.

Arti Sharma is a Fellow of the Indian Institute of Management, Indore (India) and is currently working as Assistant Professor at Jindal Global Business School,

O.P. Jindal Global University, Sonipat, Haryana (India). She studied the impact and implications of group affective composition in her dissertation. She is a recipient of Junior Research Fellowship (JRF) awarded by University Grants Commision (UGC), India. She has also qualified for the National Eligibility Test for Lecturership conducted by UGC, India. She has presented her work at different national and international conferences, such as, the European Group of Organisation Studies, British Academy of Management, the Australia & New Zealand Academy of Management, the Indian Academy of Management, and the PAN IIM conference. She has published papers, case studies, and book chapters in national and international peer-reviewed avenues. Her research interests lie in emotions, affective compositions and diversity.

Bhawna Tushir, is currently working as an Assistant Professor of Psychology in the Department of Psychology, School of Humanities and Social Sciences at Christ (Deemed to be University). Dr Bhawna has worked with various universities like the University of Delhi, Manipal University Jaipur and Chaudhary Charan Singh University in the last five years. Over the past few years, she has worked on various projects and consultancies as a trainer with agencies like India Vision Foundation, Christ consultancy and the Brain Behavior Research Foundation of India. Currently, she is working on a collaborative research project with Banaras Hindu University and Mississippi State University. She is a qualified team player with a voracious appetite for new information and concepts, and a belief in work priorities aligned with the organizational goals. Organized and driven with an impressive list of achievements excelling within high-pressure environments.

Chandan Maheshkar is one of the founders of the East Nimar Society for Education (2019), dedicated to quality improvement in higher education and the development of educator competencies. As a Senior Consultant, he has served the Centre for Internal Quality Assurance (CIQA), Madhya Pradesh Bhoj (Open) University, Bhopal, India. He is associated with several management institutes in central India, including the University of Indore, India, in various academic roles. Dr. Maheshkar earned his MBA and Ph.D. from the University of Indore, India. In 2014, the University of Indore awarded him *Golden Jubilee Research Scholarship* on the occasion of the completion of its successful 50 years. Business education, HRD, Cross-Culture Business, and organizational behavior are his core areas of research interests. His research papers and book chapters have been published in journals of international repute and edited collections by Sage, Emerald, Taylor & Francis, IGI Global, Vernon Press and others, respectively.

Eisha Rahman is a Research Associate, at Military Mind Academy, Pune, India. She recently worked as a Senior Research Fellow (UGC-SVSGC) at the Department of Psychology, Aligarh Muslim University, Aligarh, India. She has received Sajida Nabi Award for Excellence in Psychology at the UG level and University Gold Medal for standing first in MA in Psychology. Moreover, she has received a certificate of excellence in scientific writing from the Excelgate Accreditation Research and Employment Services Pvt. Ltd. Besides, she possesses a PG Diploma in Guidance and Counseling and is a lifetime member of the Counsellor Council of India (CRN6125076). In a nutshell, she is an ardent learner and a keen researcher interested in expanding her research horizon in the realm of social, health, and positive psychology.

Ezgi Gül Ceyhan graduated from Anadolu University Vocational School of Justice (2011-2013). She received a Bachelor's degree (2009-2014) and a Master's degree completed with 'A Conceptual Research on Relation to Emotion-Policy' (2015-2017) from Muğla Sıtkı Koçman University Department of Public Administration, respectively. Ph.D. graduated, at the same university, with the name dissertation Political aestheticization: 'Aesthetics and internal tensions' (2018-2022). Her academic interests are the relationships between human and macro values, political psychology, and political sciences; "emotions, violence, power, consent, obedience, aesthetics, politics". Currently, she is working on sociological, psychological, and political aspects (aestheticization) of change, transformation, and integration.

Farooq Shah is a Lecturer of Statistics, University of Peshawar, Pakistan. Dr. Shah earned his doctoral degree in Statistics while advancing the methodological developments towards the attainment of more feasible data masking strategies, especially focusing on self-reported data.

Feba Thomas, is currently working as an Assistant Professor in Xavier Institute of Management & Entrepreneurship, Kochi. Specializes in Human Resource and Organizational Behaviour. She holds an MBA and Doctoral Research from Vellore Institute of Technology (VIT) on the topic "A Moderated Mediation of Acculturative Stress and the Influence of Resilience and Social Support among International Students". She has published research papers in the field of Management in International Journals and also presented research papers in National and International conferences. Published International Book Chapters in the field of Management.

Garima Joshi is an Assistant Professor in the Department of Psychology, School of Humanities and Social Sciences, Christ (Deemed to be University), Delhi, NCR. She has completed her Ph.D. in Clinical Neuropsychology from All India Institute of Medical Sciences, New Delhi. She was awarded the prestigious Junior Research Fellowship by the Indian Council of Medical Research for the tenure of her graduate studies. She has many international and national peer-reviewed publications in renowned high-impact factor journals and has collaboratively worked in the field of neurosurgery, oncology and neuropsychiatric disorders. Her areas of interest are schizophrenia, neuropsychology, neurorehabilitation and neurocognitive interventions.

Hari Narayanan V is an Associate Professor in the Department of Humanities and Social Sciences, IIT Jodhpur, Rajasthan (INDIA). He did his Ph.D. at IIT Kanpur. His major research interests are embodied cognition, nature of the self and mindfulness

Irene Hudson is the Professor of Statistics and Data Analytics, Royal Melbourne Institute of Technology (RMIT), Australia and Conjoint Professor, University of Newcastle Australia. Prof. Hudson is elected fellow of the Royal Statistical Society. She has co-authored two books and numerous book chapters. Her collaborative research interests include Health surveillance, Gender studies, Causal inference and Climate change analytics. Over the years, her collaborative research work has been appreciated by a wide range of research audiences.

Janelle Christine Simmons earned a BA in psychology with a minor in pre-law from Michigan State University, and MA in Forensic Psychology from John Jay College of Criminal Justice (2002). Thereafter, she earned an M.Div. from Torch Trinity Graduate School of Theology (now known as TTGU) in Seoul, South Korea (2006). Then she earned an Ed. S. in Curriculum and Instruction and an Ed. D. in Educational Leadership from Liberty University (2013 and 2016, respectively) and was a member of Kappa Delta Pi. Recently, she completed a certificate in Creativity and Innovation from William Paterson University in Wayne, NJ. Currently, Janelle works as a consultant with her own company, Janelle Christine Simmons, Ed.D., Sole Proprietorship. In addition, she serves as a VISTA for the AARP Foundation in Washington, DC. Her research interests lie in spiritual matters, matters of diversity, multicultural leadership characteristics, multicultural education, and leadership in general.

Jayant Sonwalkar is a professor of marketing and international business at Devi Ahilya University, Indore (formerly known as the University of Indore). As a Vice-Chancellor (2018-22), he served Madhya Pradesh Bhoj (Open) University, Bhopal, India. He served various institutions in different roles, including the All India Management Association (AIMA, New Delhi), Directorate of Distance Education (DDE-DAVV), and SJMC-DAVV. Dr. Sonwalkar earned his Ph.D., MBA and MA (History) from the University of Indore, India and MA (Social Work) from Delhi University. Marketing Management, International Marketing, Advertising and Brand Management, Product Policy Management, Human Resource Management and Business History are his core areas of academic interest. He has made a significant contribution in promoting higher education through the Open and Distance Learning (ODL) mode in central India. He published nearly 85 papers in various journals of national and international repute.

Michael CSERKITS completed his MA in Sociology as well as Social and Cultural Anthropology at the University of Vienna, Austria, and holds a Ph.D. in African Studies from the same institution. Currently, he is an independent post-doc researcher and participates in the General Staff Course of the Austrian Armed Forces. Aside from research connected with conflicts and nation-building in the broader Sahel, he has published several articles dealing with the role of Armed Forces in societal change, strategic paradigms across different ages and actively researches in the field of Visual Studies.

Mokoena Maepa holds the following qualifications: Ph.D. in Psychology, Master of Arts in Clinical Psychology and Bachelor of Psychology. Dr. Maepa is currently employed as a senior lecturer in the Clinical Psychology Department of Sefako Makgatho Health Sciences University. She is also a registered independent Clinical Psychologist with the Health Professions Council of South Africa since 2011. She has experience of working as a Clinical Psychologist in the public sector. Her research interests include HIV/AIDS, mental health, trauma, risk-taking behavior and self-harm, parenting styles and working with vulnerable populations. At the Sefako Makgatho University, her work entails training Clinical Psychologists (lecturing and supervision) and Psychiatrists.

Mpho Maotoana is a lecturer and Clinical Psychologist in the Department of Psychology, University of Limpopo (Turfloop Campus), South Africa. She holds a Bpsych degree, MA in clinical psychology, and a Ph.D. in psychology. Her research focus is on Social Psychology and mental health issues. She is registered with the Health Professions Council of South Africa as a Clinical Psychologist-Independent Practice.

Mubashir Gull is working as an Assistant Professor in the Department of Applied Psychology, GITAM School of Humanities and Social Sciences, Visakhapatnam, India. Prior to this, he worked as an Assistant Professor at the Department of Psychology, Akal University, Talwandi Sabo, Punjab. He did his M. Phil and Ph.D. from the Aligarh Muslim University, Aligarh, and has been awarded a national fellowship from the Indian Council of Social Science Research (ICSSR). Related to his topic of expertise, he has successfully presented and published papers in National and International Journals. He also holds a PG Diploma in Rehabilitation Psychology and has been registered as a Rehabilitation Psychologist by the Rehabilitation Council of India (A50125). His research interests are Rehabilitation Psychology, Psychometrics, and Disability studies.

Muhammad Naveed Rana is Statistical Officer at Faisalabad Medical University, Pakistan.

Namrata Chatterjee is a driven entrepreneur and Co-Director of Sulhaa, a mental healthcare organization. After completing her bachelor's degree in psychology from Delhi University, she embarked on a mission to make mental healthcare accessible in India. Alongside pursuing her master's in psychology, Namrata has extensively engaged with research in psychology and psychosocial healthcare, making significant academic contributions to the field. With a strong passion for her work, she continues to lead her company, Sulhaa, towards its vision of transforming mental healthcare in India.

Odirin Omiegbe is a Senior Lecturer with the University of Delta, Agbor, Nigeria, Special Education Unit. He obtained a Bachelor degree in Religious Studies Education from Bendel State University, Ekpoma, Nigeria, a Master's degree in Special Education from University of Ibadan, Ibadan, Nigeria, and a PhD in Curriculum Studies from University of Benin, Benin, Nigeria and has been lecturing in tertiary institutions across Nigeria since 1991. He is a member of some learned professional associations, has attended conferences within and outside Nigeria and written over 30 articles in some learned journals including over 5 books (sole author and chapter contributor) of national and international repute in special education, psychology, guidance and counselling, curriculum and other related disciplines within and outside Nigeria.

Rajib Ghosh is a doctoral candidate in the Department of Applied Psychology, Kazi Nazrul University. He is also a faculty of Psychology at Raniganj Girls' College, West Bengal (INDIA). His research interests are in Positive and Cognitive Psychology, and especially in Wisdom.

Roshan Lal Dewangan is an Assistant Professor in the Department of Applied Psychology, Kazi Nazrul University, Asansol (INDIA). His specialization is in Clinical Psychology. He has been working in the area of wisdom research for the last six years.

Salman Cheema is an Assistant Professor of Statistics, Department of Applied Sciences, National Textile University Faisalabad, Pakistan. He gained his Ph.D. degree from the University of Newcastle, Australia. He completed his graduation from Virginia Tech, USA. His research interests include data masking and privacy issues, choice behaviors and utility determinants and negotiation strategies.

Siboniso Collin Gumedze is a graduate of a Diploma in Education from the Southern Africa Nazarene University (SANU) in Eswatini (Swaziland). Holds Bachelor's degree in psychology at the North-West University (Mafikeng Campus), South Africa. He has completed his honours degree in Sociology at Sol Plaatje University in South Africa. He is currently studying his Bachelor of Education honours degree in educational psychology at North-west University, Potchefstroom campus.

Sushant Bhargava finished his Ph.D. in Organizational Behavior and Human Resource Management in 2022 with a concentration in Team Studies from the Indian Institute of Management Lucknow (India). He pursues rigorous research and teaching in various areas of management scholarship, such as sustainability, experimental methods, innovation, organizational change, and post-COVID work experiences. Dr. Bhargava has previous work experience in the Indian public sector banking sector. Currently, he is working as an Assistant Professor at the Indian Institute of Management Jammu (India) and pursues language learning and cultural studies as a hobby.

Tuan Van Vu gains experience in the field of cross-cultural communication, mostly resulting from his own teaching profession and daily work in a multicultural environment. His great passion for research methodology enriches his overall knowledge of teaching methodology. As a qualified teacher of English at Hanoi Law University, Vietnam, he makes himself available in English-speaking countries frequently to keep himself updated. He specializes in English teaching –especially legal English, Law, and education management. In addition, he is also an author of many research papers published in national and international journals.

Vatsal Priyadarshi Pandey is currently working as an Assistant Professor of Psychology at the Government Girls PG College Rampur. He has worked previously in CHRIST (Deemed to be University) Delhi NCR, Ghaziabad and Amity University Madhya Pradesh, Gwalior. His expertise is in the area of thyroid dysfunction and cognition. Additionally, he has also worked on procrastination and time perception. Dr. Pandey has earned his Ph.D. in Psychology from Banaras Hindu University and also worked on a DST-sanctioned project on Attentional networks in healthy aging and Alzheimer's disease.

Wandile Fundo Tsabedze is a graduate in B Soc Sci in Psychology, Honours Degree in Psychology, Master of Social Science in Psychology (research) and Ph.D. in Psychology, all qualifications obtained from the North-West University, South Africa. He is currently a postdoctoral fellow at the University of South Africa, South Africa (UNISA). He serves as a Community Representative Member at North-West University Human Social Sciences Research Ethics Committee (HSSREC). His research focus areas are African Psychology (Indigenous Knowledge), Adolescents Emotions/Emotional Intelligence, mental health, and psycho-social well-being of incarcerated population in correctional centers, mental health and psycho-social well-being of LGBTQI+ population, and neurodevelopmental disorders (focusing on; Dyscalculia, Autism, dyslexia and ADHD).

Zawar Hussain is the Professor of Statistics, The Islamia University of Bahawalpur, Pakistan. Prof. Hussain specialized in randomized response techniques. His research work elaborates methodologies dealing with privacy protection, loss of information and dynamic modeling.

Index

A

Acculturation theory, 223, 227
Acculturation, 182, 184, 186
Adams' Equity Theory of
    Motivation, 259
Albinism, 202
Alderfer's ERG Theory, 256
Alms-Begging, 207
Angular Kyphosis, 205
Aspiration Values, 77
Assimilation, 183, 185
Attitude, 80

B

Biculturalism, 183

C

Collectivism, 5, 160, 165
Constructed Scapes, 103
Constructivism, 97
Critical Thinking, 14
Cross-cultural Communication,
    155
Cultural and Cross-cultural
    Psychology, 139
Cultural Dichotomies, 5
Cultural Dimensions Theory, 8
Cultural Dimensions, 8
Cultural Diversity, 24
Cultural Identity, 247
Cultural Intelligence, 15
Cultural Psychology, 40
Cultural Shock, 221
Culture, 11, 58
Culture Learning Approach, 188

Culture Scapes, 103

E

Eastern Cultures, 158
Emotions, 16, 30
Enduring Belief, 83
Epistemology of Cross-Cultural
    Psychology, 3, 4
Existence Need, 257
Extrinsic Values, 78

F

Functionalism, 98, 99, 100

G

Growth Need, 257

H

Historicism, 100
Hofstede's Cultural Dimensions, 8
Hybrid Approach, 119

I

Individualism, 5, 160, 165
Indulgence, 11
Intercultural Communication, 155
Intra-Cultural Situations, 13
Intrinsic Values, 78

K

Kufukama, 245

L

Language Barriers, 188
Leadership Values, 77
Logistic Model, 116
Long-term Orientation, 10

M

Masculinity v/s Femininity, 9
Maslow's Hierarchy of Needs, 256
McClelland's Acquired Needs
    Theory, 258
Moral Development, 40, 42
Moral Diversity, 49
Moral Dynamism, 47
Morality, 45
Motivational Imbalance, 261
Mourning Rituals, 243
Multiculturalism, 183
Multi-level Probabilistic
    Mechanism, 119

P

Perception, 15
Power Distance, 7, 8
Psychodrama, 138, 142, 143

R

Relatedness Need, 257
Restraint, 11

S

Short-term Orientation, 10
Social Constructivism, 98, 100
Societal Norm, 84
Sociodrama, 142, 143
Socio-psychological State, 262
Spiritual Values, 79

T

Temporal Influences, 47

U

Uncertainty Avoidance, 8
Universal Values, 78

V

Valence, 80
Values, 73, 74
Vocational Values, 76

W

Western Cultures, 158
Wisdom, 56, 62

www.ingramcontent.com/pod-product-compliance
Lightning Source LLC
Chambersburg PA
CBHW060151280326
41932CB00012B/1724